ABSTRACTS OF SOUTH CENTRAL PENNSYLVANIA NEWSPAPERS 1791 - 1795

Items from the York Advertiser and Carlisle Gazette, pertaining to the lives of persons living in South Central Pennsylvania

Martha Reamy

Willow Bend Books
Westminster, Maryland
2000

Willow Bend Books
65 East Main Street
Westminster, Maryland 21157-5026
1-800-876-6103

Source books, early maps, CDs—Worldwide

For our listing of thousands of titles offered
by hundreds of publishers see our website
<www.WillowBend.net>

Visit our retail store

Reprinted: 2000 by Willow Bend Books

International Standard Book Number: 1-58549-121-7

Printed in the United States of America

CONTENTS

INTRODUCTION

This book is the second in a series of volumes of abstracts of South Central Pennsylvania newspapers planned as an aid to genealogical research.

The Carlisle Gazette and Western Repository of Knowledge, generally known as the Carlisle Gazette, was founded on August 10, 1785 by George Kline and George Reynolds; Kline became the sole publisher with the August 3, 1791 issue.

The Pennsylvania Herald, and York General Advertiser was established by James Edie, John Edie and Henry Willcocks January 7, 1789. Willcocks turned over his interest to the Edie's in 1792. On July 31, 1793 John Edie became sole publisher and continued the paper until January, 1800, when it was succeeded by The York Recorder.

The (Carlisle) Telegraphe was established February 10, 1795, by James Steel and John S. M'Clean. Steel took over as sole owner in 1796. The last issue located is dated May 3, 1796. This issue is held by Harvard University which possesses 16 issues in all, over the period February 1795 through May 3, 1796. This book contains the only other issue known to exist, dated August 18, 1795, held by the Library of Congress.

These abstracts were taken from microfilm copies (at the Library of Congress) of those issues of the Carlisle Gazette held by the Cumberland County Historical Society, Carlisle. Copies of the York Advertiser are held by the York County Historical Society.

Abbreviations used in this volume:

a. - acres
adj - adjoining
admr - administrator or administratrix
co - county
dau - daughter
decd - deceased
exr - executor or executrix
Fri - Friday
Mon - Monday
Sat - Saturday
Sun - Sunday
Thurs - Thursday
twp - township
Tues - Tuesday
Wed - Wednesday
yr(s) - year(s)

F. Edward Wright

THE PENNSYLVANIA HERALD & YORK GENERAL ADVERTISER

1. Wednesday, 5 January 1791
Land for sale in York County, one tract in Mount-pleasant Twp., 600 a., other in Germany Twp., 200 a. - Patrick M'SHERRY, Little's-town.
Sheriff's sale of estate of William HUNTER, improvement & tract in Newbury Twp., 200 a., adj. lands of Frederick SWITZER.
Estate of Henry SCHULTZ, improvement & tract in Manchester Twp., 168 a., adj. lands of heirs of Reinhart BUTT, decd., Frederick EICHELBERGER.
Estate late of William BRACKENRIDGE, decd., improvement & tract in Manallen Twp., with saw-mill and oil-mill, 100 a., adj. lands of Peter STRASSBACH, Daniel NOEL.
Estate of Martin MILLER, improvement & tract in Germany Twp., 50 a., adj lands of John ECKERT & George KITZMILLER.
Sheriff's Sale: The estate of Joseph WILSON, improvement & tract of 200 a., adj. lands of Sebastian HELMAN; estate of Hans MORRISON, decd.
Improvement & tract of land in Strabane twp. of 256 a., adj. lands of George LIGHTNER, David SIMPSON; the estate of John M'WILLIAMS, Improvement & tract of land in Strabane twp. of 160 a., adj. lands of Jacob WIRTH, Jacob DIETERICH; estate of William HUNTER.

2. Wednesday, 12 January 1791
Robert BEANS, Monaghan twp., has taken up a stray horse.

3. Wednesday, 19 January 1791
Whereas my wife Elizabeth, hath, without any provocation, eloped from my bed and board, this is to forewarn persons not to trust her on my account. Andrew SPANGLE, York twp.
Robert MAXWELL, of Wilmington, Del., in a letter to the editor states that as a member of the Abolition Society he has submitted manumission for 8 negroes, to be recorded in the society's books.

4. Wednesday, 26 January 1791
To be sold, plantation of 200 a., adjoins lands of Samuel COOK & Philip BARDMESS in Warrington twp., York Co., 12 miles from York, William MORRISSON.
For sale, 350 a., 2 miles of Tawney Town, Frederick Co., Md. - J. THOMAS, living on the land.
Whereas James LONG, of Miller's town, Dauphin Co., obtained of William and Jerad G. LONG of Strabane twp., York Co., an obligation, persons are forewarned not to take assignment of same, as said bond was fradulently obtained.
John HAY & John CLARK, York-town, offering reward for slave named Toby, about 5'7-8", speaks English & German, very white for a mustee; also John SMETZ, about 5', 17 years old.
Two-story house for sale, 40' long, 39' wide; on south west corner of the Diamond, in Chambersburgh, John M'CONKEY, Chambersburgh.

5. Wednesday, 2 February 1791
On Tuesday the 11th inst., the house of Alexander M'DONALD, a tenant on David HOGE's farm in East-Pennsborough, was burned, and his wife and 2 of his children, and a girl the only child of his brother-in-law, unhappily perished in the flames. M'DONALD's brother-in-law was in the house with him and his wife, and her mother an old infirm woman.
Died Thursday last, 27th ult., at Phila., in an advanced age, the Hon. George BRYAN, Esq., 1 of the Judges of the Supreme Court of Penn.

5. Wednesday, 2 February 1791 (Con't.)

Persons indebted to estate of Mary SHETLER, decd., are desired to make payment. Frederick YOUSE, York.

For sale: Tract of 160. in Franklin Twp, York Co. The great road from Baltimore, York-town & Black's Gap, to the Western Country, passes through said tract. Has log dwelling & double barn. Terms to be known by applying to William GILLSLAND, Esq. or to David DUNWOODY, near the premises.

For sale: Two tracts, one on the great road from Phila. to Frederick town, in Germany twp, 200 a.; the other 161 a. in Mountjoy Twp., four miles from Little's and 7 from Getty's-town. Apply to Adam WINTROTH near Little's-town.

Brick-maker wanted at the flourishing town of Harrisburg - Stacy POTTS, Harrisburg.

John DONNEL proposes to let on share the farm whereon he lives, on Muddy Creek, Fawn twp., York co. Also wanted at same place a single man, a miller, who may have a merchant mill and saw mill on the shares. For anything relating to the quality of the land, please inquire of William KERSEY.

Sale of plantation in Tyrone twp., on head waters of Bermudian Creek, adj. lands of Archibald M'GREW, Bechtel's mill, 306 a., property of Maxwell & William ARMSTRONG - Alexander BROWN.

John SPANGLER, one of the Commissioners for York Co., will recieve proposals in writing from any carpenter who will undertake to rebuild the bridge across a branch of Codorus Creek 5 miles from York-town.

Sale of plantation of 632 a. in Monaghan twp., York co., adj. lands of James DILL, Matthew DILL, Thomas CAMPBELL, Joseph DIXON, whereof Andrew WILSON lately died owner & seized, about 1/4 mile from the Stone Meeting house occupied by Rev. WAUGH. John WILLIAMS, Thomas CAMPBELL, Admr's.

6. Wednesday, 9 February 1791

Adam MAURER notifies purchasers of Tickets in the Dover twp lottery that it will be drawn 4 March yet.

Whereas Henry BRADLEY of Hopewell twp., York Co., obtained 4 obligations of George BADDERS, Fawn twp., York Co., & whereas said BRADLEY did bind himself to make BADDERS a good & sufficient title to a certain tract. And as the said Henry BRADLEY is now decd., without conveying said land, BADDERS herby forewarns persons from taking on said obligations.

Persons having demands against estate of John Nicholas DEH, decd., are desired to bring them in. Philip GOSSLER, Adm'r.

Committed to gaol, a mullatto man who calls himself James CONNELL, about 5'6", well made; says he belongs to Jacob SMITH, late of York Co.

7. Wednesday, 16 February 1791

A Plan of a Lottery to raise money for erecting the Academy in the Borough of York, Godfrey LENHART of York Town, appointed Treasurer. Managers of whom tickets may be had: John REGAN, Hager's-town; Jacob Miller, Frederick-town; Barnabas M'SHERRY & Leonard EICHELBERGER, Frederick Co; Samuel RIPPEY, Shippensburg; Stepehn RIGGLER & Frederick REYMER, Chambersburg; Alexander M'GEGHAN & Jacob KREVER, Carlisle; John SNYDER, Middle-town, & John KELLAR, Lebanon, Dauphin Co; Jacob BAILEY, Lancaster; Andrew ROBBINSON, Baltimore; Col. Philip ALBRIGHT, Conrad SHERMAN, Esq., Henry WELSH, George NEBBINGER, John FORSYTH, Esq. Capt. Thomas CAMPBELL, Maj. James GETTYS, Patrick M'SHERRY, Philip GOSSLER, Maj. Alexander TURNER, Benjamin PEDAM, Esq., Benjamin TYSON, Esq., Daniel MAY, Esq., Dr.

James HAMILTON, Andrew JOHNSTON, Esq., John EDIE, Esq., Henry HAY, George Lewis LEFLER & Peter ICKERS, York Co.
Daniel KENTING, York twp., adj Burough of York, has taken up stray sheep.
Adam MAUER notifies purchaser & holders of tickets in the Dover twp. Lottery that said lottery will be drawn at the place appointed in the scheme on Friday, 4 March next.

23 February 1791 & 2 March 1791 - not available.

8. Wednesday, 9 March 1791
Sheriff's Sale: Estate of William OWINGS, late Collector of Heidelberg Twp, improvement & tract in Heidleberg Twp, of 200 a., adj lands of Rev. James PELENTZ, Robert OWINGS.
Estate of William M'KISSON, late Collector of Hamilton's Bann Twp., improvement & tract in Hamilton's Bann Twp., 200 a., adj lands of Joseph M'KEE & Alexander M'KISSON.
Estate of Elijah HART, late Collector of Hamilton's Bann Twp., improvement & tract of 150 a., adj lands of Reynold RAMSEY & David AGNEW.
Estate of George KUNTZ, late Collector of Germany Twp, improvement & tract in said Germany Twp, 100 a., adj "Diggs's Choice," the heirs of Peter FEESER, decd.
Estate of Philip BOYER, late Collector of Windsor Twp, improvement & tract of 120 a., adj. lands of George WILLIAMS, Matthias MILLER, Jacob MEYER.
Estate of Christian GROVE, late Collector of Heidelberg Twp, house & lot on the North side of York-Street in Town of Hanover, adj lot of Francis HEIM.
Benjamin ELDER, his dray-horse Steady, to cover mares this season at his farm in Hamilton's Bann Twp.
To be sold, plantation of Jacob SLAGLE, decd., in Reading twp., York co., on Big Conowago Creek, adj. lands of William LONG, John NEELY; 213 a., Jacob RUDISEL, Henry SLAGLE, Junr. Exr's.
I hereby forewarn persons from crediting my wife Jenny LONG, otherwise M'CONNEL on my account, as I am determined to pay no debts of her contracting. John LONG
Sheriff's sales: Estate of Valentine GRAFF, improvement & tract in Paradise twp., 60 a., adj. lands of Andrew TRIMMER, Christian HEIM.
Property of Henry BEECHER, late Collector of Germany twp., a cow & sundry articles of household & kitchen furniture.
In Cumberland twp., property of William M'CREARY, late Collector of Cumberland twp., a waggon & gears, horses, cows, sheep.
In Tyrone twp., property of George MEAL, late Collector of Tyrone twp., a waggon & gears, horses, cows, sheep.
In Shrewsbury twp., property of Martin KURTZ, late Collector of Fawn twp., a waggon & gears, horses & cows.
In Hopewell twp., property of James GIBSON, horses, cows & sheep; estate of James WELCH, late Collector of Newbury twp., improvement & tract in Newbury twp., 300 a. adj. lands of Andrew WELCH, James MILLS.
Plantaton of 358 a. for sale in Tyrone twp., York co., 1 mile from the road from Carlisle to Baltimore, 1 mile from road leading to York Town, & 1 mile from Christian BICHEL's Merchant-mill. On premises are a good dwelling house, spring house, double barn, malt kiln in which 2000 bushels of barley may be made into malt in 1 season, brew house & copper with every other kind of utensils necessary for carrying on brewing business, with hop-yard for raising hops, orchard of about 100 trees, 100 a. cleared, 20 a. of meadow made - William DELAP.

8. Wednesday, 9 March 1791 (Con't.)

Henry BURKHOLDER has taken in a stray bull, Huntington Twp, York Co.

Plantation & tract of land to be sold, 400 a., "Carrolsburgh," in Hamilton's Bann Twp, York Co, with 2 dwelling-houses, barn & outhouses. William & Andrew COCHRAN.

Sheriff's Sale: estate of Samuel NELSON improvement & tract in Monaghan Twp, 160 a., adj lands of Jacob SMITH, Daniel WILLIAMS, James HUNTER; also horses, wagon & gears, cows, sheep &c.

Sheriff's Sales: Estate of Joseph ELLIOT, 2 improvements & tracts in Monaghan Twp, together 247 a., adj lands of James DILL, John WILSON, John WILLIAMS.

Property of Daniel WILLIAMS, collector of Managhan Twp, livestock &c.

9. Wednesday, 16 March 1791

Reported from Georgetown: On Tuesday, 11th inst., died, near the North Mountain, Frederick Co. (Md.) ---- ZOLL, aged 19 years. His death was occasioned by a slight cut in one of his feet with an axe. No method could be devised to stop the bleeding--if the wound was bound up, the blood gushed out his mouth & nostrils. Five of his brothers have bled to death at different periods from simple accidents. The father of the above had has 2 wives, & by each of them, several children, & all who have died in this manner were all by the first wife.

Thursday, the 17th inst. at midnight, the dwelling-house of George SCOTT in Washington Co. took fire (the wind being fresh at NW) & was soon consumed, with 2 brick buildings adjoining. Mr. SCOTT escaped from an upper-story window, but his 2 sons expired.

Jacob PFLIEGER, York Borough, offers reward for apprentice lad, Thomas HEINS, blacksmith by trade, about 18 years of age, 5'9", sandy complexion, brown hair, speaks good English & some German.

Andrew JOHNSON to sell at his dwelling house in Borough of York, furniture, Madeira & Lisbon wines, spirits.

10. Wednesday, 23 March 1791

Persons indebted to estate of George STAKE, Esqr., decd., are desired to make payment - Catharine STAKE, John HAY, Henry MILLER, Exr's.

Several houses & lots in town of Green-Castle to be rented by George CLARK, Green-Castle.

Those who have subscribed sums for the use of Dickenson College, either to Rev. John M'KNIGHT, the late Robert M'PHERSON, Esq. or John BLACK of Marsh-Creek, & have not yet paid, are requested to do so.

Persons indebted to estate of Philip RICE, decd., late of Hellam twp., are requested to make payment - Valentine LIPHART, Adm'r.

To be sold or rented, 2 small improvements on 1 tract in Huntington twp., York co., 2 miles from WIREMAN's Mill, 239 a. - Alexander BROWN, Tyrone twp., near the premises.

David DRIMMER, notifies that whereas a tract of land in Paradise Twp. of 50 a., adj. lands of Andrew DRIMMER, Christian HEIM &c., has lately been advertised for sale as the property of Valentine GRAFF, he gives notice that he is in possession of title to said land & that he means to hold the same until legally dispossessed.

William M'PHERSON, at his farm on Marsh-Creek, York Co., his horse, Silver-Tail, to cover mares this season. He was bred by Samuel CALLOWAY of Md.

11. Wednesday, 30 March 1791

Andrew JOHNSTON informs the public that he will continue to keep Tavern at the sign of the Black Bear, next door to John GREER's store. York-Town.

John GRIST, Huntington twp., forewarns persons from taking assignment on a Judgement Bond given him to John COMER.

Silver watch found on great road from Winchester to Miller's Town, Va. - Georg WORLEY, Cordous Twp., York Co.

Whereas John SHEKLEY gave unto Peter VANDYKE of Mount-pleasant twp., 2 bonds, therefore warns all persons from taking assignment on them.

Timothy COLLINS, Germany twp., requests those indebted to Patrick M'SHERRY to make settlement.

12. Wednesday, 6 April 1791

(Salem) Samuel OGDON, of Pa, has contracted with the General Court for the purchase of two-thirds of the Western Territory of this Commonwealth, not held by Messrs. GORHAM & PHELPS, for which he is to pay one hundred thousands pounds specie.

Sheriff's sale: estate of Joseph EDMUNDSON, late Collector of Newbury twp., improvement & tract in Newbury twp., 300 a. adj. lands of Thomas LEECH, John WRIGHT.

Estate of James NEELY, late Collector of Tyrone twp., improvement & tract in Tyrone twp., 200 a., adj. lands of John WHITE, Samuel WALKER.

Estate of William NEELY, late Collector of Tyrone twp., improvement & tract in Tyrone twp., 200 a., adj. lands of Jackson NEELY, Samuel WALKER.

Estate of Andrew M'ILVAIN, late Collector of Mt. Pleasant twp., a grist mill & saw mill on Conewago Creek in Mt. Pleasant twp.

Estate of Robert Johnston CHESTER, decd., late Collector of Berwick twp., a tavern, house & lot in Town of Berlin, adj. lots of George SMITH;

Estate of Charles HEIM, late Collector of Paradise twp., improvement & tract in Paradise twp., 150 a., adj. lands of Christian HEIM.

Estate of Robert TAYLOR, late Collector of Cumberland twp., improvement & tract in Cumberland twp., 100 a., adj. lands of Thomas BIGHAM, William M'CREARY.

Estate of Martin SHETTER, late Collector of Newbury twp., improvement & tract with grist & saw mill in Newbury twp., 174 a., adj. lands of heirs of John SHETTER, decd., George MILLER.

Property of Daniel WILLIAMS, late Collector of Monaghan twp., livestock.

Estate of Richard BROWN, late Collector of Strabane twp., improvement & tract in Strabne twp., 300 a., adj. lands of Barnabas GILBERT, Hugh KING.

Estate of Christopher STAIR, late Collector of Borough of York, house & lot on east side of Beaver st., in said Borough, adj. lot of Jacob GARTNER, Junr.

Estate of Jacob RYBER, late Collector of Monaghan twp., improvement & tract in Monaghan twp., 162 a., adj. lands of Charles BOYER, Benjamin CABLE.

Estate of Thomas LEECH, late Collector of Warrington twp., improvements & tract in Warrington twp., 200 a., adj. lands of Samuel COOKSON, Peter UFFSTATT, William MORRISON.

Estate of Christian GROVE, late Collector of Heidelsberg twp., house & lot on North side of York st., in Hanover, adj. land of Francis HEIM, also a stove with pipe, clock & case, clock maker's tools & furniture.

Whereas my wife Catharine did some time ago leave my bed & board, without any just cause, I do hereby forewarn persons from trusting her on my account - Philip HEISER, Warrington twp.

12. Wednesday, 6 April 1791 (Con't.)

Whereas I gave a note of hand unto Frederick or David LITTLE, and as I consider the same to have been fradulently obtained, I hereby forewarn persons from taking assignment on it. - Jacob LANDMEASURE

13. Wednesday, 13 April 1791

A portmanteau & blanket was delivered to John HERIN, waggoner, about 28 March by a Frenchman near Berlin in Bedford Co., to being on for him to Chambersburg or York-town.; The above portmanteau & blanket being now in the possession of Joseph DOBBINS, Waggoner, York-town, he requests the owner may call for them & pay the charges.

Jacob SITTLER, York-Town will receive in payment for stills, certificates of any of the U.S., or mechantable Country produce.

Sheriff's Sale: estate of Thomas CLINGAN, improvement & tract in Hamilton's Bann twp., 230 a., adj. lands of heirs of William WITHROW, decd., David AGNEW.

Sheriff's Sale: estate of John HUGHES, improvement & tract in Cumberland twp., 170 a., adj. lands of Archibald FINDLY.

Estate of George KERN, 2 improvements & tract in Strabane twp., 200 a., adj. lands of John SAMPLE, Archibald M'ILVAN & other tract on Marsh-Creek, Franklin twp., 100 a. adj. lands of heirs of Philip SHEFFER, decd. & Daniel SOWER.

Estate of John M'WILLIAMS, improvement & tract in Strabane twp., 160 a., adj. lands of Jacob WIRTH, Jacob DIETERICH.

Came to the plantaton of Leonard FLOWER in Franklin Twp, York Co, a dary Bay Horse.

14. Wednesday, 20 April 1791

Acts enacted the first sitting of the first session of the Legislature of Pa.: An act to compensate Robert KING. A supplement to an act to provide payment to Dr. Francis ALISON for supplies furnished in 1775. An act to establish a Ferry over Swatara creek, near the town of Williamsburgh (Dauphin Co) & for vesting the rights in Christian SELTZER, his heirs and assigns. An act for the relief of Blackall William BALL. An act to enable Eleazer OSWALD, guardian duly appointed to Jane, Blaithwaite, Mary & Gibbs JONES, minors under the age of 21 years, to sell & convey property. Acts for the relief of Abraham LUKENS, James OFFICER, Philip PETER. An act for the relief of Robert CUNNINGHAM, a prisoner in the jail of the Co. of Philadelphia.

John GREER, Borough of York, now opening store, next door to Captain JOHNSTON's Tavern, at the sign of the Black bear, a large & general assortment of merchandise.

The militia of York co. are requested to attend their exercise on the days appointed by law: 1st Battalion in Battalion on the 1st Monday in May, 2d Battalion on the Tuesday following, 3d Battalion on Wednesday & so on. Wm. SCOTT, County Lieut.

To sell in pursuance of a Chancery Court decree of Rockingham Court, Va., to satisfy a debt due to M'CREA & MEASE, one undivided moiety of a tract in Rockingham Co., about 7 miles from the Court-house, 97 a. - Peachy GILMOR, Benjamin HARRISON, James CURRIE, Commissioners.

Leonard GIZEL, living in M'Sherry's town, Heidelberg twp., York Co., offers reward for missing mares.

American sickles & English Scythes for sale - Isaiah HARR.

Abraham GRIFFITH, Warington twp., York co., has taken up a stray mare.

15. Wednesday, 27 April 1791

Whereas the subscriber hath given a bond unto William Montgomery STERRET (who has lately moved from these parts) conditioned for the sum of 500 pounds, to deliver to the aforesaid STERRET, some papers which he had in his possession, but the aforesaid STERRET did not meet the subscriber at the time appointed to receive the papers and give him back his bond. He therefore forewarns persons from taking assignment on said bond - Ralph CHERRY.

Two negro men committed to gaol, York-Town, one of them calls himself Cato, says he came from Baltimore, born in Guinea, near 50 years of age; the other calls himself Wm. KYSSEY, is about 40 years of age; says he is a free man and came from Williamsburg, Va.

Andrew RUTTER, Manchester twp., York co., offers reward for mulatto man named James CONNEL, about 5'5-6", 24-25 years of age, tolerably well made, speaks both English & German, is fond of playing on the fiddle, delights in strong drink & when drunk is very apt to quarrel.

Conrad SNYDER, Manchester twp., has taken up 2 stray mares.

16. Wednesday, 4 May 1791

Abraham GRIFFITH, Warrington twp, York Co., has taken up a stray mare.

Mr. HADFIELD & David STERRET of Baltimore went out to fight a duel & before Mr. HADFIELD had got to his distance, he turned & shot David STERRET; the ball lodged in his heart & entered at the right side. Mr. HADFIELD & his second are fled from Baltimore.

Whereas John LONG has lately absconded from the presence of his wife Jane, without any just cause that she knows of & without leaving her anything for the support of herself & his child, who previous to which he had the audacity to advertise in the York-town newspaper that no persons should credit her on his account. I do hereby offer a reward of 3 pounds who will secure the aforesaid John LONG in any gaol in the U.S. Thomas M'CONNEL, Chestnut level.

Christopher HULSIZER, Hunterton Co., Bethleham twp., N.J., offers reward for negro man named Michael, 27-30 years of age, 5'10", slender, straight made, lean faced, small feet, the toes of one of his feet appear to be a good deal contracted, by reason of which it is disagreeable for him to go barefooted. He is a tanner by trade.

Nicholas MEYER, Reading twp., offers reward for William BEATY, who defrauded the subscriber of 22 pounds. He is a highlander, about 35 years of age, 5'6", short sandy hair, of a ruddy complexion.

To be sold - negro slave, registered by Leonard HATTON, Huntington twp., York Co.

17. Wednesday, 11 May 1791

David HARRIS, at his store in Caleb BALES's Brick house, near the Medical Spring in Huntington twp., York Co., formerly occupied by William HARRIS, has just received a large & general assortment of Dry goods, Ironmongery, Cutlery, Saddlery, China-Ware and Dye Stuffs, Rum, wines, molases, sugar, teas, coffee, chocolate, rice, &c.

Sheriff's sale: estate of Philip STAB, improvement & tract in Heidelberg twp., 180 a., adj. lands of Peter WILL, Francis MARSHALL, heirs of Thomas ADAMS, decd.

Estate of Hans MORRISON, decd., improvement & tract called Montgomery's Place, adj. other lands of said dec'd.

Estate of Robert ROWLAND, decd., improvement & tract in Fawn twp., 200 a., adj. lands of James EDGAR, John BOYD.

17. Wednesday, 11 May 1791 (Con't.)
Estate of John RENEY, improvement & tract in Hopewell twp., 20 a., adj. lands of David KENNEDY, William LIGGET.

18. Wednesday, 18 May 1791
Phila., Sunday last in the afternoon a fire broke out in the kitchen belonging to the house of Mr. KENNEDY, near Ninth in Market-street.
Ludwick ECCLEBERGER, in Mountpleasant twp., York Co., has taken up a stray mare.
Sheriff's sale of two improvements & tracts in Hellam twp., 1 14 a. with tavern thereon, adj. lands of Henry KAUN, --- KAUFMAN & the other 51 a., ajd. lands of Ulrich NEWCOMER, Michael BLESSINGER, estate of Jacob COMFORT, late Collector of Hellam twp.

19. Wednesday, 25 May 1791
With the direction of Mr. HETERICK, late of our Academy, an air pump has been constructed by Jacob WELSHANTZ, celebrated gun-smith in this town.
Jacob SHELLY, Newbury twp., has taken up a stray mare.
Thomas SMITH, Hopewell twp., York co., forewarns persons from taking assignment on a bond given by him to James M'CANDLES, Merchant.
Ninan CHAMBERLAIN, Mount-Pleasant twp., York Co., offers reward for Irish servant boy named Robert THOMPSON, about 5'2-3", 16 years old, tolerably well made, speaks a little on the Scotch dialect, brown hair, fair countenance with a few small pox marks.

20. Wednesday, 1 June 1791
Whereas Isaac WEIDNER, of Strabane twp, York co., obotained from me 11 bonds, this is to forewarn persons not to take assignment on said bonds, until he shall clear the premises, which I purchased of him, of all incumbrances. Leonard KNAB.
Thomas FISHER retracts statement regarding PAXTON. Apparently his neighbour misunderstood & demanded payment when PAXTON merely wanted im to enquire about the bond.

21. Wednesday, 8 June 1791
Died last Thursday morning in his 51st year, after a long & painful illness, Michael HAHAN, Esq. (York)
A gold locket was lost on Captain STAKE's porch, York-town.

Wednesday, 15 June 1791 Issue available; no new local data.

22. Wednesday, 22 June 1791
Col. Alexander ANDERSON, of Philadelphia, a native of Chestertown, Md, has built a machine for threshing grain that is so perfect as not to leave a single grain in the ear; can replace 15 or 20 men threshing.
Notice is given not to credit any persons on my account, not even my wife Barbara, as I will not pay any debts contracted to may name after this date, Edward TOPPIN, Newbury twp., York co.
Whereas Alexander BROWN has lately advertised for sale a certain tract of land in Tyrone Twp., on the head waters of the Bermudian, this is to forewarn persons from purchasing said tract, as I have a title to an undivided half part of moiety of same & whereas I gave a Power of Attorney to said BROWN for certain purposes, which purposes are now accomplished, I hereby revoke & make void said power. William ARMSTRONG

22. Wednesday, 22 June 1791 (Con't.)
The goods & Chattles of David SHEPHERD, having been attached, at the suit of Thomas CLINGAN & the subscribers appointed commissioners, have duly appraised & sold same according to law. They hereby acquaint the creditors that the amount for their use is 5 pounds, 6 shillings- Francis MEREDITH, Isaac ROBINSON, Commissioners, Marsh-Creek.
Daniel STULL, Hager's Town, offers reward for negro man named WATKINS, stout likely fellow, about 5'10".

23. Wednesday, 29 June 1791
The distillers of spirits in the County of York are informed that Offices of Inspection will be opened 1 July for reception of the enteries of stills. (Payment will be made on the basis of capacity or actual production.) Edward HAND, Inspector, Borough of York.
Robert DUNN has removed from Baltimore to the Borough of York to that noted stand in the centre of the town formerly known as Wolf's Tavern, now the sign of the Waggon.
Committed to the gaol, York-town, James DONNELL, an Irishman, supposed to be a deserter from the Maryland troops, about 30 years of age.

24. Wednesday, 6 July 1791
Christian ORENDORFF, of Lebanon, gives notice that last Wednesday, 22 June, about midnight, a certain young man named Lawrence ORENDORFF of Lebanon twp., Dauphin Co., was lying in his bed asleep & then & there in the most barbarous manner was murdered. Suspected is Matthias MELZ, a butcher, he having lived a considerable time in the town of Lebanon, & on the day following the murder, hath left his place of residence. Said Matthias MELZ is of a low stature, walks stooped, has yellow short hair, of a well humoured temperment, speaks the German language in a high stile, cannot speak any English. He was born in Brunswick, Germany, & came into this country at the commencement of the war with the German troops, amongst the Yawgers.
John WEAVER, living on Pipe-creek Hundred, Md., offers reward for servant man who came from Amsterdam, a mason; speaks good German, cannot speak English. About 5'6", 23 years of age, dark brown hair.

25. Wednesday, 13 July 1791
Sheriff's sale of: estate of John CHURCHMAN, improvement & tract in Windsor & Chanceford twps., 800 a., adj. lands of George BURKHOLDER, James SPROAT, William M'DOWELL, Nicholas QUICKELL, James HAYNS.
Estate of Alexander POWER, 1 equal undivided 3d part of the four following improvements & tracts in Newbury twp., 1 185 a., another 100 a. with ferry of Henry FREY, yearly ground rent of 42 lots in Frey's Town, York twp.
Estate of Christian WIRT, improvement & tract with tavern in Manallen twp., 100 a., adj. lands of Henry SHELBACK, Peter EICHERT.
Estate of Henry SNYDER, improvement & tract in Manheim twp., 250 a., adj. lands of John DOLL, Michael EHRHART.

26. Wednesday, 20 July 1791
Innkeepers of York co. are requested to pay off, at the ensuing Court, their licenses in arrears - Henry MILLER, Clerk of the Sessions.
George SHERMAN, Germany twp., has taken up a dun colored mare with saddle & bridle. She was left by a likely young negro man on his being pursued on suspicion of being a runaway.

26. Wednesday, 20 July 1791 (Con't.)

Zachariah HEIL, having bargained & sold by agreement a certain piece of land unto John THOMPSON containing 30 a. in Windsor twp, York co., adj. lands of James & Anthony HINES & George WACHTER, being part of the land bought of said WACHTER, & being about to convey the same to aforesaid THOMPSON, was prevented by a certain Jacob DRITT, Esq., forewarning said THOMPSON from taking any title for same, as he had the only right to it. I hereby give public notice to those who may have any title or claim to the said land to come forward.

James M'CALMOND, Cooper-Smith, his shop opposite Squire FISHER's Tavern or the west side of the bridge.

27. Wednesday, 27 July 1791

Last Friday morning departed this life in his 66th year, after a short illness the Rev. John ROTH, Pastor of the Moravian Congregation of York; buried in the Moravian Burying Ground. He was born in 1726 at Sarmund in Germany & landed at New York 3 June 1765; he preached the gospel amongst the Indians for 15 years.

George LIGHTNER, Junr. & Peter RUMEL of Strabane Twp, York Co, gave 3 Notes of Hand to Andrew HOOVER of Mt. Joy Twp; warn persons from taking said Notes, as they are determined not to pay as he did not comply with their contract.

Henry FRY warns all who have Lots laid off to them by him not to pay any Ground Rent to Margaret FRY, widow of Godfrey FRY, the elder, decd, or to Samuel FRY but to pay the rent to him.

All persons indebted to George FRITZLEN of York Borough & all who have demands against him to settle before Oct. 1.

28. Wednesday, 3 August 1791

A Vacancy having taken place in the Senate of this Commonwealth by the death of Sebastion GRAFF, Esq. Deputies were appointed from York & Lancaster counties to recommend a replacement and met at Wright's Ferry and unanimously agreed to recommend Alexander LOWRY.

To be sold at public vendue at the late dwelling of Wendel KELLER, merchant in the town of Hanover, York County, a variety of furniture. Also sale of the house of Philip MEYER, innkeeper, in Hanover a large assortment of merchandise, consisting of broad cloths, coatings, stuffs, velvets, calicoes, etc. all the late property of the said Wendel KELLER. Conrad LAUB, Agent for Assignees.

Jonathan M'CREERY, having purchased tract of land of Joseph LONG, of Manallen Twp., York Co. for which said LONG has not been able to make sufficient title. Therefore, persons are warned from taking assignments on said notes.

Came to the farm of D. John MORRIS, a Black Mare, intermixed with gray. She is about 13 or 14 hands high, 13 years old & a natural trotter.

William REED of "Carroll's Delight" advises to all such as had teams employed in the Public Service in 1780, under the direction of Col. James CHAMBERLAIN, that their accounts have been brought forward by Mr. REED and are now liquidated & inquiries may be directed to him at his house or at Gettysburg.

Frederick HARMAN warns the public not to credit any person whatever on his account, not even his wife Magdalene. (Warrington Twp.)

William TOWNSLEY informs the public that he is setting up the business of a Coverlid Weaver at the late house of John TOWNSLEY in Mt. Joy Twp., York

Co., 4 miles from Little's town and near to Mr. TWEED's Mill, where he will weave double plain coverlids, lined & float lined, rugs, etc.

Howell's small map of Pennsylvania & the parts connected therewith relating to roads and inland navigation may be had at EDIE's & WILLCOCK's Printing office.

George FRITZLEN of the Borough of York informs his debtors that if they do not pay by 5 October their accounts will be put in suit. (Jul 26)

For sale a Plantation & Tract of Land of 632 acres in Monaghan Twp., York Co., adjoining lands of James DILL, Matthew DILL, Thomas CAMPBELL & Joseph DIXON, whereof Andrew WILSON lately died owner & seized. Contains 400 apple trees, 3 dwelling houses & land situated on the great Road from York to Carlisle, passing through on one Side & the great Road from Carlisle to Baltimore passing through on the other side, & meeting at one corner, where there is a House erected well calculated for a Tavern or Store, being 10 miles from Carlisle, 20 from York, 18 from Louisburgh and 1/4 mile from the Stone Meeting House, occupied by Rev. Mr. WAUGH. John WILLIAMS & Thomas CAMPBELL, Adm'rs. Thomas CAMPBELL, who lives adjoining the farm will show. (June 1)

29. Wednesday, 10 August 1791

Yesterday departed this life, Col. Michael RYAN, late a member of Lodge No. 3 of Philadelphia. (Rest of pages for this issue missing.)

30. Wednesday, 17 August 1791

On Friday evening 29th ult. Maj. Abraham LATCHA, of Northumberland Co., with his 2 sons and son-in-law, in attempting to cross the west branch of the Susquehanna with a canoe loaded with stones--the canoe sunk & Mr. LATCHA and sons were drowned.

On Friday last, the barn of Capt. John AYRES, of this county (Harrisburgh), took fire by lightning & together with all his crop was entirely consumed.

On Tuesday afternoon, Timothy PICKERING, Esq., arrived in Phila. from the Indian country, whither he had been sent by the President of the United States to negotiate a treaty with certain Indian tribes.

Died last week at the Pa. Hospital, Phila. the old horse called Braddock, supposed to be 41 or 42 years of age. There is no reason to question his being one of the horses employed in the expedition of General Braddock in the year 1755. He was blind with age & his teeth being worn down.

Frederick KINT has taken in a sorrel mare & black horse at his plantation in Paraside Towp, York Co.

Michael GRAYBELL, Gaoler has taken into custody, a Negro Man who calls himself Jack, a likely fellow, 5'6" high, wore a brown jacked lined with red & says he came from near George-town, Md. & brought a horse with him to near M'Alister's-town where he was taken up. Also holding a Mullatto fellow who calls himelf Spencer or Paca, 5'9" high, 25 years old, had on old linen trowsers & gray cloth jacket, was taken up in Peter Little's Town & says he belongs to Thomas FITZHUGHES, in Farquier Co., Va. On the 31st of July a Negro Man who calls himself Harry was committed; he is about 5'9" high, 29 years of age & says he belongs to a Mr. CHIZLEY, Montgomery Co., Md. & brought a horse with him. On the 3d of August a broken back'd Mullatto Man was committed who calls himself Tom. About 5' high, 22 years old, very poorly clothed, says he belongs to a Mr. WILLIAMS in Md.

John WALLS, boot & Shoe-Maker has removed to the west side of the Bridge, nearly opposite Squire FISHER's Tavern thanks his customers.

30. Wednesday, 17 August 1791 (Con't.)

My wife Love, having acted in a manner dishonorable, by leaving my bed & board without just cause, I hereby caution all persons not to credit her on my account, Adam MEIRISE. (Germany Twp., York Co.)

Whereas I bought a certain tract of land of Jacob MINIG, for which he promised me a good title, said land was incumbered by a debt due from said Jacob to Simon MINIG, which I have since assumed to pay. Michael MINIG.

Simon CRONE of Newbury Twp., York Co., obtained of Jacob CRONE 9 Bonds, the first to fall due 29 Nov. next. Cautions persons from taking assignments on these bonds until he makes a good title for the land.

31. Wednesday, 24 August 1791

Died Wednesday morning last in Chanceford Twp. this Co., after a long illness, Mrs. Sarah LAIRD, consort of Col. John LARID, a lady highly respected for her many virtues & accomplishments.

32. Wednesday, 31 August 1791

Died on Thursday morning last at Wright's Ferry at an advanced age, after a short illness, Mrs. Ann JEFFERIES, wife of Joseph JEFFERIES, from whence her remains were brought to this borough (York) & interred in the Episcopal Burying Ground. An excellent serman was preached by Rev. Mr. CAMPBELL.

Reward for runaway offered by George SHERMAN of Germany Twp., York, Co. An indented Irish servant Woman named Martha BROWN, about 30 years of age, grey-eyed & down look, 5'9" high, sandy hair, short & very much curled. She had on & took with her 1 brown gown, striped petticoat, large shaw, 1 pair of new calf-skin shoes lined with linen & silver buckles marked C.R., 1 large black fur hat. It is suspected that she went away in the company of a certain William COMPTON, a noted villain, who calls himself William JOHNSON & has been cropt at York for felony. He is about 6' high, 30 years of age, wears his hair tyed & rolled with an eel skin.

33. Wednesday, 7 September 1791

The Governor from Philadelphia mentions that contracts are concluded for improving the navigation of the rivers Delaware, Schuylkill, Lehigh, Lechawaxen; for opening & improving roads from Wilkesbarre to the Windgap, from KEPLINGER's mill to the Susquehanna, from Catawessy to Hamburgh, from Middle-creek to GRUBB's furnace, from Daniel TITUS's to Poplar-run; & for opening & improving the roads through the Long Narrows, and through Jack's and Igow's Narrows & through the Canoe Narrows.

The Governor of PA has made the following appointments: William BRADFORD Jr., Esq. one of the Judges of the Supreme Court. Jared INGERSOLL, Esq., Attorney-General of PA in the room of Mr. BRADFORD promoted. James BIDDLE, Esq., President of the Courts of Common Pleas in the Circuit, of the city & county of Phila. & the counties of Berks, Montgomery & Delaware. William Augustus ATLEE, Esq. President of the several Courts of Common Pleas in the Circuit of the counties of Chester, Lancaster, York & Dauphin. Jacob RUSH, Esq. President of the Courts of Common Pleas in the Circuit of the counties of Berks, Northampton, Luzerne & Northumberland. Thomas SMITH, Esq. President of the Courts of Common Pleas in the Circuit of the counties of Cumberland, Franklin, Bedford, Huntingdon & Mifflin. Alexander ADDISON, Esq. President of the Courts of Common Pleas in the Circuit of the counties of Westmoreland, Fayette, Washington & Alleghany.

33. Wednesday, 7 September 1791 (Con't.)

Lately invented by Thomas DUNCAN of Hamiltonbann Twp. in this county, a water machine. It is a whirling pump made to raise water by the principles of centrifugal force & the application of the principles of Mr. RUMSEY New Mill at the lower end of the body of the Pump.

Died Tuesday the 30th ult. in the 66th year of his age, after a short illness, Mr. George GARBER. He was a good neighbor & a remarkable man. The most part of his life had been chiefly devoted to the study of Astronomy & Philosophy, in each he was self-taught & was said to have arrived to a degree of eminence. He was interred in the Lutheran burying ground.

William M'CLEAN, Thomas CAMPBELL, John SPANGLER, Commissioners give last notice that collectors of townships in the county of York who have not settled off their State & County Duplicates are desired to give their attendance at the house of David CANDLER in York Town.

Whereas Matthias COPELAND of Frederick County, Md., gave a note of hand unto William BINGHAM, he warns all persons from taking this note as he is determined not to pay unless compelled by law.

Frederick & Jacob LETHER selling 475 acres situated in Dover Twp., York Co., on big Conawago Creek, 10 miles from Borough of York, 20 from Carlisle, 16 from the river Susquehanna & 60 from Baltimore Town. Has a large stone building containing of an oil-mill & saw-mill & room for erecting a fulling-mill, all supplied with water from Conawago Creek. Near the premises is a smith's shop. Likewise, another tract of 100 acres, lying contiguous to the above tract whereon there is built a complete merchant mill, the mill-house is stone. On said premises are 2 good dwelling houses, one of stone & newly built with a barn, stables & orchard.

34. Wednesday, 14 September 1791

To acquaint your readers & Thomas DUNCAN of Hamilton-bann Twp. that the Whirling Pump is not of late invention, nor upon the principles of centrifugal force, nor the application of the principles of Mr. RUMSEY's New Mill at the lower end of the body of the pump. The effects of the Whirling Pump depends on the pressure of the atmosphere & requires a valve in the lower end of the perpendicular shaft. Mr. RUMSEY's Mill depends on the pressure of a column of water & requires no valve.

Andrew JOHNSTON, unwilling, if possible, to add to those indebted to him, once more requests that they pay up.

William BRACKENRIDGE, Mt. Joy Twp., York Co., has taken up a sorrel mare, 8 or 9 years old.

To be rented, a Fulling Mill situated in Huntington Twp., between the Mill, formerly known by the name of Stephen FOULKE's & Nicholas WIREMAN's Mill on Bermudian Creek; together with a convenient Dwelling house & garden. Anthony SWISSER.

Benjamin KURTZ selling that noted Tavern now in the tenure of Elizabeth RANKIN, widow, situated on the north side of High Street, a few doors above the Court House in Borough of York. Also 2-story house & half lot, the property of Jacob GARTNER, situate on the east side of Beaver St., opposite Philip GOSSLER's Tavern in the Borough of York.

35. Wednesday, 21 September 1791

We are informed by a gentleman from Lewis-Town in Mifflin Co., that while the Court was sitting on Tuesday the 13th inst., about 200 men in arms assembled with the design to take the Hon. Samuel BRYSON, one of the

Associate Judges, off the Bench, & compel him to resign, & march him before them, barefooted, down the Long Narrows, to his farm; but were prevented by the spirited exertions of the Hon. Judge ARMSTRONG, the Gentlemen of the Bar & the worthy Citizens of that place.

For sale, valuable tract of land of 225 acres in Hamilton-bann Twp., York Co., part of "Carroll's Delight;" late the property of Thomas CLINGAN, Esq. Apply to Dr. George CLINGAN of Baltimore, David AGNEW, Ebenezer FINDLEY or Moses M'CLEAN, near the Premises, Trustees.

Jacob HAHN has opened in the house lately occupied by Michael HAHN, dec'd. a large & general assortment of dry goods & groceries.

For sale Plantation & tract of land in Manallen Twp., York Co., together with a good Merchant & Saw Mill thereon erected. Tract contains 203 acres. Land lies on each side of the Great Conawago, dwelling house & Mills are near the centre, both Mills are in good order. Good Dwelling-house with double barn, ready for roofing. Apply to Robert M'CONAUGHY on premises or John EDIE in York-town.

Three pounds reward offered by John IRWIN, living in Westmoreland county, near to Pittsburgh for two runaway indented Servants, one of then named John SOUDER, alias BOARDER, a smooth, round faced, likely young fellow, with short brown hair, about 18 years of age. He is a shoe-maker by trade & a very capable workman in both men & women's work. He is a native of Pa., & was bread up to Phila. The other a young woman about 20 years of age, named Sarah WILSON. She has a good countenance, a fresh complexion & short brown hair, of low stature & remarkably strong made for one of her sex. She was born in Ireland & is an excellent spinstress, but has lived in Phila. some years & will talk much about that city. There is no doubt but they will pass themselves for man & wife, as some criminal conections were suspected for some time before their escape. Give information to John SCULL, Post Master in Pittsburgh to receive full reward.

Whereas my husband, Adam MYRISE, by advertisement in this paper has cautioned all persons from crediting me on his account, as I have left his bed & board &c. It now appears to be a day of distress with many of our married females, the newspaper is made the vehicle to expose their names when the fault is chiefly the husbsand's: how much this maybe my case I leave the public to judge from his conduct, for by his lazyness, sloth, indolence & staying from home without providing the necessary sustenance--obliged me to go out & work amongst my friends, for to get a morsel of bread for myself & my helpless infant; at which period he happened to come home, & not finding me in the house, immediately locked the door, put up advertisements at all the taverns & sent a copy of it to the Printer to expose me in a newspaper, lest as he says, I might run him in debt, when he well knows he would not be trusted to the value of six-pence in the whole neighborhood. I would forgive him if he would forsake his licentious way of living & return to his duty, until then I caution all persons from trusting him on my account. Love MYRISE, Germany Twp.

36. Wednesday, 28 September 1791

James SHORT, just imported in the Ship Louis from Liverpool, a large assortment of merchandise suitable to the season, particularly a large quantity of broad cloths.

37. Wednesday, 5 October 1791 (Front page missing)

Chambersburg meeting in Franklin County, on Monday the 26th inst. at M'CORMICK's Tavern the following were nominated & ballots taken, viz:

For Congress, James M'CLEAN 60 - Thomas JOHNSTON 49. Assembly: James JOHNSON, 79; John RAY, 73; John M'CLAY, 44. Commissioner: Isaac BAIRD, 58 & Daniel BOYER 48.

Recommended Ticket to be run at the next General Election: Representative in Congress: Thomas HARTLEY. Representatives in The General Assembly: John STEWART, Henry TYSON, William M'PHERSON, Thomas LILLY, Alexander TURNER, Thomas THORNBURGH. For Commissioner: John MORROW. Deputies for 1st District: Yost HARBAUGH & Conrad LAUB Deputies for the 3d District: George SMITH & Henry WELSH. Deputies for the 4th District: Benjamin PEDAN & Alexander TURNER. Deputies for the 5th District: George M'MILLAN & Abraham BOWER.

Sheriff Conrad LAUB gives notice that a Senator will also be chosen in the room of Alexander LOWRY who resigned 4 October 1791.

The creditors of Matthew HARTFORD are desired to attend at the house of Baltzer SPANGLER in York-Town to present claims. Godfrey LENHART & Martin KREBER, Auditors.

William CRAWFORD of Gettysburg, again solicits those in his debt to come forward & settle their accounts.

Selling valuable plantation, late property of Robert M'KEEN, dec'd., in Cumberland Twp., on the great road from Gettysburg to Chambersburg, contains 250 acres. Stream called Willobv's [sic] Run passes through it. Apply to Thomas KERR for terms, who lives now on the premises or William M'GAUGHY, near it or to Thomas M'KEEN or Alex. M'KEEN.

Wants a person who understands the distilling business, apply to Alexander TURNER in Chanceford Twp.

38. Wednesday, 12 October 1791

John GREER, Borough of York, is now opening his store selling a large assortment of merchandise & hardware & cuttlery, boulting cloths &c.

Jonathan JESSOP informs the public that he continues business at that noted stand formerly occupied by Elisha KIRK, decd., where he makes all kinds of Clocks. As he has been absent for some time, he fears the workmen left in the shop has not given general satisfaction in watch repairs; therefore engages to rectify such deficiencies gratis.

Sheriff's Sales: Estate of David POTTER, 2 improvements & tracts of land, adjoining each other in Strabane Twp., one of them containing 200 acres & the other 100 acres, adjoining lands of William KING & William ROSS.

Estate of George LIGHTNER, improvement & tract of land, situate in said Strabane Twp., of 186 acres, adjoining lands of David SIMPSON, William COOPER & Hugh MORRISON.

Estate of Adam BLACK, improvement & tract of land, in Franklin Twp., 200 acres, adjoining lands of John GUNDY & Nicholas YOUNG.

39. Wednesday, 19 October 1791

Philip WAGNER selling on the premises 2 miles 1/2 from the borough of York, a plantation & tract of land of 269 acres in Manchester Twp., York County, late the property of Jacob WAGNER, dec'd. Log house, barn & stables & out houses.

40. Wednesday, 26 October 1791

General Election Returns for PA: Return of Northumberland Co.- Congress--Andrew GREGG; Assembly--Samuel MACLAY & John WHITE. Sheriffs--Favel ROAN, Thomas GRANT. Return of Northampton Co., Congress--Daniel HEISTER. Assembly Jacob EVERLY, Thomas MAHORTER, Thomas HARTMAN & Peter BURKHALTER. Return of Lancaster Co., Assembly--Joseph WORK, Abraham

CARPENTER, Abraham WHITMER, John BRECKBILL, James MORRISON & James OLD. Sheriff--John MILLER. Return of Delaware Co.--Assembly--Nathaniel NEWLAND & Hugh LOYD. Return of Dauphin Co.--Assembly--John A. HANNA, Stacy POTTS, Jacob MILEY. Return of Bucks Co.--Assembly--John CHAPMAN, Gerardus SYNKOOP, James BRYSON & Ralph STOVER.

John FORSYTH, speaks for the Governor & informs that he is collect the Arrears of Excise due.

John LEAS has taken up, trespassing on his premises in Tyrone Tpw., York Co., a bright Bay Horse, 14 hands high, 8 or 9 years old.

Thomas S. LEE selling 607 1/2 acre tract lying on Rock-Creek, Mountjoy Twp., York Co., 7 miles from Taney-Town (Md.), 7 from Little's-Town (Pa.) within a mile of the Merchant Mill. Apply to James BOLTON, Surveyor, in Hanover-Town or to Samuel SMITH, living near the land.

The Trustees of Franklin Co. propose to build a Court House in Chambersburgh. Also selling the Old Prison in Chambersburg. James MAXWELL, James M'CALMONT, Josiah CRAWFORD, John JOHNSTON, David STONER, Trustees.

41. Wednesday, 2 November 1791

John DONNELL, selling Spring Valley Farm, in Fawn Twp., York Co., contains near 400 a., dwelling house, out-houses & barn. 18 miles from the head of the tide at Rock Run, 45 from Christian Bridge & the same distance from Baltimore; Muddy Creek runs through the place, which form large beds of mud, suitable for manuering of hemp. Convenient to Presbyterian & Quaker Meeting houses. Also 1000 acres of land within 6 miles of Lexington, on the north side of Kentucky river. Tract can produce help & tobacco of 1st quality; also large number of uncultivated tracts of land in the country of Holston & Kentucky.

Notice is given to the Collectors of the County of York, whose names are hereunto annexed, who have not settled & paid off their respective State & County Levies, to attend the house of David CANDLER in York-town at the next Orphan Court, 23 Nov. next. Collectors names who have not settled off their Duplicates from the year 1781 to the year 1789: John LYNN, in right of Samuel GETTYES, Cumberland Twp.; Robert CRAIG in right of John CRAIG, Cumberland Twp; William ORR, Mt. Pleasant Twp; Michael DEISS, York Twp; Charles HEIM, Paradise Twp; Robert TAYLOR & William BREDEN, Cumberland Twp; David WILSON, Hamilton Bann Twp; Peter MILLER, Tyrone Twp; John SHULTZ, Germany Twp; Andrew SMITH, Shrewsberry Twp; Henry ZIEGLER, Huntington Twp; Jacob ARNDT, Franklin Twp; William M'BRIDE, Manallen Twp; George RUDY, Paradise Twp; George FLEMMING, Strabane Twp., Robert WRAY, Tyrone Twp; James COCHREN, Hamilton Bann Twp; Rudolph SPANGLER, Berwick Twp; Peter DINKLE, York-Town; Michael MILLER, Cororus Twp; William JOHNSTON, York Twp; Frederick SHAFFER, Paradise TWP; John CROWL, Corodus Twp; George ILGENFRITZ, York Borough; James M'NAUGHT, Menallan Twp; Nicholas MEYER, Reading Twp; Adam LEVINGSTON, Strabane Twp; George MITCHELL, Fawn Twp; Bernard SPANGLER, York Twp; Christian HEINLER, Germany Twp; John M'GREW, Huntington Twp; Michael WILL, Heidelberg Twp; Ebenezer FINLEY, Hamilton Bann Twp; William DOUGHARTY, Chanceford Twp; John SWEENY, Cumberland Twp; Joseph MORRISON, Franklin Twp; Frederick STEIN, Newberry Twp; John RUDISELL, York Borough, Jacob LEFAVER, York Twp; Jacob HERBAUGH, Germany Twp; John NEELY, Huntington Twp; Peter FRIED, Heidelberg Twp; Andrew M'CLEARY, Chanceford Twp; George KERR, Hamilton Bann Twp; Robert WORK, Cumberland Twp; John FLETCHER, Franklin Twp; John SHOEMAN, Newberry Twp; Isaac JONES, Fawn Twp; John GALBRAITH, Menallan Twp; Jacob HAFFNER, Codorus Twp; George JACOBS, Paradise Twp; James DENISTON, Warrington Twp; Gutleip KUNTHLE, Hellam Twp; Francis

SEIGRIST, Hopewell Twp; Nathan M'GREW, Tyrone Twp; Jacob WEIGET, Dover Twp; Godfrey KING, Manchester Twp; David MEYER, Monahan Twp.

For sale by William MITCHELL: No. 1, tract whereon he now dwells in Monahan Twp, York Co, 308 1/2 a. with square log house & double barn, about 18 miles from York, 12 from Carlisle & 10 from Harrisburgh. No. 2 in Northumberland Co on the 2d Fork of Pine Creek, 372 a., all wood land. No. 3 Tract on the 4th branch of Tioga, 306 a., all wood land.

Mills for sale in Franklin Twp, York Co, upon the great road, 2 miles from Black's Gap; with the Mills are 91 a., house & barn. Apply to David HOSACK on the premises.

John GRAHAM has taken up a brown horse. Lives in the South Mountain, Hamilton-bann Twp, York Co.

Whereas John STEEL, Esq. is offering for sale a tract of 150 a. in Huntington Twp, York Co, Alexander BROWN of Tyrone Twp gives notice that he is entiteled to it and is determined to have it.

42. Wednesday, 9 November 1791

The Partnership of EDIES & WILLCOCKS, Printers of this Paper, will be dissolved 28 December next. Subscribers who live at a distance with monies due can make payments to: William ROSS in Chanceford Twp; Capt. John CAMPBELL, Fawn Twp; Robert M'ILHENEY in Germany Twp; Barnabas M'SHERRY in Taney Town (MD); Robert BLACK in Mountjoy Twp; William PORTER & Ebenezer FINLEY in Hamilton Bann Twp; David EDIE in Cumberland, Franklin & Manallen Twps; James DICKSON in Tyrone & Strabane Twp; David BEATY in part of Strabane & Mount Pleasant Twps; Andrew THOMPSON, Huntington Twp.

John TOULERTON of Nelson's Mill, York Co, has just received an assortment of dry goods & groceries of European, East & West India Manufacture.

43. Wednesday, 16 November 1791

John DOLL, Junr., Notary Public, commissioned to reside within the Co of York; performs his duties at his house on the North side of High Street, Borough of York, opposite the German Reformed Church.

44. Wednesday, 23 November 1791

For sale tract of land in Hamiltonbann Twp, York Co, within 1/2 mile of Samuel COBEAN's lower mill on Marsh Creek, adj lands of Henry ROWAN & heirs of David M'CLELLAN, decd, 221 a. Large dwelling house, double barn. Apply to Alexander RUSSELL, Marsh Creek.

IRWIN & COBEAN at their store in Gettysburg selling a general assortment of merchandise.

Peter WHITESIDES seeks sober, industrious man who understands the Blue-Dying Business.

Tract of land for sale in Baltimore Co, (Md) on the great road from Baltimore town to little York, near Joseph SUTTONS; 500 a. Apply to John TELBOTT living on premesis.

Mountjoy BAYLY, near Frederick Town (Md.), has for sale 24,000 a. of land in the state of Georgia, on the waters of the Ogeechee River, 70 miles from Savannah.

Jacob HAHN of York, informs that he has opened in the house lately occupied by Michael HAHN, decd, a dry goods & grocery store.

45. Wednesday, 30 November 1791

David MILLINGER, Farrier, has discovered that there is a distemper prevalent among horses at present called yellow water, which proves very dangerous and thinks himself capable of curing same. For particulars enquire of Peter ICKES, Abbott's Town; Frederick WOLF, Henry BALSLEY, Charles GOOD or the subscriber near Abbott's Town.

46. Wednesday, 7 December 1791

All indebted to the estate of Jacob WAGNER, late of Manchester Twp, decd., to discharge same to Frederick YOUSE. YOUSE & Philip WAGNER, Admr's.

To be sold at the late dwelling of Jacob MEYER, decd., in Dover Twp; about 1 mile from Dover Town, grains, 4 horses, a waggon & gears & said decd's late dwelling plantation will be rented to the highest bidder. Peter MEYER & Martin CRONEMILLER, Executors. Also to be sold a tract of woodland containing 100 a. in Manchester Twp., on Codorus Creek, adj lands of Thomas DUNN, Philip I. KING & Baltzer RUDISELL.

Committed to custody of York gaol, a Mulatto Man who calls himself John DICKISON, says he belongs to William ROBINSON of Old Town, Md; a young fellow, 5'5" high; he also had a sorrel horse with him.

Edward DRINKER was born in a cottage in 1680 on the spot where the city of Phila now stands, which was then inhabited by Indians, a few Swedes & Hollanders. He remembered William PENN arriving there his second time. He died 17 November 1783, aged 103 years.

Wednesday, 14 December 1791 (Front page only, no local data.)

47. Wednesday, 21 December 1791

Alexander HANNA has taken in a red cow, came to his Plantation in Monaghan Twp, York Co, near DILL's Tavern.

Ludwig ECCLEBERGER has taken in a sorrel horse on his Plantation in Mount-Pleasant Twp., York.

(Lancaster) 13 December, a most dreadful fire broke out here opposite the store of Jacob FREY in King Street. Valentine KRUGH's dwelling-house, brew house, barn & kitchen & Jacob KRUGH's new barn with over 300 bushels of wheat & a large quantity of hay were reducted to ashes.

A meeting of inhabitants in the upper part of York Co, met in Hunter's Town on the 13th inst. Col. WALKER, Chair & William M'GREW, Clerk: The question, "Is a Division of York Co necessary?" was unanimously carried in the affirmative. The said line of division should commence at the mouth of Dogwood Run, thence in a direct line to Christian CLOSES' Mill, thence to ECCHELBERGER's Tavern, on the road from Hanover to York Town; thence in a 4th direction to the Md line.

O. H. WILLIAMS has for sale a tract of land on the west side of Kitcoclon Mt., (Cactoctin) 6 miles from Frederick Town (Md.); contains 368 a.; there is a noted tavern on the place. He also has 2 other tracts for sale; one of 315 a. the other 170 a. Both have good farm houses, barns, orchards &c. They are situated near Minocasy (Monocacy) 6 & 8 miles from Frederick & on the road to York. The land is $12 per acre.

A dark colored chestnut horse was taken up by James & Andrew ANDERSON in Hopewell Twp, York Co.

48. Wednesday, 28 December 1791

This day's Publication will conclude the Partnership of EDIES & WILLCOCKS, Printers. John EDIE, James EDIE & Henry WILLCOCKS. The business will be carried on as usual under John & James EDIE.

Richard MUMMERT has taken on to his plantation in Paradise Twp, York Co, stray cattle.

48. Wednesday, 28 December 1791 (Con't.)
Valentine STEAR has taken in an iron grey horse at his plantation in Germany Twp, York Co.
Michael BRESSEL has taken in at his plantation in Berwick Twp, a steer.

Wednesday, 4 January 1792 (Missing)

49. Wednesday, 11 January 1792
James COLEMAN & John JENKINS offer reward for 2 negro men named Phil & Daniel who ran away from them (living on Sugarland Run, Loudon Co, Va). Phil is 30 years old, 5' 5-6" high, apt to smile when spoken to, has flat nose, large mouth, wrinkly forehead with small scars on it, has the marks of the whip on his back; is a blacksmith by trade. It is supposed he has a pass & has a general acquaintance, having for many years worked on the road from Alexander to Leesburg. Daniel is a low well set lad, 19 years of age, 5' 4-5" high, is used to plantation work. He also has a pass & is supposed to be in company with Phil.
Peter ICKES seeks a person capable of teaching an English school. Abbetts Town.
Henry GROSS has taken in a small brindled cow at his plantation in Reading Twp, York Co.

50. Wednesday, 18 January 1792
Died, last Sunday at 10 a.m., in Lancaster, Nelly WRIGHT, aged 11 years & 8 months, niece to the lady of Gen. James EWING. Interred in the Friends' burying ground at Wright's Ferry, Susquehanna. She was deprived, while quite an infant, of both her parents.
Last Monday night James TATE of Marsh Creek settlement (York Co) was attacked by 2 armed foot pads on the road from Peach Bottom Ferry, within a mile of York & robbed of his saddle bags which contained a large sum of money in cash & bank notes. In the same issue James TATE offers $50 reward to secure the villians.
Edward O. WILLIAMS, living in Shepherd's Town, offers reward for runaway Negro Man named Gabriel, 31 years of age, 5' 8-10" high.

51. Wednesday, 25 January 1792
Richard KEYS, Dr. John WATSON, Thomas BAILEY, of Donegall & James HOPKINS of Lancaster & John GREER of York-Town, proprietors of a Tract of land on the east side of the Susquehanna River & the south side of Conawago Creek in Lancaster Co, have laid out a town called Falmouth, of 146 lots, of which they propose to dispose of by lottery. Each person who draws one or more Lots, shall have a good Deed in fee simple, without ground rent. Alexander LOWRY, John HALDEMAN & John WHITEHILL will supervise drawing.

52. Wednesday, 1 February 1792
Sale of plantation & Tract of 632 a., in Monaghan Twp, York Co, adj. lands of James DILL, Matthew DILL, Thomas CAMPBELL, Joseph DIXON &c; whereof Andrew WILSON died owner & seized. On premises 400 apples trees, 3 dwelling houses & land conveniently situated, having the great Road from York to Carlisle passing through one side & road from Carlisle to Baltimore passing through on the same side & meeting at one Corner, where a house is located. 10 miles from Carlisle, 20 from York, 18 from Louisburgh & 1/4 from Stone Meeting House, occupied by Rev. WAUGH. John WILLIAMS & Thomas CAMPBELL, Admr's. To view apply to Thomas CAMPBELL who lives adjoining same.

52. Wednesday, 1 February 1792 (Con't.)
Commissioners will receive proposals in writing from any Carpenter who will undertake to build a bridge over Conawago Creek, on the great road from York through Getty's Town, 1 1/2 miles from Henry KOON's Tavern. Thomas CAMPBELL, John SPANGLER, John MORROW, Comm., Co of York.

53. Wednesday, 8 February 1792
William Augustus BOWLES, who some time ago appeared in London in the character of an Indian Chief, who not an Indian by birth, but an Anglo American from Md; who being of an unsettled, roving disposition, attached himself to an Indian nation, became enamored of a savage life, married a savage girl & settled among her friends, & is now by adoption, though not by birth, an Indian warrior.
Married at Green-Castle on Tuesday last, Chaistopher [sic] WIEDER to Mrs. Margaret HAWSON. Their ages together make 132 years.
A duel took place on Monday the 16th inst. in Delaware, near the Md line, between James MATTHEWS & Richard HEATH, both young gentlemen of Cecil Co. (Md) of very respectable families. The former fell at the first fire & instantly expired. Reports say Mr. HEATH gave the challenge in consequence of his father (Daniel C. HEATH, Esq.) having been violently assaulted by the unfortunate Mr. MATTHEWS.
Married, on Tuesday 31 January last, Patrick CAMPBELL, Junr. of Franklin Co. to the much admired Miss Fanny STOCKTON of York Co.

54. Wednesday, 15 February 1792
Sheriff's Sale: Estate of James M'COSH, 2 improvement & tracts of land, in Franklin Twp, one of 117 a. adj lands of heirs of Philip SHEFFER, decd., Daniel SOWER & others; the other of 20 a. with an Oil-Mill thereon erected, adj John REED & others.
Estate of William BRENDEN, late Collector of Cumberland Twp., improvement & tract in Cumberland Twp, 120 a., adj lands of William M'PHERSON, Esq; Andrew BOYD & others.
Estate of George GILBERT, late Collector of Menallen Twp, improvement & tract in said Twp, 240 a., adj lands of Jacob GREENEMEYER, Samuel M'CONAUGHY.
Estate of Rudolph SPANGLER, late Collector of Berwick Twp, improvement & tract in said Twp, 150 a., adj lands of Adam & Michael MILLER, Jacob WIEST & others.
Estate of Matthew KILGORE, late Collector of Chanceford Twp, improvement & tract in said Twp, 200 a., adj lands of John M'CALL & John MARTIN.
Estate of Samuel CROSS, late Collector of Franklin Twp, improvement & tract in said Twp, 143 a., adj lands of William CROSS & John JOHNSTON.
Estate of William M'BRIDE, late Collector of Menallen Twp, improvement & tract in said Twp, 200 a., adj lands of William VANCE & Felix ARNDT.
Estate of John WILSON, late Collector of Monaughan Twp, improvement & tract in said Twp, 200 a., adj lands of Joseph ELLIOT & John WILLIAMS.
Estate of John HERMAN, late Collector of Newbury Twp, 200 a. with Grist & Saw Mill thereon erected, adj lands of John CLARK, Esq. & Eli LEWIS.
Caleb KIRK & Samuel UPDEGRASS near York Town selling clover seed.

55. Wednesday, 22 February 1792
On Friday last in East Pennsborough twp on George FRIDLEY's plantation: Two young men, one Mr. FRIDLEY's son, the other a son of Mr. FISHER of said twp, in digging a well the side caved in. Excavations continue, but both are assumed dead.

55. Wednesday, 22 February 1792 (Con't.)
Michael HOLTZ & Philip HOBACH gave William DONALSON, formerly of Dover Twp, York Co, 8 bonds, which he has not made good title to land purchased of him by the subscriber. They forewarn all persons not to take the bonds.

56. Wednesday, 29 February 1792
Jared IRWIN, Lisburn, Cumberland Co, has a number of lots in the Town of Lisburn to dispose of. There is no doubt but that the State Road from Philadelphia to Fort-Pitt will go through it.
Peter KURTZ selling plantation of 185 a. in Strabane Twp.; has tolerable good house & barn. The road from Hunter's Town, through Little's Town to Baltimore intersects the York road at the house & a public house has been kept there many years past. Apply Peter KURTZ, York Town.
All persons who have demands against the estate of Col. David M'CLELLAN, decd, to present them. Jacob & William M'CLELLAN, Exr's.
Selling 2 plantations & tracts of land in Manchester Twp, York Co; one 4 miles from Borough of York on Cororus Creek & about 200 yards from a Grist Mill, containing 200 acres; log dwelling house, barn, spring & still houses. The other is about 3 miles from Borough of York, 1 mile from aforesaid place, 192 a., log dwelling house, barn, &c. Peter DIEL & Philip J. KING, Exr's.
Gentlemen who have subscribed towards erecting Bridges over the Big & Little Conawago Creeks, on road from Carlisle to Hanover by Mr. WIREMAN's & Mr. LONG's Mills, are required to meet at Mr. LONG's to elect managers. Signed William LONG, Strabane Twp.

57. Wednesday, 7 March 1792
To be rented, plantation in Reading Twp. The Great Road from Carlisle to Baltimore passes through. Marmaduke WILSON & James CHAMBERLAIN, Guardians.
Dr. BLAIR's Sermons being reprinted by subscriptions in 2 volumes. Subscriptions taken in by Rev. John CAMPBELL of York Borough, Thomas CROSS of Franklin Twp, Mr. Seth DUNCAN Abbet's Town, Samuel EDIE, Esq., Cumberland Twp & the printers hereof. Rev. Mason L. WEEMS, editor.
For sale tract of land in Mountpleasant Twp, York Co, 6 miles from Little's Town, 4 miles from Getty's Town, adj lands of Hezekiah HAUGHTAILN, Robert YOUNG & others. Dwelling & spring house, large barn. Thomas JOHNSTON.

58. Wednesday, 14 March 1792
Godfrey LENHART, York Borough, & William M'CLELLAN; candidates for the office of sheriff.
The young horse Farmer, will stand this Season at William LONG's Mill on Big Cannowago Creek at $1 and a bushel of oats the single leap; $2 & a bushel for the season & $4 & a bushel of oats to ensure a colt. Jared G. LONG, Strabane Twp.
Selling tract of land on Possom Creek, 1 mile from Peter ECKARTS mill in Manallen Twp, York Co; 130 a., dwelling house, orchard, barn. Apply to Archibald M'GREW.
Whereas John M'PEAK of Cumberland Twp. obtained of James M'PEAK 2 judgement bonds; persons are warned not to take assignment on any of said bonds, as James is determined not to pay no part of either of them.

59. Wednesday, 21 March 1792
The President of the United States (George Washington) has appointed the following gentlemen, officers of the 12 companies of Rifle-Men to be

raised agreeable to an act passed the 5th inst. for more effectual defence of the frontiers: Pa: Captains--Edward BUTLER of Allegany; John GUTHRIE of Westmoreland; Richard SPARKS of Allegany, William FAULKNER of Washington, Uriah SPRINGER of Fayette, John COOK of Northumberland. Lieutenants--William SMITH of Washington; John CUMMINGS of Westmoreland, Samuel VANCE of Fayette, Nathaniel HUSTON of Washington, William STEEDMAN of Northumberland, Daniel T. JENNIFER of Allegany. Ensigns--Robert PURDY of Mifflin, John KELSO of Dauphin, Robert LEE of Northumberland, John STEEL of Cumberland, David HALL of Westmoreland & Reason BEALL of Washington. The following are appointed officers of the Squadron of Cavalry: Captain--John CRAIG of Pa. Cornet--James TAYLOR of Pa.

We hear that a Mr. POND, said to be a native of N. London, a man of bold & enterprizing character, who has lived in, and for a number of years has traversed all the Indian country to the north west & who is well acquainted with the Indians, their manners, customs and languages, has been sent for by the Secretary of War & is now set out for the western country upon some secret embassy.

To be sold a plantation & tract of land in Dover Twp., York Co, 13 miles from York Town & 3 from Berlin, with Merchant & Saw-Mill thereon. 190 a. with stone dwelling house, double barn lately built, two apple orchards. Land lies along the side of the Great Conawago Creek. Also selling Mill-stones, a boulting-cloth, waggon, 8-day clock, cows, rye, &c. Catharine GUNKEL & Jacob GUNKEL, Ex'rs.

Selling plantation in Berwick Twp. 1 1/2 miles from Conawago Bridge, between 2 - 300 a., held by patent; Conawago Creek runs through tract. Apply to John MENTIETH living on the premises.

Wednesday, 28 March 1792 (Missing)

60. Wednesday, 4 April 1792

John DICKSON, Conawago; Ignatius LIGHTNER, Borough of York, candidates for sheriff.

A. STEEL informing the public that he has removed his family from Lancaster to York Town, to that noted stand lately kept by George M. SPANGLER, known by the sign of the Sorrel Horse. He also informs the Distillers of York Co that he will attend at said House to receive money due, & flatters himself that without any trouble they will comply as quick as possible. (A. STEEL, Collector of the Revenue)

Selling 2 plantations in Huntington Twp, York Co, one 120 a., held by patent, dwelling house on farm. The other is held by warrant & survey, 150 a. with small house. Apply to Alexander BROWN in Tyrone Twp.

David MILLINGER informs persons indebted to him to settle. He is noted for curing the Ringbone, Spavin & Yellow-Water & other disorders to horses.

For sale, tract in Cumberland Twp, York Co, 1/2 mile from Getty's Town, on the west side of the waters of Rock Creek, 200 a., dwelling house, double barn &c. Apply to William or James TATE, Getty's Town.

Any person who will undertake to build 2 sufficient Bridges; one over Great Conawago at Mr. LONG's Mill & the other over Little Conawago near Mr. John MENTEETH's, attend at Henry KOON's Tavern. John HENDERSON & John CHAMBERLAIN of Berwick Twp.

To be rented for 3 years, that noted Tavern known by the Brogue, 15 miles from the Borough of York, on main road from thence to M'CALL's & Peach Bottom Ferrys, 180 a. John LAIRD

To be sold 1 May next, plantation & tract of 130 a. in Mount-pleasant Twp. adj lands of Benjamin WHITTLEY, Jacob BRINKERHOFF &c., late the property of Martin NEVOUS. Good dwelling house & barn. John MONFORE & George WILLIAMSON, Executr's.

61. Wednesday, 11 April 1792

For sale on the premises a plantation & tract adj Col. M'CALLISTER's land, near Hanover Town, York Co, 149 a., log dwelling house, barn & spring house. The great road from York through Hanover to Frederick Town passes through. Samuel & Jacob FORNEY.

Small pox has been found in the vicinity of York Town & Dr. ROBINSON will innoculate persons for $1 each. The poor to any number he will Innoculate gratis. Application to be made as soon as possible at Mr. SPANGLER's, 1/4 mile from York Town.

Michael HAHN, Esq., decd, Elizabeth, John & Jacob HAHN, Admr's.

Died Friday last of the Lock Jaw in York, William BROWN, aged 19 years, he received a wound in one of his feet, which was followed by his death.

Capt. Jacob SLOUGH has commenced recruiting a company of infantry to serve in the 3d Regiment for 3 years unless sooner discharged. Each recruit to receive $8 Bounty, $3 per month free of all deduction & articles of uniform. The Rendezvous is in the Borough of Lancaster.

Alexander UNDERWOOD is a candidate for the office of Sheriff.

Sheriff's Sale: Estate of Martin SHEETER, late Collector of Newbury Twp, improvement & tract with Grist & Saw Mill thereon in said twp, 174 a. adj lands of heirs of John SHETTER, decd, & George MILLER.

Estate of Robert Johnston CHESTER, decd, late Collector of Berwick Twp, a Tavern House & lot in Town of Berlin, adj lots of George SMITH & others.

Estate of Henry ZEIGLER, late Collector of Huntington Twp, improvement & tract in said twp., 149 a., adj lands of Henry BUCKHOLDER & Alexander SANDERSON.

Estate of Peter MILLER, late Collector of Tyrone Twp, improvement & tract in said twp, 100 a., adj lands of John NEELY, the Glebe & William WALKER.

Estate of Michael MILLER, late Collector of Codorus Twp, improvement & tract in said twp, 200 a., adj lands of Peter MEYER & Christian RUBEL.

Estate of Jacob MEYER, late Collector of Reading Twp. improvement & tract in said twp, 130 a., adj lands of Ludwick MEYER & Robert POLLOCK.

Estate of Jacob ARNDT, late Collector of Franklin Twp, improvement & tract in said twp, 180 a. adj lands of Jacob BEAR & Thomas CROSS.

Estate of Alexander POWER, the 1 equal undivided third part of the 3 following improvements & tracts, to wit, one contains 100 a, with a Ferry on the river Susquehanna; one other contains 42 a. & the third is 88 a.

Estate of William BRACKENRIDGE, decd, improvement & tract in Menallen Twp, with a Saw & Oil-Mill thereon, 100 a., adj lands of Peter STRASSBACH & Daniel NOEL.

Estate of Francis CLAPSADDLE, one equal undivided 7th part of improvement & tract in Mountpleasant Twp, 160. adj lands of James MASTON, Joseph POAK & Andrew M'ILVAIN.

Estate of Hans MORRISON, decd, improvement & tract of patented land, 424 a., adj lands of John FORSYTH, Esq., Samuel HADDEN & other lands of said decd. All seized & taken in execution to be sold by Conrad LAUB, Sheriff.

David CREMER offers reward for runaway apprentice lad, Jacob BILLMEYER. He is 14 - 15 years old, has red hair & freckled in the face, has an impediment in his speech & down cast look when questioned. (York)

62. Wednesday, 18 April 1792

From Pittsburgh the following intelligence by a party of men from Muskingum, a small station between Bellprae & Bellvile, on the west side of the Ohio, the Indians killed the wife & 3 children of one Deliverence BROWN, who being some distance from the house with his son, made their escape. The same account says that a house occupied 2 or 3 days before by one Samuel M'COLLOUGH, opposite the mouth of Possom Creek, 30 miles below this place, was burn by Indians.

From New York: In the Brigantine Army, Capt. BRAINE, came John ROBINSON who says that on 13 June 1785, an Algerine Corsair captured the ship Dauphin of Philadelphia. Richard O'BRIEN, Master; Andrew MONTGOMERY, Mate, Charles CALDWELL, Carpenter; Philip SLAWEN, James HALL, Peleg LOWRING, William PATTERSON, Jacobus FENNING, John ROBINSON, Edward O'RYLLEY, John DEERING, Peter SMYTH, Robert MCAKINESS, William SWEED & Mr. COFFIN of Nantucket a passenger. That the last 6 have died with the plague--that himself & Charles CALDWELL have been ransomed by their friends.

John HAHN is a candidate for sheriff.

In pursuance of last Will & Testament of Philip JACOB, decd, late of Paradise Twp, York Co., to be sold a tract in aforementioned Twp, adj lands of Christian HIMES, Jacob SARBAUGH, decd, Nicholas ENDRES & others, 276 a. the whole is patented. Good dwelling house, large barn, young bearing orchard of mroe than 300 trees, spring house. Also to be sold livestock, farming utensils & household goods. Samuel ARNOLD, Sen. & Philip ALTLAND, Sen. Execr's.

The creditors of Matthew HARTFORD are desired to attend at the house of Baltzer SPANGLER in York Town to exhibit claims. Godfrey LENHART & Martin KERBER, Auditors.

Wednesday, 25 April 1792 (Part of issue missing, no new local data.)

63. Wednesday, 2 May 1792

Michael KRYDER arrived in Baltimore on Monday with 104 barrels of flour, which he brought from his mill above the standing stone, on the Juniata, down that river to the Susquehanna, completing the voyage in 5 days.

War Department Appointments & Promotions in the Army of the United States (from Pa, Del & Md): Quarter Master-Gen. James O'HARA, Pa; Ensigns to fill vacancies in 5th & 2nd Regiments: Peter SHOEMAKER, William Marcus MILLS, Jacob KREEMER, John MICHAEL, Felix LONG all of Pa; Samuel B. TURNER & John WHISTLER of Md. Majors of Infantry appointed: Thomas BUTLER & John CLARKE of Pa: Henry GAITHER & Alexander TRUEMAN (promoted from Capt. in 1st Regt.) of Md. Surgeons appointed: Charles BROWN, James WOODHOUSE, William M'KROSKEY & James MEASE (MEAFE?) from Pa & Frederick DALCHO, Md. Surgeons Mates for the garrisons on the western frontiers & extra services: Thomas HUTCHINS of Pa, John SELLMAN of Md, & William A. M'CREA & James CLAYTON of Del.

Fredericksburg: Married on Tuesday the 6th ult., the Hon. Paul CARRINGTON, Esq., one of the Judges of the High Court of Appeals, in the 65th year of his age, to Miss SIMMS of Halifax co., age 15.

64. Wednesday, 9 May 1792

Philip WAGER continues the wine business at the stores late of WAGER & HABACKER.

House & lot in Gettysburg to be sold; 8 rooms with good kitchen, stable & garden. John SHEKLEY.

64. Wednesday, 9 May 1792 (Con't.)
Whereas Michael HARNISHT gave to John DRIVER 8 bonds conditioned on payment of 25 pounds each payable on 1 May 1792; this is to warn persons not to take said bonds as he is determined not to pay.
Resin HAMMOND of Elk-Ridge in Anne Arundel co (Md) offers reward for 2 young negro men, viz. Davy & Charles, brothers, who went off together. They are about 5'9" high, both knock kneed & Davy's ankle joints are very large.

65. Wednesday, 16 May 1792
Andrew JOHNSTON informs that he has renewed his former business at the sign of the Bear & Cub, next door to where he lived before, opposite Maj. BAILEY's in a commodious house which he has lately built.
William HARRIS has received at his store in York Borough a neat assortment of merchandise which he will sell at reasonable terms. (Books)

66. 23 May 1792
Sheriff's Sale: Estate of John POTTER, improvement & tract in Mountpleasant twp, 149 a., adj lands of Benjamin WEAKLY, John RANDG & Henry STURGEON.
Estate of John ABBETT, house & lot in Abbett's Town, Berwick twp, York co.
Appointments by the President of the U.S., by & with the advice & consent of the Senate has made the following appointments & promotions in the Army: Otho H. WILLIAMS, Brigadier General of Md. Infantry: William POWERS, Captain & Hartman LEITHEIZER, Ensign (both of Pa). Surgeon's Mates: John C. WALLACE of Pa.

67. Wednesday, 30 May 1792
To be published next Monday, A Sermon by John BLACK, Pastor of the Upper Presbyterian Congregation of Marsh-Creek Pa.
Nathan WORLEY has at his store, 2 doors from the Sign of the Indian Queen, for sale madeira, sherry, &c. wines of the best quality.
Committed to custody of the York gaol, a negro man who calls himself Peter BROWN, a young likely fellow, 4'6" high, very badly clothed, can play the violin & says he came from Havre-de-grace (Md).
Whereas the Sheriff of York co hath advertised a certain house & lot of ground in Abbett's Town, Berwick Twp, York Co to be sold as the estate of John ABBETT at Public Venue; this cautions all persons from bidding as the money said to be due in the Sheriff's hands has long since been paid William BAILEY, late Sheriff, by the sale of said Abbett's Lands & a motion will be made at next Court to stay the proceedings. Thomas ABBETT.

68. Wednesday, 6 June 1792
Extract of a letter from Ensign MURPHY, Reed's Station (Pittsburg, 22 May) This morning about sunrise Reed's blockhouse was attacked by Indians & one Gasper GEDICK & a child of John HARBESON's killed & HARBESON's wife & 2 children taken prisoners. John CURRIE's house is burnt & his cattle killed & a Mr. MILLEN's house was seen on fire.
A vocal & instrumental concert to be given under the direction of Mr. DYCHE at the Academy in York Borough. Tickets 1/4 dollar each.
John TOULERTON at Christian WERTZ's Tavern, York Co, has just received an assortment of dry goods & groceries. Cash or country produce.
Whereas David HOWDENSHELL & Henry KNELL gave 4 bonds to John GALLASPIE of Warrington Twp, they are determined not to honor.
A dark bay mare came to the plantation of William KERR, living near Marsh Creek, York Co, Hamiltonbann Town.

68. Wednesday, 6 June 1792 (Con't.)

Those who have just demands against the estate of Henry WALTER, late of Yorktown, decd., to bring in their claims. Michael GUNDACKER & Christopher LAUMANN, Exrs.

William BAILEY gives notice that the advertisement signed by Thomas ABBETT, forbidding the sale of John ABBETT's house &c. for the Residue of debt due James BLACK, & that said debt was paid by sale of ABBETT's land to William BAILEY, late Sheriff: I will support that the Debt & Costs paid by me, amount to 283 pounds 11.2 (accounting given).

69. Wednesday, 13 June 1792

Jacob REDHEFFER (Whitemarsh) digging in a lime quarry, removed a stone causing a cave in upon him & put an end to his existence. He has left a large family of children to lament his loss.

70. Wednesday, 20 June 1792

Samuel NEIDIG of Manheim Twp, gave his bond to John NEIDIG Sen of Heidelberg Twp, York Co, condition for payment, which bond Samuel has fully paid off, but does not known whether said John has delived up said bond & he does not know where said John is.

Whereas Elizabeth DUNWOODY, Berwick Twp, York Co, gave a bond to William DONALDSON for payment, persons are cautioned from taking said bond.

71. Wednesday, 27 June 1792

Was found, on the 12th inst. not far from Abraham FORNEY's tavern, in Earl Twp, Lancaster Co, in the woods, a dead man, who was almost putrified. Signed Emanuel CARPENTER & Jacob JOHNS.

Adam KENDICH, of Conestoga Twp, Lancaster Co, offers reward for runaway servant man John BEACH, 20 years of age, 5' 9-10" high, pretty stout with black hair & a bold smart look. He passed the river Susquehanna at Burkholder's Ferry Monday morning last.

72. Wednesday, 4 July 1792

Died on Monday the 2d inst, at the house of Caleb KIRK, about 2 miles from this Borough (York), William M'KENNERY, a young & very healthy man. His death was occasioned by drinking cold water before breakfast in the harvest field.

Wednesday, 11 July 1792 (Issue available, no new local data.)

Wednesday, 18 July 1792 (Missing)

73. Wednesday, 25 July 1792

Hannah MATHEWS, Executrix of William MATHEWS, late of Borough of York, merchant, dec'd.

A dark bay mare strayed from the farm of John FREY in Franklin, about 2 miles east of Chambersburg. Reward offered.

In answer to publication by Thomas ABBETT. William BAILEY, late Sheriff makes no doubt that it was published to injure his character. The sheriff went to see ABBETT's honest father, now decd, & prevailed on him to sell part of his land to keep said Thomas out of jail, and he, a good man, agreed & delivered to the sheriff which land was assigned for sale. Debts have long been disposed of and included payment to: Michael GRAYBELL, gaoler; Daniel BARNETZ, tavernkeeper, Hanover; Andrew JOHNSTON, taverkeeper, York and John EDIE, Esq.

73. Wednesday, 25 July 1792 (Con't.)

William BAILEY, Coppersmith of the Borough of York informs that he carries on his business in all its various branches as usual at his dwelling house opposite to Andrew JOHNSTON's Tavern, Sign of the Bear & Cub--at Chambersburgh under direction of his son William,--at Hager's Town, next door to Jacob HARRY, Hatter, in Partnership with his Son-in-law, Mr. William REYNOLDS,--and at Frederick Town, near the Poor House, in Partnership with his Brother-in-Law, Robert M'CULLY. He will attend every quarterly Court week at Thomas FOSTER's Tavern in the Borough of Carlisle.

Susanna WHITELY of Louden Co., Va., 20 miles from Nolen's Ferry on the Potomac, offers reward for runaway Mulatto Slave named James MURRAY; about 40 years of age, 5' 10-11" high.

James HAMILTON of Franklin Township agreed some time since to sell a house & lot of ground in Hunter's Town to William M'KEEN, gives notice that he has not made a Title to said house & lot, nor will he until M'KEEN fulfills engagements to him.

Thomas DUNN has taken up a bay Horse come to his plantation at Dunn, in the Borough of York.

74. Wednesday, 8 August 1792

Edward BUTLER, Capt. Rifle Infantry, gives notice that he has left a soldier authorized to engage Recruits in his Company of Rifle-Men who will be quartered at Robert WILSON's in York.

Thomas ABBETT answers the late sheriff William BAILEY & informs the public to pay no regard thereto as it was done by said BAILEY to blindfold the public & keep the balance due ABBETT in his own hands; also that a balance of money is still due him by said BAILEY.

75. Wednesday, 15 August 1792

Sheriff's Sales: Estate of John ALTSHOE, late Collector of Monaughan Twp, improvement & tract of land in said twp, 200 a., adj lands of William BELL & Thomas EVANS.

Estate of Samuel CROW, late Collector of Fawn Twp; improvement & tract in said twp, 200 a., adj lands of George NICKELL & Benjamin CUNNINGHAM.

Estate of John SCHREIBER, late Collector of Mountpleasant Twp, improvement & tract of land in said twp, 100 a., adj lands of Ludwick SCHREIBER & John M'CREARY.

Estate of John SWEENY, late Collector of Cumberland Twp, improvement & tract of land in said twp; 227 a., adj lands of Robert M'KEAN & David RIDDLE.

Estate of Michael WILL, late Collector of Heidelberg Twp, improvement & tract in said twp, 130 a., adj lands of Martin WILL & Peter FRIED.

Estate of Robert ELLIOT, late Collector of Monaghan Twp, 2 improvements & tracts in said twp; one 159 a. & the other 60 a., adj lands now or late of Joshua ELLIOT & Thomas CAMPBELL.

Estate of Adam LIVINGSTON, late Collector of Strabane Twp, improvement & tract of land in said twp, adj lands of John SAMPLE & John M'CLURE.

Estate of Robert WORK, late Collector of Cumberland Twp, improvement & tract in said twp, 400 a., adj lands of William M'CREARY & Robert M'CURDY.

Estate of Jacob KEHRBACH, late Collector of Germany Twp, improvement & tract of land in said twp, 200 a., adj lands of Mathias BAKER, Joseph FLASH & John RIEGEL.

75. Wednesday, 15 August 1792 (Con't.)
Estate of James DENNISTON, late Collector of Warrington Twp, improvement & tract of land in said twp, 350 a., adj lands of Brice BLAIR & Catharine KEPPELY.
Estate of Thomas ARMOR, the elder, decd., 1 equal undivided 3d part of improvement & tract in Paradise & Codorus Twps, 120 a.; also 60 a. in Huntington Twp, adj lands now or late of Henry WIREMAN & Henry SEAFRID.
Estate of William PETTEGREW, improvement & tract of land in Fawn Twp, 33 a., adj lands of Cunningham SEMPLE, Nathaniel WILEY. All being seized & taken in execution as the estates aforesaid & to be sold by Conrad LAUB, Sheriff, York Co.
Henry SLAGLE states that David MELLINGER of Berwick Twp, York Co., Farrier, has lately cured his horse that had destructive distemper called the Yellow Water. Other owners that likewise testify are: Peter ICKES, Benjamin WIREMAN, Thomas COOPER, Michael SIVER, Peter GRUP, James NICKEL, Thomas NEELY & Joseph DODDS.
Whereas Jacob WISE, Senr, living in York Co, happened to be some time in June last in Harrisburg on business, & was, by Conrad DERR of Dauphin Co, forced in a most deceitful & fraudulent manner to sign a judgement Bond payable to saidd DERR. All persons forewarned not to take said bond.
Jacob HERBAUGH gives notice to all indebted to him to pay up as he is to leave the county immediately after 20 September next.
John M'KAISSAN & Abraham MOSSER of Windsor Twp warn persons from taking assignment on a Note given by them to Nicholas MURPHEY of Chanceford Twp, York co, as they are determined not to pay.

76. Wednesday, 22 August 1792
Sheriff's Sale: Estate of James Porter EWING, improvement & tract of land in Fawn Twp, 61 a., adj lands of Nicholas COOPER.
Thursday the 16th inst., in Philadelphia, was found the corpse of a young woman in one of the docks near Kensington. Inquest verdict was wilful murder by persons unknown. Her name is Elizabeth REEVES, about 17 years of age--handsome--apprentice to a mantus maker & courted by a young tradesman of the vicinity.
William BAILEY, York Borough, seeks journeymen coppersmiths.
Whereas John SCHULLIAN, Borough of York, has been legally declared a Lunatic by Commissioners of Lunacy, by the Court of Common Pleas for Co of York. Said court has appointed Andrew JOHNSTON, William WELSH & Christian HECKENDORN a Committee to take charge of the person & estate of said Lunatic. Samuel RIDDLE, Attorney.
Alexander UNDERWOOD is a candidate for sheriff, Co of York.

77. Wednesday, 29 August 1792
Andrew BILLMEYER, Chief Burgess, Ephraim PENNINGTON, Burgess & John DOLL, Jun, Town Clerk, (York) inform the public of Ordinance enacted 24 August regarding the driving of horses, waggons, carts & drays faster than a slow pace or trot in Borough streets.
John M. GANTT, Clerk for the Commissioners, advises that a number of lots in the City of Washington will be offerd for sale by the Commissioners.
James M'KNIGHT, Franklin twp, York Co, has taken in a stray mare.

78. Wednesday, 5 September 1792
George NEBINGER is a candidate for sheriff of York Co.
David DEMPSTER, Gettysburgh, due to want of an Apothecary Shop in the neighborhood, has laid in a small assortment of Medicines.
Philip ALBRIGHT of York Town offers $6 reward for an indentured servant man named Francis Henry FOSE, born in Germany, about 20 years of age, 5'6" high, stoop shouldered.
Thomas DICK, Hamiltonbann Twp, York Co, offers reward for runaway apprentice boy Joseph ROBINSON, 19 years of age, 5'9" high, swarthy complexion, very talkative & shews his teeth much when he laughs.
David SIMPSON, James GETTYS & Alexander IRVING, Auditors appointed by the Court of Common Pleas in York, notify creditors of John POE, late of Cumberland Twp, York Co, to meet at the house of Henry HOKE in Gettysburgh to get their dividend of said POE's estate.
Stolen last night, out of the pasture of Henry STRICKLER living in Hellam Twp, York Co, a black mare. Reward if delivered to Baltzer SPANGLER or Jacob OBB, Tavern-keepers in Borough of York.

79. Wednesday, 12 September 1792
Married on Thursday evening last, by the Rev. Daniel SHROEDER, James M'ALISTER of Hanover to the Amiable Miss Eliza WEEMS, both of this co.
John MICHAEL, Ensign, 1st U. S. Regt., offers reward for Elias SULLIVAN who deserted from Carlisle on Tuesday night, 4 September inst. He is 5'8" high, 23 years of age, short curly light hair & says he was born in St. Mary's Co, Md. Also Richard HARRIS, 5'10" high, 23 years of age, dark complexion, a little stoop shouldered, black short bushy hair, he was likewise born in St. Mary's Co.
The partnership of KERR & WORK will dissolve by mutual consent. George KERR intends keeping as usual a general assortment of dry goods & groceries. Gettysburgh.
Jacob MARCH & Daniel MAY, Exrs. of the estate of George MARCH, late of Dover Twp, decd.
To be sold, 200 a. of tract of land in Strabane Twp, on great Conawago Creek, 3 miles from Hunter's Town on the great road from Carlisle to Baltimore, property of Richard BROWN, Senr.
Came to the enclosure of Conrad SMITH, Newbury Twp, York Co, on Arthur ERWINS plantation, a dark brown cow.
Commissioner's Office, York Co, legal notice of all such tracts of land where the owners have neglected to discharge taxes levied; also there appears to be a very considerable sum of money due on lands of nonresidents in the county of York from the year 1763 until the year 1789, signed Thomas CAMPBELL, John SPANGLER & John MORROW, Commissioners.
Mountpleasant Twp State & County Levies. Acres: William GETTYS, now in the tenure of Patrick M'SHERRY; George FARRIES & Barnabas SMOCK.
Chanceford Twp: Abraham BURKHOLDER, Abraham NEWCOMER, STONER's land; Conrad LOOKUP; Joseph BROWN; Joseph CATHCART; Walter ROBISON; Richard CORDS; James MILLHORN; CHURCHMAN & LYNCH; William EMMIT; PAIN's heirs for land in Hopewell & Fawn Twp; Samuel PATTERSON.
York Borough: Henry KEPPELY, Junr & Richard STILLINGER for 1/2 lot of ground.
Paradise Twp: Jacob STIFFLER.
Windsor Twp: Charles KLUG; Zachariah SHUGART in Windsor & York Twps; Jacob KREIDER; Ulrick REIBER; John ARND, John CHURCHMAN.
Cumberland Twp: Alexander ORR; Joseph MARK; Hugh HAMILTON; Peter SWEITZER; John WILLIAMS; Michael ROWDEBUSH; Patrick VANCE; Barnabas SAINTMEYER;

Adam HOPE; John BRIGGS; Samuel GETTYS; Thomas M'CLEARY; Jacob CHRIST; Jacob OYLER.

Codorus Twp: ESCHELMAN's land & Anthony M'CAWL.

Fawn Twp: Hannah BRODLEY; Elijah FORSYTH; Eleazer BROWN; Jeremiah BRANITZ; Jacob GILES; Lavan HOPKINS; Hugh WHITEFORD; Isaac WHITELOCK; Patrick EWING; Jarret JESSE; John COX; George STEPHENSON's Heirs; John MOODY for ROBINSON's land; William W'CASKEY [sic]; James STEVENSON; William GEMMILL.

Houses & lots in Little's Town, Germany Twp: Joseph FLAUTH, formerly John BLOOM; Widow M'SHERRY in possession of William REED; Patrick M'SHERRY, in possession of Christopher STEALY; Patrick M'SHERRY formerly Henry MOORE.

Newbury Twp: William BLUMSTEAD; James SMITH, Esq. in Newbury & Chanceford Twps; William PASSMORE; John MEYER; John LEMON, John HARRIS; Matthew PATTERSON; James M'CRACKEN; Jones CHAMBERLAND; John CLEMSON; William UPDEGRASS; Christian OBERHELSTER; Christian REEB's estate; Owne HUGHES; GIBSON's heirs; Conrad SHAFFER; George ATHBRIDGE a balance in Newbury & Hamilton Bann twps; Thomas SHARP; Jacob HORSE; Robert & Ellis LEWIS; Thomas REED; Marcus HULIN; Thomas WARTON; Samuel RICHARDS; John LOGAN; Peter RHOADS; George DUNDORE; Adam WEAVER; RICHARDSON & MILLS; Moses RAMBO; Andrew RAMBO; George FREY; Thomas JENNINGS.

Hopewell Twp: Philip TANNER; Thomas PINN's land; Israel MORRIS's land in Hopewell & Fawn Twps; Henry BRODLEY; FUGIT's land; John LEWDEN; Moines MOODY; James M'MACHEN; Moses BENENINGTON; James SWEENY; KIRKHART's land; William MATTHEWS; Frederick BROSE; John CROSS; William MILLER; James M'FARLAND; David LATHAN; Walter WILEY; BROWN's land; Henry DOHM; SAINTCLAIR's Orphans; GROVER's land; CHURCHMAN's land; Thomas ARMOR, sen. for lands in Hopewell, Newbury, York & Berwick Twps.

Dover Twp: EDMONDSON's land.

Menallen Twp: Thomas COOKSON; Henry CREIGHTON; David M'CLURE; Samuel RENDALS; WHITEHEAD's land; GAUT's land; HAMMELL's land; Joshua HARLIN; Samuel M'CREARY; Joseph HUBLY; Hans MORRISON; Nathan GRAHAM's estate.

Tyrone Twp: Jacob VAGDES.

Manchester Twp: LOGAN's land; John CALHOON; John GREAF; George ROSS; Adam SHANK; Mary LOLLAR; Isaac NORRIS; Jacob GOOD; Bartram GALBRAITH, Esq; Joseph DONALDSON; Julius BRUCKHART; John HAGNER, Botts Town.

Monaghan Twp: William BLONK; Thomas KITON; Nicholas RILON; Robert ROSEBERRY; James BEATY; Samuel BETTEN (this land was sold to William RANKIN & is confiscated); Andrew PETERS; John BOYLE; Lewis LEWIS; John CLARK; Richard PETERS, Esq. for land in Monaghan & Berwick Twps.

Huntington Twp: George ARMSTRONG; Robert or David CURRY; Jesse LUKENS; Alexander BROWN.

Manheim Twp: John BOOS, sen; Mark FURNEY; Mark FURNEY & M'ALISTER; Edward MILLER.

Reading Twp: Peter LEIGHTLY; Thomas GRAY; Henry JACOB in Reading & Paradise Twps; John M'COY; Peter FANISTOCK.

Shrewsbury Twp: Issabella WADDLE; John LAWSON; John ORR; Frederick HOBIES.

Hamiltonbann Twp: David KENNEDY; Benjamin GUIST or GAUST; James ELLIS; Barnabas LINKART; David LISTER; John REIDER; John FERGUSON; John JACK; James BOSTON; John RIDDLE; Jacob GORMAN; COMMER's land; William HART, Widow M'GAUGHY; William ASKEW; John ENGLISH; Seth DUNCAN; William M'CORD.

Warrington Twp: Peter SHUGART; Christopher MILLER; William BAIDEN; Samuel ENGLAND; Joshua BROWN; Joseph COOK; Joseph STEER; Samuel EDMONDSON; Jonathan LITTLE's estate; Thomas CULLEN; James PECKER; William FELL; Mary HOLLAND; Matthew BLACKFORD.

Heidelberg Twp: DIGGS's land; Christian HERR; Martin KERBACH.

York Twp: Francis Jacob MILLER; Andrew GROFS (GROSS?) for land near Peter PETER's.

80. Wednesday, 19 September 1792

A meeting of District Deputies of York County made the following nominations: For Representatives in the General Assembly: Thomas LILLY, John STEWART, William M'PHERSON, Philip GARTNER, Thomas THORNBURGH, Alexander TURNER. Conferrees: Henry MILLER, John HAY & Henry SLAGLE, Esqrs. Commissioner: William NELSON. George BEARD, Jacob BARNITZ, George P. ZEIGLER, Abraham MILLER, 1st District. William GILLILAND & William REED, 2d district. Paul METZGER, Conrad REINACKER & Frederick BAUGHER, 3d district. William ROSS, William NELSON 4th district. Elihu UNDERWOOD & John FICKES, 5th district.

Tracts of land for sale by Thomas HARTLEY, York Town: One Tract called "Huff's Cabbins" 9 miles up north branch of Bald Eagle; Two tracts in Nittany Valley, adj or near Capt. CONNELLY & Clary CAMPBELL. Iron works are erecting within a few miles of lands. Two tracts on Brier Creek, not far from Mr. SHIPPEN's Land, on the north branch of the Susquehanna. Mr. Richard MALONE, who lives near the Bald Eagle's nest, will be as good as to show the land on Spring Creek & the Bald Eagle. Capt. CONNELLY or Mr. CAMPBELL, those in Nittany valley. William MONTGOMERY, Esq. or Northumberland will show tracts on Brier Creek.

Sheriff's Sale: Estate of Daniel M'CURDY, late collector of Monaghan twp, improvement & tract of land in said twp; 100 a., adj lands of Richard PETER's Esq.

Estate of William COWAN, improvement & tract of land in Chanceford Twp; 50 a.; adj lands of William ROSS, Esq., William HENRY, George SPANGLER.

Estate of William MITCHELL, Esq., improvement & tract in Monaghan Twp; 308 a., adj lands of Richard PETERS, Esq., William CONTRY & Andrew WILSON.

Ranaway from Alexander Johnston EDMISTON, living in West Nottingham Twp; Cecil Co, Md, a Negro man named Jack, about 22 years of age, 5' 10-11" high; with scar on one side of his face near the corner of his eye; has a large nose. It is supposed he went with Negro Bill, who was sold from this place to North Carolina & has run away from his master. It is thought he will head to Marsh Creek, where Bill has 2 brothers; one free, the other the property of Nathaniel GELLISPIE.

Creditors of William KERSEY are desired to meet at Thomas FISHER's, Borough of York 18 October next.

81. Wednesday, 26 September 1792

At a Conference in Lancaster 20 September inst., for the purpose of proposing names of suitable persons to represent Pa in Congress of the U.S. & to serve as Electors of President & Vice President: Philadelphia City: William LEWIS & Robert WAIN. Co. of Bucks: John BARCLAY, Abraham STOUTS, Gerardus SYNKOPP & William BUCKMAN. Chester: Richard THOMAS, William GIBBONS, Samuel EVANS & Thomas ROSS. Lancaster: George ROSS, John HUBLEY, Robert COLEMAN, Abraham CARPENTER, Charles SMITH, Thomas BOUDE. York: Henry SLAGLE, Henry MILLER & John HAY. Berks: Gabriel HEISTER, Caleb JONES, Jacob BOWER, Peter FELBERT, Nicholas LUTZ. Northampton: William HENRY & Robert BROWN. Montomgery: James MORRIS, John SHOEMAKER Junr, Edward SHIPPEN Junr. Dauphin: Cornelius COXE & John KEAN. Delaware: William GRAHAM & John Jonas PRESTON. Gerardus WYNKOPP, Chair. Thomas ROSS, Secretary.

81. Wednesday, 26 September 1792 (Con't.)

The above also recommend: Thomas FITZSIMONS, Charles THOMPSON, William BINGHAM, Frederick A. MAHLENBERG, David HESTER, John W. KIDDERS, Samuel SLEGREAKER, Thomas HARTLEY, William IRWIN, James ARMSTRONG, Robert ??MSTON, Phenias SCOTT, William FINLAY & the following as Electors of President & Vice President: Thomas M'KEAN, William ATLEE, Daniel CLYMER, Robert COLEMAN, John WILLIS Junr, James ROSS, (Washington) Henry MILLER, William HENDERSON, David RITTENHOUSE, John BOYD, John M'DOWEL, (Chester) John CARSON, Samuel DAVIDSON & David STEWART. Signed, John ARMSTRONG, John MONTGOMERY, Stephen DUNCAN, Samuel POSTLETHWAIT, Ephraim BLAME, Thomas SMITH, Samuel A. M'COSTRY, William ALEXANDER, Thomas DUNCAN & George STEPHENSSON.

Also, the citizens below for members of Congress: Thomas FITZSIMONS, Thomas SCOTT, Frederick A. MUHLENBERG, William IRVINE, James ARMSTRONG, Thomas HARTLEY, John Wilkes KITTERA; Henry WYNKOOP, William BINGHAM, William FIUDLEY, Samuel SITGREAVES, Peter MUHILENBERG, Daniel HEISTER.

The following ticket for Electors of President & Vice President: James ROSS of Washington, Robert COLEMAN of Lancaster, Henry MILLER or York, John BOYD of Northumberland, William HENRY of Northampton, Thomas BULL of Chester, John WILKANS of Alleghany, Cornelius COX of Dauphin, David STEWART of Huntington, James MORRIS of Montgomery, George LATIMER & Robert HART, City & Co of Philadelphia, Joseph HIESTER of Berks, Hugh LLOYD of Delaware & Robert JOHNSTON of Franklin.

Patrick CRETIN, proprietor of a lottery with the prize a plantation in Harford Co, (Md) near the Lower Crossroads; also prizes of livestock. To be drawn at James's CRETIN's at the Black Horse Tavern on the York Rd, under the direction of the following managers: Edward PRALL, John Lee GIBSON, Mrs. FREE, B. BROWN, Joseph BROWNLY, Thomas GIBSON & Patrick DORAN.

Thomas S. LEE selling tract of patented land on Rock Creek, in Mountjoy Twp, York Co, 7 miles from Little's Town, 3 from Gettys Town & 7 from Tawney Town (Md). 607 1/2 a.; apply to James BOLTON, Surveyor, in Hanover Town. Samuel SMITH living near will show.

Property of Peter WINEBRENER, decd, to be sold. Lot of ground with 2-story frame house, good cellar, kitchen & barn thereon. On York Street in the town of Hanover.

Came to the Plantation of Frederick LITTLE, living in Germany Twp., York Co, a gray mare.

For Sale, two-story house & lot of ground. Enquire of Jacob HINKLE & Jacob HERRETIN, Hanover.

82. Wednesday, 3 October 1792

Mary KENNEDY passed & gave a note of hand to Godlieb ZEIGLE, of the Borough of York, she forewarns persons that she will not honor same.

Jacob SITLER gives notice that creditors of William KERSEY are desired to meet at his house, Borough of York.

Thomas GIST of Baltimore Co, Md, near Owings Mills, offers reward for runaway Negro lad named Fill, 16 - 17 years of age, straight & slim made, 5' high, round faced & has down look when spoken to.

Conrad LAUB, Sheriff, selling improvement & tract in Monaghan Twp, 308 a., adj lands of Richard PETERS, Esq., William CONTRY, & Andrew WILSON. Seized & Taken in execution as estate of William MITCHEL, Esq.

Peter PIPER, of Marsh Creek settlement, Franklin Twp, offers reward for return of runaway indented German servant, Daniel HELLAM. 5'2" high, 18 years of age, swarthy complexion & pitted with the small pox.

Wednesday, 10 October 1792 (Issue available; no new local data.)

83. Wednesday, 17 October 1792

John DOLL executed 14 bonds to Nicholas BITTINGER to purchase land in Paradise Twp; said land is now claimed by the representatives of John ABBETT, decd, he warns all persons not to take assignment on said bonds.

Selling at public auction a large collection of new & old Books, and Robert WILSON, York Borough, intends to hold an auction of books as may be delivered to him for that purpose every second Saturday.

84. Wednesday, 24 October 1792

Notice given by Anthony BUTLER, Atty, for John PENN Junr. & John PENN, that business matters for the PENNs should be applied to atty in Phila.

The ship La Fayette of Philadelphia, Andres MILLER, Sen. Master, to sail 1 December next. For freight apply to James CRAWFORD.

John MORRIS has been appointed a Notary Public for the Co of York.

Sale on the premises a tract of land in Dover Twp, on the great road from York to Carlisle, 8 miles from former; 130 a., dwelling & spring house, barn; in pursuance of will of Samuel KNISELY, decd. John KNISELY, Tobias KEPLER & Jones YONER, Exr's.

Peter BRILLHARD, in Shrewsberry Twp, has taken up a stray steer.

John CAMPBELL has removed from Peachbottom Ferry to that noted stand, known by the name of M'CALLS Ferry, on the river Susquehanna, where he has good entertainment & accomodations for travelers.

Orphans court sale, Co. of York, one undivided third part of tract in Menallen Twp, York Co., 300 a., being real property of Alexander M'LURE, decd, bounded by lands formerly belonging to William BELL & Moses HARLIN. John M'LURE, Adm'r.

85. Wednesday, 31 October 1792

Conrad LAUB, Scrivener & Surveyor, Borough of York, Office opposite the public building near the Court House.

Ranaway from William ALLISON living in Franklin Co, Pa, a Negro man named Tom, 24 years of age, 5' 10-11" high, stout made.

Robert RYAN, living in Warrington Twp, near CARPENTER's Tavern, has taken in a dark bay horse.

Andrew WAIMER, living in Manchester Twp, York Co, has taken up a stray horse.

86. Wednesday, 7 November 1792

To be sold to the highest bidder, at Hanover Town, the Houses & Stores formerly owned & occupied by Wendle KELLER, in Town of Hanover, commonly called M'CALLISTER's Town, being one of the best houses in the town. Also plantation with improvements near Gettys Town, York Co, late the property of Wendle KELLER. POULTNEY & WISTAR, Ellis YARNALL, George ASTON, Assignees.

A man & his wife, and his son, and a cat, and a cock, and a hen, and 3 pigeons, and 4 pigs, and a large bear, a badger, all live snugly in a single room in Chester, about 3 yards square. They improve the salobrity of their enviable apartment by the fragrant trade of herring smoaking.

Was broke open on the night of 30 October, store of Mordecai M'KINNEY, and taken were cloths, scissors, gloves &c. stolen. (Middletown) There is reason to suspect a certain John WISE (alias) Indian John & William COMPTON, who were lately liberated from York gaol.

86. Wednesday, 7 November 1792 (Con't.)

Those who have subscribed towards building bridges over the Great & Small Conawago Creeks, are requested to pay their subscriptions to William LONG & Henry KUHN. John HENDERSON & John CHAMBERLAIN, Trustees.

Whereas I have reason to suspect my wife Elizabeth RATFOHN of adultery, for which I intend to be divorced from her, I warn persons from trusting her on my account. Christian RATFOHN, Windsor Twp, York Co.

87. Wednesday, 14 November 1792

Sale of 200 a. land in Strabine Twp, 2 miles from Hunter's Town, York Co. Head & main stream of Rock Creek runs through land near dwelling house. Apply to James BLACK or to John SAMPLE near same.

For sale, Mulattoe Wench, 21 years of age & a child aged 1 year. Apply to John LAIRD, Brogue Tavern.

John ECKERT, Germany Twp, York Co, has taken in a stray bay horse.

Where James M'KINLEY illegally obtained a bond from John WEBB, Hamiltonbann Twp, said WEBB refuses to pay unless compelled by law.

Andrew JOHNSTON & Jacob GARTNER, Admr's., estate of William JOHNSTON, decd.

As the suit of Valentine GROVE, for the use of William MUMMERT against Andrew DRIMMER, on which attachment John EDIE, John FORSYTH & Jacob HAY, Auditors request that they will meet at house of Baltzer SPANGLER, innkeeper, Borough of York.

John SCOTT, obedient & very humble servant, of Hunter's Town, informs subscribers for lots in said Town that lots will be drawn at the house of Hugh MORRISON in said town.

Sunday night, the 11th inst, stolen out of the stable of Ludwig GOODYEAR, living in Warwick Twp, Lancaster Co, 1 mile from LEEDET's, a bay horse.

88. Wednesday, 21 November 1792

A number of robberies has lately been committed in & near the Borough of York, & in Middle Town, Dauphin Co, by a certain William COMPTON & John WISE, (alias) Indian John. WISE is a tall stout man, of a sandy complexion, thick lip, broad face & has on a deep blue coatee. COMPTON is a stout, well made man, has dark hair which he sometimes wears tied, both his ears cropt & has on a deep blue cloth coat. Reward offered by Mordecai M'KINNEY, John STUART, Conrad WELSHANTZ & John SPANGLER, York Town.

Samuel WITHEROW selling tract of 400 a. in "Carrol's Delight," Hamiltonbann Twp, York Co, the title indisputable.

89. Wednesday 28 November 1792

The Governor of this Commonwealth (Pa) has issued a Proclamation declaring that William HENRY, Joseph HEISLER, Thomas M'KEAN, Henry MILLER, John WILKINS jun., Robert COLEMAN, Thomas BULL, Cornelius COXE, Robert JOHNSTON, John BOYD, David STEWART, George LATIMER, Hugh LLOYD, James MORRIS & Robert HARE are duly elected & chosen Electors of a President & Vice President of the United States.

Last Notice by Elizabeth, John & Jacob HAHN, Admr's, asking persons indebted to the estate of Michael HAHN, Esq., decd, to pay up.

William BOYL, selling tract of land in Strabane Twp, York Co, on great road between Hunter's Town & Gettysburg, 184 a., with dwelling house, double barn, well finished after the German manner & still-house; adj lands of George BRINKERHOOF & Hugh CAMPBELL.

90. Wednesday, 5 December 1792

John STUART gave a note the latter end of May last payable to a certain William ATCHESON & warns persons from takins same. (Chanceford Twp)

William EMMIT selling farm of 200 a., in Carrolsburg, within a mile of Emmitsburg (Md).

91. Wednesday, 12 December 1792

Thomas DUNN, of York Co, selling plantation in Manchester Twp, 2 miles from York Town, 112 a., good log dwelling house, barn, stables, apple orchard. For terms apply to Robert DUNN in Borough of York, or DUNN on premises.

Archibald TWEED, living about 5 miles from Little's Town, selling land with mill, 153 a., square log dwelling house, double barn, merchant mill with 2 pair of stones.

John STEWARD, Atty in fact for John M'CHORD, selling plantation in Fawn Twp, 100 a., dwelling house, barn &c. adj lands of Hugh EDGAR & ONNION's Ferry upon the Susquehanna. For terms apply to Capt. James EDGAR, who lives near & will show the premises. (Chester Co)

Whereas Michael HAHN, in his life time, obtained a bond from Henry REIGEIL, Manheim Twp, York Co., conditions of said bond have not been met.

John MAFFET, in Manallen Twp, York Co., has taken up a stray steer.

Sheriff's Sale: Estate of Christian BOLLINGER, house & lot of 8 a., in Cumberland Twp, adj Gettysburg, land of Henry WEAVER.

Conrad BLANCK, Menallen Twp, York Co, offers $2 reward for return of stray cow.

Martin & Adam GEMINTER, have purchased a plantation of Adam BLACK in Franklin Twp, free & to be kept free of all incumbrance.

92. Wednesday, 19 December 1792

James COOPER selling plantation & tract of land of 150 a., in Mountpleasant Twp, York Co, within 8 miles of M'Allister's Town, whereon is erected large frame dwelling 31x26', large kitchen, barn, orchard. For terms apply to Conrad LAUB, Scrivener, Borough of York or William BAILEY near the premises, or owner, James COOPER.

Selling 60 a., laid out in 10-a. lots; one lot has small house & double barn. 1 1/2 miles from York Town, adj land of James SMITH, Esq., Col. Philip ALBRIGHT's mill &c. Land was formerly property of William BAILEY, Esq. & sold to George ASTON & George WESCOTT, who will give sufficent title.

Whereas my Wife, Philibena STIVESON, has left me without any just cause, leaving behind 2 small children, the youngest not yet 2. Warns persons from giving credit on my account. George STIVESON, Huntington Twp.

Henry KOON, proprietor of the Town of Oxford, lately laid off by him in Berwick Twp, Co of York, assures lot holders that Oxford will be affected by the creation of a new county & it shall become a County Town & lays down ground rents.

93. Wednesday, 26 December 1792

Died Saturday the 15th inst. at Hanover, in this County, in the 40th year of his age, Mr. Abdiel M'ALISTER, son of Col. Richard M'ALISTER.

94. Wednesday, 2 January 1793

The Governor of this Commonwealth has appointed Conrad LAUB & William M'CLELLAN, Esquires, Justices of the Peace, Borough of York.

Samuel FANISTOCK, had left at his house, Borough of York, about 6 months ago, by Waggoner unknown, a cask of Dry Goods, marked J. KIMMELL.

94. Wednesday, 2 January 1793 (Con't.)

For sale, plantation of 105 a. in Dover Twp. on the great road from York to Carlisle, 8 miles from former; whereon is erected stone dwelling & spring house, double barn & apple orchard. A Tavern has been kept on the premises for 8 years. Indisputable title will be given by John KNISELY, Tobias KEPLER & Jonas YONER, Exer's. Sold in pursuance of will of Samuel KNISELY, decd.

Christian BUSHEY, of Reading Twp, giving reward for runaway indented servant boy named John SHEAFFER, about 19 years of age, 5' 3-4".

Came to Plantation of Sarah M'PIKE, living in Cumberland Twp, York Co, 2 red & white heifers.

95. Wednesday, 9 January 1793

Whereas Ann NEILSON fraudulently received a note from Brice BLAIR, he warns all persons not to take said note. (Warrington Twp)

The partnership of Lewis & Wendel MICHAEL is dissolved by mutual consent.

John SPANGLER, John MORROW & William NELSON, Commissioners give notice to all delinquent Collectors of the County Levy imposed on the twps of the Co of York for 1792, & they are asked to attend the house of David CANDLER, Borough of York.

Inhabitants of the several twps, included in the proposed line for the division of the Co of York are desired to meet & appoint 2 persons from each twp. to represent them at a meeting to be held at house of William BAILEY in Mountpleasant Twp.

96. Wednesday, 16 January 1793

The partnership of AGNEW & FLEMING to be dissolved, all debtors asked to pay as FLEMING intends leaving this co. (Hamiltonbann Twp)

David AGNEW, of Hamiltonbann Twp, has taken up a stray mare.

97. Wednesday, 23 January 1793

Pursuant of last will of Archibald M'CLEAN, Esq, decd, selling 2-story brick house & a 4th part of lot of ground, Borough of York, being the corner house & part of the north east corner Lot adjoining thte center square, whereon is also a brick kitchen & stables, cellar under whole house, good well & pump convenient to kitchen. Moses M'CLEAN, Jacob BARNITZ & Baltzer SPANGLER, Exec'rs.

To be sold pursuant to will of Christian HARMAN a tract of 84 a. in Manchester Twp, 2 miles from Borough of York, adj lands of Emanuel HARMAN, Harman UPDEGRASS &c., with log dwelling house & double barn. Emanuel HARMAN & Jacob SMYSER, Exec's.

Wednesday, 31 January 1793 (Missing)

98. Wednesday, 6 February 1793

To be rented, plantation & tract belonging to heirs of John IRWIN decd, now in tenure of John BIEAK(?), in Reading twp, the great road from DEARDORF's Mill to Baltimore passes through. Marmaduke WILSON & James CHAMBERLAIN, Guardians.

Tract of land of 390 a. to be sold, late the property of Robert M'MULLAN, decd., in Warrington Twp, York Co, on great road from York to Carlisle, 11 miles from former, on which is erected dwelling house, kitchen, double barn & stabling. Also another dwelling house & half barn 1/2 mile from former. Col. NELSON, Samuel & Robert M'MULLAN, Admr's.

98. Wednesday, 6 February 1793 (Con't.)
Sheriff's Sale: Estate of Robert ROWLAND, decd, in the possession of Jonathan BURGES & Margaret his wife, improvement & tract in Fawn Twp, 200 a., adj lands of James EDGAR, John BOYD &c. Godfrey LENHART, Sheriff.

99. Wednesday, 13 February 1793
Sheriff's Sale: Estate of Jacob HERTZEL, improvement & tract in Franklin Twp, York Co, 150 a., adj lands of John GOUDY, Michael BITTINGER, Thomas CROSS &c. Also tract in said Franklin Twp, 70 a., adj lands of Michael BITTINGER, Nicholas MARKS, Nicholas BITTINGER &c.

Wednesday, 21 February 1793 (Missing)
100. Wednesday, 27 February 1793
Mary WOLGAMOT, 5 miles from Hagerstown (Md.), offering reward for runaway Negro man namned Eel, 23 years of age, 5' 3-4" high, stout & well made, can play the violin.
For sale, 1500 a. of land on waters of Rock Lick Creek in Jefferson Co, Ky, in 2 tracts, one 648 a. & other 853 a., 40 miles from Salt works on Salt River. Apply to Conrad LAUB, Esq, Borough of York.
Philip GOSSLER, Jacob HAY & John HAHN, Auditors give notice to creditors of Henry FISHELL to attend house of Philip GODSSLER, Borough of York, to receive share.

101. Wednesday, 6 March 1793
Jacob HAY, Eli KIRK & John FORSYTH, Auditors, give notice to creditors of John STRAYER, late of York Co., to meet at the house of Jacob UPP, innkeeper in the Borough of York.
James KERR, Hopewell Tpw, York Co, has taken up a stray bull.
Plantation for sale on the waters of Tom's Creek in Hamiltonbann Twp, York Co, adj Carrol's Lower Tract & the South Mountain, 392 a., dwelling house & barn. William PORTER

102. Wednesday, 13 March 1793
List of appointments made during the Second Session of the Second Congress of the United States (Local appointments only): Henry VOIGHT, of Pa, Chief Coiner in the Mint of the U.S. Henry COOPER, of Pa, US Consul to the island of Santa Cruz. David Matthew CLARKSON, of Pa, Consul of th U.S. for the island of St. Eustatius. Benjamin Hamnell PHILIPS, of Pa, Consul of the U.S. in the island of Curracoa. Timothy PICKERING, of Pa, a Commissioner on the part of the U.S. for holding a treaty with the hostile Indians.
John SPANGLER, John MORROW & William NELSON, Commissioners, give notice to all persons in the Co of York whose Lands have been regularly advertised for six months, for arrears of taxes are notified that the sale is adjourned until 26th this inst, & unless such delinquents are paid the Lands will be sold. Also notify the delinquent Collectors of said Co, who have not dsettled their respective Duplicates, to attend the house of David CANDLER, Borough of York.
Sheriff's Sales: Estate of Thomas ARMOR, jun. decd., in possession of Robert BIGHAM, adm'r of said decd, improvement & tract in Shrewsbury Twp, 28 1/2 a., adj lands of Henry KORBMAN, being seized & taken .
Catharine BRUNNER, Administratix for Peter BRUNNER, late of Dauphin Co, decd, requests creditors to attend house of John DOLL, junr, Borough of York.
Hugh MORRISON, Strabane Twp, has taken up a stray steer.

103. Wednesday, 20 March 1793
For sale 800 to 1000 a., with convenient houses for a farm; land to be shown on applicant to Samuel LONE, Merchant, in Loudon C, Va. Land is situated about 28 miles from Alexandria & same from Washington City.
Philip AMENT, York Borough, offering reward for runaway apprentice boy named William HYDE, 19 years of age 5' 7-8" high, stout made & walks a little stooped.
John MYLER, renting for 1 or more years, to a good Blacksmith who has a family, 3 a. in Reading Twp, 2 miles from town of Berlin.
Richard M'ALLISTER, asks persons indebted to estate of Abdiel M'ALLISTER, decd, to make payment. Also selling large brick house, adj center square.

104. Wednesday, 27 March 1793
Whereas my wife Philibena hath been, without any just cause, absent from me since the middle of December last, as I then published, & as I wish her to return & live with me in a proper manner, she shall on such conditions be kindly received; should she neglect this notice, no debts of her contracting shall be paid by me. George STIVESON, Huntington Twp.
To be sold, hay, wheat, 10 plate stove with pipe, 2 sadler's brushes, &c. attached as property of John STRAYER, late of York Co, to be sold for the use of his creditors. Jacob HAY, Eli KIRK & John FORSYTH, Auditors.
John HALL, late an inhabitant near George Town, Montgomery Co, Md, being a free Negro, having lately moved into Warrington Twp, York Co, Pa; & whereas I cannot get employ in any kind of labor by reason of a doubt that has arisen in the minds of some people, touching on my being free. I notify any person that can have claim to me to come forward.

105. Wednesday, 3 April 1793
Married, on Tuesday the 26th ult. John SWENEY, of this Co, to Miss ---- LYTLE, of Franklin.
Henry MILLER, Prothonotary, is directed by the Judges of the Courts of York Co to make known when court will be held next.
Thomas SCOTT, living in Cumberland Twp, near Gettys Town, seeks a Journeyman Blacksmith, a sober man of good character.
James JOHNSON, Franklin Twp, York Twp, has for sale a Negro man about 40 years of age & a woman, his wife, about 35.

106. Wednesday, 10 April 1793
Dr. David RITTENHOUSE, our Astronomer (Philadelphia) has discovered a Comet in the Constellation Cipheus.
Died on Friday last, Mrs. Lydia UPDEGRASS, wife of Herman UPDEGRASS of this Borough.
Archibald STEEL informs that he has removed from the House he formerly lived in, to that elegant 3-story brick building on the Main Street, Borough of York, next door to John GREER's store, where he continues to keep the sign of the Sorrel Horse, agreeable accomodations.
Philip GOSSLER informs that he has removed from the House he formerly occupied, at the sign of the Lyon, to the House lately the property of Maj. William BAILEY, next door to George IRWIN, where he now keeps the Sign of The Buck.
William MACKEY, Abbett's Town, found a bank note in his house.

107. Wednesday, 17 April 1793

In pursuance of will of Archibald M'CLEAN, Esq, decd, selling 2-story brick house & a 4th part of a lot in Borough of York, being the corner house & part of the northeast corner lot adj the center square. Moses M'CLEAN, Jacob BARNITZ & Baltzer SPANGLER, Exec's.

For sale, improvement, messuage & tract of Land, 100 a. part in Tyrone & part in Huntington Twps, York Co, ajd lands late of John PAPER, John WILSON sen. & Valentine FLECK, being the late dwelling plantation of John WILSON Jun, forfeited to the state by his attainder. William MITCHEL, Agent for forfeited Estates.

108. Wednesday, 24 April 1793

List of the Laws passed in the 3d Session of Assembly of Pa: An act to confirm Daniel LEET's survey of a town & out-lots at the mouth of Beaver Creek. An act for the relief of John ALEXANDER as relates to the imprisonment of his person. An act to authorize Adam HAMAKER to rebuild a mill dam over Swatara. An act to authorize John WALKER to erect a wing dam on the Connodogwinnet Creek, Co of Cumberland. An act to authorize Simon SNYDER & the heirs of Anthony SELIN, decd, to erect a dam on Penn's Creek, Co of Northumberland. An act for the relief of Fleming WILSON. An act to authorize Andrew PIERCE, of Alleghany Co, to keep in repair a mill dam across past of the Monongahela river. An act to sell to Abraham RANKIN & Ann NEBINGER, wife of George NEBINGER, 2 children of James RANKIN, such parts of his forfeited estates as have been sold for benefit of the Commonweath.

George FRITZLEIN informs that he has removed from the house he formerly lived in, & now occupies a House next adj to Dr. John MORRISS, south side of High Street, Borough of York, where he continue to keep the sign of the Lamb.

Patrick M'KAIG, offers reward for bright bay mare, who strayed from his place in Hamiltonbann Twp, York Co, near Samuel COBEAN's lower mill on Marsh Creek.

109. Wednesday, 1 May 1793

John NICHOLSON asks the public to suspend judgement on his impeachment until he has the opportunity to be heard.

110. Wednesday, 8 May 1793

From Winchester, Va: Thursday last arrived in this town, a man named William PRESTON, who belonged to the Pa levies & was wounded & taken prisoner by the Indians. He was carried to the Sandusky towns, where he remained until he made his escape.

Whereas the Hon. William Augustus ATLEE, Esq., President of the several Courts of Common Pleas, Cos of Chester, Lancaster, York & Dauphin, the Hon. Henry SLAGLE, Samuel EDIE, Wiliam SCOTT & Jacob RUDISELL, Esq., Court of Common Pleas Co of York; Godfrey LENHART, Sheriff informs the public of court dates.

Archibald STEEL, Collector, gives notice to distillers & others having stills in their possession in Co of York that they must register. Also he is selling at his house, Borough of York, a quantity of contraband whiskey.

111. Wednesday, 15 May 1793

A steer, property of Jacob HILTZHEIMER, Esq., now 5 years 5 months old, weighed at Mr. PENROSE's hay-scales at 2356 pounds.

111. Wednesday, 15 May 1793 (Con't.)

HARRIS & DONALDSON inform that they have just received & are now opening in the store lately occupied by William HARRIS, a elegant assortment of seasonable goods.

John GREER selling spring goods at his store next door to Archibald STREET's Tavern, Sign of the Sorrel Horse.

Robert DUNN, continues keeping a public house of entertainment for traveling gentlemen & others at the Sign of the Stage Waggon, York Town.

James M'CALMOND, coopersmith, on the Main Street, Borough of York, opposite the Ship tavern near the bridge.

John CLARK, having moved next door to Doctor FAHOESTICK's begs leave to inform that he keeps his Office at the house of John FORSYTHE, Esq., 2 doors from Mr. DINKLE's on High Street, Borough of York.

112. Wednesday, 22 May 1793

Edward O. WILLIAMS, living near Shepherds Town, Md, offering reward for runaway Negro fellow named Gabriel, about 5' 8 or 10" high, down look, flat nose & has a scar on one of his arms.

John EICHELBERGER, at the house of Doctor John MORRIS, on the South side of High Street, Borough of York, opposite George LEWIS, selling dry & wet goods of every species & hardware.

Doctor John MORRIS has just received a fresh supply of drugs & medicines of every denomination, which he will sell on low & reasonable terms.

James FORWOOD & James KELLY, living in Harford Co, Md, on Deer Creek, offering reward for runaway small sized Negro man named Parowey, about 40 years of age & has a halt in his walk. He had on & took with him middling good clothes. Also a likely Mulatto Wench named Rebecca, of small size, about 17 years of age, went with him, which is his wife; they were married last fall & is most likely they will keep together.

Came to the plantation of Abraham KING in Germany Twp, 2 miles from Little's Town, a black mare branded on the shoulder wi

Came to the plantation of Abraham KING in Germany Twp, 2 miles from Little's Town, a black mare branded on the shoulder with the letters T.K. & a dark gray colt. George Junr. & Adam LIGHTNER.

The whole manor of Pompfret, consisting of 16 farms, 300 a. each, to be sold at Public Venue at the house of Martin WITHINGTON in Sunbury. Farms contain good log houses, with barns & stables on all of them. They are adjacent to the town of Sunbury, Co of Northumberland. John PENN & John PENN Junr. late Proprietaries of the State of Pa.

Philip ALBRIGHT, came to his farm 1 mile from the Borough of York, 4 ewes & 3 lambs.

James SHORT, George DUFFELL, Jacob TREAT, Jacob CARPENTER, Samuel M. FOX & John HANNUM are commissioned to open books & receive subscriptions for the purpose of building a permanent Bridge over the Susquehanna at or near the Blue Rocks, below Wright's Ferry. They are to meet at the house of Baltzer SPANGLER, Borough of Lancaster & at Strasburg at the house of John FUNK.

Whereas many persons under cover of their Rights, are in possession of vacancies of land, which are studiously concealed from others who would be desirous of purchasing same from the late Proprietaries: Notice is given that within six months the persons in such possession must apply to purchase same. Anthony BUTLER, Attorney for John PENN Junr. & John PENN.

113. Wednesday, 29 May 1793
Whereas I gave a bond onto John RIDDLE, living near Elizabeth Town, Md, (Hagerstown) find that said RIDDLE intends of disposing of the bond & I warn all persons from purchasing same until he makes settlement. John GROSSCOST, Berwick Twp.
Mordecai MILES wants 2 journeymen coopers & an apprentice lad.

114. Wednesday, 5 June 1793
Pittsburgh, a Court of Oyer & Terminer & Gaol Deliver & of Nisi Prius, Co of Allegheny, was held at this place by the Chief Justice & Judge YEATES. The only criminal business was the trial of Capt. Samuel BRADY who had been indicted for murder, in killing certain Indians near the mouth of Beaver Creek in the spring of 1791. It was determined that recently before the killing of the Indians, for which BRADY was not tried, several people from Ohio County, BOGGS, PAUL, RILEY's family, & Mrs. VANBUSKIRKE, had been put to death. The jury acquitted the prisoner.
William COX obtained a note payable to Ralph BOWIE & James HAMILTON, Attys at Law & he has not received any value for said note, but perplexity, loss & disappointment, & he warns all persons not to take said note.
Whereas my wife Rebecca WRIGHT had eloped from my bed & board; Take notice that I mean to pay no debts of her countracting. James WRIGHT, Manallen Twp.
HUMES & PEIRKINS, Chair & Spinning Wheel Manufactory, between the sign of the Indian Queen & the Sign of the King of Prussia, in High Street, Borough of York.
Ran away from Union Forge, in Hanover Twp, Dauphin Co, a Negro Man named Jack, about 5' 5 or 6" high, took with him a new brown cloth coat, pair of velvet breeches & new velvet waistcoat. He can work at the coppersmith trade & is a tolerable good blacksmith. Samuel JAGO. Said Negro formerly belonged to Mr. BAILEY of York Town.
Roger WALKS, proposes to practice physic, surgery & midwifery in the Gettysburgh area.
This is to give notice to all persons intending to emigrate to the Genesee country this season, that the waggon road from Pa to the Genesee country is now opened for the passage of waggons. Mr. WILLIAMSON, the Proprietor of 1 million and 1/2 acres in the Genesee country holds his Land office at the Town of Bath, on the Cohooton Creek, in the center of the tract. For particulars inquire of Robert DUNN, Tavernkeeper, York Town James TOWER, merchant Northumberland Town.
William BAILEY, Copper-smith & Tin Plate Worker, has removed from Borough of York, to Market Street in the Town of Baltimore, next door to George REINECKER's, near Congress Hall, where he carries on his business--also in Calvert's Street near the County wharf: In Hager's Town, Frederick Town & Chambersburg, as usual. He will constantly keep stills & washing kettles at Philip GOSSLER's in York Town, at the sign of the Buck, the house he formerly lived in.
Joseph HUGHES gave 15 Notes unto Nicholas GLAZIER, lately of Dover Twp, warns persons from taking said notes as agreement has not been met.

115. Wednesday, 12 June 1793
Notice to creditors of John STRAYER to meet at the house of Jacob OBB, innkeeper, Borough of York. Jacob HAY, John FORSYTH & Eli KIRK.
Whereas my wife Hannah eloped from my bed & board without just cause, I warn all not to harbor or credit her anything on my account. William MARSHALL.

115. Wednesday, 12 June 1793 (Con't.)
Wanted, an active lad about 14 years of age as an apprentice to the clock & watch making business. he will be taught the Iappanning of clock faces. Apply to Jonathan JESSOP, Clock & Watch Maker, Borough of York, a few doors west of the bridge.

116. Wednesday, 19 June 1793
Mr. BLANCHARD will repeat his experiment with the Parachute, for the last time, Monday next at his Rotunda in Chestnut Street; tickets half a dollar, may be had at Mr. ORLLER's Hotel. (No city given.)
Wanted, as soon as possible, an active lad of genius, 13 or 14 years of age as apprentice to clock & watch making business. John FISHER has worked as clockmaker for upwards of 40 years. East side of George Street, near the Court House, York Borough.
Was committed to the custody of Michael GRAYBELL a Negro Man who calls himself Jack BUTLER, 5' 6" high, stout made. Says he came from Alexandria in Va & that he is a free man.
Levi M'CLEAN, Ensign, 3d SLWSRC, offers reward for a certain John SNIDER, who deserted from this post. He is about 6' high, sandy hair. He will make for Alexandria in Va, as he has a wife & family in that place.

117. Wednesday, 26 June 1793
Persons indebted to William BAILEY are to make payment to Conrad LAUB, Scrivener, Borough of York.
Eloped from Dennis M'GREGOR, his wife Nancy, a woman of low stature, dark short curley hair, has lost her foreteeth. She went in company of a certain Thomas WRIGHT, a man of dark complexion & is short sighted. Before their departure they robbed him of 2 shirts, a piece of linen not made up, &c. Reward offered. Conawago Canal.
Came to the Plantation of Henry KUHN, 2 stray bulls, Berwick Twp.

118. Wednesday, 3 July 1793
A red cow of James CAMPBELL, Borough of York, strayed & reward offered.
Peter BUTT & George Philip ZEIGLER, Exr's. of estate of Jonas BUTT, late of Manchester Twp, decd.
Whereas my wife Susanna eloped from my bed & board without just cause, leaving a child of four years & took off with her several articles of bedding & cloaths &c. I warn all persons not to harbor her on my account & will pay no debts of her making. Peter BUSZ, Senr. Germany Twp.
Whereas my wife Eve will live no longer with me, I hereby warn all persons from harboring or crediting her on my account. Philip SMITH, Paradise Twp, York Co.
Reward given for a certain Conrad SMITH & Abraham ROCHESTER, who deserted from this post. SMITH is a German & speaks very bad English, is 5' 5-6" high, short sandy hair, has lost 2 of his foreteeth; it is supposed he will make for Lancaster. ROCHESTER is a Spaniard, speakes broken English, 5' 5-6" high, thin visage, short black hair, by occupation a Tinkere; formerly followed the seafaring business & is expected to make for some seaport. Levi M'CLEAN, Ensign.
To be sold a lot of ground with 2-story log house & smith shop, on the Main Avenue of Abbetts Town, adj the centre. Apply to Conrad LAUB, Scrivener, Borough of York.
Committed to custody of Michael GRAYBELL, Gaoler, John TAYLOR, says he is an apprentice to John WEIGHTMAN of Alexandria, Va, by trade a Taylor. He is about 5'4" high & well made.

118. Wednesday, 3 July 1793 (Con't.)
Stolen Sunday night, 23d inst, from the plantation of Daniel WELLER, living in Frederick Co, Md, 3 miles from Creager's Town & 1/4 mile from the Moravean Meeting-house, a black mare. $12 reward given for the mare; $20 given for mare & thief.

119. Wednesday, 17 July 1793
Strayed from Joseph ESINGTON, living at Codorus Forge, a bay horse. If found bring horse to subscriber or to Thomas NEILL, York Town for reward.
The ingenious & philosophic Mr. CHAMBERS of Mercersburgh PA favored the people of Elizabeth Town, Md, with a few experiments of his new invented Fire Arms.
Died Thursday the 11th inst. at his house, 2 miles from Borough of York, Thomas DUNN, in the 64th year of his age. His sudden & unexpected exit affords an instructive lesson to all of the uncertainty what time we shall be called from this life.
William CRAWFORD of Marsh Creek solicits those in his debt to come forward & settle.
Called at the house of Robert TOWNSLEY, living in Cumberland Twp, near Gettysburg, a certain person named John BOWMAN, who had with him a sorrel horse; upon offering to part with said Horse under value, was detected and seen cause to make his elopement & leave the horse behind, where he will remain till some person comes, proves property, pay Charges & take him away.

120. Wednesday, 24 July 1793
Whereas a certain Mary CORSWELL, sometime last fall, left with me, John NITCHMAN, 5 head of sheep & 3 lambs to keep for the shares, & took them away again about the middle of May, last without my leave, to a certain Jacob WAGGONER's; & where Mary has since obtained a certain Catharine SHRIVER, who in a slanderous manner, deposed before a Magistrate, that my wife said she would fetch away a share of the wool from said WAGGONER's, which never was mentioned by us; this is therefore to give notice to Thomas CORSWELL, Senr (father to said Mary) that he may, if go, or send to said WAGGONER's & take away the said wool, for the use of his children, which he has with & by a certain Nelly CONAWAY, as I will have no share, nor part thereof. John NITCHMAN, Reading Twp.

121. Wednesday, 31 July 1793
All persons indebted to KERR & WORK are asked to settle up. (Gettysburg)
The partnership of John & James EDIE is now dissolved. (Borough of York)
To be rented, that ancient and well-accostomed ferry, Wright's Ferry, on the west side of the Susquahanna, in York Co. Lot of 7 a., 3 suitable boats & the Tavern. James EWING, York Co.
Sheriff's Sale: Flavel ROAN, Sheriff, Sunbury, Northumberland Co. 2400 a. divided into 7 tracts in Washington Twp & said co, adj lands of PLUNKERT, DUMIAS, M'CORMICK & others. 3 of said tracts are improved, one now occupied by David ALLISON & one by William GRAY. Also 2 tracts on the 4th west side of the west branch of Susquehanna river, 800 a. in Loyal Sock Twp, on the waters of Lycoming Creek, near Eel Town, held in partnership with Thomas HARTLEY, Esq., seized & taken in execution & to be sold as the property of Joseph DONALDSON.
Also 1100 a. of land, divided in 5 tracts, each improved, well watered & timbered, in Buffaloe Valley, adj lands of Jacob GROZANG, IRWIN & others & one other tract on the west branch of the Susquehanna, 1 mile below

Derr's Town, adj George DERR. Seized & to be sold as property of Thomas RERS.

Ignatius PIGMAN has for sale Lands & Mills in Montgomery Co, Md, on the waters of Seneca, 22 miles from Frederick Town, 34 from Baltimore & 23 from George Town & the Federal City. The merchant mill is new, the mill house brick, 3-stories high, calculated for water wheels. Also a saw Mill, store house, dwelling, stables &c. PIGMAN, living on the premises.

Whereas a certain Henry SPINOVER, by virtue of Warrent of 18 October 1743, had surveyed to him 249 a. adj lands then of Henry HEISKY on Little Codorus Creek, Co of Lancaster, now in Paradise Twp, Co of York; & whereas said Henry sold & conveyed the said lands to a certain Philip HELTZEL, who died owner & possessed thereof intestate, leaving Tobias HELTZEL, his eldest son & heir at law to survive him; & whereas by virtue of sundry orders & decress of the Orphans Court of said Co of York, the said Tobias HELTZEL became owner & seized of said Land & died possessed thereof, having first made a will & therein appointed John BEYER & John JOSEPH his Executors; & whereas the said conveyance from said Henry SPINOVER to the said Philip HELTZER hath been lost & cannot be found, & a bill hath been perferred to the Court of Common Pleas York Co, to supply ths daid defecit in the Title: Therefore all persons concerned are required to appear at the Court House in York by order of the Court.

Ezekiel JACK, a runaway Negro, has been committed to the custody of Michael GRAYBELL, Gaoler. He is 6' high, stout made. If owners do not claim within 8 weeks, he will be sold for his fees.

122. Wednesday, 7 August 1793

Sheriff's Sale: As the estate of Henry GOOD, decd, in possession of Catharine GOOD & Bernet GOOD, improvement & tract of land in Chanceford Twp, 80 a., adj lands of Jacob GROVE, Daniel BARTHOLOMEW & Conrad LUCOB. Estate of Frederick MYER (one of the Heirs & legatees of Adam GOHN, decd) in possession of Henry GOHN, surviving Executor of said decd, 1 undivided 11th part of improvement & tract of land in Windsor Twp, York Co, 251 a., adj lands of Michael KAUSSELT (KAUFFELT), Andrew BILLMYER, Esq., Frederick LEHMAN, John REINDLEY. Estate of Philip HENRY, improvement & tract of land in Dover Twp, York Co, 113 a., adj lands of William WILLIS, John RITCHCREEK, Daniel MOONY & John EICHELBERGER. Estate of Alexander RICHEY, improvement & tract of land in Huntington Twp, York Co, 209 a., adj lands of John BRANEN, Nicholas WEAVER & David WORLY. All being seized & taken in execution as estates to be sold by Godfrey LENHART, Sheriff.

Also sheriff's sale of improvement & tract of land in Hamiltonbann Twp, York Co, 400 a., adj lands of Patrick REED & Widow COCHRAN. Being seized & taken in execution as the estate of William COCHRAN, Esq., now in possession of Henry WEAVER & to be sold subject to to a mortgage to John HOPSON.

Jacob COBLE offers reward for return of a dark bay mare, strayed from his plantation in Donegal Twp, Lancaster Co.

Joseph KRATZER offers reward for bay gelding stolen out of his pasture, about 5 miles from the Court House of Rockingham Co, Va.

123. Wednesday, 14 August 1793

On the 16th ult. Capt. Elisha ALLEN, of Princeton, was most inhumanly murdered by Samuel FROST, the person who was tried in the town of Worcester for the murder of his father. Capt. ALLEN had left his house in order to set out some cabbage plants & ordered FROST, who had lived with him several years, to go with him. Having gone a way he recollected that he wanted a hoe, sent FROST back to get one & he himself went on & began his work. FROST returned with the hoe & as is supposed, got over the fence behind the Captain & struck him on the head with the edge of the hoe, knocking him down, & continued striking him until he was dead & in pieces. The murderer made his escape into the woods & had not been taken yesterday morning. He is a short man of dark complexion, short black hair, 28 years of age. He will easily be known by his constantly shrugging up his shoulder, stretching out his arms, and shaking his head.

The Male white inhabitants, ages 18 to 45, residing within the bounds of the several Battalions to which they heretofore belong, are to meet to choose their Field & Company Officers & include Battalions lately commanded by: Lt. Col. Henry MILLER Borough of York, Lt. Col. John LAIRD at Major TURNER's Mills; Lt. Col. George DEHL at DEHL's Mill; Lt. Col. Daniel MAY at ELIFRITZ's Mills; Lt. Col. Samuel NELSON at William MITCHELL's Esq; Lt. Col. James CHAMBERLAIN at the late dwelling place of Michael MILLER, decd; Lt. Col. John KING at Hunter's Town; Lt. Col. William RIED at the Old Tanyard Place; Lt. Col. Henry SLAGLE at Hanover. Alexander RUSSELL, Brigade Inspector for Co of York.

Whereas the Hon. William Augustus ATLEE, Esq, President of the several Courts of Common Pleas, in the Circuit consisting of Cos of Chester, Lancaster, York & Dauphin, the Hon. Henry SLAGLE, Samuel EDIE, William SCOTT & Jacob RUDISELL, Esq., Judges of the Court of Common Pleas, York Co, will hold Court 8 June.

124. Wednesday, 21 August 1793

Samuel FROST, the murderer of Capt. ALLEN, mentioned in the last paper under the York head, is taken, & confined in Worcester gaol.

The Post Office is removed from the Printing Office to the house of Robert DUNN, Innkeeper.

William HARRIS has for sale at his distillery, 1/2 mile from Borough of York, excellent Rye Liquor & Gin, which he will dispose of at his Still House or at HARRIS & DONALDSON's store in York. He has declined the dry goods business & requests all persons indebted to him for shop goods to make immediate payment. He is also looking for an apprentice.

David AGNEW given notice (once more) that the Partnership of AGNEW & FLEMING is dissolved & requests debts to be paid up.

Handbills being circulated publishing a Fair at Woodstock, formerly Hunter's Town; the same being done without the knowledge of the subscriber, he takes this method of informing the promoters that if by fair means they will not be dissuaded from the their Intention, 'tis his to interpose in such way as will prove disagreeable to the persons concerned. William SCOTT, Woodstock

For sale, plantation & tract in Mountpleasant Twp, York Co, 121 a., with log dwelling house & large barn almost new. About 25 miles from Borough of York, near road to Gettysburgh. Apply to Robert IRWIN on the premises or to Conrad LAUB, Scriver, Borough of York, near the Court House.

William MORROW, of Hopewell Twp, lost a pair of saddle bags between York Town & Major TURNER's Mill, containing 2 pocket Bibles, Philadelphia print & Cotton Handkerchiefs with other articles. Return to subscriber or to James SHORT, Merchant, York Borough for reward.

Came to the plantation of John ROBINSON, living in Martix Twp, Lancaster Co, & now running at large with his cattle, 2 steers & 1 cow.

125. Wednesday, 28 August 1793

Roads from Lancaster to Chambersburg, total of 73 miles: To Wright's Ferry from Lancaster 10 miles; 12 miles to York; 5 miles to White Horse; 6 miles to Unicorn; 4 miles to Abbet's Town; 4 miles to Bull; 5 miles to Hunter's Town; 7 miles to BLACK's Tavern; 8 miles to THOMPSON's; 8 miles to M'KEAN's & 4 more to Chambersburg - total 73 miles.

Made his escape from the Constable of Strabane Twp, Monday the 19th inst, a traveling men who calls himself Wilson BROWN; was apprehended on suspicion of having a stolen horse; he left his horse, saddle & bridle, 1 shirt & pair of stockings. The horse is very old. George BURNETT, Constable.

Robert WILSON, York Town, informs that he has removed to the Red Lion Tavern in Beaver St, formerly kept by Philip GOSSLER & provides liquors, beding, hay, stabing &c.

A stray mare came to the Plantation of John SCOTT, living in Hamiltonbann Twp, York Co.

Wednesday, 4 September 1793 (Missing)

126. Wednesday, 11 September 1793

Died on the 6th of this inst., Borough of York, Mrs. Elizabeth KELLY, wife of James KELLY, Esq., & d/o James SMITH, Esq., Consellor of Law, after a tedious & painful illness.

Hon. William Augustus ATLEE, Esq., President of the Courts of Common Pleas of West Chester, Lancaster, York & Dauphin Cos, died Monday last, at his seat near Wright's Ferry.

Isaac BASSET, Surgeon Dentist in Gay St, Baltimore, is in possession of a remedy for the cure of cancers.

Thomas THORNBURG, Warrington Twp, declines nomination to the Legislature.

IRVINE & COBEAN give notice that their partnershop will be dissolved by mutual consent 1 October next. Alexander COBEAN proposes to open for sale at his Mill on Marsh Creek (where his store was formerly kept) a neat assortment of goods on reasonable terms.

Roger BROOKE, living near Taney Town (Md) offering reward for runaway dark Mulatto Man named Anthony, 34 years of age, 5'2" high, very smooth spoken fellow, plays on the violin, chews tobacco, grey eyes & a very bushy head of hair, which he seldom combed when at home.

Madeline PAINTER has taken in a stray cow at her plantation in Mountjoy Twp, York Co.

Adam LITTLE offers reward for recovery of dark bay mare to be returned to him in York Co, or to Michael SMYSER, Esq., 2 miles from York.

127. Wednesday, 18 September 1793

Baltimore: In Market, near Light St, a boy playing in a backyard in which was a well lately uncovered for the purpose of cleaning, a young lad dropped his hat in it, attempted to go down for it, but on descending 10 or 12' he was suffocated. Mr. Gaulter HORNBY, Junr., s/o Gaulter HORNBY cabinet maker went down to bring the lad up & met with the same fate; & a negro lad who was let down after him was very near dead when brought up.

Philadelphia: Sunday morning, 15th inst, a very alarming fire broke out in the back buildings of Mr. KENEDY's house, in second between Market & Chestnut Sts, which soon communicated to Mr. DOBSON's Printing Office & stables & warehouses contiguous thereto, all of which were entirely consumed. Had it not been for the maneuverings of the crews of the

French frigate La Precieuce & the India ship Le Ville de L'Orient, the fire might have burned out of control. Two persons were killed.
William FINDLEY, finding his name mentioned as a candidate for the office of Governor, declines. (Westmoreland Co)
Whereas James GALLAWAY, now of the state of Ky, obtained 4 bounds from William DUNWOODY, Marsh Creek, Franklin Twp, Pa; Mr. DUNWOODY refuses to honor such.
Abraham ARNOLD, living in Reading Twp, York Co, offers 3 pence reward! for return of runaway apprentice lad, Leonard LOWER, bound to learn the house carpenter business.

128. Wednesday, 25 September 1793
Sheriff's Sale: Estate of John M'MECHAN, decd, in possession of Thomas LARIMORE, executor of said decd, improvement & tract in Mountjoy Twp, York 10, 181 a., adj lands of John DIEFENDAL, James BEAR, Matthias RISSELL & Peter ZELL. Estate of John ALBERT, improvement & tract with Grist & Saw Mill thereon erected, 25 a., in Newbury Twp, York Co, adj lands of William HUNTER. Estate of Nicholas GLASSER, in possession of Joseph HUGHES, improvement & tract in Dover Twp, York Co, 10 a., adj lands of Philip BEERBOWER, Joseph HUGHES & Nicholas MARSHALL. All being seized & taken to be sold by Godfrey LINHART, Sheriff.
George DOUDLE, York Town, offers reward for bay mare strayed from him; Deliver to Jacob DOUDLE in York Town.
George RIFFLE, Adm'r of Matthias RIFFLE, late of Mountjoy Twp, decd.

129. Wednesday, 2 October 1793
The Deputies of the several Districts of Co of York, present the following nominations: For Representatives in the General Assembly: Thomas LILLY, William M'PHERSON, John STUART, Philip GARDNER, Alexander TURNER & Thomas CAMPBELL. Coroners: Dr. John MORRIS & Henry WELCH. Commissioner: Joseph WELCHANTZ. Jacob SMYSER, Jacob BARNLITZ, Jacob UPDEGRASS & Dr. John MORRIS, 1st District; Henry HOKE, John MORROW & John SEMPLE, 2d District; Henry SLAGLE, Frederick BAGER & Jacob HOSTETTER, 3d District; John CAMPBELL & John KELLY, 4th District; Elihu UNDERWOOD & Henry HULL, 5th District. Candidates for Governor: Thomas MIFFLIN & Frederick A. MUHLENBERG.

130. Wednesday, 9 October 1793
The Presbytery of Carlisle met at Paxton near Harrisburgh last week, & Ordained Messrs. Robert CATHCART & Nathaniel R. SNOWDEN. Mr. CATHCART was installed Pastor of the United Congregation of York Town & Hopewell & Mr. SNOWDEN was installed Pastor of Harrisburgh, Paxton & Derry.
Henry MILLER, Clerk, by order of the Court gives notice of sale of a Grist & a Saw Mill & 25 a., in Newbury Twp, York Co, adj lands of William HUNTER, late the estte of John ALBERT, decd, who died intestate, by Joseph GLANCY, Administrator of said estate.
The Creditors of William KERSEY are requested to meet at the house of Robert DUNN, Innkeeper, Borough of York. Daniel RAGEN & Michael DOWDEL, York Borough.
Wanted, as soon as possible, 2 active lads as apprentices to the scythe & sickle making business. Apply to Isaiah HARR, living on the North side of HIgh Street, on the West side of Codorus Creek, York Borough.
The Partnership of the subscribers will be dissolved by mutual consent, 1 November next. Thomas LOW & Co.

130. Wednesday, 9 October 1793 (Con't.)
Ranaway last night from Ridgley's Forges, 16 miles from Baltimore Town, a Scotch Servant man named Thomas COOK, a well made fellow, 5'8" high, about 27 years of age, yellow hair, grey eyes, down look, fair complexion, has a sear on his lip & 2 on his shoulders. He went away in company with a certain John GIBSON, an Irishman, & formerly worked as Iron-works in the State of Pa. Charles JESSOP, Baltimore Co.
Came to the plantation of George FINK, Dover Twp, 2 large bullocks.

131. Wednesday, 16 October 1793
Dr. ROBINSON, using the science of Animal Electrity & Magnetism to effect cure of headache, sore eyes, lock jaw, toothache, strains, bruises, and burns. Apply at Mr. SPANGLER's, 1/4 mile from York Town.
Joseph BUTLER, living 4 miles from Bath, offering reward for runaway Mulatto Daniel, 19 years old, 5'10" high, stout & well-made, full faced, larg scar on outside of one of his legs.
Peter SHEINFELTER, of Heidelberg twp, York Co., offers reward for runaway Apprentice Boy named Michael DOTTERO, bound to learn the Blacksmith trade. Took with him a Pocket Pistol; had on a new wool hat, gray coat & blue striped trowser, & shoes.
The Partnership of KERR & WORK is now dissolved. George KERR, Gettysburg.

132. Wednesday, 23 October 1793
James WARD, living in Harford Co, near Underaill(?) Mill, offering reward for runaway Negro Woman named Rose, with child named Mose, a boy 20 months old, well grown. The Woman 5'6" high, healthy & well looking, has lost her foreteeth & lived sometime with Mr. ORNSY and Mrl Thomas AYER near the Black Horse Tavern. It is supposed she is now concealed in the barrens of York Co.
William ALLISON, living in Franklin Co, Pa, offers reward for runaway Negro Man named Tom, 5'9" high, 24 years old, stout.

133. Wednesday, 30 October 1793
Michael GRAYBELL, Gaoler, York, committed to his custody a certain person who calls himself John HOOBER, 24 years of age, 5'9" high, slender made; was taken in suspicion of having stolen a number of clothes found in his custody. Owners are desired to come within 5 weeks from this date, prove their property, otherwise he will be sold.
Stephen HAYES offers reward for strayed or stolen dark bay or brown Horse, about 15 hands high, taken from his pasture, adj Middletown, Dauphin Co. It is supposed he was sold at the sale in York town.
Three-pence reward. Absconded from Michael TAYLOR, in Shrewsbury Twp., York Co, an apprentice lad named John CUNNINGHAM, bound to learn the trade of a Shoemaker.

134. Wednesday, 6 November 1793
The partnership of John COX & Isaac ROBINSON has been dissolved by mutual consent, Marsh Creek.
Reward for runaway from Philip DECKER, living in Hellam Twp, a young lad named Thomas FALASKEY, 12 years of age, black hair & dark complexion; speaks English and German.

135. Wednesday, 13 November 1793
22 October, Mr. LEVEZY's Mill, about 3 miles from Germantown, Pa, burnt together with 200 barrels of flour & about 1000 of wheat.

135. Wednesday, 13 November 1793 (Con't.)
On Friday last (23 October) 3 men who were at work at Robert MORRIS's quarries, on Schuylkill, were killed by the sudden explosion of a rock.
Reward for runaway of David DOUGLASS, Chanceford Twp, York Co, an indented Irish Servant Man named John M'GINNIS; about 2(?)5 years of age; 5'5" high, well made, straight & short black hair.
Robert TAYLOR has just opened a general assortment of fall goods at his store in High Street, next door to Robert DUNN's Tavern.
Pursuant to the last Will of James MATTHEWS, decd, sale to be held of plantation of 344 a. of patented land, within 3 miles of Carlisle, on which are 2 dwelling houses & 2 barns. John CAMPBELL & Daniel MORRISON, Exr's.
Sheriff's Sale: Estate of Michael HERMAN, improvement & tract in Manallen Twp, York Co, 60 acres, adj lands of James HAMMOND, James LEACH & John SPEARAND. Estate of Jacob MILLER, 2 houses & lots in Peter Little's Town, York Co; 1 adj lots of Philip LONG & other adj lots of Andrew HERTZIG & Widow M'SHERRY.

136. Wednesday, 20 November 1793
The City of Philadelphia has proclaimed 12 December next to be throughout the Commonwealth a day of general Humiliation, Thanksgiving & Prayer to celebrate the return of Health to the citizens of the city. They had been suffering a yellow fever epidemic.
Christian HECKENDORN, Borough of York, offers reward for indented servant lad, Michael RUTCH, 19 years of age, 5' 4-5" high, thin visage, strong limbs, a down look, dark hair & brown eyes; a little knock-kneed. He is a German and a weaver by trade. It is supposed that he has gone toward Baltimore & will take shipping.
Hugh LINN, Ex'r. to estate of John LINN, decd, late Collector of Taxes for Cumberland Twp.
Dr. HUMUROS's Last Will; . . . in the Co of Lancaster, 24 December 1733. To all practicing attornies I bequeath the following proverb: "Honesty is the best policy." To all within the Cities of London & Westminster I leave despair & rotten reputation & the contempt of every man; and to all prudes within the cities aforesaid, I from my soul bequeath virginity & wrinkles; or if they prefer having a bastard by their father's butler, groom or coachman, I desire my executors may give them their choice. To the armies of Great Britain & Ireland, I leave the bad roads to be mended. To the Parson of my Parish, & all other Parsons, I leave the following advice: that they would not any longer expose their own weakness & absurdity, by attempting to explain things which are mysteries. I leave the whole tribe of polite coxcombs in London, to sharpers, surgeons and taylors. Lastly, to my 3 brothers, Thomas, Henry & John, I leave my whole estate to be divided equally.

137. Wednesday, 27 November 1793
Carlisle: The trial of Ensign John MORGAN is concluded. No verdict has been announced.
John SHOEWAY, Cumberland Twp, has taken in 2 stray Bulls.
Ran away from John LEBER, living in Windfog Twp., an indented Servant Lad named Jacob ALLBRIGHT, 20 years of age, 5'10" high, a weaver to trade; he has long hair & tied.
John M'CRACKEN selling plantation in Hamiltonban Twp, York Co, adj lands of Robert RAY, Samuel KNOW, in Carrols upper Tract, 300 acres. Has log

dwelling house & barn with other buildings. Apply to Ebenezer FINLEY, Robert RAY or to M'CRACKEN living near Taney Town, Fredderick Co, Md.

All issues for December 1793 missing except below.

138. Wednesday, 25 December 1793

Just published in German: "Controversy or written Dispute, Which took place in Hanover Town, York Co, in the Year 1725 between A Lutheran Minister & A Number of poor Tradesmen Who hold the Doctrine of Universal Salvation." This curious Book may be had of Andrew BILLMYER, John GREER & John MORRIS at the West side of the Bridge, York-Town; John HOLLAR, Bott's-Town; George SMITH, Paul & Jacob METZGAR, Matthias NACE, David NEWMAN, Jacob BOSE, & James BOLTON, Hanover, M'Alister's-Town.

Robert WILSON, proposes at his House, Sign of the Lion, Beaver St, Borough of York, to open an Office of Intelligence, where he will procure Money on Loan, give information to such as want to dispose of Bonds, Notes or other property, including real estate. He will procure intelligence of stray Cattle and Horses for those who have creatures either stolen or strayed.

John ALBERT, living in Huntingdon Twp, York Co, has taken in a stray Red Heifer; has no ear marks.

Elijah HART & John MENTIETH, Admr's. to the Estate of Andrew HART, dec'd, York Co.

Andrew RUTTER & James LOVE, Admr's. to estate of Thomas DUNN, dec'd, York Co.

Archibald STEEL, Collector of the Revenue, will attend at the House of Daniel BARNITE, in Hanover, to settle with distillers in twps adjacent.

Catharine SHULTZ, her husband, Joseph, did advertise her as eloping from his bed & board without just reason or cause, she does publically declare that she can, by good proof, shew that he, as a barbarian, hath always, when drunk (which is pretty often) beat and abuse her in cruel manner; That before she left him she applied to the Hon. Henry SLAGLE, Esq. for redress of such conduct & bounded her husband to settle the matter & he should dispose of his liquors & cease from beating and abusing her; but contrary to which has since kicked and abused her that she was obliged to apply to a surgeon to get cured.

Strayed to the plantation of William GARRETSON, in Managhan Twp; a red cow with a white face & a heifer.

To be sold, that noted Tavern, the Sign of the Indian Queen, & 2 lots belonging thereto in Abbett's Town, York Co, now in the possession of William MACKEY.

To be sold, Wingfield Mills with plantation. Mills constructed by merchant from Wilmington, run 2 pair of bores; likewise a saw mill under the same roof; on Chartier's Creek, 10 miles from Pittsburgh, the western metropolis. 200 acres of excellent land besides the mills. The Mills have run about 3 years. Apply to John WOODS, Esq. in Pittsburgh or Alexander FOWLER, on the premises. Gen. Edward HAND, of Lancaster, is well acquainted with the situation & will satisfy such as may apply.

139. Wednesday, 1 January 1794

An accident a few days since in Newbury Twp, about 10 miles from the town: Matthias SURGAR accidently shot Andrew SCIPE and put an immediate period to his existence.

John HENRY, Esq. appointed President of the Courts for the district of Chester, York, Lancaster & Dauphin in place of William A. ATLEE, Esq.

decd. William BINGHAM, Esq. elected Senator of Pa in place of Samuel POWELL, Esq. late Speaker of the Senate, decd. Alexander J. DALLAS, Esq., is re-appointed Secretary of State for Pa, & that John HANNUM, Esq. is appointed Register & Recorded of Wills for Co. of Chester.

John FORSYTH, Atty. for Heirs of Thomas CORBYN, decd., selling tract of patented land called the Diamond, in Fawn Twp, Co of York; 96 acres, adj lands of Robert DIXON.

William HARRIS, has for sale at his distillery, 1/2 mile from the Borough of York, excellent Rye Liquor & Gin. Selling foreign Geneva, which he will dispose of by the barrel or hogshead. Also on sale at HARR's & DONALDSON's store in York. Also wants distillary worker.

Wednesday, 7 January 1794 missing

140. Wednesday, 15 January 1794

Robert HORNER, York Co., paid a Note of Hand unto Andrew GELWICKS, of Franklin Twp., he is determined not to pay as GELWICKS committed a fraud.

Michael GRAYBELL, York, offers reward for a Negro Fellow, who calls himself Bill, made his escape on the 10th inst.; about 5' 8-9" high, stout built & speaks slow. He says he belongs to Edward RIDGELY of Md.

Charles PALMER, York, October last executed a Bond to a certain Nicholas BENEDICT, of the Borough of York, blacksmith, warns persons against purchasing such Bonds.

William NELSON begs to inform his customers that he has lately laid in at his Store at the mouth of Muddy Creek, York Co, a large assortment of wet and dry goods suitable for the season.

Last night from the stable of Stewart HERBERT in Hagerstown (Md) was stolen a deep sorrel horse.

The partnership of Jacob SHEAFFER and Peter BOSS, being dissolved. Pay monies owed to Jacob SHEAFFER at his Store in the Borough of York.

John MORROW, William NELSON & Joseph WELSHANS, Commissioners, Co of York, now taking proposals from carpenters willing to undertake rebuilding a Bridge across Codorus Creek, adj the Borough of York, on the Harrisburg Road. (Length of bridge 130', width 15', with 3 Pillars to support it.)

ROBERTS & TWAMLEY inform their friends & customers that they are now opening at their Store, No. 83, Market St, Phila, a large assortment of ironmongery, sadlery, cutlery, etc.

The rest of January, all of February and the beginning of March all missing.

141. Wednedsay, 12 March 1794

For sale or rent, plantation where Samuel HADDEN now lives in Strabane Twp, York Co, adj lands of the Hon. William SCOTT & Col. James DICKSON, 273 a. On premeises 2-story low dwelling house, large bank Barn & other out Houses. The great road from Philadelphia & Baltimore to the westward goes through. Also for sale 2 young Negroes, one is a slave, the other will be free at the age of 28.

Adam SHENBERGER, living in Windsor Twp, York Co, executed a Note of Hand to George GALLAGHER; said note cannot be found.

William WADSWORTH, Heidelberg Twp, York Co, has taken in a stray horse.

John JACK & Benjamin REED, Exe'rs of James JACK, decd, selling decd's. property, tract in Hamiltonban Twp, near Marsh Creek, 150(?) acres.

James MARSHALL, Junr, renting Merchant Mill on the waters of Middle Creek, with 2 pairs of stones, one of them burs & the other round tops, etc.

141. Wednedsay, 12 March 1794 (Con't.)
Came to the plantation of Adam GEMINTER, living in Franklin Twp, 4 stray sheep, two of which are not marked.
Elisha RIGG & Joseph HUBLEY, Admr's of the estate of the Hon. William Augustus ATLEE, Esq., decd, selling 2-story Brick House & 2 tracts of land adjoining each other in Hempfield Twp, Co of Lancaster, 1/2 mile below Wright's Ferry, total 59 acres, bounded by the River Susquehanna & lands late of Nathaniel BARBER & Thomas PATTON.
George DEITZ, Ex'r. to the estate of Michael FREISZ, late of Windsor Twp.
Lewis MICHAEL & Co. wants 2 young lads to learn the store keeping.
Peter BOSS, late of Baltimore Town, informs that the partnership between him & Jacob SHEAFER is dissolved & that he continues to keep the store lately occupied by said SHEAFER on the west side of George Street, near the corner of Philadephia in the Borough of York.
Proposed for printing by subscription, a new work "The Life of Dr. Thomas Feeling," a novel in 4 volumes, by Eli LEWIS. Apply this office.
By decree of Orphans Court of York Co, sale of Plantation of 111 a. in Manchester twp., about 2 miles from Borough of York, adj. lands of Jacob FAHS, Codorus Creek; late property of Thomas DUNN, decd., who died intestate; by Andrew RUTTER & James LOVE, Amdr's. of said Intestate.
To be sold, 2-story log dwelling-house with valuable lot of gound on the east side of Water St, lately occupied by John HECKENDORN, dec'd, & to be sold by William LANIUS, Ex'r. For terms apply to Christian HECKENDORN, York Town. Also 100 acres of woodland in Dover Twp, 9 miles from the town. Apply to Robert WILSON at his Office of Intelligence.
Charles WRIGHT, Hamiltonbann Twp, informs that his wife, Thompson WRIGHT, otherwise LITTLE, hath acted in a dishonrable manner by eloping from his bed & board without just cause & he is determined to honor no debts.
John CLARK intends to invest a considerable part of his property in trade & offers for sale Merchant & Saw Mills on the waters of March Creek, York Co. On the premises a log dwelling house, barn, garden & pump. Also plantation with stone dwelling house & barn 65' long with tract of 150 acres. Apply John CLARK, York Town.
My son, Thomas RYLE, as been absent from me for about 14 or 15 years past, & I have heard nothing from him for a considerable time. Any person giving information as to where he is will be rewarded. Hannah RYLE, living near Deer Creek, about 6 miles from Bellair, Harford Co, Md.

142. Next issue available Wednesday, 18 June 1794
Robert WILSON, Office of Intelligence, Sign of the Blue Bell, Water Street, York selling land in this county.
Samuel MERS gives notice that he, a Black Man, formerly owned by Rebecca MURRAY of Baltimore Co, Md, is now in York Town, Pa, & maybe found by applying to Members of the Society for the Abolition of Slavery.
Ran away from Thomas CROMWELL at Bedford Furnace, a Negro Man named Tom, about 25 years of age, 5' 9" high, well made with a sour contenance & a down look. He was purchased April last from William ALLISON near Green Castle & will most likely head towards Philadelphia or Baltimore.
For sale, patented land in Warrington Twp, York Co, on the great road from York to Carlisle, about 15 miles from each, known by the names of Stephenson's or Carpenter's Tavern, 413 acres. On premises 2 dwelling houses & 2 barns & may be divided into 2 farms. Apply to Michael KEPPELE at Philadelphia or Charles SMITH & Joseph HUBLEY at Lancaster.
John OVERHOLSER, Jr., Reading Twp, York Co, has taken in stray steers.

142. Wednesday, 18 June 1794 (Con't.)
My wife, Peggy HOOVER, having eloped from my bed & board without provocation, I caution the public from crediting her on my account. Peter HOOVER.
Christian WERT, Mannallen Twp, has taken in a stray bay horse.
William BELL, selling farm of 427 acres, about 4 miles from Battle Town, on the main road to Bryer's Ferry, & about 12 miles from Winchester. Dwelling house, barn &c. Also new stone merchant mill & store house. The mill is 55' x 40', with 2 overshot wheels 20' diameter on never-failing stream. Store house is 30' x 22'.
Jacob ZIMMERMAN warns all persons from taking assignment on 2 Notes of Hand given to him, one payable to Solomon SCHMUKE, the other to Daniel MOODY, as such notes were fraudlently obtained.
John HERBAUGH, Adm'r. to estate of Jacob HERBAUGH, decd.
Ran away from Christian KUNTZ, living in Donegal Twp, Lancaster Co., near Anderson's ferry, an apprentice lad named Henry HINGLE, bound to learn the weaving business; about 5' high, 17-18 years old.
Jacob BAWN, a Black Man, who formerly lived with Josiah KETCHCOCK in York Co, Pa, takes this method of informing that said KETCHCOCK moved into Md, & took the said Jacob with him contrary to law. He conceives himself a freeman & he now lives with Abraham MOSSER, innkeeper, on the great road from York Town to the Brogue Tavern, 5 miles from York Town.
John MACKLEY selling tract of land in Manallen Twp, York Co, on head waters of Great Conawago, 500 acres, adj lands of William BOYD, Frederick WARREN & lands late property of Hans MORRISON, decd. Has dwelling house & barn, also a compleat saw mill in excellent order.
For sale by Bernard O'NEIL, Charles STEWARD, Normand BURCE & William DIGGES, about 3000 acres of land at Emmitsburgh in Frederick Co. Contains farm of 300 acres on Tom's Creek & adj to Emmitsburgh, 60 or 80 acres of which are mostly cleared, with good dwelling house. One other tract of 150 acres contains saw mill & other improvements. Land is situated 50 miles from Baltimore, to which place a main road from Franklin & Cumberland cos passes through the tract first mentioned.
Stolen from Jacob LEHMAN, living in Mountjoy Twp, Lancaster Co, a black Mare with a star in her forehead about the size of a dollar.
John DOLL, Junr., Notary Public, informs that he has removed his office next door to the Sign of the King of Prussia, kept by Frederick RUMMIL, on the north side of High Street, Borough of York, where he continues to draw Deeds, Mortgates, Wills, Bills of Sale, etc.
James PURDY has taken in a stray mare at his plantation in Hopewell Twp.

143. Next issue available, Wednesday 18 February 1795
Eli LEWIS of Newbury Twp. & Nicholas GELWICKS of Hanover, candidates for office of sheriff.
Ran away from Philip GARTNER (December 1794), of York, a Negro man named Thomas COTTON, about 5'-8-9" high, 17 years of age, has a remarkable bald spot on the right side of his head near the size of a dollar, has lost one of his foreteeth, speaks English & German, plays on the violin & is supposed to have one with him. $8 will be given if he is taken 10 miles from home & secured in any gaol.
For sale - noted tract of land, late the property of Archibald TATE, decd., in Cumberland Twp., York Co., on the west side of the waters of Rock Creek, within half a mile of Gettysburgh, 217 a. On premises a log dwelling house & barn. Apply to William & James TATE on the premises.

143. Wednesday 18 February 1795 (Con't.)

All persons who have any judgements against the estate of Martin SHETTER, Esq., late of Newbury Twp., York Co., decd., are requested to bring their accounts, duly proven to George SHETTER or Henry KRIEGER, Adm'rs.

Conrad LAUB, Collector of the Revenue for York Co. gives notice to distillers of spirituous liquors within the Co. of York that the first half yearly payment of duties on Stills become due.

Conrad LAUB, scrivener & surveyor in Borough of York informs that he intends to follow his former profession at his office opposite the public building near the Court House, where he draws deeds of conveyances, wills, mortgages, bills of sale, etc. He also makes private surveys & divides Lands, sells real estate, &c.

To be let, the farm on which Ebenezer FINLEY now lives. Also selling a negro woman & two children, the woman is 35 years of age, well acquainted with house work, one of the children is 4 years of age, the other 2. Also a negro man 25 years old, well acquainted with farming. They are all registered according to law. Apply to FINLEY on the premises in Carroll's Delight, York Co.

To be sold, a plantation tract in Windsor Twp., York Co., late the property of Adam GEYER, decd., adj. lands of John CROSBY, Christian HOUSMAN &c. Includes dwelling house, barn & stables. Paul GEYER, Surviving Ex'r.

William MACKEY requests all those indebted to him by bond, note & book account, to make payment on or before 1 March next. Those to whom he is indebted are requested to make application for payment. He has for sale 38 1/2 a. of land in Berwick Twp.

Owing to the Susquehanna not being passable, the last week's Mail has not arrived.

James GETTYS of Gettysbugh is a candidate for Sheriff of York Co.

George NEBINGER of Newbury Twp. is a candidate for Sheriff of York Co.

Selling plantation & tract, late the property of Conrad BAKER, in Manchester Twp., near to Philip BAKER's Mill on little Conawago Creek, 215 a. & allowance. Includes dwelling house, barn & stables. Also sold the same day a waggon & gears, livestock, plughs & a good Still, 8 day clock, weavers loom & kitchen dresser & Clothes press &c. George EICHHOLTZ & Mathias BAKER, Ex'rs.

John MORRIS, Notary Public & Conveyancer, informs the public that he continues to transact business in the above branches at his office, 2d door from the Bridge near the sign of the Ship, in the Borough of York.

Sheriff's Sales: Estate of Hans MORRISON, decd., in the hands & possession of Hugh MORRISON, James MORRISON & John SAMPLE, Exc'rs., land in Manallan Twp., York Co. of 350 a. adj. lands of William HAMILTON & Andrew BOYD. Godfrey LENHART, Sheriff.

The Exc'rs. of Col. David GREER, late of the Borough of York, set time to settle accounts of decd. (no names of Exc'rs. given)

Tavern Keepers of York Co. must renew licenses in the hands of John HAY.

To be sold by venue on the premises in Chanceford Twp., within 6 miles of M'CALL's Ferry & near William ROSS's estate (?), plantation of 398 a.; also 2 worthy young Negro Women & several other articles too tedious to mention. Apply to James LAIRD.

To be sold - plantation & tract of Patented land of 350 a., late the property of Robert M'MULLIN, decd., in Warrington Twp., on the great road from York to Carlisle, 11 miles from one & 19 from the other. Has dwelling house, barn & other buildings. Samuel NELSON to give details.

143. Wednesday, 18 February 1795 (Con't.)

For sale - tract in Windsor Twp., York Co., between 4 & 5 miles from York Borough on the great road from York to Peach Bottom Ferry, 264 a. adj. land of Abraham MOSER, Rudolph MILLER & others; on premises large log dwelling house, good double Barn, large stone stable & 2-story log still house with spring house. Also a new Oil Mill, a Powder Mill & an eligible seat for a Grist Mill with water sufficient for all. Also on the premises a town laid out called New Windsor, containing 59 lots under a ground rent, also a brick yard already made & excellent clay for bricks.

Another tract of land in Hopewell Twp. for sale, 15 miles from York Borough of 200 a., adj. land of Francis WENIMILLER, near to Andrew FINLEY's. Large dwelling house with large spring in the cellar. Meadow is watered by Codorus Creek; also double barn, peach & apple trees.

Also a tract of limestone land in Manchester Twp., 2 miles from York Borough, 55 a. adj. lands of James WORLEY, Eli KIRK.

Also 2-story log house & lot in M'Allister's Town, on the southwest side of Baltimore St., with a 2-story brick kitchen & 2 rooms well finished above, brick spring house, slaughter house with brick floor & large stable, all under one roof, now in tenure of Nicholas KOCH. Apply for all the above to Philip WAGNER, York Borough.

Henry KING selling 133 a. in York & Manchester Twps., 4 miles from York. Tract includes Merchant Mill, Saw Mill on Codorus Creek, double barn, sheds, out houses. Also another tract of 100 a., with dwelling house & stable on premises.

Sheriff's Sales: Estate of Mark MILLIGAN, improvement & tract of 200 a. in Franklin Two., adj. lands of Alexander THOMPSON & the heirs of John DELLOW.

Estate of James EDGAR, improvement & tract of 150 a. in Fawn Twp., adj. lands of James GORDON, Hugh EDGAR & Samuel BUCHANAN. Also an equal undivided half part of an improvement & tract of 25 a. in Fawn Twp., adj the river Susquehanna & lands late of Stephen ONION & Robert ROWLAND, decd.

Estate of Jacob KAUSSELT, 60 a. of woodland in Windsor Twp., adj. lands of Ulrich WEAVER & widow HERSHINGER.

Estate of John NEELY, late Collector, improvement & tract in Huntingdon Twp., 250 a., adj. lands of Thomas NEELY & Nicholas MILLER. Seized & taken into execution as the estates & to be sold by Godfrey LENHART, Sheriff.

To be sold - plantation & tract in Reading Twp., York Co., late the property of Christian CLOSE, decd., 154 a. & a 1?2, together with allowance of 6 a. for roads, &c. There is erected on said tract Merchant Mill with 4 pair of Stones, saw mill on Conawago Creek, on which the mills stand, 2-story dwelling house, stone double barn, stables, sheds &c. Also same day selling livestock, waggons, farming utensils, household & kitchen furniture. John CLOSE, Abraham CLOSE & Wendal GIGER, Adm'rs.

Andrew JOHNSON has just received & is now opening at his house next door west of Col. Archibald STEEL's & opposite Capt. Philip GOSSLER's Tavern in the Main St., York Town selling Madeira, sherry, Jamacian Spirits, cordials, best wine vinegar, pickled salmon, anchovies, wine bitters, pepper & alspice, F.F. gun powder, shot, cloves, &c. Will furnish Country Tavern Keepers & others with liquors cheaper than they can have them in the City of Philadelphia. Also looking for a young lad of 14-15 years of age, who can write a good hand & understand book keeping.

143. Wednesday, 18 Feburary 1795 (Con't.)
Benjamin CARPENTER of Warrington Twp., finds it necessaray to settle his accounts & hereby requests all those indebted to him to make payment.
Samuel FAHNESTOCK, at his medicine store, on the East side of Beraver St., Borough of York, has genuine drugs & medicines, viz. Aloes, Borax, Castor Oil, Foenugreck Seed, flower of sulphur, camomle, galls, mercury, Quicksilver, tartar rub &c. & patent medicines. Also has Limners & Painters Colours of the first quality.
Tempest TUCKER & Christian HERSHEY, Ex'rs. selling on the Premises plantation & tract in Paradise Twp., 9 miles from Borough of York, late property of Peter DICKS, decd., 137 a. Has stone dwelling house, log barn, stone spring house on bank of Codorus Creek.
John MILLER & Sebastian HEFFER, Adm'rs. selling on the premises a tract of land, late the property of John HEFFER, decd., 185 a. in Dover & part in Warrington Twp., York Co., adj. lands of Henry GARDNER, Thomas SHENK, Jacob ROLLER. Has dwelling house. Sold in pursuance of a decree of the Orphans Court of York County.
In pursuance of will of George STAKE, Esq., late of Borough of York, decd., will be sold noted 3-story brick house & half lot of ground known by the name of the Indian Queen Inn, on the North side of High Street, Borough of York, adj the said Borough lands, to be laid off in 10 a. lots. Catharine STAKE, John HAY & Henry MILLER, Exec'rs.
Collectors of arrears of Taxes on the twps. of York Co. who have not yet settled & paid off their duplicates to the County Treasurer are to do so before 6 March. William NELSON, Joseph WELSHANS & Henry WELSH, Commrs.

144. Wednesday, 25 February 1795
To be sold by public vendue, improvement & tract in Newbury Twp., York Co., adj. lands of Jacob BEAR, George SHERTER, 40 a. with 2-story dwelling house & stabling, merchant mill & saw mill on Great Conawago Creek. Apply to Henry KRIEGER or George SHETTER, Admr's.
Six Pence Reward offered by Abraham KOONTZ, living in Codorus Twp., York Co., for return of runaway apprentice named William SCHWARTZ, bound to learn the weaving --, -7 years of age.

145. Wednesday, 4 March 1795
Robert DUNN continues keeping a Public House of Entertainment for Travelling Gentlemen & others at the sign of the Stage Waggon, Yorktown. Also wants sober lad who can write a good hand.
From the Knoxville Gazette: On the 5th inst. John TYE, jun. was killed & John TYE, Sen., John BURLINGTON, Sherard MAYS & Thomas MAYS wounded by Indians on the frontiers of Hawkins County.
Isaiah HARR begs leave to inform the public that he has removed from his dwelling house in Borough of York to his Tilting & Blade Mill on the East branch of Codorus, 7 miles from Borough of York, between Nicholas SENTZ's Grist Mill & John JONES's Fulling Mill, where he has for sale 500 dozen of sickles & grass & kradling scythes.
Andrew JOHNSTON of York announces as a candidate for sheriff.
To be let - plantation known by the name of the Huntington Glebe, inquire of John CAMPBELL, York.
Andrew PORTER, Peach Bottom, wants to purchase a large quantity of merchantable wheat, for which he will give the highest price in cash at his new store, a few perches south of Nicholas COOPER's Ferry.
To be sold at the dwelling house of Ebenezer FINLEY, in Carrol's Delight, a number of horses, cows, sheep & hogs, waggons & harness, &c. Wheat, corn

& potatoes by the bushel; an 8-day clock & feather beds, household & kitchen furniture. (York Co.)

Lots in Shepherd's Town, Berkley Co., Va., large corner lot rented quarterly for $25; also 2 grass lots near it in the main way westward & near 4 Grist Mills & 2 saw mills; 206 a. in limestone adj. the Potomac River, 5 miles below the town. Apply at the Antietum Iron Works in Md., near the said town to Richard HENDERSON.

To be sold, a good log house with 3 rooms--a kitchen & Stable in Abbett's Town, York Co., together with a lot in said Town in the Main Street. Michael & Valentine PRESSEL, Ex'rs.

Selling plantation in Straban(?) Twp., York Co., within 2 miles of Gettysburgh, 220 a., late the property of William M'CREARY, decd., adj. lands of Hugh CAMPBELL, Widow KEYS &c. Has log house, barn, orchard. Also selling livestock, waggon & windmill &c. Robert CAMPBELL, Ex'r.

Whereas a certain Garret VORIS, living now in Buffaloe Valley, obtained from Valentine FALER of Manallen Twp., York Co., two promissary notes, said notes being fradualently obtained, FALER refuses to honor.

Tobacco, wholesale & retail, manufactured & sold by John FORSYTH, living opposite to the German Presbyterian Church, Main Street, York Borough.

Tobacco manufactured & sold by Philip WALTEMEYER at his dwelling house on the south side of High street, borough of York, opposite Andrew BILLMYER's Esq., & 2 doors above Lewis MICHAEL's Store, near the Court House; such as Pigtail, superfine ditto, Plug; &c.

146. Wednesday, 11 March 1795

Plantation adjoining Hunter's Town to be let for 3 years (known as "Green's Place"), 300 a. Apply to Alexander RUSSELL, Esq.

Alexander RUSSELL announces as a candidate for sheriff.

Those indebted to the estate of James DICKSON, Esq., late of Strabane Twp., decd., to make payments. John DICKSON, Adm'r.

For rent - that noted Stand for a Tavern, formerly occupied by William MORROW in Town of Chambersburg. Two large stone houses, brick kitchen, stabling &c. John MORROW & Samuel RIDDLE, Chambersburg.

Plantation & 250 a. for sale in Cumberland Twp., York Co., adj. lands of David DUNWOODY, John SWENEY & lands formerly of Col. Hans HAMILTON, late the property of James M'CLURE, decd. Apply to Samuel EDIE, Esq. near the premises or to John EDIE, York Town.

Plantation & tract of 160 a. in Dover Twp., York Co., within 11 miles of York Town, has new Saw Mill & house. John OVERDEER.

Peter DANNER of Dover offers $4 reward for runaway negro man named Jonathan LACKSON, a fiddler; 4 1/2' high & is hump back'd.

George LECRONE of Dover Twp., has taken stray hogs.

147. Next issue available, Wednesday, 27 May 1795

Alexander RUSSELL, Brigade Inspector of the Militia of York Co., Marsh Creek gives notice to persons belonging to the Militia who have been fined by the Court of Appeal for not performing their tour of duty on the late Western expedition.

Peter HEILSAMER gave 5 bonds unto a certain Robert CUNNINGHAM, which bonds will not be honored until CUNNINGHAM fulfills his end of the contract.

Valentine BERYER of Manallin Twp., York Co. has taken in a stray mare.

Philip WAGGNER signed a note to a certain Adam MOURER, which note was obtained by fraud; & WAGGNER will not honor.

The horse Eclipse will stand to cover mares this season at the stable of Thomas GIBSON in Taney Town (Md.).

147. Wednesday, 27 May 1795 (Con't.)
Andrew SMITH of Shrewsbury Twp., York Co. has taken in a stray cow.
William EHRHART of Shrewsbury Twp., York Co. hasa taken in a stray mare.
Henry SCHRIBER, in the month of October last, died at the house Zacharias DERSS(?) in Newbury Twp., York Co., & whereas Zacharias administered on the estate of the said Henry, I said Zacharias do now give Public Notice to all persons who have any demands against the said decd., to bring in their accounts properly.
HARRIS & DONALDSON have just received & are opening at their store near the bridge, a large & handsome assortment of seasonable goods.
A farm in Chanceford Twp. to be rented on shares, 259 1/2 a., dwelling house, barn &c. Apply to Ralph BOWIE in York Borough.
John FLINCHBAUGH warns all persons from giving credit on his account to a certain Catharina WALTMAN (or Catharina FLINCHBAUGH), as he will not pay.
Whereas a certain Valentine HOLLINGER of York Co. obtained a note of Adam DENTLINGER 25 or 26 December 1793, DENTLINGER refuses to pay.
Robert WILSON occupies the Tavern kept by Robert DUNN, the sign of the Waggon, on the North side of High St., Borough of York, where Travellers can be entertained.
William M'CLELLAN is a candidate for sheriff of York Co.
Sheriff's Sales: Estate of James Porter EWING, tract & improvement in Fawn Twp., 61 a., adj. lands of Nicholas COOPER.
Estate of John POFFENBERGER, one equal undivided half part of improvement & tract in Mountpleasant Twp., York Co. of 180 a., adj. lands of Martin BOTOSFF(?), Nicholas LENGLE, & John BEEGHER.
Estate of Thomas ARMOR, Jr., decd., in hands & possession of Robert BIGHAM, Adm'r. of decd., improvement & tract in Shrewsbury Twp., 28 1/2 a., adj. lands of Henry KORBMAN.
Estate of Peter MILLER, late Collector, 100 a. in Tyrone Twp., York Co., adj lands of John NEELY, the Glebe, William WALKER.
Estate of WIlliam BREDEN, late Collector, tract with improvement 120 a. in Cumberland Twp., York Co., adj. lands of William M'PHERSON & Andrew BOYD.
Estate of John SWENEY, late Collector, 227. a. in Cumberland Twp., York Co., adj. lands of Robert M'KEAN & David RIDDLE.
Estate of Samuel CROW, late Collector, 200 a. in Fawn Twp., York Co., adj. lands of George NICHELL & Benjamin CUNNINGHAM. Seized & taken into execution as the estates aforesaid & to be sold by Godfrey LENHART, Shrf.
William KERSEY, D.S., York, has removed his office to the sign of the Lyon & expects to be from home some time; has left it under the care of his son, Joseph, who will pay strict attention to the surveying business & with cases of particular difficulty will call on his cordial friend John FORSYTH, Esq. to assist him.

148. Next issue available, Wednesday, 17 June 1795
Conrad LAUB, Collector of the Revenue notifies owners of stills of regulations & taxes due.
J. G. D. KERLKGAND, living in Frederick Town, Md., offers $10 reward for runaway Negro Wench by name of Kitty, about 40 or 42 years of age, 5'6" high, had on a red cloth Cloke, green woolen jacket, brown woolen petticoat, white hat & is likely she has a pass & is now in some part of Pa. She walks bold & straight, speaks English & German Languages & a little French; is supposed she has been with child since the runaway.
Peter MORETZ, of Franklin Twp., has taken in a stray bay horse.

148. Wednesday, 17 June 1795 (Con't.)

All having legal claims against the estate of William M'CREERY, decd., should make immediate application. Robert CAMPBELL, Ex'r., Strabane Twp.

Tempest TUCKER, of Paradise Twp., York Co., has taken in a stray black cow.

Ulrich PETER of Menalon Twp, has taken in a stray bay horse.

Jacob BUSER of Codorus Twp., offers reward for runaway apprentice born of German parents named Jacob DECKHR, who was bound to learn the Taylor Trade; about 15 years old, 5' & perhaps an inch high, black hair, much pitted with the small pox.

Sign of the Bear in York Borough kept by Henry SCHAEFFER, 6th door above the Public Building, on the South side of High St. leading from York Town to Wright's Ferry, continues keeping a public house of Entertainment. Also carries on at the place aforesaid, a Tobacco Manufactory.

John TAYLOR offers $30 reward for a young Negro Man named Peter who ran away in Dec. 1790. About 20 years of age when he went away, a likely faced fellow, has a beautiful set of teeth, strait in his body, square sholdered. He is supposed to be from 5' to 5' 10-11" high.

John TAYLOR, living at the lower Cross Roads, Harford Co. Md., also offers $30 reward for runaway young Negro Man named Cato, about 22 years of age, 5' 8-9" high, stands well on his legs, tolerable good shoe maker & very handy with carpenter's tools. A certain Charles GALE (alias HOPKINS), a whiteman; by trade a hatter dressed in sailors cloaths is supposed to have gone with said negro.

149. Wednesday, 24 June 1795

A very unhappy circumstance occurred (June 17th) in Baltimore. A person who calls himself Patrick REARDON & says he has a wife & family in Alexandria, was discovered a few miles from town in the desperate act of suicide. He had just given himself 2 strokes across the throat with a knife & made a third into the windpipe. He declines giving any reason for this rash attempt, more than that a voice in the woods bade him. He was treated, but it is much doubted that he will survive.

John LEE, Coppersmith informs the public thata he carries on his business in the shop late in the occupation of James M'CALMOND, decd., partly opposite the ship Tavern, near the Bridge, Borough of York.

150. Next issue available, 22 July 1795

Richard Bland LEE selling tract of land in Frederick Co., Va., 9-10,000 a. being the greatest part of Greenway Court Manor. If not sold will be divided into tracts 5-800 a. each.

Distillery to be rented 1/4 mile from Borough of York, stone house 43x21 1/2' with extensive floor over head for the reception of Rye, &c. William HARRIS, York Borough.

Robert WILSON selling horses for saddle or draught.

John THOMAS, Hanover, York Co., has taken up 2 stray steers.

William CRAWFORD, Marsh Creek, being under a necessity of leaving that part of the country wherein he now resides early in the Fall, his return thereto uncertain, expects all in his debt to come forward by 11 Sept. next to settle. So there will be foundation for excuse or offence afterwards, he will be at home every Wednesday & Saturday.

John WALLS, Borough of York, has taken in a stray heifer.

Dr. Daniel WALDENBERGER has the best wine bitters & headache snuff at the sign of the Prince of Poland, York Town.

Conrad REINICKER renting that large commodious 3-story brick house & lot in Town of Baltimore, Market St., known as the name of Congress Hall with stables for 30 horses, at present occupied by REINICKER as a Public House. There are 14 rooms with kitchen & wash house & good cellar.

Persons indebted to the firm of ELDER & M'ALLISTER are requested to make payment before 10 Aug. next, as said partnership will then disolve by mutual consent. Renting house also. (Gettysburgh)

House & lot for sale in Waynesburgh, upper end of York Co., Francis HARBISON.

All persons indebted to estate of John HOSHAR, late of Manheim Twp., York Co., decd., are desired to make payment. Samuel HORNISH & Peter BURKHART, Adm'rs.

151. Next issue available, Wednesday, 5 August 1795

For sale - That excellent Stage, Skinners Tavern, on the top of Sideling-hill: also a tanyard with good spring & 200 a., with said stage. Log House with 4 rooms lower & 5 bedrooms on 2d floor, kitchen in back & kitchen & cellar in house. 22 miles from Bedford & 1 mile above the fork of the Roads from Philadelphia to Baltimore. Enoch SKINNER, Bedford Co.

All who bought anything at my vendue who has not paid before 12th inst. can expect to be sued for same. Andrew JOHNSTON, York Borough.

John THOMAS, Hanover, York Co., has taken up two stray steers.

152. Next issue available Wednesday, 25 November 1795

Sheriff's Sales: Estate of Henry WEAVER, improvement & tract in Cumberland Twp., York Co., 150 a., adj. lands of Rev. Alexander DOBBINS, Andrew BOYD, William M'PHERSON, Esq. & others also 130 a. in Cumberland Twp., adj. lands of James GETTYS, Archibald TATE lands late of Robert SCOTT & others. William M'CLELLAN, Sheriff

Forgemen wanted immediately for a new Forge just completed at the Great Falls on the Potowmack River. Apply to the Manager at the Works or to John POTTS in Alexandria.

Ran away from Moses THOMPSON, living in York Co., South Carolina, 2 likely Negroes viz. Toney about 22 years of age 5'9-10" high, light made & very active, he is of yellow complexion & wore long hair when he ran away, he is much market with the whip on his Body. Wench named Lidia, of a course visage, about 25 years of age, much pitted with the small pox, very stout made, has been bred to house work & is active at her business. Give notice at William BAILEY's Coppersmith in Baltimore for reward. N.B. Said Negroes were apprehended in June near Woodstock, Va. & put in gaol; in November they were taken out by their Master & in a few days made their escape again, they pass for Free Negroes & said they were going for York Town in Pa. Alexander LOVE for Moses THOMPSON.

All indebted to the estate of William DOUGLASS, late of Strabane Twp., decd., are to pay up to Daniel MENTEITH or David DEMAREE, Ex'rs.

Jos. WELSHANS & Henry WELSH, Commissioners, are willing to receive proposals in writing at their office from any workmen who are willing to undertake to erect a substantial stone bridge across the Codorus Creek, on High St., Borough of York; the bridge to be 20' in breadth, 130' long.

Robert WILSON, Borough of York, selling healthy Negro Woman & Child; she is about 25 years of age & has 9 or 10 years to serve; well acquainted with housework.

John TREICHLER, living in York Twp., has taken up a stray steer.

David MOORE, Inspector of flour for the Port of Baltimore, announces that he has discovered the Perpetual Motion [machine]. It operates by Wedge, Screw, Lever or dead weight from a clock to a forge & will apply to all smooth water Navigation & even certain Carriages.

152. Wednesday, 25 November 1795 (Con't.)
John WOLF, Junr. of York Borough, gives notice of Lottery.
To be sold- 190 a. near Conowago Creek, Heidelberg Twp., York Co. half a mile from Conowago Chapple. Has large stone house, barn, smith shop & sickle mill, spring house. Apply to Robert OWINGS, living on premises.
Tavern Keepers are notified that their Licenses are in the hand of John HAY, Esq., Treasurer for York Co.
Charles BRADSHAW has taken in a stray mare, Chanceford Twp.
John FORSYTH, living opposite to the German Presbyterian Cnutch, Main St. Borough of York, sells tobacco wholesale & retail.
Selling 12 a. of limestone land under good fencing, in Manchester Twp., 1/4 mile from Borough of York. Has thriving hop yard of 150 hills, good barn & stable; Stone Still House 43 x 22' with apparatus. Apply to William HARRIS, York Borough
James RIDDLE, renting for 3 or 4 years, plantation adj. Hunter's Town, known by the name of "Greens place," 314 a. Apply to Alexander RUSSELL, Esq. near Gettysburg or to RIDDLE in Chambersburg.
Alexander COBEAN, now living on the premises, wants to let his merchant mill on the waters of Marsh Creek, Cumberland Co. about 3 1/2 miles from Gettysburgh, together with upwards of 100 a., dwelling house, store house with shelves & counter, still house with 2 stills, barn & stables. He also offers for sale a tract of land adj. the above of 154 a., on which are a new Saw Mill, stone dwelling house 2-stories high, double barn. Also, all persons indebed to Alexander COBEAN are requested to make payment before 1 Jan. next, as the plan of business which he intends pursuing will not admit of longer indulgence.
Wanted at the Conowago Canal, a millwright for a saw mill; also labourers who are willing to be engaged at the Canal. Apply to James THOMPSON, at the Canal.
Nathan PATTERSON selling 103 a. & 111 perches in Strabane Twp., York Co., adj. lands with George HAYS, William FLEMING & others. There is erected a small dwelling house on tract. Also to be sold on the same day, grains, livestock & farming utensils & household furniture.
For Sale- 565 a. in Frederick Co., Md., 40 miles from Baltimore & 6 from Frederick Town. 20 acres cleared, the rest mostly timbered & a large quantity of Meadow Ground, has dam & saw mill. Will either be divided into Lotts or sold altogether. Apply to Joel WRIGHT or Allen FARQUHAR, living on Little Pipe Creek, Frederick Co., Md.
To be sold at the house of Samuel FAHNESTOCK, Town of Berlin, a variety of store goods, one cow, some household goods, the apparatus of a pottery with some crackery. Daniel BROWN, Herman BLAZER & Samuel ARNOLD.
Selling part of Stevenson Garden, 1000 a. of rich limestone land on Little Pipe Creek, Frederick Co., Md.; about 35 miles from Baltimore & 40 from the Federal City. Has 300 bearing apple trees, some log houses, corn house, barn & stables. Apply to Andrew ROBINSON, York Town or Christopher JOHNSTON in Baltimore.
Whereas Adam BROWN did make over all debts, dues & demands in his books to the subscribers, this is to caution persons against paying over to the said Adam any sum of money they may owe him. Instead they are to call upon the subscribers or upon Gabriel SMITH, Esq., of Berlin (who has his books) for the purpose of discharging same. Daniel BROWN, Herman BLAZER & Samuel ARNOLD.
Whereas my Wife Agness ADAMS hath eloped from my bed & board without any just cause, the public are cautioned not to give her any credit on my account. William ADAMS.

153. Wedesday, 5 January 1791 (Vol. VI, No. 283)
George KLINE, Postmaster gives notice of the post from Philadelphia.
Sheriff's Sales: 253 a. with gristmill & improvements in Tyrone Twp. sold as the property of John DAVIDSON.
Square log house & lot on corner of Queen & Water Sts., now in the possession of Daniel M'GRIGER; another square house & kitchen adj. aforesaid on the east now in possession of John KIRKPATRICK, both in the town of Chambersburg (Franklin Co.); sold as the property of Jeremiah TALBOT.
150 a. in Derry twp., Ferguson's valley, now in Mifflin Co., sold as the property of James BURNS.
100 a. with saw mill in Greenwood twp., to be sold as property of John CRAIN.
150 a. with grist mill &c. in Derry twp., 3 miles from Lewistown, Mifflin Co.; sold as property of Abraham STANFORD. Thomas BUCHANAN, Sheriff.
Stolen or strayed from Ephraim BLANE in Carlisle, dark sorrel horse.
Sheriff's Sales: 560 a.in Middletown tsp., 3 miles below Carlisle, Cumberland Co.; bounded on one side by the Conedoguinet Creek & on the other by the Letart Spring; sold as property of Robert CALLENDER, dec.
200 a. near Shippensburgh in Franklin Co.; property of James DUNN.
200 a. with improvements in Eastpennsboro two, on the Conedoguinet creek, adj. lands of --- COFFMAN, near the mill fording, property of Henry NEFF.
Two tracts in Rye twp. (500 a.) adj. lands of Samuel ROBESON, property of David MOORE.
200 a. in Wayne twp., now Huntingdon Co., property of James ARMSTRONG.
House & Lot on York St., opposite the sign of the Seven Stars (borough of Carlisle) property of Jacob ISSETT.
200 a. in Hamilton twp., now Franklin Co., adj. lands of Samuel GUTHRIE; property of William M'CUNE.
120(?) a. with merchant mill in Fannet twp., now Franklin Co., adj. lands of Hugh M'CURDY, property of Robert GRAY.
400 a. in Lurgan twp., Franklin Co., property of Benjamin ALSWORTH, dec.
Nicholas FREDERIC, Tuskarora Valley Mifflin Co., paid 3 Bonds to a certain William STURGEON & is unwilling to honor.
Three tracts of land (750 a.) in Derry Twp., Mifflin Co., to be sold, the plantation where John GAUGHEY & Robert ANDERSON now live. Enquire of Thomas FRANKLIN, Philadelphia.
Sold or Leased: House & 2 lots in borough of Carlisle, on south extremity of York St., lately occupied by William BARKER; apply to Jonathan WALKER; John WALKER or Stephen DUNCAN.
Charles LEEPER requests persons indebted to him to make payment.
Ran away from Joseph WALLACE near Elkton, Cecil Co., MD, a Negro Man named Will, about 5'10" high, well set, wears his hair platted & cued. Has a considerable sum of money with him, is fond of playing the fiddle.

154. Wednesday, 12 January 1791
For printing by subscription Sermons on Practical Subjects by Robert WALKER, late Minister of the High Church of Edinburgh, with a character of the author by Hugh BLAIR, D.D. Subscriptions received by John CREIGH, John WEBBER & Samuel TATE in Carlisle.
Came to the plantation of Benjamin HENDERSON, 2 1/2 miles from Carlisle in Middletown twp., stray mare.
Came to the plantation of David REED, 1 mile from John MOOR's Mill in West Pennsborough twp., Cumberland Co., dark bay mare.

154. Wednesday, 12 January 1791 (Con't.)

Came to plantation of Edward MORTON, living in East Pennsborough, a small black cow.

Joseph STEEL, clock & watch maker & silversmith, has commenced business opposite to Samuel LAIRD, Esq. in Hanover St., between sign of the Black Horse & Seven Stars; borough of Carlisle.

A quantity of goods, the property of Maj. William GOFORTH & Dr. GANA, lost in Carlisle. Contains quantity of medicine. Reward offered. Contact Capt. William RIPPEY in Shippensburgh.

Thomas & John STEPHENS, Fullers, thank public for past patronage at Callender's Mill.

155. Wednesday, 19 January 1791 (next issue on available)

Sheriff's Sale: 120 a. in Armaugh twp., adj. lands of William DICKSON, property of William YOUNG.

150 a.in Derry twp., Ferguson's valley, now Mifflin Co, property of James BURNS.

200 a. with sawmill in Greenwood twp, property of John CRAIO.(?)

On Tuesday instant at 9 a.m. the house of Alexander M'DONALD, a tenant on Mr. David HOGE's farm in East-Pennsborough, was burned, & his wife & 2 of his children & a girl, the only child of his brother-in-law, perished in the flames. He & his wife's mother escaped.

Died Monday last in Chambersburgh, Franklin Co., after a short illness, Jeremiah TALOT, Esq., late High Sheriff of that county.

Richard CARSON offering reward for bay mare of James WILSON, living on Dogwood Road in Monagban twp., York County.

Thomas & Henry MOORE have had a shipment of sugar left with them by a wagoner who could not recollect the owners name. Plese claim. (Middletown, Dauphin Co.)

Came to the plantation of John GARBER in West Pennsboro twp., Cumberland County, a small steer.

William HUNTER, blue-dyer, thanks past customers. He continues to live in Pomfret St., opposite to Mr. John HUNTER's at the sign of General Washington, immediately opposite to a Locust Tree, where he also carries on the Weaving Business.

156. Wednesday, 26 January 1791

House & Lot to be sold on York St., next door to but one to the corner of Pomfret St., borough of Carlisle. And all indebted to the subscriber requested to pay up. Nathaniel WEAKLEY, Carlisle.

Peter KAUFMAN passed 4 bonds to a certain David PFOUTS, in part to pay for a tract of land in Greenwood Twp., Cumberland Co., which said PFOUTS promised to clear of all judgements & mortgages, which he did not.

Robert MILLER, Jr.& John HUGHES, admin. of the estate of John MILLER, late of the Borough of Carlisle, to let the mansion house & lot of decd. or that part now occupied by Mr. HUSTON, which is the Shop, Store-house & cellar.

Whereas my husband, Philip DELANCEY hath exploited me in the public news papers on 29 April 1790, I think it reasonable the public should know the real cause I had for leaving him; (although a quire of paper would scarce contain the many miserable abuses I have received from him by blows from his fists & kickings from his feet) that narrow space of a news paper would not be adequate to the dreadful castrophe which I could relate. . . . I wrought plantation work like a man, and my house work I was obliged to do after night, and my spinning also at night . . .

and in wet weather I was obliged to assist in quarrying stone & heaping them . . . and when it rained very heavy, and I not able to fulfill my task he would curse and imprecate shocking expressions. . . . Margaret DELANCEY.

For sale: 2-story stone house, 40' long, on South West Corner of the Diamond in Chambersburg. Apply to John M'CONKEY, Chambersburg.

157. Wednesday, 2 February 1791

The house now occupied by John DEAN in the town of Huntington, to be leased.

To be sold: lot on which the Meeting House of the late Rev. George DOFFIELD formerly stood; corner of York & Pomfret Sts., opposite the new house of Mr. Stephen DUNCAN on York St. This lot is sold for the use of the Presbyterian Congregation of Carlisle.

Persons indebted to estate of John REYNOLDS, Esq. decd., are requested to pay. Hannah REYNOLDS, Robert PEEBLES, Mathew HENDERSON, Adm'rs. Shippensburgh.

Died in East Pennsborough on Thursday night, the 27th of January, Isabel HOGE, wife of Jonathan HOGE, Esq. in the 64th year of her age. On the Saturday following her remains were attended by a large and respectable train, and interred in the burial ground at Silver-Spring. Her husband was absent, attending his duty in the Legislature of the state. Her health had been for a long time declining.

158. Wednesday, 16 February 1791

All persons indebted to the estate of Daniel DUNCAN, Sr. of Shippensburgh, county of Cumberland, decd; are requested to make immediate payment. James DUNLOP, Thomas DUNCAN, Robert COLWELL, Admin.

The same administrators as above selling at the late dwelling house of Daniel DUNCAN, in the Town of Shippensburgh, household goods & kitchen furniture, farming utensils, livestock, etc. An excellent housewench will be disposed of & 5 young Negro children, who have to serve until they arrive at the age of 28 years. Also to be sold, a lease of 5 years for 40 a. of land adjoining the town. Also, to be rented for 3 years, a plantation 2 miles from Shippensburgh, on the great road to Carlisle. Also a tract on the Walnut-Bottom Road about 4 miles from Shippensburgh; likewise a tract in Mifflin Co. James DUNLOP, Thomas DUNCAN, Robert COLWELL.

John WEBBER, intending to quit the Woolen branch of his business, every article to be sold without reserve at first cost for ready money. Also selling or renting 2-story log house & lot in Pomfret St., near the College, very low for cash.

Philadelphia: On the 27th instant, departed this life after a short illness, in the 60th year of his age, the Hon. George BRYAN, Esq. of the Supreme Court of this Commonwealth. He was a native of Dublin, Ireland & the eldest of an ancient family of that place. He had resided in Philadelphia for nearly 40 years.

To be sold at Moystons Coffee-house in Philadelphia, 100 a. at the forks of the Great Meadow & Big-glade-run, formerly Westmoreland, now Fayette county, called Millseat. The road to Benson(?)town and Redstone passes through this tract. 314 a. in Rye twp., Cumberlandcounty, on little Juniata creek. These lands are the property of John PATTERSON, whitesmith, of Philadelphia, for the use of his creditors. Apply to Thomas ARMAT, assignee, Philadelphia.

158. Wednesday, 16 February 1791 (Con't.)

Alexander M'KEEHEN, Esq. Treasurer of Cumberland Co., directed Thomas BUCHANAN, Sheriff to sell land in Fannet Twp., 150 a. with a house & barn thereon, property of Samuel MEARS, delinquent collector of the State Taxes for Fannet twp., now in Franklin County.

159. Wednesday, 23 February 1791

Sheriff Sale: Tract of Land called Ramage, in Rye twp., Cumberland Co., 103 1/2 a., property of Robert RAMSAY.

Tract of Land called Lovesburgh, in West Pennsborough twp., Cumberland Co., adj. lands of William CLARK, 138 a., property of John LOVE.

Tract of Land called Billy-Willing, in Newton twp., Cumberland Co., adj. lands of Samuel WILLIAMSON, 331 a. Property of Thomas MARTIN.

House & Lot in Louther St., Borough of Carlisle, now in tenure of John MORRISON. Apply to Andrew HOLMES.

Whereas Benjamin BROWN of Derry twp., Mifflin Co. obtained a note of bond from Captain William ARMSTRONG, of the same twp. & county; William ARMSTRONG, Jr. has reason to believe that they were fraudulenty obtained by taking advantage of his father (Captain William) and refuses to honor.

Came to the plantation of John KINKEAD living in Middleton twp., Cumberland County, a stray steer.

Came to the plantation of James YOUNG, living in Middleton twp., within one mile of Carlisle, a stray steer.

160. Wednesday, 2 March 1791

New York (Feb. 21): Among the unfortunate slain, at Muskingum, by the Indians, Jan. 2, were 2 sons of Col. STACY, New-Salem; a son of Major Ezra PUTNAM and John CAMP of Mass.; Jonathan FAIRWELL, from New-Hampshire; Zebulon TROOP, from Barre; William JONES from Conn.; Joseph CLARK from Rhode Island; and one MEEKS from Va. with his wife and two children.

Robert MILLER, Junr. Clerk, Union Fire Co. of Carlisle, gives notice of exercising the engines; all members required to show up with buckets.

George CLARK renting several houses & lots in the town of Green-Castle, one of which has been occupied by Mr. CLARK for several years at the sign of General Greene.

Land to be sold in Franklin Co., Southampton Twp., 270 a. 3 miles from Shippensburgh; apply to William REYNOLDS or Francis GRAHAM.

Was found in trespess, a little chunky brown horse, somewhat old. James BELL, East Pennsborough, Stonney Ridge near Callenders- mill.

The elegant horse Dobbin, to cover mares this season at the stable of John STEPHENS at Callender's Mill. Dobbin was got by Young Chester Bell, his dam was of the dray breed. Jacob WEAVER.

161. Wednesday, 9 March 1791

Sheriff's Sale: 200 a. on which is a cabin & still house in Fannet twp., Ambersons valley, Franklin Co., 2 miles from John WARDs; property of Patrick M'GEE.

200 a. with improvements in East-Pennsborough twp., adj. lands of Jacob MILLER; property of Ludwick FRIDLEY.

Following properties, all property of delinquent Collectors of state taxes for said townships: Millford twp., Mifflin Co. 200 a. Robert TAYLOR; 100 a. with Tanyard, Thomas TURBETT, 200 a. Thomas HARDY.

161. Wednesday, 9 March 1791 (Con't.)
Armaugh twp., Mifflin county, John M'NITT. 200 a. in East Pennsborough twp., James BELL. 200 a. in Tyrone township, with sawmill, John DUNBAR. 200 a. in East Pennsborough twp., Abraham LONGNECKER.
All persons indebted to William WILSON, requested to make payment before 25 March, as he intends removing from this town to Harrisburgh.
Ran away from Alexander OFFICER in West Pennsborough twp., Cumberland Co., an Apprentice lad, Samuel MILLER; about 19 years, 8 months old, 5'10" high, fair hair.

162. Wednesday, 16 March 1791
Tract for sale, late the property of Allen LEEPER, decd. 150 a. in West-Pennsborough twp., Cumberland County; on which is a square log dwelling house, double log barn, stone still-house. James & Charles LEEPER, Executors.
Mr. Lucas CARTER, being possessed of full powers to transact the business of Messrs. Penn within the counties of Cumberland & Franklin &c., will attend at the house of Joseph POSTLETHWAITE, Borough of Carlisle for the purpose of selling all tracts of land within any of their Manors & Islands in the river Susquehanna, which have hitherto been undisposed of. Anthony BUTLER, Attorney to John PENN, jun. & John Penn, Esq. Phila.
Sheriff's Sale: 329 a. formerly lying in Tyrone but now in Rye twp., adj. lands of Samuel M'CRACKEN, Mathias BURD & Charles DOWNEY, sold as the property of David MOORE.
Stolen last night (Mar. 15, 1791) from the stable of Jacob RUPLEY, living in East Pennsborough twp., Cumberland Co., a gray mare; there is a lump on the top of his head which appears as if she had the pole evil. Also taken was a saddle, new bridle with silver plated tips & buckles, & the head piece faced with red silk ribbon. All of the above was stolen by a fellow who was employed as a hireling, he called himself John LANDIS, alias John HOFFMAN. About 5'6" high, about 40 years old, thick set, dark complexion, short black hair.
To be sold at the late dwelling house of Major Alexander PARKER, decd. in Middleton twp., a number of horses & breeding mares, milch cows & young cattle, Swine, waggons, ploughs & harrows, etc.; the farm of 200 a. to be rented. Rebecca PARKER, John M'DANNEL & Samuel POSTLETHWAIT, Admrs.

163. Wednesday, 23 March 1791
Stolen Friday evening last from Robert SEMPLE, Mt. Rock, a bay horse.
To be sold, at the dwelling house of William APPLEBY, Hopewell Twp., near Shippensburgh, hogs, cows, horses, etc.
Young Canadian will cover mares at the stable of Bartholomew WHITE, living at Mt. Rock, West-Pennsborough twp.
Alexander MURRAY, Esq. & Alexander MURRAY, admrs. selling plantation in Toboyne twp., Sherman's Valley, 210 a. with house.

164. Wednesday, 30 March 1791
Dr. STINNECKE, who arrived here from Germany, informs that he has removed from Pomfret St. to the house now occupied by Mr. KLINE, Printer, the next door but one to Dr. STEVENSON.
A ferry, tavern & smithshop kept in Long Narrows on the road from Carlisle to Lewistown in Mifflin Co.--enquire from the Run Gap to squire BEAL's forge, then to John HARDY's, then JORDON's ferry, where you will be

kindly received and quickly waited on & thankfully acknowledged for your custom by David JORDON.

A number of labourers & carters at Col. James CHAMBER's Iron Works in Franklin Co. James TRIMBLE.

Sheriff's Sale: 202 a. in West Pennsboro twp., Cumberland Co., adj. lands of William MOORE, Edward WEAKLEY & Michael EGE & the South Mountain; property of James DAVIS.

200 a. in Lacktown (?) Mifflin Co., with improvements, property of Alexander FARRIER.

200 a. adj. Lewistown in Derry twp., now Mifflin co., one undivided part thereof, property of John MAGEE.

236 a. Allen twp., adj. lands of James GREGORY, John WILLIAMS; property of Alexander HAMILTON.

200 a. with valuable improvement thereon in East-Pennsboro twp., on the Connedoguinet Creek, adj. lands of --- HOFFMAN, near the mill fording, property of Henry NEAFF.

40 a. adj. the Dry Tavern, &c. 1 mile from Carlisle, property of Ralph NAILOR, decd.

150 a. in West-Pennsborough twp., adj. lands of Elendor REAGH, William EWING, Thomas GLENN; property of Alexander ROSEBORROW.

Large 2-story stone house & lot, corner of York & Louther Sts. in Carlisle; property of William WALLACE.

Selling plantation of 242 a. formerly purchased by the late Proprietaries from George ARMSTRONG, Esq., about 1 mile from borough of Carlisle, on both sides of the road leading to Shippensburgh in Cumberland Co. Anthony BUTLER, Atty. for Penns.

John WORMLE now occupies the ferry nearly opposite Harrisburgh, where John MONTGOMERY did live, & was generally known by the name of Montomgery's Ferry.

Wanted at Pine Grove Furnace, a number of workmen. Arthur THORNBURGH & Co.

165. Wednesday, 6 April 1791

For sale: 300 a. of patented land on the South Eastside of the North East Branch of Susquehanna, 9 miles from town of Sunbury & nearly opposite Montgomery's Mill at the mouth of Machoning creek, nearly half a mile front on creek; house & barn; in tenor of a Mr. EWING, who has lived on it for 13 years past. 300 a. ditto adj. the back part of the above, & land late Dr. John MORGAN's; also house & barn, now in tenor of a Mr. IRWIN, who has lived on it for 13 years.

300 a. ditto, including the mouth of Briar Creek, which is on the North West side of the North East Branch, about 16 miles above Northumberland, adj. lands of Joseph SHIPPEN & George IRWIN; house & barn; now in tenor of Mr. Thomas ELLIS.

304 a. ditto, 4 or 5 miles above the Falls of Neseopeek (Nefeopeek?), in the North East Branch, nearly opposite the mouth of Wappalipan creek, about 1 mile back from the river, now supposed tobe settled by some people of the name of WOLF--who are making good improvements.

25 a. rich bottom land under location & survey in the summer 1769, adj. lower end of the mannor of Pomfret, on the South East side of the North East Branch of Susquahanna.

50 a. ditto, opposite above, entirely cleared.

315 a. under warrant & survey, adj. the back of the mannor of Pomfret, on each side the old road from Wiaming to Easton. For terms apply to Messrs. Francis & John WEST in Philadelphia or to William WEST, living in Baltimore Town, MD.

165. Wednesday, 6 April 1791 (Con't.)

Sheriff's Sale: Unimproved tract of 150 a. lying on Sherman's Creek, adj. lands of Stephen DUNCAN; sold as the property of William THOMPSON, decd.

50 a. in Derry twp. lying on the Juniata River, adj. lands of David STEEL. Contains 15 a. of cleared land & cabbin, sold as the property of John JOHNSTON, decd.

200 a. in Greenwood twp., adj. lands of John LONG, has improvements; sold as property of John, Robert & Benjamin CRAIN.

600 a. in Middletown twp., 3 miles below Carlisle, with grist mill, saw mill & fulling mill. In Cumberland Co., is bounded by the Conedoguinet Creek on one side, on the other by the Letarr Spring; sold as the property of Robert CALANDER, decd.

The undivided 2/5 and 1/3 of 1/5 in Fannet twp. Franklin Co., taken in execution at the suit of John SMITH of Baltimore, as the property of William & Benjamin CHAMBERS, decd.

200 a. on which is a cabin & stillhouse, in Fannet twp. Ambersons Valley, Franklin Co., 2 miles from John WARD's; property of Patrick M'GEE.

Tract in Fermanagh twp., house & double barn, sold as the property of Epenetus HART.

Two-story frame house, and lot of ground in York St., property of James WILLIAMSON.

The partnership of Thomas STEPHENS & Son, being dissolved. The fulling business to be carried on by John STEPHENS. Cloth will be taken in at Thomas STEPHENS, the lower end of York St., Mr. John HUNTER's tavern, Mr. Robert SMITH's tavern & at Mr. CRAVERS tavern in Carlisle.

Pittsburgh March 26: On Friday the 18th instant, a party of Indians murdered a certain Robert CHAPMAN at the House of Thomas DICK, about 3 miles from this place, on the West side of the Allegheny river & took DICK & his wife prisoners; and the same day another party took a boy by the name of BRICKEL. Another account has been received that several families, to the amount of 12 persons have been killed by a party of Indians about 20 miles from this place, up the Allegheny on the west side.

George COINERD informs all indebted to his father, Michael COINERD, to discharge same.

Mary M'CORMICK, having removed from the Main Street, has taken residence in the house lately occupied by Mr. RAINEY, in the alley leading from Mr. Ephraim STEEL's dwelling, where she continues her milinary business.

With regret, and shame, the subscriber finds himself under the necessity of advertising his wife. Although it is practised by some white people, yet he, though black, blushes at the thoughts of declaring to the world that his wife has run away. But, disagreeable as it is, he does make known that LUCY, his wife, has eloped from his bed & board & forbids all persons harbouring & trusting her. Prince HULL (Hartford).

166. Wednesday, 13 April 1791

Trustees of the Public School in the Town & County of Huntingdon give notice that they have opened a Grammer School under the direction of the Rev. John JOHNSTON. John CANAN, President of the Board.

Sheriff's Sale: 300 a. at the mouth of the Juniata River, Rye twp., now in the tenor of William BEATTY, Esq.; sold as the property of Mitchell BARKINS.

100 a. on the Bigspring in West Pennsboro twp., adj. lands of David BLAINE, James BROWN, with merchant mill (stone springhouse) and saw mill,

farm house & millers house. Sold as property of James IRWINE.
30 a. near Sherman Creek; the property of Joseph ROSE. (paper creased & name of twp obliterated.)

Joseph T. JAMES informs that he is opening at the House of Mr. George KLINE in York St. 2 doors from Dr. STEVENSON, a general assortment of merchandize.

Negro Man named Sambo ran away from Conrad SHERMAN of Mankeim twp. About 21 years of age, 5'7 or 8" high, has a scar on one eyebrow; smart & active, fond of strong drink, plays a little on the fiddle, talks both English & German.

William THOMPSON, watchmaker, informs that he has removed from his former stand in High St. to Louther St., nearly opposite John ANDERSONs store & next door to the house formerly occupied by Peter LETREETT, silversmith.

167. Wednesday, 20 April 1791

Sheriff's Sales: By virtue of Precepts of sale from under the hand of Alexander M'KEEBEN, Treas. of Cumberland Co., for public sale: (All the property of delinquent Collectors of State Taxes in the respective twps.) 200 a. in Millford twp, Mifflin Co, with improvements; property of Robert TAYLOR.

100 a. in Millford Twp., Mifflin Co. with tanyard & other improvements thereon, property of Thomas TURBETT.

200 (?) a. in Millford Twp., Mifflin co; property of Thomas HARDY.

200 a. in Armaugh Twp., Mifflin Co, with improvements; property of John M'NITT.

200 a. in East Pennsborough twp., with improvements, property of James BELL.

200 a. in Tyrone twp. with saw-mill, property of Abraham LONGNECKER. All of which to be sold by Thomas BUCHANAN, Sheriff.

Sheriff's Sales: 202 a. in West Pennsborough Twp., Cumberland, Co., adj lands of William MOORE, Edward WEAKLEY & Michael EGE and the South Mountain; well timbered. Property of James DAVIS.

200 a. in Lack township, Miflin Co., property of Andrew FARRIER.

200 a. in Hamilton twp. now Franklin Co., adj lands of Samuel GUTHRIE, sold as property of William M'CUNE.

150 a. with grist mill, farm house & miller's house in Derry twp.;, 3 miles from Lewis town, in Mifflin co; sold as property of Abraham STANFORD.

Acts of the Legislature of the State: An Act for granting $800 to Corn-Planter, Half-Town & Big-Tree, Senaca Chiefs, in trust for the Seneca Nation. An Act to empower the Governor to grant a patent to Big-Tree, a Seneca Chief, for a certain Island in the Allegheny river.

An Act providing payment to Dr. Francis ALISON for supplies furnished in the year 1775.

An Act to establish a ferry over Swatara creek, near the town of Williamsburg, in Dauphin Co., & for vesting the right in Christian SELTZER, his heirs and assigns.

An Act for the relief of Blackhall William BALL.

An Act to enable Eleazar OSWALD, guardian duly appointed to Jane JONES, Blaithwaithe JONES, Mary JONES and Gibbs JONES, minors under the age of 21 years, to sell and convey the property therein mentioned for the benefit of said minors.

Acts for the relief of Abraham LUKEN, James OFFICER, Philip PETER, Robert CUNNINGHAM, a prisoner in the Jail of the County, Philadelphia.

167. Wednesday, 20 April 1791 (Con't.)

Died at Middle Octorara, of a lingering illness, in the 73rd year of his age; on the 10th of March, 1791: The Rev'd. John CUTHBERTSON, Minister of the Gospel.

To be sold on the premises in Tyrone Twp., Cumberland Co., the undivided half part of 400 a. whereon Samuel LEONARD now lives, adj Col. Thomas HARDY on the South, John ELLIOT on the West, the Heirs of Mary BUCHANAN on the East, and a baron hill on the North. Property of Isaiah HESTON, decd. to be sold by Ann STOCKDAL & Ann HESTON, Administratrix.

Regarding plantation for sale in Greenwood twp., Cumberland co, recently advertised in the Carlisle Gazette, adj John LONG, as the property of John, Robert, and Benjamin CRANE, to be sold by Thomas BUCHANAN, Sheriff. Abraham SIFER, wishing that the innocent public may not be deceived or wronged, does hereby offer a true statement of the title of the land. A warrant issued by the proprietors of the then province unto Valentine KEMMEL, on 3 February 1755, and KEMMEL by his conveyance dated 14 June 1756, has made over the land to John RESH, his heirs & assigns, and said John RESH's heirs have by their convenience dated 17 June 1771, made over the land to Leonard PFOUTZ, who by his conveyance dated 20 June 1771 has sold the land to John & Jacob WEISER, who sold the land 1 October 1789, have sold and conveyed the land to George CRANE, who by sold the land to the subscriber, Abraham SIFER, who feels himself to be justly and legally possessed of the land.

168. Wednesday, 27 April 1791

Whereas my wife Elizabeth LARMUR hath behaved not becoming the character of a prudent wife; has obliged me to leaver her. Hugh LARMUE of West-Pennsborough twp. cautions the public not to give her credit on his account.

Died at Philadelphia, much lamented, the Hon. Nicholas EVELEIGH, Comptroller of the Treasury of the U.S.

On Saturday, the 9th instant, departed this Life, at Elizabeth-Town, Washington Co. Md. (Hagerstown) Col. John STULL, funeral service by Rev. Mr. George BOWER of that Place.

Plantation of 242 a. formerly purchased by the late proprietaries from George ARMSTRONG, about 1 mile from the Borough of Carlisle on both sides of the roading to Shippensburgh in Cumberland Co., has lately been divided into convenient parts. Same to be sold at public vendue to be held at the house of Jacob POSTLETHWAIT, in said Borough. Anthony BUTLER, Attorney to John PENN.

A number of deeds and mortgages are amongst the papers of John AGNES, late of the Borough of Carlisle, left with him while he was acted as Recorder for the co of Cumberland. These are to give notice that the said deeds and mortgages are now in the hands of Samuel POSTLETHWAIT of Carlisle, who requests those concerned to call and pay the recording fees and take them away.

For sale on long credit, or to be rented, a merchant mill with 2 pairs of burrs on a fine stream, joining Martinsburgh in Barkley Co., Virginia. A good miller is wanted. Apply to Adam STEPHENS on the premises.

For sale; price Six-pence: A Choice Drop of Honey From the Rock Christ, of A Word of Advice to all Saints & Sinners by Thomas WILCOCKS.

169. Wednesday, 4 May 1791

Thomas STEPHENS informs his friends & the public in general that he has set up a Blue-Dying in the Warm Fatts, at the 4th corner of York Street near the Dutch Church in the borough of Carlisle. He secures & cleans gentlemens cloaths without ripping the seams.

John STEPHENS returns his thanks to his friends & the public in general and says that he still carries on the Fulling Business at Callanders mill. Cloth taken at Carlisle by Messrs. John HUNGER, Jacob CREAVER & Robert SMITH, Tavernkeepers, and Thomas STEPHENS the corner of York-Street.

William LYON of Carlisle offers reward for return of a bright bay Filly, which strayed from the Carlisle Commons.

Samuel POSTLETHWAIT seeks small sorrel Mare, strayed from the Commons of Carlisle 8 April last.

The famous horse High Flyer will cover mares at the stable of Matthew LAIRD on Letart Spring, 2 miles from Carlisle. James YOUNG.

Strayed from the commons of Carlisle 22 April last, a bright bay filly; John CREAVER offers reward.

170. Wednesday, 11 May 1791

A ferry, tavern and smith shop kept in the Long Narrows for the accommodations of travellers, and much the nearest road from Carlisle to Lewistown, in Mifflin Co. Enquire from the Run Gap to Squire BEAL's forge, then to John HARDY's, then JORDON's ferry, where you will be kindly received. David JORDON.

A shocking murder was lately committed at Guilford by Soloman FOSTER and his wife, an infant child of theirs was murdered. FOSTER is in jail.

171. Wednesday, 25 May 1791

Deserted from the Barracks, near the Borough of Carlisle, the following soldiers belonging to 2d. Regiment Levies, Commanded by Col. George GIBSON. Richard BRYAN, born in Ireland & still retains a smack of the brogue, 45 years of age, 5'11" high, short hair a little grey, and is stoop shouldered. John REITHER, about 5'5 or 6" high, black hair, grey eyes, talks English and German, American born. Philip FREEZE, about 5'5 or 6" high, very yellow complexion, black hair and brown eyes, talks English and German, American born. Jonathan PACKER, about 5' 6 or 7" high, black hair, stoop shouldered an American born. James M'BRIDE, about 5'7" high, born in Ireland, sandy complexion, freckled in the face and grey eyes. John KITZMILLER, 5' 5 or 6" high, black complexion, speaks German only.

Deserted from Captain Zebulon PIKE's Company of the 2d. Regiment of Levies, commanded by Col. George GIBSON on the night of the 20th instant from the Barracks near Carlisle: Thomas GUTHRIE, 5'11" high, slim and straight made, dark complexion, black eyes, dark hair, by trade a nailer or blacksmith. John HAYS, 5' 8" high, well proportioned, fair complexion, brown curled hair, by trade a nailer or blacksmith. James VAN DOREN, about 5' 7" high, fair complexion, light brown hair, trade unknown. These deserters passed Mr. R. STERETS, Croghans Gap, early on Saturday morning last and enquired the Road to Junieta.

Alexandria, April 28. Died on Thursday last, of a madness occasioned by the bite of a mad cat, Miss Betsy SANFORD, only daughter of Mr. Richard SANFORD of Fairfax-County. She had been bitten about two months before the hydrophobia appeared.

Strayed or stollen on the night of the 16th instant, from the plantation of Christain WOHLGEMUTH, in Mt. Joy Twp., Lancaster Co., 3 miles from Elizabethtown, a mare.

172. Wednesday, 1 June 1791

Messrs. G. WALLACE, R. ELLIOT, W. AMBERSON, A. TANNEHILL, J. WILKINS, Jr. and J. IRWIN have offered a reward of $100 for every hostile Indian's scalp, with both ears to it, taken between 17 May and 15 June by any inhabitant of Allegheny county.

Natl. WEAKLEY is opening a neat assortment of dry & wet goods in the house of William RAINEY in York-Street, opposite to Mr. FORSTERS Tavern, to which place he has lately removed.

173. Wednesday, 15 June 1791

Ran away from Valentine EGOLFF, living in Borough of Carlisle, an apprentice girl, 12 years old.

Patrick CAMPBELL, Secretary, seeks a person of character who can be well recommended as a teacher of the English language, Arithmetic and the Mathematics. The Union School of Chambersburgh.

Strayed or stollen from the Commons of Carlisle, a sorrel mare, belonging to Joseph KELSO. Give information to Joseph GIVEN in Carlisle or KELSO living within one mile of Carlisle.

Daniel SMITH, Cumberland county, Toboyne twp, has taken up on the north side of the far Mountain, near Road crossing to Shippensburgh, a sorrel mare.

For sale by virtue of writ 200 a. with grist mill and other improvements thereon, in Fannet twp., now Franklin, formerly Cumberland Co., adj land of Hugh M'CURDY, taken in execution as the property of James POTTS. To be sold at the same time & place: 200 a. adj Lewistown, in Derry twp., now Mifflin Co., one undivided 9th part thereof, property of John MAGEE. Also a house & lot in York-street opposite to the sign of the seven stars, Borough of Carlisle, property of Jacob ?ett & to be sold by Thomas BUCHANAN, Sheriff, Carlisle.

Whereas an undivided 4th part of a tract of land, and a grist mill thereon, in Fannet twp, now in the co of Franklin, is advertised to be sold, by the sheriff, as the property of James POTTS. Notice is given that the said 4th part undivided is vested in Robert POTTS, by a Deed duly recorded in the county of Franklin. Alexander POTTS in behalf of Robert POTTS.

Came to the plantation of John STONE, 3 miles from Hurley's Gap, Tyrone twp., Cumberland County, a light coloured bay horse.

174. Wednesday, 22 June 1791

Deserted from my company, William M'COY, native of Ireland, 5'8" high, short hair, fair complexion, 28 years of age, a little round shouldered, is fond of liquor & talkative when intoxicated. Lived for some time at the Iron Works at Carlisle. John ARMSTRONG, Capt. 1st US Regt.

Deserted at Carlisle from the detachment under my command, John HECMAN, a German, 5'9" high, talks broken English.

James M'CORMICK, an Irishman, 5'9" high.

William SMITH, an Irishman, 5'7" high, stout made and much marked with the smallpox.

Paul Hamilton WILLIAMS, an Irishman, 5'4" high, inlisted as a fifer. William PRATT, Capt.

To be sold, 2-story house & lot in York-street, Borough of Carlisle. Has been kept as a Public House these six years past; has 2 rooms & small shop below, 5 rooms above with 1-story stone kitchen & bake-house, cellar & stable. Apply to Godfrid LUTZ, Carlisle, living on the premises.

175. Wednesday, 13 July 1791

Sheriff's Sales: 250 a. of land adj lands of James & Benjamin M'KEEHEN in West Pennsborough twp, with 2-story log house, (good limestone land), 9 miles from Carlisle & 3 (?) miles from Big Spring, property of John WEIGHT/WRIGHT?.

300 a., house and barn thereon, sold as property of Robert GILLISPIE.

200 a. on the Juntaia River in Rye twp., adj lands of Andrew BEATTY (?), house & double barn, sold as property of William ?

580 a. in Greenwood twp., grist mill, saw mill & other improvements, also plantation of 170 a. property of Stophel MONTZ, decd.

As undivided 8th part of a tract in Allen Twp. late the property of Alexander TRINDLE, decd. of 230 (?) a.

250 a. in Middleton twp. with improvements, 1 mile from Calenders mills on north side of Conedoquinett creek, sold as the property of William WEAVER.

30 a. in Rye twp., adj lands of James POWERS, late the property of John BEATTY, decd.

A tract of land in Rye twp. with -------, sold as property of Robert JOHNSON(?).

Undivided half of 150 a. ---- twp. Cumberland County, adj Benjamin JUNKINS, Jacob WAGGONER & Sherman's Creek, with log house; sold as the property of Joseph ROLE.

200 a. withimprovements, 1 mile below the Long Narrows in Fatmona(?) twp., now Mifflin Co., on the road leading to Lewis-town; sold as the property of James PURDY.

Lot in Borough of Carlisle, bounded on the south by High-street, on the west by a lot of William LYON, Esq., on the east by a lot of John HENRY, and on the north by a 20' alley; on which is erected a large house & kitchen with other outhouses. A tavern has been kept in this house for many years, formerly by John POLLOCK, and now by James DAVIS--Also, 202 a. in West Pennsborough twp., Cumberland County, adj lands of William MOORE, Edward WECKLEY and Michael EGE, and the South mountain. Sold as the property of James DAVIS.

200 a. in Lack twp., Mifflin County, with improvements thereon; property of Andrew FARRIER.

70 a. with loghouse. Has been kept as a tavern for many years, in Tyrone twp., about 8 miles from Carlisle, sold as property of James M'CABE.

Tract of 300 a. on little Juniata, adj Robert PORTER on the west & Charles QUNN on the East. Another tract of 200 a. on said creek, adj lands of Robert PORTER on east, and William STEWART on the West. Another tract of 250 a. adj John KERNS on the West & Nathan ANDREWS on the South, in the Limestone Valley, sold as property of David ENGLISH.

Whereas Sheriff BUCHANAN advertised that he will expose to sale the property of James DAVIS, house & lot in Borough of Carlisle; the public are desired to take notice that John POLLICK of Carlisle (Malstar) on 3 July 1767 was the owner and proprietor of the above-described house and lot, and on that day did convey the same to Jeremiah WARDER, William WEST and Richard PARKER (since deceased), of the city of Philadelphia, merchants. The claim of said James DAVIS is founded on conveyance from the same John POLLOCK given long since the above mentoned deed. John WEST, Agent for the heirs & representative of Jeremiah WARDER, William WEST & Richard PARKER.

All persons indebted to William WILSON are requested to pay to John JORDON, Esq.

175. Wednesday, 13 July 1791 (Con't.)

Whereas Thomas BUCHANAN, Sheriff of Cumberland Co, hath advertised for sale a plantation in Wayne twp., Mifflin County, as the property of James ARMSTRONG, I do hereby forewarn against purchasing said land, as said ARMSTRONG has not ever had a title in law to said land, but I hold the title & intend to hold the same unless legally dispossed. James CARMICHAEL.

John WOLSON & William HUNTER, inform that they have opened a tavern at the sign of the Sorrel Horse, No. 3, 6th Street, between Market & Chestnut Sts.

Stolen or strayed from James SMITH, living in Frankstown twp., Huntingdon County, a sorrel horse. Deliver to Alexander M'CONNELL in town of Huntingdon, James KARR, on Spruce Creek, Justice COULTER in Cumberland Valley, Bedford county, Col. John ALLISON, near Green-Castle, or the subscriber, James SMITH.

Ran away 3 July from John WEAVER, living on Pipe Creek, near Jacob MORTAR's tavern, an indentured servant man named Laurance FRIED, a High German by birth, 24 years of age, 5'5" high, light complexion, long hair cued with a black ribbon; he can speak no English.

Whereas parts of Cumberland & Northumberland Counties have been made into Mifflin county; Trustees were appointed to get a tract of land on the river Juniata for the purpose of laying out a town for the seat of Justice for said county. The Trustees give notice that they have received by bargain a quantity of land at the confluence of the river Juniata and the Kithacoquillas creek and confirmed thereon a town for the seat of Justice called Lewis-Town. The lots are now offered for sale. John OLIVER, William BROWN, Andrew GREGG & James ARMSTRONG, Trustees. Apply to Samuel EDMINSTON, Samuel MONTGOMERY or James POTTER.

Edward HAND, Inspector, gives notice to the distillers of spirits in counties of Cumberland & Dauphin that the Offices of Inspection for the Entry of Stills are opened at the following places: Cumberland Co.: Joseph POSTLETHWAIT's borough of Carlisle; Robert HAMMEL's, Shippensburgh; Samuel M'GACHEY's, Tyrone twp.; Archibald LAUGHLIN's, West Pennsborough twp: Hugh MILLER's, Rye twp.; and Jacob GEHR's, Lisburn. Dauphin cunty, at Henry VALENTINE's, Shaffer's Town, Heiddleberg twp--Philip GREENAWALT's, Lebanon--William CAMPBELL's, East Hanover Twp., --William CRAB's in the Borough of Harrisburgh--John LITTLE's, Upper Paxton twp., and at Henry MOORE's, Middletown.

In pursuance of the last Will & Testament of John AGNEW, decd. selling 4 lots of ground enclosed with a good fence and a double barn thereon, situated on Letart Spring. Bounded on the north by a 20' alley, on the west by Louther St, on the South by Pomfret St. and on the East by the said spring. Samuel POSTLETHWAIT & Samuel LAIRD, Execut.

Strayed from the plantation of the Widow REAGH, at the head of Yellow Breeches, dark gray mare & mare colt. Matthew ADAMS, living on above plantation.

Stolen, a surtout coat, almost new, of a light winestone color. Likewise stolen, a body coat, homemade cloth, dark silver colour. Reward offered by Archibald LOUDON, Carlisle.

Found, a small bundle tied up with 15 yards of curtain calico, shirts & smocks. Jonathan WALLACE found near his back door. Also wants journeymen shoemakers, a womans woman and a mans man, generous wages will be given.

176. Wednesday, 27 July 1791

Strayed from George WILT, living in Newtown twp., Cumberland County, at Mr. M'CRACKEN's mill at the head of Big Spring, 2 cows. George WILT.

Mifflin County Distiller information can be obtained at David WALKER's, Vermanagh twp.: John STEWARD's, Lack township; Capt. John CULBERTSON's, Wayne Twp.; James ALEXANDER's, Lewistown; James POTTER's store, Potter's twp.; Malcolm ANDREW's (coll. of the Revenue for the County) Armaugh twp.

Whereas my wife, Ann BYERS, has eloped from my bed & board, without any reason or just cause, and gone with a certain John METZ; I forewarn all from giving her any credit on my account. (Middletown twp, Cumberland County.) Jacob BYERS.

Strayed or stolen from the commons of Shippensburg, a black horse, deliver to George SPRECHER or Joseph CAMPBELL for reward. (Shippensburg)

Andrew GALBRAITH & James ANDERSON, Overseers of the Poor for the twp of East Pennsborough, ask residents to report stray cattle, horses, sheep or swine so that they might be sold for the benefit of the poor of said twp.

Strayed or stolen from the commons of Carlisle, a bay horse belonging to Samuel LAIRD of Carlisle.

Sheriff's Sale: 200 a. in Greenwood twp. Cumberland County, adj lands of Michael WILT, with improvements; sold as property of John PFOUTZ, Sr. Also, one other 150 a. tract with saw mill and log house; sold as property of same.

The undivided half of 200 a. in Farmanagh twp, adj lands of Rev. Hugh MAGILL; sold as property of William COCHRAN.

200 a. in Rye twp, on Shearman's creek, adj land of Robert HAGARTY; sold as property of Patrick MATTAIN. Thomas BUCHANAN, Sheriff.

Deserted from the company of Patrick PHELON, Capt. 2d. US Regt. on night of the 23d inst. at a place called Mount Rock, 7 miles to the westward of Carlisle: John Fitzgerald ELLIS, an Irishman, 5'7" high, red hair and light complexion.

John MOGER, an American, about 5'9" high, fair complexion & light hair.

Augustus WILLARD, American, about 5'9 1/2" high, thin face, dark eyes, short dark hair.

John BURTON, 5'8" high, brownish short hair & rather light complexion. It is supposed they have gone to Baltimore.

177. Wednesday, 3 August 1791

Whereas Jacob STITLE, of Sherman's Valley, Tyrone Twp. passed 2 bonds payable to Robert CAMPBELL in consideration for land, which said CAMPBELL was to clear of all incumbrances, which has not been done; he forewarns all persons against taking said bonds.

Carlisle, Aug. 3: Died on Friday night last after a short illness, Mr. John HARRIS of Harrisburgh.

Whereas Thomas BUCHANAN, Sheriff of Cumberland published for sale 200 a.of land in Greenwood twp, adj Michael WILT, as the property of John PFOUTS, Sr., I do therefore notify all who might become a purchaser, that I do hold the possession and title in right of --- HENNING, who formerly possessed the premises. Frederick LEINHART.

Came to the plantation of Patrick LEGIT, living in West Pennsborough Twp., Cumberland County, a dark bay mare.

178. Wednesday, 10 August 1791

Reward offered for 2 deserters from the encampment at Bedford, on the night of the 30th instant. William KERLTON, a Drummer, 5' 7 or 8" high, short curly hair; dark complexion, is very talkative. Daniel FAILING, 5'9" high, fair complexion. Hugh PURDY, Ensign; 2d Regiment of Levies.

Peter SMITH of Middletown offering reward for runaway Negro man named Harry. About 37 years of age, fond of strong drink. It is supposed he has a forged pass.

Whereas Joseph STITLE, Shearman's Valley, Tyrone twp., passed 2 bounds to Robert CAMPBELL for a tract of Land, wich the said CAMPBELL was to clear of all incumberances, which has not been done.

179. Wednesday, 17 August 1791

Carlisle, August 17: Departed this life, at Dover, in the State of Delaware, in 69th year of his age, Rev. John MILLER, Pastor of the Presbyterian Churches of Dover and Duck Creek in said state. He was born and educated in Boston, Mass. The same day, departed this life at York-Town, in this state, in the 65th year of his age, after a short illness, Rev. Mr. John ROTH, Pastor of the Moravian Congregation in that Borough. He was a native of Sarmund in Germany, came to this country in 1765.

Died at Providence, on the 19th ultimate, after a short illness, the Rev. Mr. James MANNING, S.T.D. President of Rhode Island College, in the 54th year of his age.

Died at Philadelphia on the 4th instant, Col. Michael RYAN, late Member of Lodge, No. 3, of that city; the first military character to teach the militia of that city in the use of arms to oppose the wanton designs and arbitrary encroachments of Great-Britian.

John M'CORMICK informs that he makes sacking bottoms for beds, and arnons for doors, upon the lowest terms. He lives in the house formerly occupied by Mr. RAINEY, 2 doors from Mr. Ephraim STEEL's.

Daniel WALDENBERGER, School master, informs that he has opened an English and German School in the house of Mr. Philip PENDERGRASS in Pomfret St.

John EVERLY informs & forewarns against taking bonds which he passed to a certain George WOODS, late of East-Pennsborough twp, in consideration for a tract of land.

Gilbert SEAWRIGHT, Middletown twp, Cumberland Co, offers reward for stray mare, which broke out of his pasture.

Robert GILLESPIE found tresspassing in his inclosure in Newton twp,Cumberland County, a horse colt.

180. Wednesday, 24 August 1791

Thomas WHITE of Shearman's Valley, has taken up a stray cow.

Carlisle: Departed this life on Thursday the 11th instant, aged 39 years, after a long & lingering illness, which she supported witha great degree of fortitude & resignation, Mrs. Mary PEEBLES, wife of Col. Robert PEEBLES, at his seat near Shippensburgh.

Died suddenly, on Monday morning last, Mrs. BROWN, wife of Mr. John BROWN of Carlisle. Mrs. BROWN was hearty & well on the Saturday evening preceeding. On Sunday morning she was taken ill & remained so until next morning, when she expired. On the evening of the same day, her remains were deposited in the burying ground adjoining this Borough.

Isaac ATLEE, living in Salisbury twp, Lancaster Co., seeks runaway servant boy named Hugh WILSON, about 17 years of age, has lite brown hair, is firm made, sloop shouldered, 5'6" high.

181. Wednesday, 31 August 1791

On Thursday evening last the house of John STEEL, Esq. now occupied by Mr. Joseph GIVEN in this Borough (Carlisle) was struck by lightning and sustained considerable injury; the top of the chimney being thrown down, the rafters next the chimneysplit, etc.

Came to the house of John STEEL a few days ago, a certain John MULHOLLAN, an indentured servant to John FOREHELLER of Franklin Co., PA, who is requested to come and take him away.

Whereas John CULBERTSON executed an obligation to a certain James GOLD, which obligation GOLD returned to him to dissolve the contract, CULBERTSON forewarns persons not to take any assignment, as he is determined to contest the payment.

Deserted last night from the detatchment under the command of John BUELL, Captain: John RUSSELL (of Capt. HUGHES' company) an Irishman, about 24 years of age, 5'8" high, light complexion, light short hair, grey eyes, freckled face, has a down look when spoken to; supposed to have gone to Baltimore.

Thomas CUSHMAN (of Capt. NEWMAN's Company), an American, 35 years of age, 5'9" high, stout built, short dark hair and eyes, has a remarkable small foot and is a little lame occupied by a sprain.

Hugh DUNCAN (enlisted by Lt. HOWE of New York) a Scotchman, about 26 or 28 years of age, 5'8" high, dark hair and eyes, very fond of liquor.

Henry O'NEIL (enlisted by Lt. HOWE) an Irishman, a stout likely young fellow, about 23 years of age, 5'9" high, long hair which he generally wears cued.

John WILSON (enlisted at Philadelphia) an Irishman, about 40 years of age, 5'10" high, thin visage, and large blue eyes.

James GALLAGHER (of Capt. BUELL's company) an Irishman, about 26 years of age, 5'6" high, light eyes, dark hair, ruddy complexion.

182. Wednesday, 7 September 1791

Samuel A. M'COSKRY has received a quantity of drugs & medicines of the first quality. Carlisle.

The following Gentlemen have been appointed by the Governor, Justices of the peace for the County of Cumberland: Maj. William ALEXADER & George LOGUE, Borough of Carlisle; Runnel BLAIN & James M'FARLANE for West-Pennsborough twp; Alexander LAUGHLIN & Maj. Samuel FINDLEY for Newton twp; James M'CUNE for Hopewell twp., John HEAP for Shippensburgh; Samuel IRWIN for Middletown twp.; Christopher QUIGLY for Allentown twp; John CAROTHERS & Maj. Andrew GALBREATH for East-Pennsborough; Thomas HULING & --- HEARTER for Greenwood twp; James POWER for Rye twp; David M'CLURE for Toboin twp; William BLAINE for Tyrone twp.

Thomas WHITE, Shearman's Valley, has taken up a stray black cow.

183. Wednesday, 14 September 1791

William M'CLINTOCK of Toboyne twp, Cumberland co, has taken up a stray dun sorrel horse.

To be sold at private sale, a large log house & lot in Pomfret St., near the College, Borough of Carlisle. Apply to John TRAU.

A Negro fellow was taken up in Shippensburg Sunday evening and committed to the gaol of Carlisle, who calls himself Benjamin THOMAS, and says that he belongs to a gentleman of the name of "Josiah CRAWFORD" of the Quaker Society, living about 2 miles from Redstone Fort, in Monongalia county, state of VA. He is 5' 8 or 9" high, of a yellowish color, says his father was a mulatto and the property of David ROGERS, who now resides in

KY; has a scar on thin of his left leg, lively and well made. He says he left his master towards the close of the last harvest, and has since worked at Turnbull's Iron Works.

184. Wednesday, 21 September 1791
On Wednesday, the 14th instant, departed this life at his own house, after a few weeks painful illness, James SMITH; and on Friday following his remains were conducted to the burying ground at Carlisle.
Sheriff's Sales: 200 a. in Greenwood twp, Mifflin co, adj lands of Robert ARMSTRONG, George HAYS, and lying on stony run, a small cabbin thereon, sold as the property of Thomas REARDON.
500 a. 1 mile from Lewistown, property of James BURNS.
200 a. with a grist mill and a saw mill thereon, a good house. This land is in Rye twp, about 2 miles from General WATTS; sold as the property of John & William M'COY.
200 a. in Greenwood twp, on the Juniata river & adj lands of Jacob AULL; sold as the property of John & William ENGLISH.
Lot of ground in Borough of Carlisle, bounded on the south by High St., on the west by a lot of William LYON, Esq., on the east by a lot of John HENRY, and on the north by a 20' alley, on which is erected a stone house and kitchen. A tavern has been kept in this house for many years, formerly by John POLLOCK and now by James DAVIS.
202 a. in West-Pennsborough twp., Cumberland Co, adj lands of William MOORE, Edward WESKLEY, and Michael EGE, and the South Mountains; sold as the property of James DAVIS.
200 a. on the Juniata River, Rye twp., adj lands of Andrew BEATTY, sold as property of William BEATTY, deliquent Collector of Taxes.
A house & lot in Shippensburgh, Lot No.82; sold as the property of James BROWN.
A house & lot, Borough of Carlisle, No. 155, good log house, stable and garden; now occupied as a tavern, has the sign of the bull; sold as property of Francis SHUERKEUTERGER & Godfried LUTZ.
140 a.in Newton tpw., adj.lands of John BARTON & the North Mountain. Sold as the property of Alexander RACHFORD.
300 a. in Tyrone twp; sold as the property of Alexander RODDY.
To be sold by public venue, at the dwelling house of David & James M'CURDY, in Newtown twp, near the head of Three Springs; livestock, tools, farm implements, as well as 330 a. adj. James PATTERSON, Joseph BROWN.
Selling large log house & lot in Pomfret Street, near the College, Borough of Carlisle. Apply to John TRAU.

185. Wednesday, 28 September 1791
Committed to the gaol of Carlisle Thursday the 22nd of September, a Negro fellow who calls himself Harry, alias Henry; about 5'8" high, stout and well make, not very black, an excellent set of teeth, is very bold and foreward in giving answers to questions, but very contradictory; he says that he belongs to Thomas SONGSTER, living about half a mile from Winchester, VA, that he left his master about 3 years ago and about the middle of last harvest was apprehended & committed to Yorktown gaol, from which he says he was sold Mr. LAUB of Yorktown and remained with him 2 or 3 weeks. He says he left Yorktown with a certain Jack CAIRNS, who took him towards Fredericktown, with a view of selling him, from whom he run when he was offered for sale, which was near Frederick. He further says he belongs to a certain Thomason ELFEY, living in Fairfax Co., VA, about

19 miles from Alexandria; whom he left about 9 weeks ago. It is uncertain which of the above stories are true.

From William STERRETT to the Public: I see to my surprise my name often mentioned in a publication in your paper of the 21 August which states an account of the late disturbances at Lewistown, Mifflin County, in such a manner as to leave the public to believe that I was equally concerned with the people who wished to oppose Judge BRYSON. He denies the charges. He was alarmed at the manner of the proceeding against Judge BRYSON (altho he knew people were much enraged at him). Mr. BRYSON thinks that he is his enemy because he has publically given his opinion of him, and it coincides with the 9/10 of the people of his acquaintance in Mufflin County; that he was very unfit for office in a republican government. (See Extra below.)

Mr. Joseph GIVEN now opening a store in York street, opposite Dr. George STEVENSON's.

186. (Insert) Wednesday, 21 September 1791 - SUPPLEMENT EXTRAORDINARY TO THE CARLISLE GAZETTE

The Governor has lately appointed Samuel BRYSON Second Associate Judge of the Court of Common Pleas in Mifflin County. Mr. BRYSON, having been Lieutenant of the co of Mifflin had excited the determined enmity of 2 men who were ambitious of being Colonels of the Militia; and against the commissioning of whom (as unfit persons) Mr. Bryson as co. Lt. had made respresentations. Enraged at the promotion of Judge BRYSON one William WILSON, brother to the Sheriff of Mifflin county, one David WALKER, levied 'a considerable force' and marched at the head of 40 armed men with a fife playing to Lewistown, and determined to seize upon the person of Judge Bryson, drag him from the bench and oblige him to resign his commission and march with them many miles along the rugged Narrows of Juniata River. Mr. CLARK and Mr. HAMILTON, 2 attornies of the court at the request of some of the Judges who knew the mob was coming, remonistrated with Mr. WILSON, who was on horseback within a few paces of the court house at the head of the troops. Mr. WILSON was dressed in a military state, with a cockade in his hat; and was armed with a horsemans sword and pistol. He observed that nothing would divert him from his purpose, and he immediately drew his sword and marched to storm the courtroom, where Judge ARMSTRONG and others were stationed at the door; the rioters followed with a cry of Liberty or Death. Mr. ARMSTORNG hollowed[sic.] out repeatedly "Villains come on, but you shall first march over my dead body before you enter." Wilson was invited to disarm and enter the courtroom, to which he acceded. A meeting was agreed to with assent of some members of the court and William STERETT, who appeared on behalf of the rioters. It was hoped to prevent the person of Mr. Bryson from injury and to that end it an offer was made that Mr. BRYSON would not sit duting that week on the bench. When this did not work, WILSON & WALKER insisted that Mr. BRYSON accompany them down the narrows. In the meantime, Judge BRYSON had sent for a horse & affected his escape. At this point Mr. William STERRETT exclaimed with an oath, we are out generalized. Maybe just say Mr. S Spoke for the rioters.

187. Wednesday, 28 September 1791 (Con't.)

Whereas a notice in last week's paper exposes for sale a tract described as the property of John & William ENGLISH, and whereas Samuel WORLEY is legally in possession of the land by legal title before any judgement had been entered against them, Samuel WORLEY forewarns purchasers not to buy but at their own risque.

188. Wednesday, 5 October 1791

Stolen out of the stables of William ELLIOT in the Path Valley, Franklin County, a sorrel horse.

To be sold at public vendue at the dwelling house of Mrs. PARKER in West-Pennsborough twp, 3 copper stills by Rebecca PARKER, John M'DONALD & Cam POSTLETHWAIT, Administrators.

189. Wednesday, 12 October 1791

On Saturday the 1st instant departed this life after a few days illness, Robert Davidson COOPER, a very promising child, aged about 4 years, the son of Charles COOPER of Carlisle. The same parents lost a child of the same name with this, a few years ago; and another, a few weeks since, named Samuel M'Coskry COOPER; both very young.

On Thursday, the 29th ult. departed this life, Henry MILROY, of Mifflin county. This man had left his own house, on Wednesday morning, in health, and came to the house of Mr. William BROWN. Being taken suddenly ill with a cholic about 1 o'clock, he was called into eternity the next evening about 6! He left a distressed widow and 6 small children, with the prospect of a 7th.

Whereas Thomas BUCHANAN, Sheriff of Cumberland County hath advertised that he will expose at sale the property of James DAVIS, a house & lot in the Borough of Carlisle, bounded on the south by High St., on the west by a lot of William LYON, on the east by a lot of John HENRY's, & on the north by a 20' alley; the Public are desired to take notice that John POLLOCK of Carlisle on 3 July 1767 was the owner and proprietor of the above described house & lot, and that on that day, by his deed, did convey the same to Jeremiah WARDER, William WEST, and Richard PARKER of the City of Philadelphia. John WEST, Agent for the heirs of WARDER, WEST & PARKER.

John BROWNLEE desires to inform the public that he has commenced the business of reed-making at the house of George BROWNLEE, Tanner, North in Carlisle, next door but one to the widow M'DONALD. As he is both Weaver and Reed-maker, he flatters himself that he can make to the best advantage for the purcheser.

A small box of Blacksmith's tools were left some years ago at the ferry on Susquehannah. The owner is requested to call for same. William KELSO.

All persons indebted to he estate of John REYNOLDS, decd. are once more requested to make speedy payment. Hannah REYNOLDS, Robert PEEBLES, Matthew HENDERSON, Admin. Shippensburg.

Strayed or stollen from Robert CLARK living in Hopewell twp., Cumberland Co., a brown mare.

190. Wednesday, 19 October 1791

Reward offered for recovery of sorrel horse, strayed from the plantation of Martin BRAND in Allen twp., Cumberland Co.

Hugh SMITH, living in Middleton twp, Cumberland Co., has taken up a stray sorrel horse.

Acts passed by the PA Legislature: An act to grant restitution in value to Thomas GORDON, for lands sold by the commissioner for the sale of forfeited estates, late the property of T. GORDON. An act for the relief of Mary HARRISON. An act to exonerate Robert SMITH and William RICHARDS from the payment of certain monies found due to the commonwealth by a judgement of court and from Alexander BOYD. An act for the relief of the estate of Sarah CALDWELL, and also for the relief of Mary BEERE, James STEEN & John THOMPSON.

Married: On Thursday last, William TURNBULL of Pittsburgh, to the amiable Miss Maria NISBET, d/o Rev. Dr. Charles NISBET, Principal of Dickinson College, Carlisle.

Died: on Friday night last, Mrs. HERR, wife of Mr. David HERR, of this borough.

Died: on the 15th inst. Mrs. Mary STEVENSON, in the 65th year of her age.

James MONTGOMERY of Carlisle has a large assortment of goods for sale on low terms; for cash or merchantable wheat.

Was left in the inclosure of Martin DILLER, living in Allen twp, Cumberland Co, a sorral roan mare.

191. Wednesday, 26 October 1791

Died on Tuesday the 18th inst. at his farm, about 4 miles from Carlisle, Andrew MACBETH, in an apoplectic fit, which, being the third he has had, came on & caried him off in a very sudden manner.

The Board of Commissioners of Cumberland Co. to meet to settle duplicates regarding Collectors of Taxes. Jacob CRAVER, Edward WEST, Sam POSTLETHWAIT, Commissioners.

To be sold at the house of Jacob CREAVER, Borough of Carlisle, large log house & lot in Pomfret St., near the College. Apply John TRAU.

Came to the plantation of Benjamin BROWN in Rye twp., a sorrel bay mare, blind of one eye, signed John LAWSHE.

192. Wednesday, 2 November 1791

Died on Wednesday last after a short illness, Mr. Joseph GIVEN, Merchant of this town.

To be sold by public vendue at the late dwelling house of Andrew M'BETH, decd, livestock, household and kitchen furniture. Ann M'BETH & William BLAIAR, Jr. Admin.

All persons indebted to the estate of Joseph GIVEN, decd., are desired to make payment. James GIVEN & John MORRISON, Admin.

John WALKER of Shirley twp, Huntingdon co, purchased a tract of land of John JOHNSON, late of the aforesaid place; one to Rebecca JOHNSTON due in May 1791 & one to Edward JOHNSTON. He warns all persons of taking such as he is determined not to honor same.

193. Wednesday, 16 November 1791

Married: on the 8th inst. Jacob WALTERS of Chambersburgh, Merchant, formerly of this town, to Miss Patty STUART, of this town.

On the 9th, Mr. William WALLACE, of this town, married to Miss Jean GRAY, of Northumberland Co.

Died: On Thursday last, after a tedious & painful sickness, which she endured with a becoming Christian fortitude, Mrs. Margaret STEEL, aged 24 years, wife of Mr. Joseph STEEL, Clockmaker, of this town. She was buried on Friday.

James GIVEN, brother & successor to Joseph GIVEN, decd., has now opened a store at the house of John STEEL, Esq., opposite Dr. George STEVENSON. He expects by the lowness of his prices to merit a continuance of the favor of his late brother's customers.

Wanted immediately, a man that can attend a grist & saw mill, either for wages or thirds. Enquire at Col. George GIBSON's, Sherman's Valley.

Ran away from Samuel LYON in Middleton Twp., Cumberland Co., a negroe man named Peter, about 5'9" tall, light made, bow shinned, about 21 years of age, large flat feet, speaks pretty good English. It is supposed he has a counterfeit pass and that he will head for Baltimore or Philadelphia.

James M'CRACKEN, near the mouth of Aughwick, had stolen from him a blackish gray horse.

Strayed or stolen on the 7th inst., from the plantation of Hugh M'GEE in Middletown Twp., a dark bay mare. Whoever takes her up & brings her to the subscriber or Mr. Ephraim STEEL in Carlisle, Dr. JAMUSON in Shippensburg; Hugh BIGHAM in Chambersburgh or to George CLARK in Greencastle, shall receive $2 reward.

194. Wednesday, 23 November 1791

Sheriff's Sale: Plantation & tract in West Pennsborough twp, on Yellow Breeches Creek, adj lands of James WEAKLEY & Samuel WOODS, 257 a. House, barn & outhouses late the property of Samuel BRICE, decd.

Broke into the inclosure of the subscriber, in Middletown Twp. Cumberland Co., a black mare. William CLARK.

195. Wednesday, 30 November 1791

Whereas Christopher MYERS, Augusta Co., VA, gave 3 bonds to a certain Joseph HALLER of Cordorus Twp. to purchase land in Augusta Co. VA. And said HALLER signed them over to Henry KELLER. Christopher MYERS is determined not to honor same.

Came to the plantation of John CLOUSER in Middletown Twp., a bright bay mare.

By a gentleman lately from the vicinity of Sharpsburgh, Md., we are informed that Rosanna RONDORFF still continues to behave in a manner that excites the surprise of all who behold her. Ever since some time in February, she has become affected by fits once a day.

John HUGHES informs the public that he is just returned from Philadelphia & is now opening his new store in the main street, second door west of the courthouse in Carlisle.

Came to the plantation of John HAYES, some time ago, a black male colt.

196., Wednesday, 7 December 1791

Came to the plantation of William DUNCAN in Hopewell Twp., Cumberland Co. 3 sheep.

Strayed or stolen from James LAMBERTON, a bright bay mare.

Isaiah THOMAS of Worcester, Mass. informs that he has this day completed the Old & New Testament of his Royal Quarto Edition of the Holy Bible.

Married: at the seat of David HOGE, Esq. Mr. James BLAINE to Miss Jean HOGE, d/o David.

Louisiana: The garden of America, which is celebrated by all writers as a Terrestrial Paradise. 300 to 1000 acres of land will be secured to every family gratis. A. FOWLER will descend the Ohio the ensuing March. Those who wish to accompany his to share the Golden Advantages now offered may apply to Wingfield Mills on Chartiers Creek, Allegheny Co, 9 miles from Pittsburgh.

197. Wednesday, 14 December 1791

John HUGHES has opened his store on the main street on the second door west of the Court House on the left hand in Carlisle. The kitchen and garden, also one vacant lot.

Married at Shippensburgh on Friday last, Mr. Joseph DUNCAN to Miss Ruth RIPPEY, d/o Capt.Wm. RIPPEY.

197. Wednesday, 14 December 1791 (Con't.)
Sheriff's Sales: 300 a. with improvements in Tyrone twp, property of Alexander RODDY.
234 a. in Allen twp. adj. lands of James GREGORY, John WILLIAMS, property of Alexander HAMILTON.
Unvidived 2/5 and 1/3 of 1/5 of a Furnace and the lands adjacent in Fannet twp, Franklin Co., taken at the suit of John SMITH of Baltimore, as the property of William & Benjamin CHAMBERS, decd.
A 2-story house & lot on corner of York & Louther Sts, borough of Carlisle; has been occupied for some time as a tavern at present in tenure of Robert GRAYSON, to be sold as property of Thomas KENNEDY, decd.
200 a. (formerly Hopewell) adj. land of Col. James DUNLAP, David MAHON & the south mountain; sold as property of Conrad BEAMER.
300 a. in Milford Twp, now Mifflin Co, adj. lands of Andrew FARRIER, Ezekiel DUNNING & William BAILEY; sold as property of Alexander RAMSEY.
100 a. in Milford Twp, now Mifflin Co., a branch of the Tulkarora (?) runs through premises; sold as the property of John BOGGS & John HARRIS
Whereas Joseph OGDON & Samuel HUTCHINSON gave a note to a certain John O'BRYAN, they forewarn all from taking said notes.

198. Wednesday, 21 December 1791
Sheriff's Sales: 100 a. within 1 mile of Shippensburgh, adj lands of widow M'CALL, sold as property of John COAPLEY.
200 a. in East Pennsborough twp, 5 miles from Harrisburgh, adj land of James BELL. Sold as property of John STEVENSON.
100 a. in Milford twp, now Mifflin Co, a branch of Tuskareta Creek runs through premises; sold as property of John BOGGS.

199. Wednesday, 28 December 1791
Josias BROWN offers reward for stolen gold watch.
Alexander BEERS, took in Bay mare at his plantation, adj. Carlisle.
Ranaway from James BYERS, living in Lower Paxton twp., Dauphin Co., 2 indentured Irish Servant men, viz. Bryan DOUGHERTY, 23 years of age, 5'8" high, blackish short hair. Andrew CRAWFORD, the other, about 18 years of age, 5'6" high, dark brown hair.
Whereas John AGNEW being possessed of 2 notes of hand passed by John REED of West-Pennsborough Twp., the notes will not be honored untii AGNEW fulfills his contract.
John CARSON has taken in a stray brown steer in Newtown Twp., Cumberland Co.
Sheriff's Sale: Lot with improvements on Pomfret St., adj Jacob SINGER, being lot No. 205, formerly occupied by Mr. POLLY.

200. Wednesday, 4 January 1792
James WALLACE announces as a candidate for sheriff.
Peter CREAMER living in Hopewell twp., has taken up a black horse.

201. Wednesday, 11 January 1792
Ran away from Mary LONG living in Dromore twp., Lancaster Co. Irish servant girl Nancy DEVIN, of low size, fell faced and black hair.
Robert GALLISPIE & William MONTGOMERY, Auditors, give notice to those indebted to the estate of William FENTON, late of Newtown twp., to call Tuesday at the house of Robert LUSK in Newville on the Big Spring to settle.

201. Wednesday, 11 January 1792 (Con't.)
Jacob CRAVER, Edward WEST & Samuel POSTLETHWAIT, Commissioners, to meet to settle tax disputes.

202. Wednesday, 25 January, 1792
Robert SMITH, at the sign of the Seven Stars in Carlisle, selling writing paper of all sorts, also Wrapping & Pasteboards.
Edward O. WILLIAMS (Shepherd's Town) offers reward for return of Negro man Gabriel, 31 years of age, 5' 8" or 10" high, flat nose & down look; has scar on one arm occasioned by the cut of an axe.
John BUCHANAN requests all indebted to him to come forward and make payment to Thomas CREIGH, Esq. without delay.

203. Wednesday, 1 February 1792
Thomas SMITH & Thomas DUNCAN, having recovered some time since a sum of money for the heirs of Peter REIGHTER, decd, and having frequently written to John REIGHTER, one of the sons of said Peter, addressed by his direction to the care of Mr. John HOLMES, jun. Merchant, in Baltimore; & having reason to believe that said John has removed from Baltimore, give notice that they will pay to the said children or guardians, the money recovered by them.
Ephraim STEEL gives notice to the subscribers for the "Universal Asylum" & "Columbian Magazine" that they now will be regularly delivered at his store in Carlisle.
Alexandria, Loudoun Co., Short Hills (VA) Last Sunday was delivered of her first born, Mrs. Elizabeth CARNYHAM (wife of Adam CARNYHAM) without ever conceiving a thought of such a thing. The woman is about 40 years of age and has been 20 years married. The child weighs near a pound & is still living.
The excellent beer manufactured in Carlisle by Jacob & John CRAVER promises to be of advantage to the public. We should contribute to the establishment of Breweries in that part of this state.
Came to the plantation of Archibald M'COLLOUGH, living within 2 miles of Mount-Rock Tavern in Westpennsborough Twp., Cumberland Co. a bay mare & he has taken her up as a stray.

204. Wednesday, 8 February 1792
(Elizabethtown, NJ) William Augustus BOWLES, who, some time ago appeared in London in the character of an Indian Chief, was not an Indian by birth, but an Anglo-American from Maryland; who being of an unsettled, roving and enterprising disposition, attached himself to one of the Indian nations, became enamoured of a savage life and, of a savage girl, whome he married; then settled among her friends, is now by adoption an Indian warrior.
Married on Tuesday 24th of January last, at Trindle's Spring, William GILSON of East Pennsborough twp., to Mrs. Sarah TRINDLE, Widow of Capt. Alexander TRINDLE. (Carlisle)
Married Tuesday 31st at Carlisle William TRINDLE to Miss Betsy GILSON, son and daughter of the above.
On Friday last an accident happened in East Pennsborough twp., on George FRIDLEY's Plantation: 2 young men (a son of Mr. FRIDLEY & a son of Leonard FISHER in said twp), in digging a well, the well gave way and closed them in. All hopes of getting them out alive have been given over.

204. Wednesday, 8 February 1792 (Con't.)
Samuel JACKSON, opening at his house in Carlisle, a Register Office for persons out of employment and prospective apprentices.
Anthony SHOEMAKER, living in Lorgan Twp., Franklin Co, has taken in a red heifer.
David MILLER, living in Fermanaugh Twp., Cumberland Co, has taken in a sorrel mare, which has been lately sold by John O'BRIAN to Joseph OGDEN, for which said OGDEN disputes payment.
William M'CONNELL of Shippensburg, selling plantation in Lurgin Twp, Franklin Co, on Conodoguinet creek, adj. lands of William HUNTER, John SNIDER, of 217 a., barn, dwelling house & out houses.

205. Wednesday, 15 February 1792
Stephen DUNCAN, renting stone house & kitchen on the southeast corner of York & Pomfret Streets, now in tenure of James POLLOCK, belonging to DUNCAN. Also brick house & kitchen now in possession of Hugh PATTON in High Street, above the court house adj Mr. DAVIDSON. There is likewise a HARTER's Frame Shop on this lot.
Whereas several judgments of very old standing appear on the dockets of this county against Robert NELSON of Farmanaugh twp., for which no satisfaction is entered; therefore notice is given that the money arising from sale of the said NELSON's Land is now in my hands & will be paid to persons in whole favour. Thomas BUCHANAN, Sheriff of Cumberland Co.

206. Wednesday, 22 February 1792
John HOLMES, living in Carlisle, has lost a sorrel mare.

207. Wednesday 29 February 1792
Henry WEALS, Admin. gives notice to those indebted to the estate of Andrew KINCAID, late of Cumberland Co. decd., to attend the house of William WALLACE, borough of Carlisle.
Came, some time ago, to the place of Patrick BORLAN, a red steer.

208. Wednesday, 7 March 1792
To Joseph HARBIN, Sir, you will please to take notice that I intend to file a Bill in High Court of Chancery, state of MD to compel you to convey the following tracts of land "Harbin's Lot" 100 a. of land, Evans's Chance, 50 a., Piney Grove, 72 a., James' Tract, 20 acres, in Montgomery Co., MD, agreeable to your bond of conveyance 25 Nov. 1791. I am with due respect, thy friend, Joseph EVANS, Ann-Arundal Co.,MD.
To be sold, agreeable to will of Samuel RIPPEY, Senr. (decd) on the premises 200 a. adj the west end of Shippensburg in Franklin Co. A Negroe man about 18 years of age. William & Samuel RIPPEY, executors.
All indebted to the estate of Robert HOW decd., are requested to make payment at the house of William KENNEY, in Lewis-town, Mifflin Co. Hannah KENNEY & John SNELL, Admin.
Gerald IRVIN has a quantity of lots in the town of Lisburn to dispose of. The lots to be laid out fronting one street, through which the main road from York, Rankin's ferry & sundry other places to Carlisle. For further particulars, enquire of James DAVIS in Carlisle or IRVIN on the premises.
Bully-Rock will cover this season at the stable of Robert SMITH in Carlisle, sign of the Seven Stars.
Deserted from the detachment under command of Thomas HUGHES, Capt. 2d US Regt, John TAYLOR, Serjeant, 31 years of age, 5'11 1/4" high, born in Rye, Westchester, NY, a blacksmith by trade, of a light complexion, has

brown eyes & dark hair. James EASTON, 22 years of age, 5'8 3/4" high, born in Suffex Co., NJ, a nailor by trade, of a light complexion, grey eyes & dark hair. William BRENEMAN, 21 years of age, 5'9" high, born in York Co., PA, cooper by trade, of a dark complexion, grey eyes & dark hair. Deliver said deserters to Richard PARKER at Carlisle.

209. Wednesday, 14 March 1792

Being about to dissolve the partnership BUCHANAN & M'CAUSLAND request all those indebted to them attend at their Store.

The elegant horse Figure will cover this season at Bartholomew WHITE's blacksmith shop at Mount-Rock & at Robert SHARP's on Conodoguinet Creek.

210. Wednesday, 21 March 1792

Sheriff's Sales: 200 a. with a grist mill & saw mill house, etc. Land is in Rye twp., 2 miles from General WATTS; sold as property of John & Alex M'COY.

50 a. in Wayne twp., Mifflin Co., adj. lands of William ROBINSON with a small cabin thereon, as property of Alexander & John MAHON.

100 a. in Milford twp., now Mifflin Co., dwelling house, small double barn, sold as property of Marion CROZZER.

A tract of land, in Rye twp., with sawmill thereon; sold as property of Robert JOHNSTON.

Samuel LYON & John ARMSTRONG, exec. of estate of William BLANE, Esqr., late of Toboyne Twp., Cumberland, selling livestock, farm utensils & household furniture, a Young Negro Man, road waggon, quantity of Wheat, Rye, Corn & Buckwheat, etc. Also for sale tract of land late property of the deceased on the south side of Shearman's Creek, adj lands of David HARKNESS, together with a small tract on the North side of said creek, adj the place where the decd. formerly lived, whereupon is erected a grist mill.

To be sold or rented: farm in Middleton Twp., Cumberland Co., near main road to Crohan's Gap, 4 miles from Carlisle: 300 a. of land, grist mill, still-house. Also 142 a. on Conodoguiner Creek, 1 mile from Carlisle, house, barn, orchard. Apply to Robert SANDERSON.

Married at Carlisle on the 20th instant, by the Rev. Mr. MEYER, Samuel SHAVER to Miss Elizabeth RITCHWINE.

Whereas Margaret M'CLEARY, my wife, absented herself from my bed & board in Feb. last, this forewarns all from giving her credit. Thomas M'CLEARY, Lack Two, Mifflin Co.

All persons indebeted to the estate of Major Alexander PARKER, late of West-Pennsborough twp., decd., are desired to make immediate payment. Rebecca PARKER, John M'DONNEL & Sam. POSTLETHWAIT, Admin.

To be sold at public venue, 1 2-story log house, likewise one other house. Both being in the main street. James KELSO, Shippensburg.

Andrew GWINN, Reed-Maker, begs to inform that he has dissolved the connexion he formerly had with Charles BOVARD in the business, & has now commenced business for himself at the house of William PETRIKIN, Taylor in this Borough, next door below Ephraim STEEL, Esq., on the 4th side of the public square, opposite the Presbyertian Church.

Broke gaol, 2 fellows, one named John HOFFMAN & the other Daniel NICKS. Hoffman is a Dutchman, a sadler by trade, about 45 to 50 years old, about 5'8" high. Nicks is about 20 years old, 5'10 or 11" high, brown hair. $2 reward, Thomas ALEXANDER, Gaoler, Carlisle.

210. Wednesday, 21 March 1792 (Con't.)
Is offered to any person who will engage to build a bridge over the Canodoquinet Creek, at the Mouth of the Letart Spring, apply to Ephraim BLANE, Wm. CHAMBERS, Alexander M'BEATH or Robert KENNY, Carlisle.
To be sold agreeable to the will of James KILGORE, late of Newtown Twp., Cumberland Co., decd., all real estate of said James KILGORE and household furniture. Tract of 150 a. and likewise the estate, real & personal, of Elizabeth KILGORE, decd. including 230 a. of land adj the above. Alex. LAUGHLIN, Esq. & William KILGORE, Exec.

211. Wednesday, 28 March 1792
Departed this life Wednesday, the 21st instant, after 3 days illness, William BLAIR Junr., of Carlisle, in the 32nd year of his age; and on the day following his remains were committed to the dust. He was a most indulgent husband & kind father; has left a wife and 4 small children.
Also departed this life on Saturday, 24th instant, in a sudden manner, without any previous complaint, John RODGERS, in the 50th year of his age. But a few minutes before his death, he was apparently in perfect health, and conversed cheerfully with his friends. It is thought he was seized with an apoplectic fit. Several other persons were also carried off, after a few days illness, in the last week in the vicinity of this place.
Sheriff's Sale: to be sold at Lewistown, 100 a. on Loss (?) creek, adj lands of John M'CLELLAND. Also 50 a. adj lands of William CORRAN. Also 30 a. adj lands of the Rev. Hugh MAGILL & John CAMPBELL. Also 100 a. adj lands of John CAMPBELL, John HENDERSON, William CUNNINGHAM, all above lands are in Fermanaugh twp., Mifflin Co., taken in execution as property of Robert NELSON.
Lasts & women's shoe-heels made & sold by James SCRANTON at the sign of the Spread Eagle in Glouster St., Carlisle.
Ran away from William KAUB about 3 miles from Borough of Carlisle, an apprentice lad named Peter KAUB, about 19 years of age.

212. Wednesday, 4 April 1792
Stolen out of the stable of Robert GIBSON, living near Carlisle, a dark bay horse.
Ran away from James ALEXANDER living in Fannet Twp, Franklin Co., a servant man, James COCHRAN, a well set fellow, 18 years old, 5' 7 or 8" high, short, fair hair.
Strayed or Stolen: from the stable of Robert FINDLEY a dark sorrel horse. $5 reward for horse; $9 for horse and thief. Isaiah ROBERTS, Tiuckling Spring meeting-house near Staunton.
Wednesday, 4 April 1792 (Con't.)
Ran away from Tomazin ELLZEY the 28th day of this inst., on the Yellow Breeches Road, about 3 miles from Shippensburgh, who lives when at home in Fairfax Co, 18 miles from Alexandria, VA & 75 miles from Williamsport, the Negro Buck NELSON, about 20 years of age, 5' 8 or 10" high, complexion rather yellow than black, very active & lively, drives horses or oxen well in a carriage, a good plowman, and an excellent hand with a sythe.

213. Wednesday, 11 April 1792
Arrived on Sunday last at his farm near Carlisle, Major Thomas BUTLER, of the 2d Regt. of Levies, who was badly wounded in the engagement of 4 Nov. last; and is in a fair way of recovery.

213. Wednesday, 11 April 1792 (Con't.)

Married on Tuesday, 3d of April by the Rev. Richard SHELDON of Cumberland Co., Iron Master, to Miss Susannah FOULK, d/o Stephen FOULK, Senr. at his seat near Carlisle.

An election will be held on Monday the 16th inst., for a major in the room of John JORDAN, Esq. who has resigned.

Joseph T. JAMES informs that he has removed from the dwelling house of George KLINE to the house of William WALLACE, where he continues to keep a general assortment of merchandise.

Just received from Philadelphia, a general assortment of drugs & medicines, dry goods & groceries. Also 240 acres of limestone land in the settlement of Big Spring, within 2 miles of Newville town & only 9 miles from Carlisle. Apply to Robert M'CALL, living in Shippingsburg opposite the Potters.

214. Wednesday, 18 April 1792

Acts of the Legislature of PA: A supplement to Act to enable Eleazer OSWALD, Guardian to Jane JONES, Blaithwait JONES, Mary JONES & Gibbs JONES, minors, to sell property for benefit of said minors.

An Act to vest in the widow of John ROBERTS, decd, & in Abraham CARLISLE, only son of Abraham CARLISLE, decd, such parts of estates as have not been sold for the benefit of the Commonwealth.

An Act to vest in Christopher ZIMMERMAN & David SOWER in trust for the use of all the legal representatives of Christopher SOWER, decd, such parts of his forfeited estate not been sold for the benefit of the Commonwealth.

A stray mare came to the plantation of Philip GORSHALL, living in Allen twp., near to James GREGORY.

Property of Major James SMITH, decd, to be sold, estate known by the name of Spring Mills, 300 a. patented land, with grist mill, saw mill, dwelling house & barn. Margaret SMITH, Charles M'CLURE & James SMITH, exec.

Nathaniel WEAKLY & Joseph POSTLETHWAIT, Overseers Poor.

Came to the plantation of John CULBERTSON, living in Toboyne twp., Cumberland Co., a bright bay mare.

Strayed from the premises of John HUNTER, living in Borough of Carlisle, a filley.

215. Wednesday, 25 April 1792

Sheriff's Sales: Tract of 300 a. on little Juniata, adj Robert PORTER on the West, Charles QUNN on the East. Another tract on same creek, adj lands of Robert PORTER on the East & lands of William STEWART on the West. Another tract of 250 a. adj John KERNS on the West & Nathan ANDREWS on the South, in the Limestone Valley, all sold as the property of David ENGLISH, Senr.

100 a. on Lost Creek adj land of John M'CLELLAND; 50 a. adj lands of William CORRAN; 30 a. adj lands of the Rev. Hugh MAGILL & John CAMPBELL; 200 a. adj lands of John CAMPBELL, John HENDERSON, William CUNNINGHAM. All lands are in Fermanag twp., Mifflin Co., taken & sold as the property of Robert TAYLOR.

200 a. in Fermanagh twp., known by the name of the Noisy Entry, with a small cabin thereon; sold as the property of Andrew BROWN, adm. of John BROWN, decd.

30 a. in Lack twp., adj lands of William BRICE & the line run by James HARRIS, adj the Huntingdon Co., handsome square log house & kitchen, on

the great road leading from Tustatora(?) to the Path Valley; and sold as the property of Benjamin WALLACE by George WILSON, Sheriff, Lewistown.
Joseph THORNBERGER, having left off business in Carlisle & intending to move out of this state, requests those indebted to him to make speedy payment in his absence to Robert & John MILLER, who do business in the store he formerly occupied.

216. Wednesday, 2 May 1792
George KLINE lists a catalogue of books sold at his bookstore in Carlisle.
John HULING, Collector of the Revenue of Cumberland Co., gives notice that he will attend the house of Joseph POSTLETHWAIT in Carlisle.
Next week in the Jail Yard, Town of Carlisle an exhibition will be performed by a company of French Dancers on the Tight Rope and then a tumbling entertainment. Tickets can be had of Mr. WALLACE and at the Jail.
Dennis HARGAN, book & shoe-maker, 2 doors from Robert MILLER, Tanner.
Dr. STINNECKE has removed from his late dwelling to the new stone house in Hanover Street, next door to the corner of Pomfret St., where he has for sale all kinds of Medicine (Carlisle).
John MONTGOMERY of Carlisle has for sale dry goods & books.
Committed to the jail of the Borough of Carlisle 29 April instant, a Negro Wench who calls herself Sall, & says she belongs to a certain John WHREAY, living about 2 miles from Mercersburgh in Franklin Co.; she is about 20 years old, 5' 3 - 4" high, light coloured linsey short-gown on and a petticoat & tow linen apron. Thomas ALEXANDER, Jailor.

217. Wednesday, 9 May 1792
Commencement for Degrees in the Arts, in Dickinson College, Carlisle. Prayers by the Rev. Dr. Charles NISBET, Principal, after which followed: Salutatory Oration in Latin by John MOORE of VA; Oration on the Insufficiency of human Laws for preventing Disorders by John LYON of Carlisle; orations by James SMITH of MD, Robert WHITEHILL of PA, Isaac WAYNE of Philadelphia, Andrew STEEL of Kentucke, John CREIGH, Jun. of Carlisle, James LAIRD of York Co., PA. After a short intermission the following orations were pronounced in the P.M. On the Connexion between a prosession of Scepticism & Licentiousness of Conduct by George DUGAN of Baltimore; orations by John M'JIMSEY of PA, John STEEL of Kentucke, James M'KNIGHT of NC, Mr. RENNELS of PA, James POSTLETHWAIT of Carlisle, Augustin SMITH of VA, Samuel DAVIDSON of PA, David CASSAT of PA, Haden EDWARDS of KY, William WOODS of PA, (On the Principles that serve as Substitutes for Virtue in bad Men) John FOULK of Carlisle & an oration by William CARCAUD of MD. Bachelor of Arts confered on: John MOORE, John LYON, James SMITH, Robert WHITEHALL, Isaac WAYNE, Andrew TEEL, John CREIGH, James LAIRD, John M'JIMSEY, David CASSAT, Samuel RENNELS, John STEEL, James M'KNIGHT, William HUNTER, James POSTLETHWAIT, Augustin SMITH, Haden EdWARDS, Samuel DAVIDSON, George DUGAN, James GILLELAND, John M'KESSON, John FOULK, William WOODS, William CARCAUD, Maxwell M'DOWELL, James HEMPHILL, Robert CALENDER, Joseph LEEK, John TODD, Charles ROSS, John BRAKENRIDGE, William STEEL & John WILSON. James M'CORMICK also received the honorary degree of Batchelor of Arts & is professor of mathematics in Dickinson College. Degree of Master of Arts conferred on the following, former graduates of this seminary: Isaac GREER, Robert DUNCAN, James DUNCAN, David WATTS, Jonathan WALKER, Steel SEMPLE, Thomas CREIGH, David M'KEEHAN, Isaiah BLAIR & James CALHOON. Degree of Doctor in Divinity conferred on the Rev. James WADDEL of VA,

the Rev. Samuel M'CORKLE of NC, the Rev. Robert COOPER & the Rev. John KING of PA. Valedictory Oration delivered by Maxwell M'DOWELL of PA.

Deserters from Major Henry GAITHER's detachment at Carlisle: John SMITH, 40 years of age, born in Ireland, 5'8" high, black complexion, black eyes, and wears his own long black hair.

James HAMILTON, 35 years of age, born in Ireland, 5'10" high, fresh complexion, light hair & gray eyes.

William BUTTON, about 30 years of age, born in Ireland, 5'6" high, pale faced down looking fellow, dark hair & eyes, speaks much on the brogue.

John JOHNSTON, 30 years of age, born in Philadelphia, 5'9" high, dark short hair, round shouldered, pale complexion & dark eyes.

James WRIGHT, 25 years of age, born in New York, 5'9" high, dark long black hair & black eyes, round shouldered, by trade a shoe maker.

Whereas David JORDON gave a bond to Thomas JOHNSTON of Allen twp., Cumberland Co., for the delivery of 60 bushels of wheat in Middletown, but JOHNSON never gave him any value for same.

218. Wednesday, 16 May 1792

Whereas my wife Mary COOPER has behaved in a very indecent & unbecoming manner & has taken up with a certain Hugh WATSON: this is to forewarn all persons not to give her credit on my account. John COOPER, Middleton twp., Cumberland Co.

Charles BOVARD, Reed-Maker, at the sign of the Weaver's Reed in York Street, South, Carlisle.

Whereas the Surveyor General in pursuance of an act of the General Assembly of PA, a supplement to the act entitled 'an act for directing the mode of distributing the Donation Lands promised to the troops of this commonwealth,' has made the following report to the Governor, stating the number of patents that have been granted for such lots of Donation Land, as have been found, since line between PA & NY, to be within the jurisdiction of the latter State. Whereas provision is made for indemnifying in kind the persons, who by reason of the premises have accidently been deprived of the bounty; and whereas for the relief for a number of persons who did not apply for same, they have extended the time for making such application until 1 July next. Return of that part of the 10th District of PA Donation Lands, that on running the Northern Boundery were found to lie within the State. Taken from the general draft of the said District, returned to the late Supreme Executive Council: (Name of patentee, rank in the Army, # of the lot, [acre] quantity of lot) Eocas (?) M. KAY, Col., 181, 500; William SPROAT, Capt., 182, 500; Arthur ST. CLAIR, Maj. Gen., 183, 500; William MACKEY, Capt., 184, 500; Francis JOHNSTON, col., 191, 500; M. MATTHEWS, widow of H. MATTHEWS, capt., 192, 500; Robert SAMPLE, capt. 195, 500; Daniel BROADHEAD, col., 196, 500; Widow & heirs of br. gen. W. THOMPSON, 198, 500; Jeremiah TALBOT, major, 96, 300; Rev. D. JONES, chaplain, 97, 300; Isaac CRAIG, major, 99, 300; Frederick VERNON, major, 100, 300; Joseph MORGAN, serjeant, 206, 250; Francis MURRAY, lt.col., 207, 250; William GRAY, serjeant, 208, 250; S. LOUDEN, assignee to R. PENDERGRASS, 209, 250; Joseph DALEY, serjeant, 190, 250; James PIPER, lt. col., 191, 250; James NEAL, serjeant, 192, 250; David EWING, pvt., 2076, 200; Thomas MURRAY, pvt., 2077, 200; George HARVEY, pvt. 2079, 200; William REYNOLDS, pvt., 2080, 200; S. LOUDON, assignee of John GREER, pvt. 2081, 200; John BENTLY, pvt., 2082, 200; Wm. M'INTIRE, pvt. 2083, 200; M. BARNET, executor of Martin O'BRIEN, pvt., 2006, 200; Joseph BANKS, pvt., 2007, 200; Wm. HUNT, pvt., 2009, 200; Joseph KINNAIRD, pvt., 2012, 200; P. BOEHM, assignee of Mortocks

SULLIVAN, pvt., 1998, 200; Abraham MORRIS, pvt. 1999, 200; Wm. WILKINSON, pvt., 1962, 200; Patrick DEVER, matross 1963, 200; John M'KEWN, pvt. 1961, 200; John STRICKER, Lt. art. 1985, 200; Peter LISK, pvt., 1995, 200; J. STUART, executor of John TRACY, pvt., 1994, 200; William WILLIAMS, pvt., 1992, 200; Wm. GILL, matross, 1990, 200; James M'FERRALD, lt., 1988, 200; Josiah THOMAS, pvt., 2022, 200; John TOM, pvt., 2023, 200; Wm. M. I. CHATTON, pvt., 2024, 200; Evan HOLT, pvt., 2025; Wm. WEBB, pvt., 2026, 200; Joshua SEDWICK, pvt., 2000, 200; Jacob DIEKS, pvt. 2001, 200; James HUTTON, pvt. 2002, 200; Edward SPEAR, lt., 2003, 200; Samuel BRYSON, pvt., 2027, [all pvts got 200 a.] Murty THOMY, vpt, 2028; Robert ADAMS, pvt., 2043; A. BEMER, assignee of Philip DENNIS, pvt., 2044; Frederick WINCKLER, pvt.., 2045; Mervin NIXON, pvt., 2047; Daniel ST. CLAIR, Lt, 2048, 200; Philip BUTTINSTON, pvt., 2050; Archibald M'LEAN, pvt., 2051; J. NICHOLASON, assignee of Chr. CROW, pvt., 2052; Anthony PETREE, pvt. 2053; Michael LYN, drummer, 2054, 200; Augustus MILLISOCK, pvt. 2055; John DUNN, pvt., 2056; John PINE, matross, 2069; Thomas M'ENTEE, pvt. 2084; James THORNTON, drummer, 2085; Wm. CLARK, matross, 2086; Robert PARKER, lt., 2087; John SHAW, pvt., 2088; A. CUNNINGHAM, pvt., 2089; John DOWNEY, pvt., 2090; Wm. HOPKINS (no rank given), 2091; John SMITH, pvt., 2092; Wm. SCOTT, pvt., 2094; Archibald MELOUE, pvt., 2095; Alexander DOW, lt., 2098; Jeremiah BANNON, 2111; John AIKEN, matross, 2112; Stephen GILBERT, pvt., 2113; Henry OVERMAN, pvt., 2114; Lawrence BURNS, pvt., 2115; Edward M'CALLY, pvt., 2117; John WARD junr. (no rank given), 2118; S. M'MURRAY, executor of Wm. MORROW, pvt., 2119; Wm. STEWART, lt., 2120; Thomas JENNY, lt., 2121; John WILLIAMS, drummer, 2122; Francis THORNBERRY, lt., 2123; John BURRAGE, pvt., 2124; John ANDREW, pvt., 2125; James CAWHAWK, pvt., 2139; David CROWLEY, pvt., 2140; Job REILEY, pvt., 2141; Patrick MURRAY, pvt., 2142; Michael WALT, pvt., 2143; Elizabeth, widow of John ROWLAND, pvt., 2144; Joseph FERGUSON, pvt., 2145; Robert CAMPBELL, pvt., 2146; Wm. BAIRD, amin. of John LAWRENCE, pvt., 2147; John M'PHERSON (no rank), 2148; Thomas CAMPBELL, lt., 2149; S. LOUDON, assignee of John SPALDING, drummer, 2150; Peter RIPLEY, pvt., 2152; Michael M'CHRISTIE, pvt., 2154; John DONNEL, assignee of Thomas VARDEN, pvt., 2167; Peter BOON, matross, 2168; Peter SUNCKLE, pvt., 2170. [All acreages from David EWING, pvt on above, to end of list are 200 acres.]

The following is a list of Surveys, through which the Northern Boundary Line [with state of New York] passes & cuts off a considerable part of them. (Patentees, rank in the Army, # of the lots, quantity in each Lot). Robert COLTMAN, capt., 185, 500; Peter BOYER, capt., 190, 500; David ZIGLAR, 199, 500; George TUDOR, major, 95, 300; Wm. LEE, serjeant, 205, 200; (all 200 acres after this) Joseph B. WEBSTER, serjeant, 196; Philip BOEHM, assignee of Jos. FLECHER, pvt., 2075, 200; John STOY, lt, 2014; John MARKLAND, lt, 1997; Widow & children of James HARROLD, pvt., 1964; Matthew SMITH, pvt., 1957; Samuel CRAWFORD, pvt., 2029; Solomon WISER, pvt., 2040; John M'CARTHY, matross, 2057; Roger M'CULLOUGH, pvt., 2068; Wm. ENT, pvt., 2099; Adam ANDERSON, pvt., 2110; Daniel M'GEE, matross, 2137; Patrick M'GROSSAN, pvt. 2138; John ECKHOLTZ, pvt. 2155; Richard BURRANCE, pvt., 2166. Total acres, 38,350. Daniel BROADHEAD, Surveyor General.

219. Wednesday, 23 May 1792

Board of Commissioners of Cumberland to meet when those Collectors of Taxes who are in readiness for final settlement are desired to attend. (Signed) Jacob CRAVER, Edward WEST, Samuel POSTLETHWAIT.

219. Wednesday, 23 May 1792 (Con't.)

Selling 2 new stills with heads and worms complete. Apply to John HOLMES in Carlisle, or the Widow GIBSON in Shearman's Valley, who has to sell a very handsome horse.

This warns all persons of taking any assignment on 3 bonds gave by me to Richard WOODS, as I am determined not to pay any of them. Witnesses to the above mentioned are E. DUNNING & Jane FRENCH. William FRENCH, West-Pennsboro twp.

Ran away from Alexander BOGGS, living in Donegall twp., Lancaster Co., a certain Negro Man named Bill, 5' 6 or 7" high, rather of the yellow than real black & his right eye has a blemish almost white.

220. Wednesday, 30 May 1792

Married on Thursday last, the Rev. Nathaniel. SNOWDEN of Philadelphia to Miss Sally GUSTAIN, d/o Dr. GUSTAIN of Carlisle.

Ran away from David DAVIDSON, living in Fermaeagh (?) Twp., Mifflin Co., an apprentice boy named William CHAPMAN, 5' 6-7" high, 17 years of age, fair complexion, light colored hair, has a remarkable scar on his left thumb. His parents live near the Big Spring above Carlisle in Cumberland co. Said apprentice is a tolerable good English scholar, and likely will make himself a pass.

221. Wednesday, 6 June 1792

Married on Thursday the 31st ult. by the Rev. Dr. DAVIDSON, the Rev. Samuel MAHON to Miss Nancy DUNCAN, d/o Stephen DUNCAN, Esq. (Carlisle),

Robert DUNCAN, living in Dickinson twp., about 6 miles from Carlisle, has taken in 3 strays.

Strayed or stolen from the commons of Carlisle, belonging Casper KROPH, a bay mare.

222. Wednesday, 13 June 1792

Andrew NELSON, Fermanaugh twp., is candidate for sheriff.

John WEBBER, has just received merchandize suitable to the season, dry goods, hardware, glass & chinaware, books, etc. (Carlisle).

Peter KOCH, Blue Ball, Buffalo Creek, selling Buffalo Spaw, a much-approved mineral too well known to need a repetition.

Wednesday, 13 June 1792 missing

223. Wednesday, 20 June 1792

Strayed or stolen from the pasture of Jacob SHONTZ near Strasburgh, a chestnut bay horse.

Wednesday, 27 June 1792 (Issue available; no new local information.)

224. Wednesday, 4 July 1792

Married Thursday last by the Rev. Dr. DAVIDSON, at the seat of Mr. Ralph STERRETT, Adam LOGUE of Carlisle to Miss Nancy STERRETT.

Deserted from the barracks at Carlisle. James GALLIGHER, about 22 years of age, 5'6" high, of a dark complexion, brown hair, thick lips, speaks in the Scotch dialect. George WALKER, about 19 or 20 years of age, a country born, 5'7" high, of fair complexion, short fair hair, by trade a black-smith, lived formerly near little York. Michael M. CASTLEN, an Irishman, 5'7" high, fair complexion, short dark hair mixed with gray; has a small lump on his forehead as large as the half of a musquet ball; by trade a weaver. Apply to Thomas BUILER, Maj. Command. A number of desertions hath also taken place in Major ASHTON's detachment.

Mary & Isabella COCHRAN, milliners & mantu-makers at the house of Robert HASLET, at the corner of York & Pomfret St., Carlisle.

Strayed from the common of Carlisle, a dark brindled cow belonging to Peter BOYLE.

Strayed or stollen from Samuel THOMPSON, living in Tyrone Twp., a bay horse.

225. Wednesday, 11 July 1792

James ROSS, next door to Dr. GUSTINE, west end of High St., Carlisle, selling a variety of merchandise.

Jeremiah MILLER, Senior, blue dyer & stamper informs that he has just begun his business in Carlisle, next door to Mr. WALLACE at the sign of the bear, and adjoining the wagon-maker's shop of Phillip MILLER.

Strayed or stolen from William ANDERSOSN, Carlisle, a black gelding.

Whereas William CHRISTY, living in Milford twp., Mifflin Co, passed bonds to a certain Michael M'CROAM, in consideration of a tract of land in said twp., bounded by lands of Thomas GILSTON, John WALLACE, John CHRISTY & by lands of the subscriber, which tract said M'CROAM bought of a certain John CROZER, which land has not been yet cleared of all incumbrances. William CHRISTY refuses to pay said bonds.

Information Wanted. Being informed that a certain John GRACIE, who has a little halt in his walk, a cabinet maker by trade, lately from Galaway in Scotland, had been inquiring for a brother he has in this State, and as I am expecting a brother of mine of the same description, do think it may be him. He may find me at the head of Big Spring, Cumberland Co, PA. Thomas GRACIE.

Whereas my wife Catherine hath eloped from my bed and board, without just cause, and refuses to return, I am determined not to pay any debts of her contracting. Isaac WOODS, Middletown twp., Cumberland Co.

By virtue of a writ of vendition the following tracts formerly in the county of Westmoreland, but now in the county of Alleghany, on the bank of the Alleghany River, about 5 miles from the town of Pittsburgh, such lands to be sold. 1. 186 a. bounded by a tract in the possession of EVALT & the Alleghany River. 2. Adj the latter, 500 a. whereon is the mansion house, late of George CROGHAN , decd. 3. Adj the last described, 228 a. 4. Plantation now in possession of Capt. HEATH of 453 a. adj tract last described. 5. Plantation of 553 a. adj. the last described place, surveyed for the said George CROGAN, taken in execution as property of George CROGAN, Esq. decd, at the request of the executors of Joseph SPEAR, Esq, decd. James GUTHRIE, Sheriff, Greensburgh, Westmoreland Co.

226. Wednesday, 18 July 1792

Saturday being the anniversary of the ever memorible French Revolution, the day was commerated by a respectable number of local citizens. In the afternoon they assembled at Robert GIBSON's farm near Letart Spring, where 20 documented toasts were drunk.

George STEVENSON has lately imported from London, a fresh assortment of drugs & medicines. (Carlisle)

Sheriff's Sale: 2 lots on the north side of Louther St., adj the Lentart Spring with a 2-story house with 2 kitchens, a brew-house and back building of logs. Sold as property of John POLLOCK, Malster.

227. Wednesday, 25 July 1792

Sheriff's Sale: House & lot in town of Shippensburgh, opposite to Squire Henderson's on the Main-street; sold as the property of Robert HAMMELL.

200 a. in Rye Twp., on South side of the Juniata River, sold as property of Robert MAGAHY (?), Thomas WILSON & James MITCHELTREE.

200 a. of land in Antrim Twp., now Franklin Co., adj lands of William RANKIN & John ROBINSON; sold as property of Samuel PERRY, Executor of David MAGAW, decd.

200 a. in Greenwood Twp., Cumberland Co., adj lands of David ENGLISH; sold as property of Michael HUFFNAGLE.

Mr. WILLIAMSON takes this method of informing all those who wish to emigrate to the Genesee that his property consists of 1 million of acres. A village called Williamsburg is laid out in a beautiful situation at the junction of the Canferaga & Genesee Rivers. We encourage in particular a brewer, tin smith, tayler, and shoemaker and a nursery man or gardener . . . will have their village lots gratis. He informs German settlers in Pa. that he daily expects to hear of the arrival at New York of 400 Germans from Saxony, who have taken up lands in the Gennessee and sailed from Hamburgh 15 April last. Enquire William P. BRADY, Surveyor, Sunbury, PA, who will show the place.

Notwithstanding the great fall of rain on July 4th, a number of the citizens of the newly-erected town of Lewis-Town met & drank toasts under the discharge of small artillery commanded by Dr. JONES. A repast was prepared at the home of John CULBERTSON.

William BAILEY, coppersmith of the Borough of York, informs that he carries on the business as usual at his house opposite Andrew JOHNSTON's tavern, sign of the Bear & Cub. At Chambersburgh under the direction of his son William. At Hagerstown next door to Jacob HARRY, Hatter, in partnership with his son-in-law, William REYNOLDS, and at Frederick Town near the Poor House in Partnership with his brother-in-law, Robert M'CULLEY.

228. Wednesday, 1 August 1792

Sheriff's Sale: 147 a. in Newtown tpw, adj lands of Ludwig CHRISTIAN, George TAYLOR with 2 cabbins & other improvements thereon; sold as property of James SMALL, decd.

200 a. in Middleton twp, adj lands of James ELLIOTT with improvements thereon; now in the tenure of Hugh M'KRE/KEE (?); all right, title, interest & claim of Samuel BINGHAM.

76 a. on Jack's Creek in Derry Twp., adj lands of Mr. SWIFT about 4 miles from Lewistown, with improvements, in Campbell's Valley, sold as property of Samuel BAIRD.

The next quarterly meeting of the Fire Company will be at the Courthouse Tuesday next. Samuel LAIRD, Clerk.

Philip ERWIN informs the public that he continues to keep that commodious house in Market Street, between 6th & 7th Sts., now next door to the Surveyor General's office.

229. Wednesday, 8 August 1792

Sheriff's Sales: 200 a. in East-Pennsborough, about 5 miles from Harrisburgh, adj land of James BELL &c., log house; sold as the property of John STEVENSON.

300 a. with improvements in Tyrone Twp., sold as the property of James & Alexander RODDY.

229. Wednesday, 8 August 1792 (Con't.)
Strayed from the plantation of Nicholas ESHWEY in Letterkenny twp, Franklin Twp, about 2 miles from Strasburgh, a bay mare. Give information to Nicholas ZOLLINGER, living near Carlisle.
John WALKER announces as a candidate for sheriff of Cumberland Co.
David LINDSAY carries on the Coppersmith business in the Main St, Borough of Carlisle next door to John POLLOCK.
Patrick M'CAFERY, living in Rye Twp, Cumberland Co, has taken up a stray roan mare.

Wednesday, 15 August 1792 (No new local data.)

230. Wednesday, 22 August 1792
Susannah THOMPSON opening for sale at the house lately occupied by John MOORE, storekeeper, a complete assortment of dry goods & spririts. Grain, bees-wax & country produce will be taken in payment.
To be sold - 2 houses & lots in High Street, Borough of Carlisle; also tract of Patented Land on the west branch of the Susquehannah, about 2 miles above the Big Island; 315 a. with front on the River of above 1 mile; about 50 a. clear with a cabin & barn. Also 315 a. of land in Nittenny Valley, 4 miles land carriage from Bald Eagle, same distance from good grist & saw mills. Also 300 a. on Turtle Creek, on both sides of said creek, on the old Pa. Road, near CAVER's Mill, in Allegheny Co, known as SMALL's Place; now in the tenure of John TIONS(?), who will shew the land. For terms apply to John IRVINE, Esq. near Greensburg, Squire FLEMING & David HANNAH or to James POLLOCK, living in Borough of Pollock.
Whereas Jacob WISE, Senr. living in York Co., when he was in Harrisburgh upon business, was by a certain Conrad DERR, of Dauphin Co, forced in a most deceitful & fraudulent manner to sign a judgment payable to the said DERR. Persons are warned that he will not honor same.
Broke gaol Thomas LOGUE, a Felon; about 25 years of age, 5' 7-8" high, short brown hair, striped cotton jacket & trousers, shoes & buckles &c. Reward of $2 offered by Thomas ALEXANDER.
Agreeable to orders from the War-Office I do hereby offer a reward of $10 for each deserter, delivered to me. Thomas BUTLER, Maj. Commanding, Barracks at Carlisle.
Gentlemen who compose the Troop of Light-Horse in Cumberland Co, are requested to mee. John ALEXANDER, L.C.C.
Whereas my wife Mary WATKINS, alias TIPPO, has behaved in a very indecent & unbecoming manner, by defiling my bed during my absence, & is now in a disordered condition, through which means I am under the necessity of warning the public to give her no credit on my account. James WATKINS.
Wanted: A number of good Working Hands, to be engaged in clearing the River Juniata. Apply to Benjamin ELLIOTT, John CANAN, David STEWART & Richard SMITH at Huntingdon.
$10 reward - Deserted from the detachment of Edward BUTLER, Captain, R.C., the 17th inst.: Jacob COFFMAN, German, about 5' 708" high, fair complexion with pale face & marked with the small pox.

231. Wednesday, 29 August 1792
William M'FARLANE offers himself as a candidate for sheriff.
Ranaway from the plantation of the subscriber in Fayette Co, one Negro Slave named Sam, about 27 years of age, 5' 6-7" high, very black, short hair, very talkative & impertinent. Also a Mulatto slave named Harry, formerly the property of James BLAINE of Carlisle, about 25 years old, 5'

6-7" high, well made, fair complexion, long frizled hair, is very fond of liquor. Reward paid by Andrew RABB.

The body of Patrick DOILE was found floating in the river Deleware on Sunday the 19th inst., an inquest held pronounced it an accidental death. A letter was found in his pocket directed to John PATTERSON, who identified the body and said that he came from Milford twp, Mifflin Co. A Philadelphia paper says he had been in the army during the late war & revolted in the Jersies. Drink was his bane, but when sober he was an active, industrious man.

On Wednesday evening last, the barns of Jacob BRENNEYMAN, Donnegall, Lancaster Co, were consumed, together with upwards of 1000 bushels of grain & 20 ton hay, a waggon &c. The fire started when Mr. BRENNYMAN intended to smoke out a wasp's nest near a strawroom of an old barn.

By virtue of writs to be sold at public sale 2 lots on the north side of Louther St, adj the Letart Spring with 2-story stone house, with 2 kitchens; Brew-house & back building of logs. Sold as property of John POLLOCK, Malster.

232. Wednesday, 5 September 1792

Whereas a certain Christopher PEELMAN obtained a note of James HAMILTON, for which he received no value, I warns all not to take said note.

Joseph T. JAMES at his store in the Borough of Carlisle, has general assortment of merchandize suitible to the approaching season.

S. BALENTINE proposes to stay in town for a few months, would during his stay teach the following instruments of music: violin, bassoon, german flute, trumpet, hautboy, french horn, clarionet, guitar. Enquire at William WALLACE's.

By virtue of a precept under the hand & seal of Christian FEBIGER, Esq., Treasurer of State of Pa., will be exposed to public sale 140 a. in Middletown Twp., 2 miles from Carlisle, adj lands of Andrew HOLMES, mortgaged by Matthew LAIRD to the trustees of the Loan Office.

Committed to the jail in Carlisle on suspicion of being runaways: One Negro & 2 mulattoes. The Negro calls himself John or George WRIGHT, about 5' 8-10" high, very black & has a broad nose & narrow chin, hair is very low to the forehead. A mulatto who calls himself George JOHNSTON, about 5' 5-6" high, very surly looking fellow, appears to be about 20 or 22 years of age, has thick lips, is stout & well made. Has lost one of his teeth out of his under jaw, from the marks on his back appears to be an old offender. A mulatto boy who calls himself Timothy JOHNSTON, about 5' high, between 15 & 17 years of age, likely & well made. The mulattoes say they are brothers & are free men & lived near M'Alister's Town in York Co. The negro says he also lived near M'Alister's Town.

233. Wednesday, 12 September 1792

Ran away from James SHARP, living in Hopewell twp, Cumberland Co., a negro man named Thomas CATON(?), about 30 years old, 5' 8" high, stout & well made; understands the German language.

L. GUSTINE has received a quantity of drugs & medicines of the best quantity. (Has printed a very long list in the paper.)

234. Wednesday, 19 September 1792

Christian KAUFMAN seeking his dark brown horse, stolen from a field in his plantation in Hempfield Two, Lancaster Co.

On the night of the 8th inst., departed this life, after a short illness, John IRWIN, at his house near Shippensburgh in Franklin Co. Remains were

interred on the Monday following in the burying-ground at Middle Spring Meeting House. He died in the prime of life, possessed of those qualities which constitute the amiable character; but which were connected with a weak & infirm body.
Jacob CREVER offers himself as a candidate for Sheriff.

Wednesday, 26 September 1792 (Issue available, no new local data.)

235. Wednesday, 3 October 1792
James LINDSEY in the Borough of Carlisle has taken up a stray black cow.
To be sold at public vendue at the late dwelling house of John YOUNG, in West-Pennsborough, decd, livestock, a wagon, farming utensils &c. Eleanor YOUNG, John DAVIDSON & Samuel LAIRD, Ad'rs.
Joseph & James M'MEEKAN, lately from Belfast, have set up the hosiery business in that house adj the vacant lot, opposite John HUNTER, on York & Pomfret Sts, Borough of Carlisle.

236. Wednesday, 10 October 1792
William GRAYSON, Clothier, has erected a fulling mill on his plantation in East-Pennsborough. Cloth &c. will be received at Maj. John WALKER's in East-Pennsborough, Robert GRAYSON & William AITKEN's, Carlisle & at Ralph STATRETT's, North Mountain.
Sheriff's Sale: 20 a. in Lack Twp., adj William BRICE. Thereon is a square log house &c. Taken in execution as the property of Benjamin WALLACE.
James GIVEN has just imported from Ireland, Irish linens, collection of Family, School & Pocket Bibles and a number of other religious books. Also Birmingham Hardware, all of which he is determined to dispose of at Philadelphia prices. (Carlisle)

237. Wednesday, 17 October1792
Ran away from Peter KREEMER, living near Shippensburgh, Cumberland Co., an Apprentice Lad named William SHOEMAN, about 18 years of age.
Died last Saturday morning, after an illness of considerable duration & great severity, which she bore with continued fortitude & patience, Miss Susanna THOMPSON d/o the late Parson THOMPSON, in the 19th year of her age. On the Sunday following, her corps [sic] was interred in the Episcopal Church in this town.
To be sold at public vendue: agreeable to will of John COOKE, decd., on the premises, 167 a., adj lands of James ATCHISON & George M'KEEHEN in West Pennsborough twp, Cumberland Co. James CAROTHERS & William LINDSEY, Ex'rs.
Strayed from the commons of Carlisle, a Sorrel colt. Reward if returned to Charles BOVARD in Carlisle. The same Charles BOVARD selling 60 a. patented land in West-Pennsborough twp, 8 miles westward of Carlisle.

238. Wednesday, 24 October 1792
Was found on the Great Road between Carlisle & Mount-Rock a linen bag containing a numberof clothes. Apply to James M'CUNE, Esq. in Hopewell by proving property. Thomas NEIKELS
To be sold by the Heirs of Alexander ADAMS, decd., tract in York Co, Hamiltonban twp, within 3 miles of Millerstown of 340 a., log dwelling house, double barn. Apply to David AGNEW & David BLYTH, near the premises or Alexander DEAN in Huntingdon.
Notice that the Commissioners of Cumberland Co, will meet to settle duplicates. Edward WEST & Samuel POSTLETHWAIT of Carlisle.

239. Wednesday, 31 October 1798

Notice is given to the owners of unseated land in Co of Huntingdon that unless taxes are satisfied that said land will be advertised for sale. Robert RIDDLE, John CADWALLADER & John BLAIR, Commissioners.

Andrew HERVEY, advertised 2 years ago that he had taken in a stray calf & no owner appeared. If not claimed, he will disposed of for the benefit of the poor of the poor of Westpennsborough.

Ranaway from William ALLISON, living in Franklin Co., a negro man named Tom, about 5' 10-11 high, stout made. To be sold by Vendue at the late dwelling house of Robert M'CLURE, decd, in west Pennsborough twp, near M'Clure's gap, horses, cows, sheep, a wagon, hay in the stack &c. William M'CLURE & James LAIRD, Ex'rs.

Died at Shippensburgh on Sunday morning last, after a severe illness, which he bore with true Christian resignation, Mr. Robert COLWELL, a merchant of that town in his 28th year.

All persons indebted to Samuel ALEXANDER are requested to make payment to William ALEXANDER, Esq.

240. Wednesday, 7 November 1792

(Baltimore) Died last Monday morning, aged 36 years, after a very long & painful illness, Mrs. Ann HOLMES, amiable consort of Mr. John HOLMES of Baltimore, Merchant; & last evening her remains were interred in the Presbyterian burying ground.

Mary PATTERSON, lost on the road from Carlisle to Harrisburgh, between Maj. John WALKER's & Jonathan HOGE, Esq., a saddle with plated buttons on which are the letters R.P. Deliver it to any of the tavern keepers on that road.

The partnership of Robert COLWELL & Co. being dissolved by the death of the former, all indebted to said partnership, please pay up. John DUNCAN

James SCRANTON gives notice that sunday articles will be sold in the market house in Borough of Carlisle, in pledge by Daniel KELLER, late of this place for certain debt due SCRANTON.

Ran away from James LAIRD, Westpennsborough, near M'Clures gap, 10 miles from Carlisle, an apprentice lad called Joseph HALBERT, 15 years of age, 5' 4-5" high, black eyes, fair complexion, dark hair tied behind, had on a round crown hat fur hat, half worn, nankeen drawers, pierced in inside of the thigh, ribbed worsted stockings, round steel buckles. He ran away before, & said that he came from Samuel M'TERRS, 10 miles below Carlisle.

A certain Matthias FLAM of upper Paxton twp, Dauphin co, obtained ten notes of the subscribers, for which we are likely not to obtain value, for which reason we have thought it proper to warn all from taking assignment on such. William LOWDEN & John LOWDEN.

Child Lost! I left my child, named Margaret HOGAN, aged about 4 years, last spring with a certain Nicholas WILLIAMS, a Frenchman, then living near Liberty-town, for him to take care of until I returned from Phila. And now, on my return, I find said Williams has moved away with my child. Any person who can give account where he now resides, convey such intelligence to the Printer in Hagerstown. Said WILLIAMS is a silversmith but mostly follows peddling & I am told that he & his wife (who is an Irish woman) call the child their own.

This gives notice to all persons having claim against the estate of Andrew THOMPSON, decd., to come & state their accounts. David WILLS & John SNODY, Ex'rs.

241. Wednesday, 14 November 1792
Sheriff's Sales: 2 tracts adj each other, one in Middleton twp, adj lands of James RAOKIN & Richard PETERS, 132 a., the other tract adj John M'DONALD, 198 1/2 a., late the property of John GLENN.
Tract called Goodhope in West Pennsborough twp, on Conodoguinet creek, adj lands of John DUNBAT & William CAROTHERS; 186 a. & 105 perches, late the property of John FORBES.
Tract in Newton twp, with a grist mill, 63 a. adj James JACK & the Condoguinet creek, late the property of James CHAMBERS.
Tract in East Pennsborough twp, adj lands of Hugh M'CABE, John MITCHELL &c., 118 a. & 139 perches, late the property of Woolrick BURKHOLDER. Also the same ay another tract in East Pennsborough called Houes (?), adj lands of William HOLMES, John QUIGLY & Shippen's lands, 71 a., property of Ulrick BURKHOLDER.
Tract in Rye twp, adj lands of John CREIGH & Sherman's Creek, 209 1/2 a. late the property of Tole M'ALISTER.
Tract in Rye twp, adj James M'LAUGHLIN's claim, John M'COY & William BASKIN's claim, 216 a., late the property of Francis WATTS.
Christian MILLER informs that he has laid out a number of Lots on the Susquehannah River and mouthof little Juniata river, for a town to be called Petersburgh. Within 1/2 a mile of Isaac JONES's Mill & another merchant mill will be erected the town. Application for lots to be made to George KLINE, Printer in Carlisle or to subscriber in Petersburgh. 20 lots remain unsold. He has also opened lately a house of entertainment.
Dr. Isaiah BLAIR, having removed to Lewis-Town in Mifflin Co, all those indebted to him in Cumberland Co., are requested to pay Alexander M'KEEHAN, Esq. in Carlisle.
By virtue of precept of sale on 24 December will be sold, tract in West-Pennsborough two, adj theConnodoguinet creek, lands of Daniel WILLIAMS, William DUNBAR,William CAROTHERS & John M'CLURE, 158 1/2 a. late the property of Alexander PARKER, decd., seized to be sold.
Died last Saturday morning, David ALLEN of Carlisle in the 58th year of his age & on the Sabbath evening his remains were followed to the grave by his relations & large group of citizens.
Married on Thursday last, by the Rev. Dr. R. DAVIDSON, William KELSO to Miss Betsy CHAMBERS, d/o Col. William CHAMBERS, near Carlisle.
On Monday the 12th inst. died in the 38th year of her age, Mrs. Susan M'COSKRY of Carlisle, consort of Dr. Samuel A. M'COSKRY.

242. Wednesday, 21 November 1792
Samuel SMILEY, living in Rye Twp., has taken in a stray steer.
Sheriff's Sale: Tract in Antrim twp, Franklin Co., adj lands of David HOOP, James POE & John ANDREW & the Conogocheague creek, 200 a., sold as the property of Andrew GIBSON.
Also tract in Mifflin co, adj lands of the Widow MOORE, Robert CRAWFORD & Archibald MOORE, 171 a., sold as the property of Robert PATTON.
George STEVENSON requests all persons indebted to him to settle same.

243. Wednesday, 28 October 1792
Sheriff's Sale: Tract called the Big Lick, in Toboyne tpw, adj claim of Alexander ROSEY, Andrew HIGHLANDS & vacant lands, 113 1/2 a., late the property of Joseph SHIELDS.
Strayed or stolen from the commons of Shippensburgh, brown mare. Reasonable charges paid by Isaiah GRAY, Shippensburgh.

243. Wednesday, 28 October 1792 (Con't.)
All persons indebted to John CREIGH are requested to make immediate payment. The said CREIGH has received at his store in Carlisle an assortment of general merchandise.

244. Wednesday, 5 December 1792
Persons indebted to John MOORE to pay up.
Mordecai M'KINNEY offers $60 reward for apprehension of those who broke open his store and stole goods from therein. There is reason to suspect a certain John WISE, alias Indian John and William COMPTON, who were liberated from York Jail.
To be sold at the Court House in Carlisle, 2 lots in said town, one in Louther St, upon which is a log dwelling adj Thomas DICKSON: the other in Pomfret St., with house, adj a lot the property of Jacob WEAVER. Ephraim BLAINE, Agent for the adm'rs. of Daniel CLARK.
Thomas GUY has taken up a stray mare, in Middleton twp, Cumberland Co.
John DUNWOODY informs his friends & the public that he had opened a House of Entertainment, the Sign of the Spread Eagle, between 7th & 8th Sts, Philadelphia.
To be sold by William DOUGLASS, attorney for excrs. of said estate, for living near the premises, a plantation in Middletown Twp, Cumberland Co., within 3 miles of Carlisle, late the property of James MATTHEWS, decd, 344 a., on which are 2 houses & 2 barns.
Notice to all indebted to estate of David ALLEN, decd,to pay up. Sarah ALLEN, Adm'r. NB: the tobacco busiess is carried on as usual by S.A.
Robert ERWIN informs that he continues to keep that House in Market St, between 6th & 7th St., next to the Surveyor General's office & directly opposite the new state treasury.
William PETRIKIN, taylor & shopkeeper, next door below Ephraim STEEL, Esq. mechandize including dry goods & groceries. He also needs 2 or 3 Journeymen Taylors.
Married Tuesday, the 20th ult. at the farm of Robert SANDERSON, by the Rev. Dr. DAVIDSON, Dr. James M'CLEAN of Leesburg to Miss Patty SANDERSON d/o Robert.

245. Wednesday, 12 December 1792
Notice is hereby given to all indebted to estate of William BLAIR, Junr., late of Carlisle, decd. to make payment to William BLAIR, Senr. Isaiah BLAIR & William G. HOLMES, Adm'rs.
John GLEN, just opening in High Street, opposite the Prison, Carlise, selling dry goods & groceries.
Sheriff's Sales: Tract in West Pennsborough twp, adj the Connedoguinet creek, lands of Daniel WILLIAMS, William DUNBAR, William CAROTHERS & John M'CLURE, 158 1/2 a., late the property of Alexander PARKER, decd.
200 a. with improvements, in Milford twp, Mifflin Co, sold as property of Robert HOGE, delinquent Collector of Taxes.
100 a. with improvement in Milford twp, Mifflin Co, sold as property of George GLASAFORD, delinquent Collector of Taxes.
300 a. with improvements in Farmannagh twp, Mifflin Co., sold as property of James BARR, delinquent Collector of Taxes.
500 a. with improvements in Newton twp, Cumberland Co, sold as property of James LAUGHLIN, deliquent Collector of Taxes.
200 a. in Lack twp, Mifflin Co, adj lands of ARBUCKLE, sold as the property of William BRICE, delinquent Collector of the Taxes.

245. Wednesday, 12 December 1792 (Con't.)
200 a. with improvements in Lack Twp, Mifflin Co, as the property of William M'CONNELL, delinquent Collector of the Taxes.
100 a. with tanyard thereon, in Milford Twp., Mifflin Co., sold as the property of Thomas ARBETT.

246. Wednesday, 19 December 1792
R. M'CALL requests all indebted to him to make payment.
Sheriff's Sale: Tract in East-Pennsbough twp, 200 a., sold as the property of Joseph STAYMAN, delinquent Collector of Taxes.
Tract of land in Derry Twp, Mifflin Co, adj lands of KEEVER & MAKEE,sold as the property of James BURNS.
Tract in Newton Tpw. co of Cumberland, adj lands of James PATTERSON, Alexander WOODBURN, John JOHNSTON, Sarah DAVIS & James EWING. 113 a., sold as the property of Mary DAVIDSON, widow & heirs & children of Samuel DAVIDSON.

247. Wednesday, 26 December 1792
Sheriff's Sales: 140 a. with improvements, bounded by Capt. FISHER & the Connedoguinet Creek; seized by Thomas BUCHANAN, Esq. late Sheriff, sold as the property of Abraham WOLF.
Undivided half of 530 a., in Fannet twp, Franklin twp, sold as the property of Robert GRAY.
Tract in Antrim twp, Franklin Co, adj lands of William RANKIN & John ROBINSON, sold as property of David MAGAW, decd.
Tract in Rye twp, 30 a. cleared, sold as property of Robert MAGAUGHY, decd.

248. Wednesday, 2 January 1793
An advertisement has appeared in Mr. KLINE's paper 10 December, signed James WALLACE, Sheriff of Cumberland Co, to sell my plantation & tanyard as a delinquent collector of taxes. This is to warn all good people from bidding as I have the Treasurer's receipt for the amount of my Duplicate in Full, which Mr. Wallace knows. Thomas TURBETT
2 tenaments & lots on the north east corner of Louther St, Borough of Carlisle, late the property of Johnny POLLOCK. Lots, which back on Letart Spring, have long been used as Breweries. Apply to John DUNCAN (Jan .9)
The subscriber, by long & severe sickness, finds his strength so much reduced as to render him unable to pursue his present business & having an assortment of goods on hand, he would dispose of them to some young man or 2, who would rent his shop, cellars &c. John HUGHES, in Carlisle. Stand is one door from the Court House in the Main Street. (Jan 9)
Jacob WEITZEL, Collector, being pressingly called on to make up his accounts for the first year, requests all who have not paid in his division to make payment in 30 days. (Jan 9)
The report that James ROSS of Carlisle intends to remove from this place is entirely without foundation, & he intends to continue to teach Greek & Latin at the west end of High st. (Jan 9)
Alexander M'BRIDE, Collector, requests of West-Pennsborough twp,to make payment of tax due.
Whereas James LAUGHLIN executed a bond to George ANDERSON of Cumberland Co., which said LAUGHLIN has paid off & received a receipt in full. (Jan 16)

248. Wednesday, 2 January 1793 (Con't.)

Adam CLELAND has disposed of his real property & moved to Newville, at which place he intends to reside for some time. Those with outstanding accounts are to see Samuel FINDLAY, Esq., in Carlise. (Jan 16)

George M'ELHENEY passed 8 bonds of 15 pounds & 1 of 10 pounds, dated 1793, to William CHRISY, of Milford Cts., Mifflin co. This warns persons not to take assignment on same. (Jan 16)

The executors of the estate of Robert PATTERSON, decd, hereby give notice to a certain William COWAN, to come or send for a watch, which was left as a pledge in consideration for a final amount within 6 weeks. (Jan 16)

249. Wednesday, 23 January 1793

Notice is given to persons desirous of holding Pews or parts of Pews in the Episcopal church in this Borough regarding pew rents. Stephen FOUCK(?), Junr. & Joseph T. JAMES, Wardens.

John DUNCAN returns his thanks to the customers of the late partnership of Robert COLWELL & Co. He proposes attending at the house of Capt. RIPPEY for the last time 4 March next for final settlement. Bonds are in the possession of Mr. S. COLWELL. John DUNCAN, Surviving partner.

250. Wednesday, 30 January 1793

Atchenson LAUGHLIN has laid off a number of lots on the East side of Big-Spring in addition to Newville, which he proposes to dispose of by way of Lottery.

Robert STURGEON, Collector of Revenue for Mifflin Co gives notice to those in arrears to settle up at his office in Lewistown.

The mildness of the present winter season is allowed to exceed that of every winter in the memory of the oldest inhabitants.

Alexander M'KEEHEN declares that he is in perfect health & is of sound mind & memory; that he never was a candidate nor had he ever any pretensions to the sheriff's office. Thomas TURBETT says that he is also of sound mind & memory & attends his Tanyard in Mifflin Co & renounces all claim to the sheriff's office in Cumberland Co. Samuel TURBET declares that he is not the least likely that he follows his business in Lancaster Co; that he never had any pretentions to the Sheriff's office in Cumberland Co. Now be it known to all whom it may concern, that James WALLACE (in whatever state he may be) or any thing that may be said to the contrary notwithstanding is bona fide the High Sheriff of Cumberland Co.

The fire company is notified of their next quarterly meeting. Samuel LAIRD, Clerk.

251. Wednesday, 6 February 1792

Sheriff's Sale: One sorrel stallion, also dwelling house of John BEAM, a quantity of wheat & a remnant of merchandise, seized & taken in execution as property of said BEAM & Baltzer WALTER.

Last night, 25 January ult. from Captain Jacob SLOUGH's detachment, deserted William BROWN, of Captain KERSEY's company. He is about 38 years old, 5' 9 3/4" high, dark complexion, black eyes & hair, by trade a stone mason. John FLAKE, of said company; 35 years of age, 5' 7" high, dark complexion, black eyes & hair, a weaver by trade. $10 reward from Thomas BUTLER, Major Commanding.

This day the partnership of BELL & GIVEN dissolves by mutual consent. Persons owing should pay up. The pot-ash manufactory is carried on by John GIVIN, Shippensburgh.

251. Wednesday, 6 February 1792 (Con't.)

Baltimore: Yesterday morning (Jan. 29) about 2 miles from this town, the post-Boy carrying the Eastern Mail, was stopped by a slender, well-dressed, armed man about 5' 10" high, who ordered him to light or he would blow his brains out; on which the boy got off the horse & was ordered to go on. The fellow mounted & rode towards town until he came to the road that leads to Mr. VAN BIBBER's place, when the boy lost sight of him. Soon after, a negro man belonging to William SMITH, rope maker, going to work, espied the horse and nearby found some of the letters torn & scattered about. One letter from John VAN LEAR of William's Port to John MORREL mentioned that it contained $60. Ditto Charles WHITLOCK to Mrssrs. John FIELD & Son, Philadelphia mentioning a draught on Mr. Peter BLIGHT for $600. Ditto William WOOD of Port-Tobacco contained a draught of Gabriel WOOD.

Carlisle: On Friday the 1st inst. departed this life in the -- year of her age, after a tedious illness, Mrs. Amelia M'CLURE, wife of Charles M'CLURE, & on Sabbath Day last, remains were interred. She has left a husband & 4 small children to lament their unspeakable loss.

William REED, living in Washington Co, Pa, offers 1 shilling reward for return of runaway apprentice boy named John DEPEW; about 17 years of age, 5' 7" high, dark complexion, very talkative.

252. Wednesday, 13 February 1793

Whereas John MOORE, Merchant, Carlisle, intends moving out of this county in the spring, he requests all indebted to him to make payment.

Married on Thursday last by Rev. Dr. DAVIDSON, at the farm of John DUNBAR, Thomas URIE to Miss Margaret DUNBAR d/o of John DUNBAR.

To be sold - dwelling house now occupied by Joseph HUDSON, next door to the printing office; also a house & lot in possession of John WALKER, opposite Robert SMITH. Apply to George STEVENSON, Carlisle.

253. Wednesday, 20 February 1793

Archibald LOUDON's new tobacco manufactory, 2 doors west of Ephraim STEEL on the south side of the Public Square, where he manufactures from inspected Leaf. Said LOUDON still carries on the Book Binding business as usual in its various branches.

Whereas Thomas HUNTER intends to leave this town, he ernestly requests all persons indebted to him to make payment. (Carlisle)

Whereas my wife Mary hath eloped from my bed & board without any just cause; & although I have since her elopement requested her to return, & in order to remove any groundless apprehensions on her part, I have offered in the presence of a number of reputable persons, to give her any reasonable security she may require . . . I am determined not to pay any debts of her contracting. William BROWN

254. Wednesday, 27 February 1793

"Mr. Kline: In our Gazette of the 20th inst. I find myself made the unfortunate object of public attention by a notice from my husband to the public, not to trust me on his account. This Notice was needless & unnecessary. I never had taken up anything on his credit, & however destitute I may have been turned from his door, after having spent upwards of 30 years of my life in his labour, I should not have had recourse to so precarious & uncertain support". She requested a divorce to the supreme court in the January term, stating her complaints against her husband & asked for support. A subpoena on that petition was served upon him by the Sheriff. The application which he alludes to & his proposed security were made to rid him of her maintenance, as "he knew that I dare not return... I had just cause to dread barbarous treatment, personal indignity & loss of my life, then I hope I shall be enabled to end my latter days in quiet & tranquillity, exempt from domestic strife, & die as I have lived, free from reproach in the arms of my dutiful & affectionate children whose lives have been too long embittered by the misfortunes of their mother and the cruelty of their father. Mary BROWN"

The partnership of SHELDON & FOULK being dissolved by mutual consent, all persons who have demands against said partnership, come forward. (Holy Forge).

Whereas Charles BOVARD intends leaving this town, requests all persons indebted to him to make payment before 15 May. (Carlisle)

Wanted, a good active apprentice to the hand-screw business. Apply to David HOUSE, Carlisle.

255. Wednesday, 6 March 1793

The horse Alleghany Farmer will cover mares this season at the house of John PARKER, West-Pennsboro twp, Cumberland Co.

To be sold or rented agreeably to will of William BLAINE, Esq., decd., farm whereon he lived, 230 a., 2-story house, double barn, grist mill & still house. Is situated on the bank of Sherman's Creek. Apply to Samuel LYON or John ARMSTRONG, Ex'rs.

256. Wednesday, 13 March 1793

Sheriff's Sales: Half part of a Messuage & lot in Shippensburgh, marked on the general plan No. 1; sold as property of John DAVENPORT.

50 a. in Tyrone Twp., with improvements, sold as property of Frederick DORMELY.

200 a. in Lack Twp., Mifflin co, adj lands of SHEARER on the east & the Tusearora Mountain, seized by John BOGGS, a late Sheriff & sold as the property of Andrew FARRIER.

Strayed or stolen from Andrew PROBST, living in Strasburgh, Franklin Co, a sorrel mare.

To be sold - tract in Huntingdon co & twp, 3 1/2 miles from Huntingdon Town, 534 a., dwelling house & other necessary buildings. Apply to Jacob WIDNOR in Huntingdon or Jacob MIER on the premises.

Was taken up in the mountain on Saturday morning last, near Godfrey's, a small brown horse with a bob tail. John KRUNDLE, York Co.

Was found in the ?? of Thomas PARKER, Borough of Carlisle, the following supposed to be stolen: 2 coverlids, one mattock, 2 axes, 2 hilling hoes & a number of bags &c. Persons who may have lost the above may call with George LOGUE, Esq. in Carlisle & prove their property.

257. Wednesday, 20 March 1793

Susannah THOMPSON, widow of the late Parson THOMPSON, opposite the house formerly James POLLOCK's Tavern, has received in addition to her former large assortment, a variety of articles in the fancy & ornamental way for ladiess, a great number of hats of different kinds, wines & spirits, cheap Irish linens &c.

Lewis FOULK requests all persons indebted to him to make payment by 20 April next, as he means to leave this state.

The elegant horse Sweeper will cover mares this season at the stable of Jeremiah M'KIBBON, town of Newville.

257. Wednesday, 20 March 1793 (Con't.)

The Dragon will cover mares at the stable of Charles M'KOY, Tyrone twp, Shearman's valley. The Dragon is a beautiful black, 16 1/2 hands high.

Young Herrard will cover this season at the stable of George ALLEN, Strasburgh.

The beautiful horse Young Chester Ball to cover mares this season at the stable of Jacob MYERS, 1 mile from Yellow Breeches, between York & Liberty Roads.

Jolly Ranter will be kept for mares at Mr. Francis DONNALD's in Cumberland Co, Newton twp, near the Big Spring. Attendance given by Joseph M'DANIEL. The grain for the season to be delivered at Samuel M'CORMICK's, John SCHOUILERS & Archibald LAUGHLIN's Mills.

This day the partnership of Alexander & Samuel JACKSON is dissolved by mutual consent. Samuel JACKSON will continue to carry on the store as formerly, Mifflin Town.

Watch found upon road leading to Shippensburgh, between Carlisle & Mount Rock, now in the possession of William THOMPSON, Watch Maker, Carlisle.

Died on Saturday morning last, Mrs. Mary KLEINHOOF, about her 80th year, after nearly 3 months illness.

Alexander M'KEEHEN, Treasurer Cumberland Co, conceives it his duty to give information that the Sheriff of this county has not in his hands by Precepts against delinquent Collectors, the return day of proceeds being issued by him having expired, the authority of the Sheriff ended with it.

Ran away from James PAXTON, living in Cumberland Co, Dickinson twp, near Carlisle, an Irish indented servant named Peter KERRIGAN, about 5' 9-10" high, pretty well made, about 26 years of age, black complexion, has traveled a good deal through Ireland, England & some parts of Scotland & is very fond of talking of his travels, professes to be a Roman Catholic, has some little of the Brogue on some words, can read, write & cypher a little, & is a weaver to the trade.

258. Wednesday, 3 April 1793

Died at Ligonier on the evening of the 24th March, Mr. John BUCHANAN, formerly a citizen of Carlisle.

John DUNCAN, surviving partner, having attended at Shippensburgh of 4 March inst., to settle the account of the late partnership of Robert COLWELL & Co., but few persons paying attention thereto, owing as he supposes to the badness of the roads, he has again appointed the 27th of May next, as the last time.

259. Wednesday, 17 April 1793 [next available issue]

Was taken out of the stable of Simon SINGER in Carlisle a sorrel horse. Horse alone reward of $2 if brought to Mr. Geo. KLINE, Printer of Carlisle or Andrew CROUS, living at Simon SINGER's.

Married on Thursday last by Rev. Dr. DAVIDSON, Samuel SIMISON to Miss Peggy DENNY, both of this town.

In Carlisle, Monday morning, in the 24th year of her age, after a short illness, died Mrs. Jane BLAINE, wife of Mr. James BLAINE.

James ROSS thanks parents of this Borough who have placed their children in his school. In Carlisle, next door to the Printing Office.

Persons indebted to John MOORE, merchant are requested to make payment to William ALEXANDER, Esq. by 1 May next.

Strayed or stolen from plantation of Capt. John LAMB in Allen twp., Cumberland Co, an Iron Grey Horse.

259. Wednesday, 17 April 1793 (Con't.)
By writ directed to James WALLACE, to be sold a tract of 90 a., in Newton twp, with a grist mill & other improvements thereon; seized & taken as property of Adam HARBISON.

260. Wednesday, 1 May 1793 [Issues out of order on film, see next entry.]
Sheriff's Sale: 2 tracts in Tyrone Twp, co of Cumberland, one of 74 a. and 16 perches & patented & other adj 1st, 15 a. & 117 perches. Sold as property of Robert GREEN, decd.
Came to the place of Isaac DEARDORFF, living in Monaghan twp, York Co, an Iron Gray horse.
John GLEN offers reward for return of mare that strayed from Commons of Carlisle 16 April last.
Strayed or stolen from John KRYSER in Middletown, Cumberland Co, near CREIGHEAD's Mill, Yellow Breeches Creek, a strawberry roan horse. Bring to Mr. LEEPER's Mill at the head of Yellow Breeches to have reward.
Ran away from William AMBERSON, living in Pittsburgh, a mullatto slave named Harry; 23 years old, 5' 8-9" high, very much adicted to drink; took no cloaths with him except what he had on; short brown coat, striped jacket, union shirt, pair of coveralls dyed purple & a blanket. Formerly lived with Col. BLAINE in Carlisle.
To be sold at public vendue at the late dwelling house of Thomas WOODS, Dickinson Twp, Cumberland Co, a young stallion. William & Nathan WOODS, Ex'rs.
Whereas James WALLACE, Sheriff of Cumberland County has advertised a tract of 90 a. in Newton twp, Cumberland Co, with grist mill &c. as property of Adam HARBESON; the public are notified that no legal demand can be alleged against said estate as all incumbrances against said land and mills have been discharged. Adam HERBESON [sic]

261. Wednesday, April 24, 1793 [On microfilm out of sequence.]
Departed this life Monday the 22nd inst. in the 42nd year of his age, after a short illness, Hugh PATTEN, for some years a worthy inhabitant of this Borough. He was a sober, industrious, honest and religious man.
On Saturday in the morning of the 20th inst. departed this life, at York Town, Mrs. Martha GIBSON, in her 81st year; her remains taken to Lancaster and interred in the family burying ground.
Strayed from the Commons of Carlisle, small dark bay horse. Reward offered by John WELLEN.

262. Wednesday, 8 May 1793
Persons indebted to Thomas JOHNSTON, late of Juniata twp, Cumberland Co, decd, to pay up. Hugh GHORMLEY, Adm'r.
John COFFEY, having passed a note to a certain Thomas NICHOL, this is to warn all persons from taking assignment on this note.
To be sold by public sale at the dwelling house of the subscriber in Southampton twp, Cumberland Co, 4 miles east of Shippensburgh, plantation now in the possession of same of 164 a. with grist house and saw mill, dwelling house, double barn, still house &c. James LEEPER.
Francis ELLIS & John BROWN dissolve their partnership by mutual consent this day. Lewistown.

263. Wednesday, 15 May 1793
Married Tuesday the 14th inst. by Rev. Dr. DAVIDSON, Mr. James FLEMING to Miss Fanny RANDOLPH.

263. Wednesday, 15 May 1793 (Con't.)
Married at this Borough on Wednesday last, George HAMILTON, aged 86 years, to Catharine BOW, aged 73. Each had been married 2 times before and had both been in the single state but a short time before this union. Their friends tried to disuade them considering their great age & infirmaries, but they could not live without each other.
To be sold at the late dwelling house of Henry BROWN, Middleton Twp, Cumberland Co, livestock, household furniture &c.; also farm to let for 1 year. Rebecca BROWN & Benjamin JUNKIN, Adm'rs.
James POLLOCK informs that he has again opened a tavern at the former house of entertainment, Carlisle.
$4 reward for runaway Irish indented servant man named Alexander HAMILTON, 5'7" high, 18-19 years of age, brown hair & down look. John DAVIDSON, West Pennsbro', Cumberland Co.
Escaped from the prison yard of this co, a certain Thomas PARKER, 45 years, 5'9" high, sandy hair & white eyebrows. Says he is an Englishman. Robert GRAYSON, Jailor, Carlisle.

264. Wednesday, 22 May 1793
George STEVENSON has imported from London a fresh supply of drugs & medicines &c. (Carlisle)
Note from William COX, payable to Ralph BOWIE and James HAMILTON, attorneys at law; said COX has not received any value for said note, but perplexity, loss & disappointment. COX therefore warns all persons against taking same.
Stolen from John HAFFER, living in Derry Twp, Dauphin Co, 5 miles from Middleton, near Conowago Creek, a fox-colored mare.
The whole manor of Pompfrett to be sold, consisting of 16 Farms, near 300 a. each, at the house of Martin WITHINGTON in Sunbury. Sold at the same time & place a number of valuable lots, 5 a. each; most of them 1st rate meadow in good fence. John PENN & John PENN, Jr. Esqs. late proprietaries of the state of PA.
Strayed from a drove of pack horses between Strausburgh and Carlisle, 2 small bay mares; one had lost her right eye and had a bell on. $6 reward to whoever delivers them to A. SCOTT & Co. store in Strasburgh or the printer in Carlisle.

265. Wednesday, 29 May 1793
Persons indebted to the estate of Andrew CROCKETT, late of Allen Twp, decd, are requested to make payment. Elizabeth CROCKET [sic], George LOGUE & Thomas CLARK, Ex'rs.
Those who know William COX will not be surprized at his advertisement in last weeks paper complaining of loss & dissappointment and requesting his note for 15 pounds due in one month to Ralph BOWIE & James HAMILTON, his attornies, might not be received by any person until he received value for same. This notice might be interpreted injuriously to the character of his attornies if it passed unnoticed. The action in which Mr. HAMILTON was originally assumed by Mr. COX terminated at the last court in his favor.

266. Wednesday, 5 June 1793
To be sold at the house of William WOOD, Junr., decd, in Dickinson twp, Co of Cumberland, on Yellow Breeches Creek, livestock, waggon & gears, grain, farm utensils &c. Samuel & Richard WOODS, Ex'rs.

266. Wednesday, 5 June 1793 (Con't.)
All persons indebted to the estate of Alexander MURRAY, late of Toboybe Twp, Cumberland Co, decd, to make payment in one month. Agness MURRAY, William FISHER & Allan NISBET, Ex'rs.
Strayed or stolen off the Commons of Carlisle, bright bay horse. Jeremiah MILLER, Carlisle.

267. Wednesday 19 June 1793
Carlisle: a great quantity of rain has falled lately, with severe winds & has injured crops of wheat & rye locally.

268. Wednesday, 26 June 1793
All persons indebted to the estate of Hugh PATTON, late of Carlisle are requested to pay. Also selling general assortment of dry goods & groceries. Mary PATTON, Ex'r.
Joseph COWGILL, Ex'r. gives notice to all indebted to estate of Zephinah STARK, late of Derry Twp to pay.
Whereas George BITZ paid his obligations dated 30 Oct 1792 to Joseph BOGLE for 12 pounds 5 shillings and one penny and for the better security of the payment of which, Philip SCKLOSSER entered with him in the obligation. George BITZ cautions all from taking same.
Susannah TOMPSON has just received elegant trinkets, ear-rings, necklaces &c. Also has dry goods & groceries (Carlisle).
Archibald RAMSAY has just opened a store next door to Thomas FASTERS, in the house lately occupied by Mr. Lewis FOULK, where he is selling goods appropriate to the season. Also, strayed from the plantation of Samuel RAMSAY, a heifer.
Ran away from Thomas FOSTER in Carlisle, an indented servant boy named Charles O'NEAL 14 years of age, small for his years, freckled face, short brown hair.
On Saturday morning last a Duel was fought near Carlisle by Messrs. John DUNCAN & James LAMBERTON, when the former unhappily received a ball through his head, which instantly deprived him of life. His wife has lost an affectionate husband, his 5 children a tender parent, and society one of its most valuable citizens. He was honest, benevolent, generous and brave.
Strayed from the farm of John WILT, West Pennsboro' twp, a bay mare.

269. Wednesday 3, July 1793
All persons indebted for the use of Golden Farmer to pay John SIMONTON by 1 August.
Thomas STUBBS, Middletown, Dauphin Co, informs that he has lately erected a Furnace for Manufacturing Iron into Blistered Steel at Middletown on the Susquehanna, 9 miles below Harrisburg, & 92 miles west of Philadelphia, on the road leading to Pittsburgh.
Committed to Carlisle jail: a Negro boy, about 15 years of age, calls himself Bill and says he was born in Annapolis (MD) but will give no account of his master. Says he had a pass from George SLY, Esq. of Fredericksburgh.

270. Wednesday, 10 July 1793
Carlisle: The 17th anniversary of independence was celebrated by the Sons of Liberty & troop of Light Horse, the company of Light Infantry, & company of Artillery, in uniform, paraded on the commons & from thence

proceeded to the banks of the Conedogainet creek, at the farm of Capt. Matthew GREGG, late decd, where they took part in a cold collation.

A petition of the name of John HART, lately a liver at Big Spring, died on the road about a quarter of a mile from town, on Sunday afternoon last.

Married: At Pittsburgh on Monday the first inst., Mr. Ebenezer DENNY, Merchant to Miss Nancy WILKINS d/o John WILKINS, Esq.

Animal Electricity & Magnatism taught by Henry ROBERTS, living at Mr.WELCH's house in York St, the corner house below Mr. HUNTER's tavern, Carlisle.

Charles STINNECKE offers reward for horse strayed or stolen from Commons of Carlisle.

271. Wednesday, 24 July 1793

John George BUTTLER of Shippensburgh, informs that he intends opening a school in September next at his house in Shippensburgh.

William REED, living in Washington Co, PA seeks runaway Negro man named Thomas DOYER, formerly lived with Mathew LOUDON in Cumberland Co. About 30 years of age, 5' 7" high, very active, talks very much, excellent at playing on the Violin. He has a pass signed by a Mr. BRADFORD, an attorney of the Western Court & a Mr. Benjamin REED, which are counterfeit.

To be leased: Grist & saw mill on the Big Spring in West Pennsboro twp, Cumberland Co. late the property of Gabriel GLEN, decd. Apply to Alexander M'KECHAN in Carlisle or to Jane GLEN or Benjamin M'KEEHAN, ex'rs. on or near the premises.

Robert LUCK offers $20 reward for strayed or stolen mare, from the plantation of Atcheson LAUGHLIN, Newville, Cumberland County.

Aquilla JOHNS of Montgomery Co, MD, near the mouth of the Sineca, seeks runaway named Negro Dick, a very black fellow, thin vissige, about 5' 10-11" high. Ran at the same time Negro Rachel, Dick's wife, about 5' high, light black, has had several children, supposed to be with child.

John MONTGOMERY, in the Borough of Carlisle, selling school pocket books and large Bibles, testaments, spelling books, grammers, etc. Also coffee, sugar, tea.

Strayed from the plantation of William MOORE, light bay horse. Reward to paid by George COOPER.

James POLLOCK informs that he has again opened a tavern at his former house of entertainment.

Robert M'CALL selling plantation in West Pennsborough Twp, Cumberland Co, within 9 miles of Carlisle & 2 of Newville, on Big Spring, 240 a.

Strayed or stolen from Daniel WELLIR, Frederick Co, (MD), near Creagerstown, black mare.

Hugh RACHFORD has passed a note payable to a certain Lawry RAFFERTY & refuses to pay. (West Pennsborough twp.)

Sheriff's Sales: One lot of 15 a. adj lands of James YOUNG. One lot 10 a., adj Stephen DUNCAN. One lot with barn in Borough of Carlisle on Louther St, near William EAKINS; all seized as property of George STEVENSON, decd.

One house & lot in Borough of Carlisle, seized as property of John IRVINE.

Tract in Rye (now Juniata) twp, 280 a., with house, barn & sawmill; property of David ENGLISH, Sr.

Tract in Newton twp, 195 a. & 45 perches, log house on the leading road from Carlisle to Shippensburgh; seized in execution as property of Isaac SKYLES.

Tract in Greenwood Twp, in possession of ---- SWEEZY, 600 as.; seized as property of Michael HUFFNAGLE.

271. Wednesday, 24 July 1793 (Con't.)
Tract in Franklin Co, in occupancy of Andrew ROBINSON, 150 a.; adj William Rankin &c., seized by former Sheriff Robert SEMPLE as property of David MAGAW, decd.
Tract 6 miles below Carmichael's on the Juniata; seized by Thomas BUCHANAN, late Sheriff, as property of John MOORE.
200 a. in Middleton twp, adj lands of James ELLIOTT, now in tenure of Hugh M'KEAS, all right, title &c. of Samuel BIGHAM thereto.
200 a. in Lack Twp, Mifflin co, adj lands of --- SHEARER on the East & the Tusearora mountain. Seized & taken as property of Andrew FARRIER.
One undivided half of 930 a. of land in Fannet twp, Franklin Co, seized as property of Robert GRAY.
Also 2 tracts about 3 miles northeast of Shippensburgh, 500 a., adj each other, stone house & 2 lots of ground in Shippensburgh & 1 tract about 1 mile north of Shippensburgh, seized as property of Francis CAMPBELL, decd.

272. Wednesday, 31 July 1793
Matthew MILLER of Middleton twp, Cumberland Co. seeks Carolina Steers that strayed from his plantation.
Carlisle: Married on Thursday last by the Rev. Dr. DAVIDSON, the Rev. David DENNY to Miss Peggy LYON, d/o William LYON Esq. of this Borough.
W. ALEXANDER, Clerk, informs that the Quarterly Meeting of the Union Fire Co. will be held.
Reward offered by Epenetus HART, Fermanagh twp, Mifflin Co, for bay horse, strayed or stolen out of paddock of Mr. RHOADS on Penns-creek.
Whereas Patrick DOUGHERTY having passed a bond to a certain James TAYLOR; he cautions that he will not pay.
Charles STINNECKE of Carlisle offers reward for return of apprentice boy named George K. KAUFFMAN; about 13 years of age.
Sheriff's Sale: House & lot in Shippensburgh with appurtenances, seized & taken as property of John COPELY.

273. Wednesday, 7 August 1793
Carlisle: Reported from Borough of Easton, PA, a free negro man name of Thomas HERCULES was chosen Town-Clerk of that Borough by a decided majority of votes.
Married: June 25th, 1793 at the farm of Mr. John WILLIAMS, by the Rev. Samuel WAUGH, Mr. Andrew PARKER of Cumberland Co, to Miss Margaret WILLIAMS d/o John.
Meeting of inhabitants at Silver Spring Meeting House, East Pennsborough Twp, raised a subscription for relief of distressed French citizens. Oliver POLLOCK, Chairman; Andrew GALBREATH, Clerk.
Mary MONTEETH gives notice that whereas Robert TAYLOR of Milford twp, Mifflin Co, has obtained of her 2 notes, she will not pay.

274. Wednesday, 14 August 1793
Abraham WELLS living in Mifford twp, Mifflin Co, has taken in a stray mare.
John HULING, Collector of Revenue gives notice to distellers of Cumberland Co, to call on Joseph POSTLETHWAITE in Carlisle to settle accounts.

275. Wednesday, 21 August 1793
Notice to persons indebted to estate of late John DUNCAN, Merchant Carlisle, pay up Sarah E. DUNCAN, Sam. POSTLETHWAIT & James DUNCAN,

Adm'rs. His surviving partner Robert CALDWELL asks your attendance at house of Capt. William RIPPER in Shippensburgh.
Charles BOVARD has opened a cheap new store in York St, next door to Dr. George STEVENSON, nearly opposite to John WEBBER's store. Where he has for sale hardware, dry goods & groceries.
Jesse ADAMS of Lewistown has taken in a stray horse.
Jacob CARVER has taken up a sorrel horse between Carlisle & his plantation.
Jeremiah LAMBERTON, came to his plantation near John MOORE's, a stray black mare. (Dickenson twp, Cumberland Co.)
Carlisle: Friday last (Aug. 1) a number of inhabitants of East Pennsborough twp, Cumberland Co, met in a Grove of Walnut Trees on Silver Spring, near the house of Oliver POLLOCK, to celebrate Harvest Home. Oliver POLLOCK, Chairman; Mr. BERREHILL, Secretary. Many toasts were drunk.
Married: On Thursday the 8th inst., at Shippensburgh, by the Rev. Mr. LONG, Joseph KERR, merchant of Strasburgh to Miss Isabella RIPPEY, d/o Capt. William RIPPEY of Shippensburgh.

276. Wednesday, 28 August 1793
Elizabeth GEMMIL, John GEMMIL, John BROWN & Lazarus B. M'CLAIN being possessed of a most beautiful spot of ground in Huntingdon co, on banks of the Juniata, 1 1/2 miles below Water St., commands the trade of Morris's Cove, Frankstown, Sinking Valley, Warrior's Mark & Spruce Creek. They now propose to lay out the same in a town to be called Alexandria. The great road from Philadelphia to Pittsburgh passes through this town, as does the road to Woodcock Valley. Apply: Samuel LAIRD, Carlisle; John COLHOUN, Merchant, Chambersburgh; Galbreath PATTESON, Esq., Harrisburgh; Samuel MONTGOMERY, Merchant, Lewistown & Lazarus B. M'CLAIN & John BROWN near the proposed town.
Joanette Chirstine [sic] KNOEHE, late KIMMEL, a native of Wisbaden near Frankford, on the Maine, in Germany, who is known to have resided a considerable time in East Pennsborough twp, Cumberland Co, PA, is requested to call on John HALSE at Bethelehem, Co. of Northampton, where she will hear something to her advantage.

277. Wednesday, 4 September 1793
Mary M'CORMICK thanks the Ladies for their custom & informs that there is lately arrived at her house a young lady from Philadelphia who is a milliner. Business is in a house of Captain John HUGHS's near the Court House in Carlisle.
John CULBERTSON, Clothier, thanks his friends & the public for past custom, & he intends in keeping a stage as usual at the house of Major Samuel MONTGOMERY in Lewistown the 2nd Monday of each month; & the same day at Mifflintown at house of John WATSON , on Friday at Huntingdon at house of Alexander M'CONNELL.

278. Wednesday, 11 September 1793
Whereas Andrew WOLFE gave notes to Jonathan HASSAN, he refuses to pay same (Middleton twp, Cumberland Co.)
Lost near Carlisle a silver faced watch; maker's name John WOOD, Philadelphia; No. 8. Bring to John RHINE, Tavern-keeper in Carliele shall have $2 reward.

279. Wednesday, 18 September 1793

Ranaway from John MOORE, Dickinson twp, Cumberland co, a certain John BRIMINGHAM from Ireland. He is short 26 years of age; 5' 10-11" high; fair hair, sandy beard with whiskers.

Deserted from the Barracks at Carlisle, Adam DE WALT, about 24 years of age, 5'5" high; by trade a cooper, served his time in M'Allister's town; has a very great halt in his walk, but supposed his lameness is only pretended. Thomas BUTLER, Maj. Com.

The Union Bands of Matrimony between Geo. & Catharine HAMILTON, formerly BOS, my wife, being mutually dissolved & intends keeping so . . . & he will not pay her debts. Signed Geo. HAMILTON.

Whereas it has been reported that persons infected with the Malignant disease now prevailing in the City of Philadelphia, have been received into and are now living in my house, I have thought it a duty which I owe to myself and to the public to remove every fear which might have arisen. Nathaniel WEAKLEY. (Carlisle). The undersigned, physicians in Borough of Carlisle, do hereby certify that they have examined the premises of the house of Nathaniel WEAKLEY. That he appears to us not to be infected with the putrid fever. Samuel A. M'COSKRY, Charles STINNECKE, Lemuel GUSTINE.

William FINLEY, finding his name mentioned as a Candidate for the office of Governor, declines. (Westmoreland Co.)

The Commissioners of Cumberland Co. to meet in Carlisle to receive returns. Edward WEST, Sam. POSTLETHWAIT, Commissioners.

280. Wednesday, 25 September 1793

All indebted to estate of Doctor John M'CLESKEY,decd, late of Huntingdon Co, are requested to make payment. Richard BEATTY & Samuel MARSHALL, Ex'rs.

2000 young apple trees of different kinds sold by David BOWER, near Pipers Mill on Big Spring.

Stolen from David TORRANCE & John BLAIR in Frankstown twp, Huntingdon Co, the following: 1 white coat with breechens of same; 1 pair jacket of carded linen, 2 black silk handkerchiefs; 1 rifle gun short in the barrell &c.

Whereas a certain Hugh GIBSON of Toboyne twp, & Cumberland Co, obtained a bond from Abraham STALL of Toboyne twp, Shearmans Valley; said GIBSON has not performed his contract.

To be sold by public vendue at the house of Philip MILLER, decd, Borough of Carlisle; all the Household & Kitchen furniture; a complete set of Waggon-Makers' tools &c. Michael MILLER & William LEVIS, Ex'rs.

281. Wednesday, 2 October 1793

Came to plantation of George ARNOLD in Toboyne twp, a sorrel horse.

282. Wednesday, 9 October 1793

(June 17, 1793) Whereas John MILLIGAN & Margaret his wife, have by their petition to the judges of court of common pleas Co of Cumberland, set forth, that the will of Robert M'WHENNY, late of said co, after being proved before he register of wills in said co, & probate of said . . Before the said Will became registered, consumed by fire in the register's office; by which said will devised to said Margaret a certain plantation in twp of East Pennsborough in said Co. of 189 a.. Praying said court to supply said defect in said title arising from the loss of said will.

282. Wednesday, 9 October 1793 (Con't.)
All persons indebted to James GIVEN of Carlisle to make payment. Said GIVEN has just received from Baltimore a fresh supply of fall goods & Groceries.
Deaths in Philadelphia: Washington WOODHOUE, Printer; Mr. BARNES; Mr.Isaac MILLER; John COTTRINGER; Mr. GILCHREEST; Mrs. SYNG; Mr. MASON; Mr. Joseph TATEM; Mrs.HOLLAND of Front Street; Mr. David HICKMAN, Jun. &c. &c. (Sept. 28) Samuel POWEL, Esq., former Mayor of that city; Mr. Nicholas FOSBGBERG Sen.; Mr. A. CLOW, Merchant; Mr. KAY, one of the partners of the House of A. CLOW & Co.; Dr. GLENTWORTH; Mr. Charles SYNG; Mr. Philip PHENTOM; Mrs. Townsend SPEAKMAN, Apothecary; Mrs. HAINES, relict of the late Mr. Reuben HAINES; Mr. PENMAN; Mr. John TODD, Sen; Mr. JOHNSON, PRINGER & many others (October 5).
Joseph T. JAMES requests all persons indebted to him to discharge their debts. In his absence call on Mr. Robert SMITH at the Seven Stars, Carlisle.
Ranaway from William AMBERSON, Pittsburgh, mullato slave named Harry, about 28 years old and lived formely with Col. BALINE in Carlisle; is much addicted to drink. His brother lives with Dr. COSKRY & a woman he calls his wife with Mr. Stephen DUNCAN, he will no doubt be lurking about them.
John DAVIDSON of West Pennsburgh offers reward for runaway Irish indented servant man named Alexander HAMILTON; 19 years of age, 5' 7-8" high; short brown hair; down look.
Robert FAUCET discharged persons from taking a note he passed to Dr. GUSTINE, which he understands is conveyed to Peter ULER.

283. Wednesday, 16 October 1793
Sheriff's Sales: Tract in Hopewell twp, 330 1/4 a. lands & tenements of Robert MEANS & Martin HOLTERBAUM, Terre Tenant.
Also 2 tracts in twp aforesaid, adj each other, one 188 a. & other 300 a., lands of John KEENEY.
Likewise a tract in Newton twp, Co of Cumberland; adj lands of James PATTERSON, Alexander WOODBORN, John JOHNSTON, Sarah DAVIS; and James EWING, 113 a. & 57 perches; sold as property of Mary DAVISON, widow & heirs & children of Samuel DAVIDSON, decd.
Tract on Twp, 300 a., property of Jonathan HASON.
William WATSON, living in Rye twp, has taken in stray sheep.
To be sold: 2-story log house in Newville, with stack of chimneys 2 fire-places below & one above, house well covered with white pine shingles. Apply to Henry ROBISON.
Accounts of the last post from Philadelphia lay 3000 inhabitants of City have fallen victims to malignant fever which is still raging. The following are among the deceased: Jonathan D. SERGEANT, Esq., Mrs. RODGERS, wife of Rev. D. RODGERS, Mrs. KEPPLE, relict of Mr. Henry KEPPLE; Mr. YOUNG and Mr. DOOSON, Booksellers.

284. 23 October 1793
William ALLISON of Franklin Co offers reward for negro man named Tom, 5' 9-10" high.

285. 30 October 1793
Andrew CROUSE has opened a manufactor for tobacco of every kind, smoaking, chewing & snuff tobacco, and black and pigtail. He lives in York St., just opposite Mr. DUNCAN's nail factory.

285. 30 October 1793 (Con't.)

Aaron GAMBLE offers reward for mare missing from the enclosure of Samuel COLHOON, decd, East Pennsborough twp, 10 miles from Carlisle.

Persons having demands against Gabriel GORDON are desired to attend in Shipensburgh at the house of George M'CANDLESS. James LOWREY, Reuben GALLISPY, Trustees.

Persons indebted to John CREIGH are requested to make settlement.

Susan BROWNLEE will carry on the Milliner & Mantua making business in the corner house opposite to John HUNTERS, with the high porch.

286. 9 November 1793

A letter directed to the subscriber was given to a wagoner about 2 months ago, which is not yet come to hand. Reward offered. Henry Daniel DAELHAUSEN, Carlisle.

James GIVEN requests persons indebted to settle their accounts.

Married at Shipensburgh, Tuesday 29th ult. by Rev. COOPER, Dr. Samuel DAVIS, of Shippensburgh, to Miss Mary NEIL, d/o William NEIL, late of Baltimore.

Persons indebted to the estate of Philip SHROM, sadler, decd, are desired to pay the same to Joseph SHROM, adm'r. of said Philip.

Francis BURK of Carlisle offers reward for indented servant named Daniel M'LAUGHLIN, about 2 months from Ireland, about 27 years old, 5'7" high, dark coloured hair which hangs loose.

Nicholas CREUTZER has taken up a stray steer.

Died at Pittsburgh Thursday last, Samuel ALEXANDER, merchant, lately an inhabitant of this town.

Robert GIBSON of Middletown twp has taken up a stray calf.

John M'CURDY of Carlisle offers reward of 100 cents for apprentice lad named John BAKER, about 19 years old, 5'6" high, bound to the blacksmith business.

287. 20 November 1793

Just imported in the last vessels from Canton, London, Liverpool, Bristol, Amsterdam and Dublin and now selling by James GALLAGHER at his china, Queensware, and glass ware-house, Philadelphia.

Whereas Thomas KELLY hath by misrepresentation and in a fraudulent manner, obtained of me an instrument of writing, empowering him to make demand of and recover all my right, title & claim, as a legatee, against the estated & property of John & Agness WISHARD, decd, these are to warn all ex'rs. or others not to comply with said Thomas KELLY's demands. David M'DONALD.

Tract to be sold on state road between Carlisle & Shippensburgh in Newton twp., 220 a. John CALDWELL, Cumberland Co.

Persons indebted to Hugh WILSON are requested to make payment.

Sheriff's Sales: Tract in Mifflin Co, adj lands of the Widow MOORE, Robert CRAWFORD & A. MOORE, 271 a., property of Robert PATTON.

288. 27 November 1793

Several stills that were bespoke by those that cannot make payment, they are to be sold yet - David LINSEY, copper & tinsmith, Carlisle. Old stills & worms will be mended at lowest terms.

Notice not to take assignment on notes payable to Sarah REED. Bartholomew M'CARTNEY, James DEARMIT, Huntingdon Co.

Persons indebted to us are to make immediate payment. BELL & GIVEN, Shippensburgh.

289. 4 December 1793
Sale in town of Newville, house & Lot & cattle & furniture. Alexander BUCHANAN.
John LAMBERTON of Carlisle offers reward for missing horse.
Elizabeth M'COY, Rye twp., has taken up stray sheep.

290. 11 December 1793
Whereas John GROSHER obtained of me bonds in part pay of a tract of land in Mifflin Co, which he was to clear of all taxes, judgments & mortgages, which he failed to do. This is to forewarn persons not to take assignment on said bonds. John KEPNER.
Robert STODART, Middletown twp., has taken up a stray cow.
William BOYD, Paxton twp, Dauphin co, has taken up a stray mare.
Pursuant to last will of Robert BOYD, decd, the tract of land on which he lived in Ray's or the Big Island in Paxton twp, Dauphin Co, 260 a. William COOKE, Ex'r.
George KLINE of Carlisle offers reward for apprentice to the printing business, Andrew BROWN, Jr., about 18-19 years of age, 5'4-5" high, stout made, his hair is a dark colour which he wears tied, can play on the flute of which he is fond.
John SIMKINS offers reward for mare stolen from the house of Robert BLACKY, Rye twp.
To be sold, 2 houses & Lots in town of Huntingdon, one in Alleghany St., the other on Hill Street. George STAGLADEN.
John WILT of West-pennsborough twp offers reward for missing mare.

291. 25 December 1793
Married at Pittsburgh, Tuesday 17th inst, Steele SEMPLE, Attorney at Law, to Miss Kitty FOWLER, d/o Capt. George FOWLER, of Wingfield, Allegheny Co.
Sales of 30 a. in Fermanaugh twp, adj lands of the heirs of John HAMILTON & others, near the Juniata river, property of James CLARKE, at the suit of John KINNARD. Wiilliam WILSON, Sheriff.
Sheriff's Sales: Four lots in Carlisle, one bounded by lot of John ANDERSON, property of John THOMAS.
124 a. in Greenwood twp, adj John BUCHANAN & Susquehanna River, property of Christopher MONTZ, decd.
126 a. with small house in Greenwood twp, property of Peter SHAW.
Sheriff's Sale of land in possession of James LAMON, in Newton twp, Cumberland Co., bounded by Joseph M'GOSSOG, James LAUGHLIN, John CARSON, & Big Spring, 73 a., property of James LAMON.
Sheriff's Sale: 144 a. on Crooked Creek in the name of Nicholas SCHAFFER, Huntingdon twp.
526 a. adj SKELLY's tract on Rayston Branch of Juniata, in Hopewell twp, in the name of Thomas BRANDON.
2287 a. between Bramble Spring & Limestone Gap, adj BUCHANAN's land & the LOOUDON land, in Hopewell twp, in the name of John FULTON.
All the property of Joseph DONALDSON in Springfield twp, bounded by George CLUGAGE & ASHMAN & Company, property of Robert CLUGAGE, decd.
50 a. of Samuel CHARLTON.
Also undivided half part of tract belonging to BARNIT & Col. Hugh DAVIDSON, adj lands of the Bedford Company & George STAINS (?).
224 a. in Springfield twp, property of Robert BARNET.
100 a. bounded by Nathaniel GERARD & John HEFFNEY in Huntingdon twp, property of Robert THOMPSON.

291. 25 December 1793 (Con't.)
Joseph THORNBURGH informs those indebted to him that his books are taken out of the hands of John MILLER & put into those of James DUNCAN, Esq.
Jacob BYERS of Middleton twp has taken up a stray bull.
Stage to be sold where the subscriber now occupies, 50 a. - Samuel COYLE, living on the premises.
Persons indebted to the Bedford Company (Bedford Iron-works, Huntingdon Co), are desired to call at the furnace. Thomas CROMWELL.
George WILSON, Barree twp, near Shaver's Creek, Huntingdon co, has taken up 4 stray hogs.
Hugh M'CORMICK has taken up a stray cow.

292. Wednesday, January 1, 1794
Sheriff's Sales: Two lots in borough of Carlisle, bounded by Pomfret st, Bedford st, & a 20' alley on the north; also two other lots in Carlisle, bounded on the west by lot of John ANDERSON, property of John THOMAS.
124 a. in Greenwood twp., adj. John BUCHANAN & the Susquehanna River, property of Christopher MONTZ, decd.
126 a. with small house & 2 a. cleared, in Greenwood twp., property of Peter SHAW.
William DAVIDSON, Middleton twp., 1 mile from Carlisle, has taken up a stray steer.

293. Wednesday, 8 January 1794
Melancholy Accident - A few days since in Newburg twp., York co., about 10 miles from York, Matthias SURGAR mistakenly shot & killed Andrew SCIPE.
Jonathan FOSTER, boot & shoe manufacturer, carries on his business in High St., Carlisle, in the house formerly the property of John AGNES, Esq., decd., opposite Robert MILLER, tanner.
Hugh KENNEDY, Pomfret St, Carlisle, has taken up a number of stray sheep.
John WEBBER has received from London & Glasgow an Elegant Collection of Books for sale.
Agreeable to the last will of Samuel RIPPEY, senior, decd., will be sold 200 a., adj. west end of Shippensburgh, Franklin co. William RIPPEY, Samuel RIPPEY, Exr's.
Morrocco pocket book lost in Shippensburg, in which is a note executed by Humphry MONTGOMERY. Thomas ALEXANDER, Shippensburgh.
James CAROTHERS, West-Pennsborough twp., offers reward for stolen horse.

294. Wednesday, 15 January 1794
David WILLIAMSON, Middleton twp., has taken up a stray cow.
Joseph HAYS has for sale, in the store lately occupied by Thomas HUNTER, York St., Carlisle, Dry Goods & Groceries.
Sales of unseated land in Mifflin co. for taxes are postponed until 4 Feb.: John M'CONNAL, Thomas ANDERSON, John WILSON, Commissioners, Lewistown.
Persons indebted to the estate of James LAUGHLIN, junior, of Newton twp., decd., are requested to make payment. Robert LAUGHLIN, Adm'r.
John LITTLE, Huntingdon co., Berree twp., offers reward of one shilling for apprentice boy named Samuel HARPER.
Stewart HERBERT, Hagerstown (Md.), offers reward for stolen horse.

295. Wednesday, 22 January 1794
John PURDY, Newton twp., has taken up a stray mare.
Strayed from the plantation of John HOGE in East-Pennsborough twp., a grey mare. Reward will be paid by Gottlieb KINZLE or John HOGE.

295. Wednesday, 22 January 1794 (Con't.)
Boatman wanted - Generous wages will be given for boatmen to go to New Orleans, clever fellows who wish to engage, will apply to James BLAINE in Carlisle.

296. Wednesday, 29 January 1794
David MILLER, Juniata, has 80 lots laid out on Juniata River, to be called Millers Town. Lots to be disposed of by lottery. Tickets may be had of John ELDER, Harrisburgh; Robert SMITH of Carlisle, George M'CORMICK, merchant at Patterson's Mills, Mifflin co., or to the subscriber, David MILLER, at the town.
James ROWNEY, Carlisle, has taken up a stray heifer.
To be rented - houses & lots in Carlisle; also building which lately belonged to John POLLOCK. Apply Samuel POSTLETHWAIT or James DUNCAN, Carlisle.
Sheriff's Sales: House & lot in Shippensburgh, taken as the property of Robert HAMMIT; also tract near Carmichals, on Juinata, property of James MOORE.
Stephen DUNCAN, Carlisle, has taken up a stray heifer.
William M'FARLANE, Big Spring, requests payments of debts.

297. Wednesday, 5 February 1794
George HEARST, Carlisle, has taken up a stray heifer.
Austin LEAKE offers reward for lost purse. Deliver to himself or to John MILLER, both living in Carlisle.
To be rented - convenient house in the Alley, near the centre square of Carlisle, now in the tenure of Mrs. M'CORMICK, Milliner. John HUGHES.

298. Wednesday, 12 February 1794
Died Friday last at his farm in East-Pennsborough twp., in his 80th year, James PARKER; his remains interred in the Old Burying Ground on Conodoguinet, about one mile from this borough.
For rent - stage & farm on Great Road between Carlisle & Shippensburgh, now in possession of William M'CRACKEN; also tavern in Shippensburgh known by the sign of the Black Horse, now in the tenure of Patrick COCHRAN; also 123 a. in Lurgan twp., Franklin co., adj. William LINN, Col. MILLER & others. Apply to William M'CRACKEN or John PEEBLES.
Nathan HAYS offers reward for mare missing from the pasture of Joseph CONNELLY, West Pennsbro- twp., Cumberland co.

299. Wednesday, 19 February 1794
Doctor M'COSKRY requests persons indebted to him to make payment.
Nathaniel WEAKLEY continues keeping a House of Entertainment at the sign of the Lamb, formerly kept by William REINEY, in York st., Carlisle.
For sale - A lot of ground with two-story log house & back buildings thereon, in Carlisle, bounded on north by High st., on east by lot in the tenure of William ALEXANDER, on south by a 20' alley, & on north by lot in the tenure of William LEVIS, property of William BLAIR, junr., decd. Isaiah BLAIR & William G. HOLMES, Adm'rs.
House & lot on South St., adj. Casper KROP in Carlisle, to be sold. Valentine EGOLFF.
Jacob WYNKOOP, at Blaine's Mill, Middleton twp, has taken up a stray horse.
Joseph CORBETT, Wayne twp., Mifflin co., has taken up a stray mare.

300. Wednesday, 26 February 1794
To be let - House & lot now in the tenure of Robert GUTHRIE; apply to Major Thomas BUTLER or John ARTHUR.
Cold Iron Manufactory, carried on by Robert HUNTER & Mr. M'MANNES, where they make all sorts of nails, near the Printing Office, Carlisle.
Mark M'CAUSLAND requests persons indebted to him to make payment.

301. Wednesday, 5 March 1794
Died on Friday last, after a short illness, in her 56th year, Mrs. Sarah ALLEN, relict of David ALLEN.
Selling house & lot in High st., adj. Robert MILLER, Esq., late the property of John HENRY, decd. William ALEXANDER & Robert MILLER, jun., Ex'rs.
Whereas John MILLHOUSE of Milford twp. passed 4 bonds of 50 pounds each payable unto William WILSON of Milford twp., Mifflin co., in consideration of a tract of land, he forewarns persons from taking assignment until said WILSON complies with his deed of conveyance.
To be sold agreeable to last will of Zephiniah STARKS, decd., plantation of 213 a., whereon he lived, Mifflin co., Derry twp., 1 mile from Lewistown. Joseph COWGILL, Ex'r.
Whereas the marriage covenant between Deborah my late wife and me, Timothy DOTY of Mifflin co., is by mutual consent dissolved, and the said Deborah is now separated from my bed & board: This is to forewarn persons from trusting her on my account, as I shall pay no debts of her contracting after this date.
Thomas STEELE, Augusta Co., near Staunton, Va., offers reward for mullato man named Rube, 5'10" high, about 23 years of age.

302. Wednesday, 12 March 1794
Married 18th February in Wayne twp., Mifflin Co., by Rev. Mathew STEVENS, William STANLEY to Miss Petty ARMSTRONG, both of the same place.
At Lewistown in Mifflin Co., married on the 4th inst. by Rev. James JOHNSTON, Thomas JOHNSTON to Miss M. PHINNES.
Died at his farm in Mifflin co., February 28th, John HARRIS, Esq., aged 71 years, after a long & painful illness, leaving wife & children. In said county, died Mrs. Martha NELSON, wife of Robert NELSON.
The horse Young Ranter will cover mares at the stable of James M'CLURE, Tobyne twp., Shearman's Valley.
Wanted as an apprentice to the Hair Dressing business, a lad of 14-15 years of age. He will be taught bleeding & tooth drawing. Apply to Frederick BOYER.

303. Wednesday, 19 March 1794
Died in her 44th year, in a very sudden manner, Monday morning last, Mrs. Mary COOPER, wife of Charles COOPER of this borough, leaving husband & 4 children.
Tract to be sold in Middleton twp., Cumberland co., 5 miles from Carlisle, 2 miles from Waggoner's, 364 a.; James HARPER, living on the premises.
Thomas HIBBEN, Shippensburgh, at the sign of the Bear, seeks too [sic] apprentices to the black smith & sickle making business.
The horse Blue Dun will cover mares this season at the stable of the subscriber, Allen twp, 2 miles from Mr. EGE's iron works, 1 mile from Yellow-Breeches. Jacob MYERS.

303. Wednesday, 19 March 1794 (Con't.)
Persons indebted to the estate of Robert GALBRAITH, decd., in Lisburn, Allen twp., are requested to make their payments. Mary GALBRAITH, James GALBRAITH, Andrew GALBRAITH, Adm'rs.
John SHEAFFER, Tyrone twp., Cumberland co., Shearman's Valley, has taken up a stray mare.
To be sold - stone house & lot on King St., Shippensburgh, property of George SPRECHER. Mathew HENDERSON, John HEAP, David M'KNIGHT, Auditors, who request persons indebted to said George SPRECHER to pay their debts to John HEAP.
To be sold at the dwelling house of the late Sarah ALLEN, Carlisle, decd., 3 tobacco presses & furniture. James ROSS, William ALEXANDER, Ex'rs.
Persons indebted to Archibald RAMSEY of Carlisle are requested to pay off their accounts.

304. Wednesday, 26 March 1794
Thomas HUMES, Middleton twp., has taken up a stray heifer.
The horse Young Irish Grey will cover mares this season at the stable on the plantation late of John YOUNG, decd., 2 miles from Mount-Rock. John & Thomas HUGHES.
Persons indebted to Christian HOLLINGER, Carlisle, shoe & boot making, are requested to make payments.
Whereas the marriage convenant between Barbara my wife & me, Ludwik CHRISTIAN, is dissolved because she hath forsaken me, this is to forewarn persons from trusting her on my account.

305. Wednesday, 2 April 1794
Sheriff's Sales: 400 a. bounded by William RAMSAY on the north, property of James BARNIT.
50 a. bounded by land of Samuel CHARLTON; also one undivided half part of a tract in the name of BARNIT & Col. Hugh DAVIDSON, adj. lands of the Bedford Co. on the north-east & George STAINS on the south-west, 224 a. in Springfield twp., both the property of Robert BARNIT.
160 a. bounded by Patrick FITZSIMONS, Robert STITT & Hugh ROBISON in Dublis twp., property of Amos MOORE.
The horse Sportsman will cover mares this season at the stable of George CLARKE, Green-castle.
Notice to distillers - John HULING, Collector of the Revenue, East Pennsborough.
Whereas John DONNELLY of York co. obtained a single bill from me for the sum of nine pounds, 15 shillings for a mare . . . this is to warn persons not to take assignemnt on said bill. Andrew MOORE.

306. Wednesday, 9 April 1794
To be sold - plantation in Milford twp., Tuscarora valley, Mifflin Co., adj. lands late of Samuel LYON & James RODMAN, 439 a. John LYON.
Robert SMYTH has commenced the blue dying business at the house of James PEEPLES, near William BARR's in Shippensburgh.

307. Wednesday, 16 April 1794
John WEBBER has removed his store to the house formerly the Post Office, directly opposite to where he did live.
On Monday last, Lieut. Richard HAZLEWOOD was thrown from his horse & killed. This accident happened on the mountain near Strasburgh; buried in the ground adj. this borough.

307. Wednesday, 16 April 1794 (Con't.)

Married on 15th inst., by Rev. Dr. DAVIDSON, John MILLER of Mount Rock, to Miss Jean SEMPLE, d/o Robert SEMPLE.

Tract for sale in Path Valley, Franklin Co., 1 mile north of the upper meeting house, adj. lands of David CAMPBLE's heirs, 437 a. Thomas BLAIR.

Whereas I understand that Robert & Matthew TAYLOR have proposed & advertised for sale a tract in Derry twp., Dauphin co., late the property of Ann ??, decd., which land the said decd. did in her last will bequeath to the heirs of her son John SAMPLE, this is to forewarn persons not to purchase said property. John SAMPLE.

John COLLET has opened a House of Entertainment on the North side of the Shade Gap, between the Burnt Cabbins & Huntingdon, where he has provided good hay, oats, chopped rye & cut straw for wagoner's horses & everything necessary for travellers.

Wednesday, 23 April 1794 [Issue not available.]

308. Wednesday, 30 April 1794

Delinquent distillers of Mifflin co. receive last notice - Robert STURGEON, Collector of the revenue, Mifflin co.

John JOHNSTON has opened a House of Entertainment at the sign of the Seven Stars, nearly opposite George M'CLELLAN's store in Lewistown. He has laid a good stock of Liquors.

William WALLACE, Carlisle, requests payment of debts.

The horse Mark Anthony will be let to mares this season at the stable of Robert SMITH in Carlisle.

William EAKEN has removed to the sign of the Black Horse, formerly kept by Robert GRAYSON, opposite William WALLACE's sign of the Bear, where he continues to keep a house of entertainment.

Persons indebted to the estate of William DUNCAN, southampton twp., decd., are requested to make payment. David DUNCAN, Ex'r.

Tract to be sold on Loss Creek, Mifflin Co., 1 1/2 miles from Mifflintown, 251 a.; excellent mill-seat. Apply to John HENDERSON on Loss Creek. John DENNY, Middletown twp.

Persons indebted to estate of William WOOD, Junr., decd., are requested to make speedy payment. Samuel WOODS & Richard WOODS, Ex'rs.

Proposals for erecting a bridge over Kishacoquillas creek to be accepted. Thomas ANDERSON & John WILSON, Commissioners.

Mary M'CORMICK, having removed from John HUGHES' house in the alley to the new house in High St., next to James LAMBERTON's store. She carries on the milliner & mantua making business.

James SPOTSWOOD, tobacconist, Carlisle, informs the late customers of the decd. Mr. & Mrs. ALLEN, for whom he carried on the business these several years past, that he will carry on as usual at the said house.

Whereas Cornelius VANDERBELT, Newton twp., passed 3 bonds payable unto Ezekiel MITCHEL of Newton Twp., Cumberland Co., this is to forewarn persons from taking assignment on said bonds, as he will not pay until Ezekiel MITCHEL complies with his deed of conveyance.

The horse High-Flyer is now standing on the farm of James YOUNG in Huntingdon Co., Shirley twp., on the Straight road leaving to Huntingdon Town, 6 miles from Col. ASHMAN's Furnace.

William PATTERSON, living at the head of Letart Spring, has taken up 4 stray sheep.

309. Wednesday, 14 May 1794
John DAVIDSON, West Pennsborough twp., Cumberland Co., offers reward for Irish indented servant, a man named Alexander HAMILTON, about 5'8" high, 19 years of age, short brown hair, looks down.
Married on Thursday last by Rev. Dr. DAVIDSON, Major Samuel JACKSON of Mifflin Town to Miss Peggy RAMSAY, d/o James RAMSAY of this town.
Married the same evening, Jehu WOODART to Miss Jane CLENDINAN, both of East Pennsborough twp.
Died Thursday last, Andrew COLHOON, carpenter of this town.
James ROSS continues to teach the Greek & Latin languages as usual next door to the Printing office & is not about to remove from this place, as it has been falsely reported.
Sheriff's Sales: Two tracts adj. each other in Greenwood twp., bounded by lands of George PFOUTZ, John LONG & Peter COFFMAN; 125 a., property of John PFOUTZ, Senior.
Tract in Newton twp., adj. lands of Robert LUSK, 115 a., property of Alexander RATCHFORD. James WALLACE, Sheriff.
Notice to purchasers of non-resident land in Huntingdon Co., John BLAIR, John SHAVER, Commissioners.
James GEDDES, Cumberland Co., Westpensborough twp., offers reward for apprentice boy named Aaron PENWEL, in his 18th year of age, 5'6" high, slim made; had on & took with him 2 shirts of hemp linen, pair of trowsers tow cloth, pair of black linsey, jacket of same, of a whitish coloured coat witht metal buttons, pair of new shoes tied with strings, a half worn wool hat.
John SIGGENS, one mile from Carlisle, offers reward for missing mare.
Harrisburgh mail stage starts from Carlisle every Monday morning at 4 o'clock from house of Thomas FOSTER, arrives at Philadelphia on Wednesday at house of Abraham SHARDINE, same week. William COLEMAN.

310. Wednesday, 21 May 1794
The partnership of Patrick M'MANNES & Robert HUNTER is dissolved. The business will be carried on at the same place by Robert HUNTER, where all sorts of cut nails may be had on the lowest terms.
Mulatto man to be sold, 21-22 years of age, registered slave sold for want of having sufficient employment, to keep him from bad company. He can plow, chop & drive a waggon. William MILLER in Carlisle.
Alexander OFFICER, Westpensborough twp., has taken up a filey.
Richard DOWLIN to apply for patent for land he now lives on, at Raystown Branch, 8 miles from Huntingdon.
William M'CLURE offers reward for missing horse. Deliver to Col. William LUSK, Dickinson twp. or himself.
Robert DAVIDSON offers reward for mare missing from the commons of Carlisle.
Tract for sale, 400 a. in Berkeley Co., Va., apply to Ezekial BULL, living on the premises.
Whereas William WHARTON gave 2 notes to William KENNY for five pounds each, for which he has paid said KENNY, but KENNY's wife has secreted said notes from him. This is to warn persons from taking assignments from her upon them, as I have paid him off.

311. Wednesday, 4 June 1794
Deserted on the night of 29 May: David CARSON, about 21 years of age, 5'7", fair hair, which he wears short, stoops much in walking; Thomas FEER, by trade a wagon maker, about 20 years of age, 5'10" high, fair

complexion, light short hair. Charles MARTIN, Ensign, U.S. Legion, Barracks at Carlisle.

312. Wednesday, 11 June 1794
Charles LEEPER offers reward for horse missing from the farm of William MILLER, near Mount Rock, Cumberland Co. Deliver to William or John MILLER, Mount, or to Charles LEEPER.
William NOBLE offers reward for horse which strayed from the plantation of James NOBLE in East Pennsborough Twp., Cumberland Co. Deliver to him or to James NOBLE, within 5 miles of Harris's Ferry on Susquehanna.
Susannah THOMPSON, opposite James POLLOCK's Tavern, has added an assortment of articles for ladies chosen by herself. Also wines, spirits, teas, &c.

313. Wednesday, 18 June 1794
Died on Thursday last, after a lingering illness, Mrs. ALEXANDER, wife of Thomas ALEXANDER, of this town.
Thomas CROMWELL, Bedford Furnace, offers reward for negro man named Tom, about 25 years of age, 5'9-10" high, well made, purchased from William ALLISON near Greencastle.
To be sold in the town of Shippensburgh, noted stand for public business, now occupied by David TATE; apply to Matthew HENDERSON, living in said town. James M'CALL.
Tobias KRIDER, near Lebanon, Dauphin Co., offers reward for mare missing from plantation of Thomas KENNEDY, Esq. in West Pennsborough Twp.
Mary & Jane MILLER, living nearly opposite to the Black Horse Tavern, to carry on the millinary business in all its branches, together with gowns, stay, riding habits, &c.
Whereas Richard WILLIAMS, Mifflin Co., Lack Twp., having passed 8 bonds to Archibald WATT of Toboine twp., Cumberland co., for a tract which WATT was to make a good title, but as there are other claims setting up for said land, I do forewarn persons from taking assignment on said bonds.
Joseph M'CLELAND, Milford twp., Mifflin co., offers 8 1/2 cents reward for apprentice girl named Mary MOORE, 14 years old, about 5' high, much freckled, sandy hair, in common linsey clothing.

314. Wednesday, 25 June 1794
Married last week, Dr. John GEDDES of Newville to Miss Elizabeth PEEBLES.
Arrived here Sunday last, on their way westward, Captain HOWE, with a detachment of about 40 troops.
Married on the 29th inst., by Rev. William CLINGAN, James CRAVAN to Miss Rachel WRIGHT, both of Fermanaugh twp., Mifflin Co.
Died on Thursday 29th inst., after a short illness, Mrs. Rebecca WILSON, aged 44 years, wife of William WILSON, Esq., High Sheriff of Mifflin Co.
The Printer is happy to inform the subscribers who are supplied with this Gazzete by post that he has engaged a rider, James FLEMING, who will ride weekly unless prevented by the inclemency of weather.
John TOULERTON, Manallen, York Co., offers reward for missing horse.

315. Wednesday, 2 July 1794
Notice of meeting of the trustees of othe public buildings for the county of Huntingdon, to meet at the house of Lodwick SELL to contract with persons to build Court House. Commissioners: Benjamin ELLIOT, George ASHMAN, William M'ALEAVY, Lodwick SELL, Richard SMITH & Andrew HENDERSON.
George CLUGGAGE, candidate for Sheriff of Huntingdon Co.

315. Wednesday, 2 July 1794 (Con't.)

Whereas an advertisment has lately appeared in the Carlisle Gazette signed James M'CALL, for the sale of that house in the town of Shippensburgh now occupied by David TATE, this is to forewarn persons from purchasing same, as the subscriber apprehends herself entitle to the premises. Ann M'CALL.

This is to caution persons from taking assignment on notes given by me to Jesse ADAMS row of Cumberland, late Mifflin Co. Alexander MOOR.

Merchant mill to be sold, 1 1/2 miles from Huntington Town, on Frankstown branch of Juniata river. She has a pair of French Burrs & a pair of country stones with four bolting cloths. The mill & store house is 81' long. Good saw mill in good repair, 3 story house, tan yard, house 30x20', with other outhouses, barn, stables, 500 a. Michael CRYDER, living on the premises.

Joseph T. JAMES offers reward for horses missing from pasture of Mrs. WILSON, 1 mile from Carlisle.

William BROWN, Kishacoquilas Valley, offers reward for stolen horse.

Charlese BOVARD requests payment of debts.

John RAMSEY, Shearman's Valley, Juniata twp., offers reward for missing horse; deliver to Archibald RAMSEY, merchant, Carlisle or himself.

No more issues for July 1794 available.

316. Wednesday, 6 August 1794

Sheriff's Sales: 800 a. on Clearfield Creek, one in the name of Cheney RICKETS for 400 a., the other in the name of Edward RICKETS, Senior, adj, for 400 a.; also undivided half part of 400 a. in name of William WALLACE on Little Juniata, held by warrant by said WALLACE & Edward RICKETS, as tenants in common, all property of Edward RICKETS.

George ROWAN has for sale at his hatters shop, next door to Charles GOVERD's store, a quantity of fine & coarse hats.

William BELL offers reward for horse missing from farm of Michael EGE, Dickinson twp., Cumberland Co. Deliver to Thomas NORTON, Walnut Bottom.

Coroner's sale of tract in Antrim tpw., Franklin Co., in the occupancy of Andrew ROBERTSON, 65 a., adj. lands of William RANKIN, taken as the property of David MAGAW, Esq., decd. James HOGE, Coroner.

If John CRAIG, brother of the late Sarah ALLEN of the Borough of Carlisle, & who it is said lived near Pittsburgh, will apply to the ex'rs. of the said decd., he may hear of something to his advantage. (Mr. SCHULL is affectionately requested to insert the above in his gazette.)

Public sale agreeable to will of Stephen DUNCAN, decd., horses, cows, sheep, waggons, furniture, negro man aged about 54 years, mulatto wench about 22 years old. Ann, Thomas, Robert & James DUNCAN, Ex'rs.

Peter STEVENS, Huntingdon town, offers reward for horse stolen out of his stable.

Brave Volunteers . . . come forward & recieve $8 bounty & everything a gentleman soldier should have & your choice of any corps, Cavalry, Rifleman, Artillery or Infantry . . . bid adieur to Militia Duty, taxes & impost of every kind, & come & live on the treasures of the United States collected & provided as the Reward of Bravery. Richard SPARKS, Captain, Commandant.

Thomas BARNES, Newton twp., to sell tract of land whereon he now lives, well for the valuable Sulphur Spring, 153 a.

Nails for sale. William PETRIKIN carries on the Taylor business as formerly.

John Marry BAIN has for sale at the store of Nathaniel WEAKLEY, Carlisle, a complete assortment of gold & silver watches.

317. Wednesday, 13 August 1794

Died Monday, 11th inst., after a few weeks indisposition & in her 20th year, Miss Betsey NEILL, d/o the late William NEILL, merchant of Baltimore.

Sale of remaining household furniture, late the property of Samuel ALEXANDER, decd. John CREIGH, William ALEXANDER, Adm'rs.

Those indebted to estate of John SEDGWICK, late of Carlisle, decd., are requested to settle their accounts. Hugh BODEN, Adam LOGUE, Adm'rs.

Persons indebted to the estate of Hugh PATTEN, decd., are requested to settle accounts. Mary PATTEN, Adm'r.

James HUSTON, near Mount Rock, offers reward for missing horse.

William FRAZER, Loudon Derry twp., Dauphin Co., offers reward for indented apprentice boy, Francis Campbell SMITH, about 16 years of age, brownish hair, blue eyes, about 5' high, thick set, large scar on the outside of his left leg & a little marked with the small pox, broke open & stole from a drawer a sum of money, amount unknown.

318. Wednesday, August 20 1794

Deserted from this post: Corporal John BROWN, about 40 years of age, stout made, about 5'8", bald headed, his hair black mixt with grey, born in France, speaks broken English, by trade a miller; Benjamin M'MAHON, about 5'7" high, about 40 years of age, stoop shouldered, weaver by trade, fond of liquor, slow of speech. Richard SPARKS, Captain, Commandant, Barracks at Carlisle.

Sale of land on the Alleghany River, late the property of Thomas SMALLMAN, 519 a.

Shop to be let adj. the house occupied by William DENNEY, in the Main st., well suited to a hatter shop, as there is a furnace ready built.

Samuel GRAY, North end York st., Carlisle, is just returned from Philadelphia with a fresh assortment of goods.

Guns made & mended by Samuel CRISWELL in Carlisle.

319. Wednesday, 3 September 1794

Carlisle - on Thursday night last, a party of armed men, who were blacked, called on Major HULING, the Collector of Excise for this county, damanded his commission & papers, which were relating to Excise; they having obtained them went off without further injury.

Deserted from the Barracks at Carlisle a certain Thomas M'ELHENEY, soldier in the 3d Sub-Legion of the U.S., excellent scholar, formerly kept school at Col. CAMPBELL's in York Co.; about 5'10", 25 years of age, fair complexion, strait & slim made, fond of strong drink, which is immediately seen in his face, it becoming very flush & red, at other times he is naturally pale. Richard SPARKS, Captain, Commandant.

Henry FORRER, of New-bury twp., York Co., offers reward for stolen horse. Supposedly taken by John WISE, alias Indian John.

Casper SINGHORSE, Mountjoy twp., Lancaster co., offers reward for stolen horse.

Daniel BOYLE, Newville, Newton twp., Cumberland Co., offers reward for apprentice lad named Thomas CRAWFORD, to learn the taylor business, about 18 years of age, black short hair, 5'8-9" high; had on a deep blue coating coatee, trousers & jacket of India nankeen.

319. Wednesday, 3 September 1794 (Con't.)
Deserted from my Recruiting party about 2 miles below Carlisle Barracks, on 17th inst., soldier named James DERMID, Irishman, about 30 years of age, 5'10" high, stout made, thick bushy black hair, fond of whiskey to excess. James STERRET, Lt., Artillery, U.S. Carlisle Barracks.
Whereas my wife Catharine has acted in an unbecoming manner & trying to ruin me by running me in debt or useless articles of no consequence to either herself or me, and her scandalous behaviour to me in many respects, lays me under the necessity of forewarning all persons from crediting her on my account, nor if they take my advice on her credit either, as I will pay no debts of her contracting. John LOGUE.
Persons indebted to the estate of Andrew BEATTY, decd., late of Juniata twp., are requested to make immediate payment. James BEATTY, Adm'r.

320. Wednesday 10 September 1794
To be rented, house in which the subscriber now lives in York St., Carlisle. James HAMILTON.
Jacob WELSH, Allen twp., has taken up a stray bull.
Persons indebted to the estate of Peter CRA-- of Huntingdon Co., decd., are requested to make payment without delay. Israel CRYDER, George FOCKLER, Ex'rs.

321. Wednesday, 17 September 1794
Dr. Charles STINNECKE has lately imported from Europe a fresh & general assortment of drugs & medicines.
Lewis & Wendel MICHAEL have just received & now opening at their new store in Main St., Carlisle, second door above the Sign of the Indian Queen, a large & general assortment of merchandise.
Drawing taught every Tuesday & Thursday at Mr. LOUDONS, bookseller.
John M'DANNEL, West Pennsbro' twp., Cumberland Co., on Conodoquinet Creek has taken up a stray milch cow.
To be sold agreeable to will of John BONNER, decd., plantation on which he lived, 300 a., in Mifflin Co., Millford twp., adj. river Juniata, 1/2 mile from George PATTERSON's Mill. James BONNER, near the premises, James BIGHAM & William BIGHAM, Lancaster Co., Chestnut Level, Ex'rs.
Conrad SHERMAN, Manheim Twp., York Co., on the great road from Hanover (M'ALister's Town) to Baltimore, offers reward for 2 negro men, one named George about 36-37 years of age & Tom, about 41 years of age.
Tract of land for sale in Tuscorara valley, Lack twp., Mifflin Co., 8 miles from Harristown on Juniata, 617 a. Apply to Samuel BARNET, tenant, on said land, John STUART, Esq., adj. Robert GALLESPIE, Newton Twp., Cumberland Co., or Stephen PORTER, Cecil Co., Md.

322. Wednesday, 24 September 1794
William GRAYSON, Junr., East Pennsbro' twp., carries on the fulling business at William GRAYSON, Senior's mill. The following places are appointed to take in work & return it drest, viz. Francis SILVERS, Silver Spring; Robert GRAYSON, at the gaol; William EAKIN, sign of the Black Horse, Carlisle; John PIGLER; Mr. JUMPER's mill; Ralph STERRETT, North Mountain; Mr. WELSH on Lisburn Road; Matthew DILL, Monaghan twp., York Co.
John OVER, East Pennsbro' twp., Cumberland Co., 2 miles from Squire CAROTHERS, offers reward for missing cows.
To be sold - Two-story log house, late the property of Alexander M'DOWEL, decd. Samuel GREY.

322. Wednesday, 24 September 1794 (Con't.)
John PHILLIPS, Carlisle, offers reward for horse missing from the commons.

323. Wednesday, 7 January 1795
James MILLIGAN, 1 mile of Carlisle, has taken up a stray cow.

Wednesday, 14 January 1795 [Not available]

324. Wednesday, 21 January 1795
John CREIGH requests payment of debts; & has received at his store in Carlisle a neat & general assortment of merchandise.
House for let on Hanover St., near the corner of Pomfret St., Nathaniel WEAKLEY.
House for sale in Carlisle, Alexander BLAINE.
Henry ZEIGLER, Middleton twp., Cumberland Co., has taken up a stray cow.
David GLEN, Southampton twp., Cumberland Co., has taken up a stray horse.
For lease - stone houses & buildings on Water St. in Carlisle, lately belonging to John POLLOCK, decd. These houses have each a separate kitchen & large enough for the accomodation of 2 families. Apply to Samuel POSTLETHWAIT or James DUNCAN.
To be rented on the shares, about 120 a. of out lots, belonging to the late Stephen DUNCAN, which will be leased together or in lots. Thomas DUNCAN, Robert DUNCAN, James DUNCAN, Ex'rs.
The subscriber, having passed 2 notes to James DICKSON, on consideration of a lease, I hereby notify persons from taking assignment on said notes. Jacob BOWER.
Mathew SCOT, Shippensburgh, offers reward for missing horse.
Alexander M'KEEHAN requests all those indebted to him to make payment.

325. Wednesday, 28 January 1795
Married Thursday 15th inst., by Rev. Dr. DAVIDSON, James BLAINE, merchant, of Carlisle to Miss Peggy LYON, d/o Samuel LYON.
John THOMPSON offers reward for colt missing from the plantation of John GRAHAM, ALlan twp., Cumberland Co.
Watch of James RAMSAY was lost in borough of Carlisle.
Persons indebted to the estate of Abraham M'KEW are requested to make immediate payment. William HARKNESS, Eleanor M'KEW, Ex'rs.

326. Wednesday, 4 February 1795
George STEVENSON, intending to remove from Carlisle, requests persons indebted to him to make payment.
Mordecai M'KINNEY has for sale at his store in Middletown, a general assortment of groceries.
Susannah THOMPSON has at her new store, opposite Mr. POLLOCK's Tavern, a fresh assortment of Dry Goods.

327. Wednesday, 11 February 1795
Died Thursday 5th inst., after a long continued scene of affliction, Mrs. Rebecca BLANE, consort of Col. Ephraim BLAINE.
Meeting of the Trustees of Dickinson College - John ARMSTRONG, President, pro tem.
William ALEXANDER, Carlisle, candidate for sheriff.
John MILLER, Mount-Rock, Westpennsborough Twp., has taken up a stray filly.

327. Wednesday, 11 February 1795 (Con't.)

Sale of noted publick house two miles of Harrisburgh known as Tobias HENDRICK's tavern, and latterly kept by the late Robert PATTERSON, decd., with 212 a. Henry FORRER, Ex'r.

Lot in Shepherds Town, Berkely Co., Va. & farm near it; apply at the Antatum (Antietam) Iron Works in Md., near said town to Richard HENDERSON.

Lots for sale in town of Jaysburg, on the bank of the West Branch of Susquehanna, Northumberland Co. Jacob LATCHA, Jaysburg.

328. Wednesday, 18 February 1795

Died Friday last, in his 71st year, Alexander GORDON, of this town; remains interred in burying ground adj. this town.

The Carlisle Light Infantry Company to meet at Nathaniel WEAKLEY's. Robert MILLER, Jun., Captain.

Dr. FRANK, intending to remove from this town, requests persons indebted to him to make payment before 4 March.

Persons indebted to estate of James STUART, late of Carlisle, breeches maker, decd., are requested to make payment. Martha SCOTT, William WALLACE, Adm'rs.

House & half lot for sale at the south corner of York St., near the Dutch Church; for further particulars enquire of John POPE, at the sign of the German Emperor, near the said house.

Adam JOHNSTON, Carlisle, offers reward for missing gelding.

Sale of 155 a., near the head of Bigg Spring, between PIPER's mill & M'CRACKENS mill, Westpennsbro' twp., Cumberland Co. Robert HUTCHESON.

For lease, old tavern formerly occupied by William EAKIN, Carlisle, now at the sign of General Washington; apply to Robert CHAMBERS or Charles COOPER. Robert CHAMBERS, Carlisle.

329. Wednesday, 25 February 1795

John WEBBER, Carlisle, being determined to remove to the westward, requests persons indebted to him to make immediate payment. He will continue to sell his remaining stock of merchandize & books.

Whereas the subscriber gave his obligation to Charles BUCK, in the sum of 80 pounds, notice is hereby given to warn persons from taking assignment of same, as the subscriber is determined not to pay. The obligation is at present in the hands of Thomas ANDERSON, Esq., of Lewistown, Mifflin Co. John RICHARDSON.

To be sold - plantation known as the Locust Hicker, in Westpennsborough twp., Cumberland Co., 85 a. late the property of George WALDENBERGER, decd., Henry SHANK, Peter DILLER, Ex'rs, Westpennsborough Twp.

330. Wednesday, 4 March 1795

Married Tuesday 24th ult. at the farm of William FLEMMING by Rev. Dr. DAVIDSON, Charles GREGG to Miss Nancy FLEMMING, d/o William FLEMMING.

Sale of the real estate of Robert CALLENDER, decd., by Thomas BUCHANAN, Esq. The court orders that the plaintiffs in the several judgments against said Robert, shew cause why the sheriff should not pay over the monies remaining.

The horse Experiment will cover this season at the stable of L. GUSTINE in Carlisle.

John HOLMES, Junr., Carlisle, intends to remove from this place and requests debts be paid. After 10 March their accounts will be lodged in the hands of George LOGUE.

331. Wednesday, 11 March 1795
Died Monday last, in this borough, in his 78th year, General John ARMSTRONG.
George STEVENSON, Carlisle, to sell at his dwelling house, books, furniture, waggon & geers.
Persons indebted to James BLAINE are requested to settle their accounts.
Smithshop to be rented, on the great road between BELLS & WALKER's Tavern, in Cumberland Co. Apply Benjamin JUNKIN, on the premises.
To be sold by public vendue, at the dwelling house of David BRIGHT, Middleton twp., living at Col. Ephraim BLAINE's country seat, at the junction of Letart Spring with Conodoquinet Creek; livestock, farm utensils, grain in the ground, desk, drawers, tables, chairs &c.

John HUGHES, finding it impossible to attend to the business of his shop & the duties of his present appointment as Revenue Officer, offers for sale an assortment of goods which he has now on hand. He also would rent his shop & cellar, the latter completely finished with granaries for all kinds of grain, salt, &c.
Jonathan WALLACE & Jacob CREVER, candidates for sheriff.

332. Wednesday, 18 March 1795
Sale of tract of land, 330 a., by Orphans Court, in Wood Cock valley, 8 miles from town of Huntingdon, on road to Bedford, part of the estate of John WILSON, decd. Terms of sale will be made known by James WILSON & Robert WILSON, adm'rs. Andrew HENDERSON, Clerk of the Orphans Court, Huntingdon Co.
William HARPER, gaoler, offers reward for Joseph RICHARDSON, who broke out of Lewistown gaol, Mifflin Co., on night of 1st inst. 5'6" high, dark complection, short black hair, indifferent apparel, committed for stealing a stud horse in Frederick Co., Va.

333. Wednesday, 1 April 1795
Land for sale, 450 a. of patented land on Juniata River, 8 miles of town of Huntingdon, formerly possessed by Jacob HARE. Enquire of Frances REID, present owner in Carlisle, or Andrew HENDERSON, Esq., Prothonary of Huntingdon Co. in Huntingdon.
Public sale in town of Newville, a number of Out Lots, adj. said town. John CARSON, Newville.
The horse Young Patriot will cover mares this season at the farm of Major William SANDERSON, Shermans Valley, every other week, and at Captain James SANDERSON on Conodoguinet creek the same. Alexander SANDERSON, Shermans Valley.
Persons indebted to the estate of William WOODS, Junr. decd., are once more requested to make payment. Samuel & Richard WOODS, ex'rs.
Coroners sale of tract in Antrim twp., Franklin Co., adj. lands of William RANDKIN, on which Andrew ROBINSON now dwells, late the property of David MAGAW, decd., seized by Robert SEMPLE, Esq., late Sheriff. Also a house & lot and Pot-Ash works in the town of Shippensburgh, property of John COPELY, taken by James WALLACE, Sheriff. James HOGE, Coroner.

334. Wednesday, 8 April 1795
George KLINE has removed his English & German Printing Office to the house formerly occupied by him, next door, but one to Dr. George STEVENSON, where printing in general is executed in a neat, correct & expeditious

manner. At said Office is given the highest price for clean linen & cotton rags.

John WEBBER's store is removed to the new brick house, next door but one to the house he formerly occupied, and opposite to Samuel GRAY's Store, where he is now opening for sale; Dry Goods, Groceries, books, etc.

Farm for sale on road from Lancaster (by RANDKIN's ferry) to Carlisle, 400 a., large dwelling house, 50' in front, with 3 rooms on a floor, kitchen, smoak house adj, barn 72 1/2 x 36', stables underneath, distillery with 2 stills, tanyard capable of containing 700 hides. Jacob WELSH.

The horse Jolly will cover mares this season at the stable of Alexander M'BRIDE, Junior, Cumberland Co., Dickinson twp., at $2 the season, or $1 the single leap, $4 for ensurance & one bushel of oats to the horse for each mare. Alexander M'BRIDE, Junr.

The horse Albany Bay will cover mares this season. Hugh SMITH.

Wanted, colliers, wood-cutters & labouring men. Daniel TURNER, Mifflin Co., Spring-creek Forge.

335. Wednesday, 15 April 1795

Died on the 9th inst., after a very short illness, in her 45th year, Mrs. Eleanor LYON, wife of Samuel LYON, living in the vicinity of Carlisle. The stroke (being of a paralytic kind) by which she was taken away, was sudden & alarming.

The following was handed some time ago for publication. Exact copy from the orginal in the hand of the printer. "York County - Whereas David JORDEN appeared before me, one Justice of the peace for said County, for to pint two good man or to apris a Stray Mare John NISPED & Samuel M'MOLLIR I Suspect will doe the same given under my hand. Daniel MESSERLY."

Joseph SHROM will give 25 shillings per cord for chestnut & spanish oak bark.

James GILFOY has removed his store to York St., opposite to the White Beard & next door to Samuel GRAY, wher he has for sale a neat & general assortment of dry goods & groceries.

Andrew MURRAY, Taylor & Ladies Habit Maker, lately from Dublin, has removed from Mr. WEAKLEY's Tavern to the Center Square, next door to Ephraim STEEL.

Notice is given to persons who are in arrearge of taxes, in Mathew LAIRD's Duplicate for the year 1781 to come forward without delay. Mathew LAIRD, Middleton Twp., Cumberland Co.

336. Wednesday, 22 April 1795

An act for the relief of Dickinson College ($5000). That there shall be annually admitted at no time more than ten students & none shall continue in said College longer than two years.

William NICHOLS, Esq. is appointed Marhsal of the District of Pa., in the room of David LENOX, Esq., who has resigned.

James PATTON, Green-Castle, offers reward for apprentice lad to the Cabinet Making Business named William HAYS, about 18 years of age, slender made, fair hair, very talkative.

Sale of tract called Washington's Bottom, in lots, one of 338 a. & two each of 300 a. Israel SHREVE.

337. Wednesday, 29 April 1795

For sale-135 a. in Middleton Twp., 1 mile from Carlisle. Also stone house & lot opposite Robert SMITH's tavern in Carlisle.

337. Wednesday, 29 April 1795 (Con't.)
David HARRIS, of Baltimore, will sell stone house & lots in Harrisburgh.
Whereas the subscriber bought a tract of land from Gabriel GLENN & David GLENN about 4 years ago, & gave his bonds for the same & this is to forewarn persons from taking an assignment on same until I get a right title for the lands. Martin WALMUTZ.
Died Sunday last, Mrs. Elizabeth PATTISON, after a lingering illness, in her 55th year; remains buried in the burying ground adj. the town.
Buying Chestnut & Spanish Oak Bark, William MILLER, at his tanyard in Carlisle.
The subscriber, having passed sundry bonds to William CLARK, in consideration of a tract on Conodoguinet Creek, I hereby request such person who is possessed of the bond payable 1st April 1795 to come forward, indemnify me, & receive payment. Jacob MUSSELMAN.
Sale of plantation in Westpennsborough twp., 9 miles west of Carlisle, 1 mile from Wood's mill, 206 a. Patrick WALLACE.

338. Wednesday, 6 May 1795
Died Saturday after a long illness, in her 54th year, Mrs. Margaret CHAMBERS, consort of Robert CHAMBERS, living near this town; remains buried in the burying ground adj. this borough.
The Trustees of Dickinson College to meet. Thomas CREIGH, Sec'y.
Whereas Joseph DUNCAN of Shippensburgh, having quit business, requests pesons pay their debts to him.

339. Wednesday, 13 May 1795
Died Thursday last, after a short illness, in the prime of life, Christly FISHER, Innkeeper, of this borough.
Deceased on Monday morning, a son of Oliver POLLOCK, Esq., Silver Spring, occasioned by a fall off a horse, which he received the day before.
The General Assembly of the Presbyterian Church will be held in the Presbyterian Church of Carlisle. Rev. Dr. Alexander M'WHORTER is expected to preach.
Exhibition of Figures in composition at full length at the house of William HEIGEL, at the sign of the White Bear, Carlisle. Price $.25.

340. Wednesday, 20 May 1795
Robert SMITH, having rented that well-known house, at the sign of the Indian Queen, west of the Court House, Carlisle, continues to keep Good Entertainment.
By virture of a precept of sale under the hand & seal of Philip REILEY, agent for the managers of the Penn. Hospital, will be sold a tract of 158 a., in twp. of Frankford, Cumberland Co., bounded at this time by John DUNBAR, John CAROTHERS, Benjamin HERSHEY & Philip BAKER, Conodoguinet Creek & other lands of Alexander PARKER, decd. James HOGE, Coroner.
To be sold at private sale, well-furnished two-story stone house, with stone kitchen, good stabling & a well with a pump at the kitchen door, Hanover St., Carlisle. The lot is 60' in front & 240' in depth, well calculated for a store & tavern & occupied as such for a number of years. At present known as the sign of the White Bear. Apply to John JORDAN, Esq., Carlisle, or the subscriber, Benjamin HARE, living in the borough of Lancaster, who also has for sale a quantity of boulting cloths.
Job BRIGGS, Luzerne twp., offers reward for mare stolen out of his stable in Fayette Co., near Redstone, Pa.

341. Wednesday, 27 May 1795

John WALLACE has opened a store next door to Dr. GUSTINE's and has for sale articles got out of the Ship Commerce from Europe, viz. Callicoes, handkerchiefs, shaws, nankeens, vest patterns, mustard in bottles, fans, teas, sugars, jarr & cask raisins, coffee, irish brown linen.

Sundry accounts & notes due the subscriber are left in the hands of James M'CORMICK, Esq. George STEVENSON.

John SMITH, taylor, late from Philadelphia, but last from Newark, Delaware, carries on business in Pomfret St., nearly opposite Jacob WEISER's Tavern.

342. Wednesday, 3 June 1795

Coroners Sales: Tract called St. John's in Newton twp., 258 a., bounded by lands of Daniel DUNCAN, David M'CURDY, James DUNLAP & Charles RODDEYS, sold as the property of John JOHNSTONE.

Tract called Spring Field, partly in Westpennsborough, partly in Newton twp., 112 a. bounded by lands of David BLAIN, John BROWN, taken as property of James IRWIN.

Tract called Belly Willing, 331 a., bounded by lands of Samuel WILLIAMSON, Andrew M'ILWAINE, John KEENERS, James M'CLINTOCK, Matthew HENDERSON, property of Thomas MARTIN.

Died Tuesday morning, Thomas STEVENS, fuller.

Committed to jail of Cumberland Co., negro boy who calls himself Caleb BROWN, alias John BROWN, confesses to be the property of Frederick BEACOM, Upper Merrion twp., Montgomery Co., about 18 years of age. Robert GRAYSON.

Michael M'CRUM, Mifflin town, offers reward for missing mare.

343. Wednesday, 10 June 1795

James BLACK, living in Juniata twp., Racoon Valley, Cumberland Co., offers reward for negro man, 25 years of age, 5'10" high, yellowish complexion.

James BROWN, carpenter, Carlisle, offers reward for apprentice boy named James MURPHEY, dark complexion, much pitted with small pox, dark hair, about 5'6" high.

Thomas JONES, Carlisle, seeks two apprentices to the bricklaying & plastering business.

Benjamin ELIOTT, Huntingdon Town, offers reward for indented servant man Peter SMITH, 5'9-10" high, dark coloured hair, about 21 years of age, talks of the Dutch dialect.

David OVER, Newville, has taken up a stray horse.

344. Wednesday, 17 June 1795

Isaiah BLAIR has just received & opening for sale in High St., next door to Alexander M'KEEHEN, Carlisle, Drugs & Medicines.

Carlisle Light Infantry Company to meet in Uniform at the Court House. Robert MILLER, Junr., Captain.

Deserted from a detcahment at Carlisle under the command of Captain Russell BISSEL, Samuel SMITH, 5'9" high, fair complexion, grey eyes, light hair, 22 years of age, born in Ct.; William RYON 5' 8 1/2", dark complexion, black eyes, dark hair, 39 years of age, born in Ireland. Deserted between Lancaster & the Susquehannah: Michael RYON, alias Michael COGEN, 5'4", 25 years of age, fair complexion, brown hair, dark eyes, born in Ireland; Dominick SERVILE, 5'6", swarthy complexion, sandy hair, black eyes, born in Canada, a mariner 39 years of age; Morris Fitz JERULA, about 5'2' high, about 30 years of age, dark hair, born in Ireland; Aaron

GRAHAM, 5'4", 26 years of age, fair complexion, dark hair, blue eyes, joiner by occupation, born in Ireland. Peter FROTHINGHAM, Ensign, U.S. Sub-Legion.

Lewis & Wendel MICHAEL have just imported in the ships Dianna & Liberty from Liverpool, Leeds & Manchester, & are now opening at their store in Carlisle, 2d door above the sign of the Indian Queen, a large & general assortment of merchandize.

James M'KINNEY & James BRATTON, living in Wayne twp., Mifflin Co., have taken up two mares.

Reward offered for two horses which strayed from the plantation of James MATHEWS; bring to Henry NEVIL or William HUNTER.

James BLACK, Junitat twp., Racoon Valley, Cumberland Co., offers reward for negro man, 25 years of age, 5'10" high, yellowish complexion.

Silver watch found at the tavern of William FORREE on Philadelphia road, 9 miles from Lancaster.

345. Wednesday, 24 June 1795

Samuel FINLEY, Newville, to superintend the building of a bridge across the Conodoquinet creek near Newville. July 3d set for contracting persons.

Samuel FINLEY & Co., Newville, to decline business, offer to sell two tracts in Newton twp.,

Married Thursday evening last by Rev. Dr. DAVIDSON, at the farm of Col. CHAMBERS, Mordecai M'KINNEY, merchant of Middletown, to Miss Polly CHAMBERS, d/o Col. William CHAMBERS.

William HENRY, living in Armagh twp., Mifflin Co., offers reward for Irish servant boy, about 1 1/2 years from Colerain in the North of Ireland, named William HUNTER, about 18 years of age, 5'6" high, well made, round faced, marked with small pox, a little out-mouthed, his upper two foreteeth middling broad, sandy haired, a little frizling & tied; took with him a short winestone coloured coat with the fore parts of his jacket of the same, the back part of light blue, half worn wool hat, not high crowned, was bound with tape, but the tape is bvroke; is talkative & fond of liquor, apt to swear. He took a scarlet jacket a little worn from a young man in his master's house.

346. Wednesday, 1 July 1795

To be sold - lot & house formerly occupied by George RIDDLE; also store house & lot formerly occupied by Stephen HAYS, now by Messrs. WILLSON & ELDER. James M'CALLEY.

For sale - stand for a tavern & store, late the property of William MORROW & at present in the tenure of Henry SHYROCK & Thomas MURRAY, on West side of Front St., Chambersburg. John MORROW, Samuel RIDDLE, Chambersburgh.

Whereas the subscriber, having passed sundry notes to John TENNIS of Fermanaugh twp., Mifflin Co., in consideration for a tract of land, to which TENNIS was to make a clear & indisputable title, but finding some doubt in the title, I hereby forewarn persons from taking assignment on any of the said notes. William JENNINGS.

Reward offered for deserter from Barracks at Carlisle, a soldier named Michael O'NEIL, belonging to the 4th Sub-Legion, about 5'6", 40 years of age, dark hair cut short to his head, has a remarkable cut over his left eye, the eye is much swelled, not being yet well. An Irishman, formerly belonging to the British Navy; had on a new linen shirt, jacket & overalls, Continental, no coat & an old hat. Charles MARTIN, Ensign, U.S. Sub-Legion.

346. Wednesday, 1 July 1795 (Con't.)
Just published & to be sold by Archibald LOUDON, book-binder & stationer, at the sign of the Bible, High St., Carlisle, "The Mother's Catechism."

347. Wednesday, 8 July 1795
Whereas the subscriber, having passed a note to a John JOHNSTON for the sum of 14 pounds, the said JOHNSTON having assigned the said note. The person now possessed of the note is requested to come forward & receive payment. Simon BOYD.
New store - John ARTHUR has just opened his store in Carlisle, formerly occupied by Joseph THORNBURGH - Dry Goods & Groceries; also barr iron, nail rods, steel & pine grove castings.
Benjamin KNOB, Allan Twp., 17 miles from Carlisle, offers reward for horse which strayed away from the plantation of Jacob KNOB.

348. Wednesday, 15 July 1795
Corner's Sales: Tract near Carmichaels, on Juniata, taken by Thomas BUCHANAN, Esq., late sheriff, as the property of John MOORE.
Undivided half of 530 a. of land in Fannet twp., Franklin Co., property of Robert GREY.
Two houses & lots in town of Shippensburgh, property of Thomas MARTIN.
Reward offered for soldiers who deserted from Carlisle Barracks: John TRUMPER, native of N.J., labourer, about 5'10", 24 years of age, fair complexion, freckled, with light brown hair; James BRYAN, Irishman, 23 years of age, 5'5" high, fair complexion, short brown hair. Charles MARTIN, Ensign, U.S. Sub-Legion.
Robert HUSTON requests persons to pay their debts to him.
Samuel HUEY, Greencastle, Franklin Co., offers reward for missing gelding.

349. Wednesday 22 July 1795
Samuel BERNHEIZEL, Shermans Valley, living in Tryone Twp., Cumberland Co., offers reward for apprentice to blacksmith business named Jacob BEYLER, about 19-20 years of age, 5'8-9", well made, speaks both Dutch & English, marked with small pox.
Person occupying or intending to occupy seats in the Protestant Episcopal Church in this borough are requested to attend at said church for the purpose of renewing their applications for pew or seats, payine one half year's rent of the same, and all arrearages due. Those who can not attend on that day will please to call on Mr. Edward MAGAURAN. Carlisle.

350. Wednesday, 29 July 1795
William KIDD, Holly Forge, has taken up a stray bay mare.
Six bank notes lost in between Carlisle & John WILLIAM's Mill, or in Carlisle; for reward leave at Joseph ELLIOTT's in Allan Twp., or the printing office.

351. Wednesday, 5 August 1795
Married Thursday evening last by Rev. DUBENDORF, Wendel MICHAEL, merchant of this town to Miss Margaret CLOUSER of this county.
Jacob SCHOENENBERGER & Philip JACOBIE have taken up a stray filly at their plantation.

352. Wednesday, 12 August 1795
Andrew NELSON, candidate for sheriff.

352. Wednesday, 12 August 1795 (Con't.)

Martin BARNHIZEL, constable of Tyrone twp., offers reward for John M'CORD, who made his escape from him. About 30 years of age, 5'7-8" high, short black hair, pitted with the small pox, born in Ireland, a weaver, says he is a mason, very talkative & in conversation called the word "if," "gif."

House for sale in Shippensburgh, with Pot-Ash works, on North side of High St., in the occupancy of Joseph DUNCAN, merchant; apply to John HEAP, Esq., Shippensburgh, Col. John WRAY of Carlisle or to the subscriber, William COPLEY.

James M'FARLANE has taken up a stray cow & calf.

James C. RAMSAY has removed his store from the borough of Carlisle to Mifflintown. Dry goods, Groceries & Hard-ware.

353. Wednesday, 19 August 1795

At a meeting of the millers in Carlisle, it was agreed to request all proprietors & owners of mills to attend a meeting at the house of John HUNTER, Carlisle. John SCOULLAR, President.

Surveyor General's Office. 76 a. in Hopewell twp., Huntingdon Co., surveyed to Richard DOULIN, on warrant dated March 22, 1785. There is an order in the name of Anthony MOUL, No. 2027 that calls for the land. Hearing of the parties on this dispute is set. David KENNEDY, Sec'y.

Deserted last night [Aug 17th] from the Barracks near Carlisle, a soldier belonging to the 4th Sub-Legion named Andrew YUHART, about 5'7" high, 35 years of age, dark complection, short black hair, very sulen countenance, much marked with small pox, shoemaker by trade, but lately worked as he said, at Mr. EGE's Forge. Charles MARTIN, Ensign.

David LINDSEY offers reward for negro wench named Sebro, 25 years of age.

354. Wednesday, 26 August 1795

William WALLACE, candidate for sheriff.

Died Friday morning last, at age of 93 years, Mrs. Agness MOORE.

On Sunday, died after a very short sickness, Mrs. Catharine WEISE, wife of George WEISE, saddler.

The Cumberland County Troop of Light Horse to meet at the Court House, Carlisle, to elect a 2d lieutenant in the room of Joseph R. POSTLETHWAIT, resigned. John ALEXANDER, Inspector.

A new paper-mill, the first in this county, erected by William DUCKET is now commencing to manufacture paper of every kind. Seeking 2 apprentices, apply at the mill, known as LEEPER's mill, 16 miles from Carlisle.

A large farm to be let on the Juniata river, 2 miles within its junction with the Susquehannah; apply to David WATTS, Esq. at Carlisle, or the subscriber, Frederick WATTS, on the premises.

Robert M'DOWEL offers reward for horse stolen out of the pasture of John CAMBLE, Fermanaugh twp., Mifflin Co.

Whereas it is made a practice by the soldiers under my command to sell their cloathing & other things, they being public property, or to exchange them for whiskey with some person in this borough . . . I do foretake this public method to forewarn persons from harbouring, buying or bartering with any of my soldiers for any articles whatsoever, without permission in writing under my hand, except they buy for cash alone. Charles MARTIN, Ensign, U.S. Legion.

Samuel COX, near Shippensburgh, offers reward for missing horse. Deliver to Patrick COGHRAN or Jacob REHM in Shippensburgh.

354. Wednesday, 26 August 1795 (Con't.)
John STEPHENS, Carlisle, having removed from the Fulling Mill of Ephraim BLAINE, Esq., to a new & most commodious one of Capt. Gilson CRAIGHEAD, on Yellow Breeches Creek, proposes carrying on fulling & dying in all its branches as usual. Clothes are taken in at the following places, viz. John HUNTER, Jacob CRAVER, Jacob WISER & William WALLACE, in Carlisle; John FRITZ, Stephen RHINE & George HACKET, Shermans Valley; Daniel LENHART, between Waggoners gap & Carlisle; Adam LONGSTAFF in the barrens; John CAROTHERS, late Mr. WALKER's, Harrisburgh road.
John DAVIDSON, Senr., Woodcock Valley, has 300 a. for sale, within 7 miles from Huntingdon.
Persons indebted to the estate of John SEMPLE, decd., are requested to make payment. William CHAMBERS, Joseph SEMPLE, Ex'rs.

355. Wednesday, 2 September 1795
Bibles, Testaments, spelling books, primers &c. [long list of books for sale], John MONTGOMERY.
Deserted from the Barracks at Carlisle, Samuel WOODWARD, soldier of the 4th Sub-Legion, about 5'8" high, slim made, short brown hair, a little hard of hearing, an Irishman, formerly served in the British Army, but lately kept school in Mifflin Co., above Lewistown, about 28 years old. Charles MARTIN, Ensign, U. S. Legion.
Samuel LAIRD, Carlisle, offers reward for apprentice lad named James KENEDY, near 20 years old, about 5'8", fair complexion, a joiner by trade.

356. Wednesday, 9 September 1795
Died Saturday, John WEBBER, merchant of this town, after a short illness.
Died Monday, Mrs. EGOLF, wife of Michael EGOLF.
Persons indebted to the estate of John WEBBER, decd., are requested to settle their accounts. Samuel GRAY, James GIVEN, John MORRISON, Carlisle, adm's.
John RAMSBERGH, Frederick-Town, offers reward for mare.
A certain person, who said his name was Edward PARKER, & that he lived in Montgomery Co., Pa., on the 30th of August last, left a horse, saddle, bridle & great coat with John FRITZ, living at Sherman's Creek, Cumberland Co.

357. Wednesday 16 September 1795
Joseph R. POSTLETHWAIT has removed from Carlisle & opened a tavern in Pittsburgh, at the sign of the Bear, in the house lately occupied by Capt. John M'MASTERS.
Whereas my wife Mary, having absented herself from my family without any cause, I am therefore under the disagreeable necessity of forwarning the public not to credit her any thing on my account. Michael GALLISPIE.
Ellis PRICE, Alexandria, offers reward for negro Stephen & mulatto wench Henny, about 18, who ran away whilst at Bath.
Fair to be held by order of the Burgesses. John M'CURDY, Clerk.
Abraham BIDDLEMAN, Shippensburgh, offers reward for missing horse.
John M'CAULAY, Hopewell twp., Cumberland Co., 3 miles from Shippensburgh, offers reward for missing mare.

358. Wednesday, 23 September 1795
Persons indebted to the estate of Peter SMITH, late of Middleton twp., decd., are desired to make payments. William BOOR, Jacob WITMORE, Admr's.

358. Wednesday, 23 September 1795 (Con't.)
Canal lottery ticket lost - John KINKEAD, Carlisle.
Agreeably to order off the Orphan Court, will be sold 22 a. adj. George MANN in East-Pennsbro' twp., part of estate of Daniel WOOMELDORF, decd. William LYON, Clerk.
Persons indebted to John HOLMES, Junr., late of this borough, storekeeper, are requested to make payment to the subscriber, Andrew HOLMES, Sen.
Oliver POLLOCK seeks to hire miller & sawyer.
Sale of Lot on Bedford St., Carlisle. Thomas BRYSLAND.

359. 30 September 1795
Deserted from the Barracks near Carlisle on the 26th inst., Charles CALHOON, soldier of the U.S. Legion; stout made, about 5'8" high, short dark hair, about 24 years of age, an Irishman by birth & by trade a tanner. Charles MARTIN, Ensign, 2d Sub Legion.
The Synod of Philadelphia are to meet in the Presbyterian Church, borough of York. Nathaniel IRWIN, slatled clk.
Tract of land for sale in Dickinson Twp., 8 miles from Carlisle, on Walnut bottom road. John M'DONALD.
Coroner's Sale of tract in Fermanaugh twp., Mifflin Co., adj. lands of A. HAMILTON & others, 200 a., property of James DAVIS; also two houses & 3 lots in Shippensburgh, property of Thomas MARTIN.

360. Wednesday, 7 October 1795
Commencement held at Dickinson College. Bachelor of Arts conferred on: David M'CONAUGHY, George REID, Samuel DONNELL, John LYON, James IRVINE, William SPRIGG, John KENNEDY, Patrick DAVIDSON, William CREIGHTON, Edward WORK & Joshua WILLIAMS, Thomas M'CLELAN, John NEVIN, Roger Brooke TANEY (of Md.), John PASSMORE (Md.), Andrew MOORE (S.C.), Walter BREDEN, Samuel BRYSON, Abraham CRAIG, James HASSON, William STERRETT (Pa.), William Aston HARPER (S.C.) & William STEWART (Del.).
Died in his chair without a pang, in his 76th year, at his farm on Juniata, General Frederick WATTS.
Take notice - That the line run part by James BUCHANAN & part by James HOGE, between the lower Election District of Cumberland Co., & the Carlisle district, beginning at the North Mountain; the dwellings of the inhabitants near the said line, and in the following manner, to wit: the dwelling of John CLENDENING, below; Jacob SHUPE, below; William GRAYSON, above, his mill below; Richard GILSON & John CHAIN, below; Andrew IRVIN, above; Archibald LOUDON, below; Benjamin JUNKIN, above; John REINECK, below; Martin LONGSTAFF, above; Philip SNIDER, William BOOR in Eastpennsbro'; in Allen Twp., George COVER, Junr., Abraham HIDE, Jacob HOLLINGER & one BOGGS on the side of Yellow Breeches Creek, below & James GREGORY above.
The subscriber, having passed a bond to a certain Lawrence SPRING of York Co., for the payment of 17 pounds, forwarns persons from buying or taking an assignment on said bond. Samuel SHURTZ.

361. Wednesday, 14 October 1795
Died Wednesday 30th ult., Col. Eleazer OSWALD, on his way from Rhode Island to Philadelphia.
Died Saturday morning the 10th inst., at his farm near Shippensburgh, after a short illness, Capt. David SOMERVILLE.

361. Wednesday, 14 October 1795 (Con't.)
Died Wednesday last, Mrs. Sarah M'DONALD of this borough; on Thursday Mrs. Jean CRAINE; on Sunday William SIMONDS, in the vicinity of this borough, all in an advanced age.
Robert JAMISON, Frankfort twp., Cumberland Co., has taken up a stray horse.

362. Wednesday, 21 October 1795
Valentine EBLING, within one mile of the Black Horse, Rye Twp., seeks an apprentice to the sickle making & black smith business.
The inhabitants of the borough of Carlisle, who are indebted to the subscribers for road taxes, are requested to call & pay same. Nathaniel WEAKLEY, John ARTHUR, Supervisors.
The inhabitants of Dickinson twp. who are indebted for road taxes, assessed for the year 1793, are requested to pay the same. John ARTHUR, Carlisle.
John EBERSOLDH, Middleton twp., has taken up a stray steer.

363. Wednesday, 28 October 1795
To be sold - 300 a. on the waters of Whiskey Run, Newton Twp., Cumberland Co. Apply to William MONTGOMERY, living near said land or to Adam JOHNSTON, living near Pittsburgh.
Sale of unseated lands in Mifflin Co. for taxes due thereon to be delayed. Thomas ANDERSON, John M'CONNAL, Commissioners.
To be sold at the dwelling house of the subscriber, adj. Carlisle, horses, cows, sheep, hogs, waggon & geers, plows, harrows &c. William HARSHE, Middleton twp.
Plantation for sale at the late dwelling house of Adam CARNAHAN of Newton twp., decd., 135 a. on south side of Conodoguinet Creek, also livestock, etc. Robert & James CARNAHAN, Adm'rs.

364. Wednesday, 4 November 1795
Married 24th October by Dr. Robert DAVIDSON, James SMITH to Miss Betsy DUNLAP, both of this county.
William PARKER on Conodoguinet Creek hs just completed a Fulling Mill for which he wishes to engage a fuller.
Michael NATCHER, Harrisburgh, offers reward for a missing mare.

365. Wednesday, 11 November 1795
Died Tuesday the 10th inst. in his 72d year, Robert MILLER, Senior.

366. Wednesday, 18 November 1795
Married Thursday last by Rev. Dr. DAVIDSON, Hance MORRISON of Pittsburgh to Miss Margaret POLLOCK, d/o John POLLOCK of this town.
Died 6 May 1795, Charles QUIN of Westpennsborough twp., in his 37th year, he having a number of books lent to different persons, his sister Margaret QUIN, now living in Newville at Capt. Archison(?) LAUGHLIN's, in said town, would be desirous that they should be conveyed to her.
To be sold at the house where Robert DUNCAN lived lately in Dickinson Twp., horses, cows, sheep, etc. Reasonable credit will be given by Joseph GALBRAITH. The farm whereon William WOODBURN formerly lived is to be let for the term of 3-4 years. J.G.
Andrew KERR offers reward for horse which strayed from the enclosure of John COOPER on Green Springs, Cumberland Co. Deliver to John COOPER, Robert LUSK, Newville or William WALLACE in Carlisle.

366. Wednesday, 18 November 1795 (Con't.)

Thomas DUNCAN, Carlisle, to sell 308 a. of limestone land in Middleton Twp., 4 miles from Carlisle, adj. lands late of General John ARMSTRONG, Robert CHAMBERS & Peter YOUNG.

Robert M'BRIDE, weaver, has commenced a cotton factory in Carlisle. Coverlids, diaper & white counterpains.

367. Wednesday, 25 November 1795

Samuel GALBRAITH, Dickinson Twp., Cumberland Co., has taken up a stray cow.

368. Wednesday, 2 December 1795

Joseph SHOWALTER, 3 miles from Carlisle, has taken up a stray mare.

Persons indebted to James M'CALLAY, late of Middletown, Dauphin Co., shop-keeper & trader, are requested to make immediate payment. Cadwalader EVANS, Alexander HENRY, assignees of J. M'CALLAY.

369. Wednesday, 9 December 1795

Whereas the subscriber passed 5 bonds to a certain Lawrence DEMPSEY, in consideration of an improved tract of land in Greenwood Twp., Cumberland Co., this is to forewarn persons from taking assignment on said bonds. Nathan JONES, Greenwood Twp.

Tract to be sold, West-pennsborough twp., Cumberland Co., by Adm'rs. of estate of James CUMMINS, decd., 256 a.

370. Wednesday, 23 December 1795

Sheriff's Sales: Two tracts in Greenwood twp., one 111 a. & the other 25 a., the first adjoins lands of Frederick RHINEHART, the other lands of Abraham KENDRICK & George PFOUTZ, property of Johannes PFOUTZ.

126 a. in Greenwood twp., property of Peter SHAW & Casper DULL.

Tract in Rye twp., 50 a. with saw mill, property of John GRAHAM.

150 a. near Carmichaels, on Juniata, property of John MOORE.

300 a. in Fermanaugh twp., now Mifflin Co., property of William M'COY, Esq.

210 a. in Rye Twp., property of Samuel WHITAKER, decd.

Persons indebted to estate of John GRAHAM, decd., are requested to make immediate payment. Jane GRAHAM, James GRAHAM, Allan twp., adm'rs.

$200 reward offered. Whereas a certain Michael HEVICE of Reading Twp., in York Co. on Friday night last about the hour of ten.

John WHISNER, living in Beggars Row, Hopewell Twp., Cumberland Co., has taken up a stray horse.

Frederick NOACRE, Middleton twp., has taken up two stray cows.

Thomas KENNEDY, Tyrone tpw., Shearman's Valley, Cumberland Co., has taken up a stray cow.

John NOBLE, Carlisle, has taken up 3 stray sheep.

Samuel BRANDYBURY, living at Holly Iron Works, offers reward for missing milch cow.

371. Wednesday, 30 December 1795

Persons indebted to David BRIGHT, late of Middleton twp., are notified that their notes & bonds will be put in suit within 3 weeks if not settled off & paid. George LOGUE, Carlisle.

George COUCHER, living in Dickinson Twp., Cumberland Co., 1/2 miles from Mr. WEAKLEY's mills, has taken up a stray mare.

James PORTER offers reward for horse missing from the plantation of Enoch ANDERSON, Toboyne Twp.

372. Tuesday (Evening) Aug 18, 1795. Vol 1, No. 28

At a meeting of the millers, in Carlisle, it was resolved to request all proprietors and owners of mills to attend at Mr. Hunter's tavern keeper in Carlisle. John Scouller, Pres.

Farm to be sold on which the subscriber, James Horrell, Tusc. Val., now dwells, 200 a., within 30 perches of Tuscarora Creek, 4 miles within Wilson's Landing on Juniata. Apply to the subscriber or Major Robert Taylor near the premises, or John Patterson, Store keeper. James Horrell.

Whereas the subscriber executed bonds to Elenor, John and Samuel Reaugh, late of West Pennsbor' or Dickinson twp, Cumberland co, and whereas they have not fulfilled their contract, this is to forwarn persons from taking assignment of said bonds. John Harper, Dickinson twp.

Aaron Cotter, Milford twp, has taken up a stray horse.

Whereas Nicholas Myers of Fermanagh twp, Mifflin Co, obtain bonds of the subscriber, this is to forewarn persons not to take assignment of said bonds. George Rombough, Greenwood twp, Cumberland co.

James Ramsay has removed his store from the Borough of Carlisle to Mifflin Town, on the Juniata, where he has for sale a neat and general assortment of dry goods, groceries and hard ware.

House and lot for sale in Shippensburgh, with pot-ash work, on north side of High St, in the occupancey of Joseph Duncan, merchant; apply to John Heap, Esq. of Shippensburgh, or Col. John Wray, Carlisle, or the subscriber, William Copley.

Samuel Huey, Greencastle, has taken up a stray gelding.

James Brown, carpenter, Carlisle, offers reward for apprentice boy named James Murphey, of a dark complexion, much pitted with the small pox, dark hair, about 5 ft 5-6 inches; had on and took with him an old fur hat with a high crown, a brown coat much worn, striped jacket with the stripes across, three old shirts, one fine thickset breeches, thread stockings, one pair of trowsers, of Russia sheeting, with a piece set in the crutch, old shoes.

Andrew Nelson, Fermanagh twp, Jonathan Wallace, Carlisle, William Wallace, Jacob Crever, John Lyon, William Alexander, Joseph M'Clelland, James Horrel, candidates for sheriff.

To be let - merchant mill and saw mill, in good repair, on the Big Spring, Cumberland Co, Westpensbro twp, property of Gabriel Glenn, decd. Jean Glenn, Benjamin M'Keehan, admrs, Big-Spring.

Persons indebted to Robert Huston, are desired to settle their accounts.

James Ross now settled at Strasburg, 9 miles from Chambersburgh, and teaches the Latin and Greek Languages. Boarding and washing included at 15 pounds per annum.

Whereas William Sterret, junr, of Messersburgh, Va, obtained a note of me, I forewarn persons not to take assignment. John Bowers, Hopewell twp, Cumberland co.

Lands for sale, 25 a., Milford twp, adj lands of Col. Thomas Turbett, Abraham Wells, 1 1/2 miles of River Juniata. William Robinson, Mifflin-Town.

APPENDIX A: LETTERS AT THE YORK POST OFFICE (Taken from the York Advertiser)

Letters remaining at the Post Office, York-Town, Pennsylvania, 19 January -1791: William BALENTINE, William BIGGAR, George BYERS, William CALLAGHAN, Mr. CETAR, John CONNELL, Samuel CORGAN, Thomas DEADY, Joseph DONAGHY, Abraham GALLAGHER, David GILLAMAN, James GRAHAM, Robert GRAHAM, Edward HARE, Wendle KELLAR, Hugh KELLY, David KENNEDY Esq., Robert KIDD, Alexander M'CARTNEY, Thomas M'CLALAN, William MILLIKIN, Ann MOORE, Samuel MOORE, James MORTON, Thomas MULLEDY, James NICKLE, John NUGENT, James OLIVER, Elijah PARKLOE, Andrew PATTON, Hugh PATTERSON, Samuel REA, Andrew ROGAN, Jean SCOTT, William SEMPLE, Messrs. John SHORB & Son, Robert SPROUL, James & Robert SPROUL, Michael STANLEY, James SWENEY, John THOMPSON, Peter TINKLE, Peter ULRICK, Moses VANSOYOC, John WHITE or Big John. A. JOHNSTON, D. P. M.

Letters remaining at the Post Office, York-Town 11 May 1791: Malcom BOYLE, Samuel COOK, Stephen CORNELIUS, Thomas CROSS, John GARDNER, Philip GRAFT, Thomas HAWKINS, Thomas M'ILHENEY - School Master, Barnabas M'KEYS - teacher of music, James M'NAUGHT, George M'NICHOL, Charles M'NOLTY, William MARSHALL, John ROBERTSON, James SMITH, John SMITH, Moses VANSCOYOC, Elizabeth VARDIN. James EDIE, D. P. M.

Letters remaining at the Post Office, York-Town, 20 July 1791: Leonard BECKRAN, William BROWN, William DUDGEON, John GALBRAITH, John GWINN Esq., Tobias HABERSTICK, Charles HEANEY, James HOLIDAY, Michael KEPSLER, Robert M'BRIDE, Robert M'CASHLIN, Barnabas M'KEYS, Rev. Robert M'MORDLE, James M'NAUGHT, William MARSHALL, John MOODY, James MORTON, Mrs. Margaret MURRAY, James NICHOLSON, Matthew ROGERS, John Preston SARGOOD, Martin SHUDY, Mrs. Christiana SLOSHAR (?), Kilyon SMALL, Peter STEWART, Archibald TATE, Alexander TURNER. James EDIE, D. P. M.

Letters remaining at the Post Office, York-Town, 12 October 1791: Robert ALEXANDER, John ANDERSON, John ANDREWS, George BAXTER, William BINGHAM, Andrew BOYD, William BRADLEY, John CAMPBELL, Robert CARSON, John CAVENAGH, James CHAMBERLAIN, Matthew CLELAND, William COLL, Robert CROAN Jr., Joseph CROWDER, James CUNEY or CULLEY, John DENISON, William DENISON, James DORRIS, William DOUGLAS, Robert DUCKER, William DUDGEON, Robert DUNCAN, Thomas DUNCAN, Joseph EDMUNDSON, Robert ERWIN, James FALLOW, Samuel of John FINLEY, Philip GERMAN, Capt. Robert GRAY, John HENDERSON - Fawn Twp., Martin HINES, Thomas HOLMES, Elizabeth JOHNSTON, Thomas KEEMAN, John KELLY, Thomas KIRKWOOD, John LEAS, Willilam LEEPER, Eli LEWIS, John LINTON, Henry LOGAN, Robert LOGON, William LONG, John LONGWELL, Matthew LONGWELL, Thomas M'CASHLEY, Samuel M'CLURE, Samuel M'CURDY, David M'ELNEA, Daniel M'ELROY, Barnabas M'SHERRY - Marsh Creek, William M'SHERRY - Marsh Creek, William MARSHALL, Edly MATSON, Thomas MILLER, Daniel MOONY, James MORTON - Taylor, Robert ORR, George OSBURN, Samuel PATTERSON, Oliver RAMSEY, Henry REBEY, Widow REED (Rock Creek), Miss Ann REED, Joseph REED Esq., Andrew RICHEY, Martin SHUDY, William SMITH, William STEWART, John SWANN, Patrick TEGART, Alexander TURNER, Messrs. VANSCYOC, William WALKER - Chanceford Twp., John WEBB - Tanner, John WEYLIE, Andrew WILSON - Hopewell Twp., Andrew WILSON - Strabane Twp., James WILSON, John WILSON.

A list of letters remaining at the Post Office at York-Town, 28 December 1791: James ANDERSON, cooper, Fawn Twp.; John BOWMAN, Codorus Forge; Richard BROWN, Esq. for Eleanor LALLY, York Twp.; James CAWOOD c/o James MURRAY, York-Town; John CLARK, near Neel's Hole; Matthew CLELAND, Huntington; James CONN, Marsh Creek; John CONNEL c/o Col. Moses M'CLEAN; John CRAIT, Chanceford; Simon CROAN, Miller's-Town; Samuel CROW, Fran; James CURRY; James DOUGHTERY at Walkin; John GALBRAITH & Peter CLARK, Canawago; William GALLAGHER, Windsor; Samuel HAYS, Chanceford; Robert HEZLIT c/o James MORRISON; Peter HOKE, Inn-keeper; George LINCH, Monaghan; James LOGUE, Chanceford; John M'BRIDE, little York or elsewhere; Mark M'CASHLAND near Peach Bottom Ferry; Mannesses M'GILEN, Strabane; Alexander M'GREGOR c/o Joseph REED, Esq.; Charles M'NULTY, Mt. Joy; John M'PIKE, Marsh Creek; John MARSHAL, York; William MITCHEL, Monaghan; James MURPHY, Chanceford; James MORTON, Marsh Creek; John MURRY, Marsh Creek; Capt. Malcas MURRY, York; Charles Wm. PORTER, merchant; George SMITH, Chanceford; John SWAN. No letters to be delivered out of the office, except they are paid for. James EDIE, P. M.

List of letters at the Post Office, York-Town, 18 April 1792: William or Alexander ALLISON, Chanceford Twp.; John ANDERSON c/o James EDIE; George BAXTER c/o Alexander TURNER; Jacob BYRE, Blacksmith, York-Town; Alexander CLETON, Marsh Creek; William COLL, taylor, c/o Joshua RUSSELL; James DAVIDSON, Fawn Twp.; John DENNIS & Co.; William DUDGEON, Monahan; Samuel & John FINLEY, Chanceford Twp.; Abraham GAILAGHER, Windsor Twp.; William GREER c/o Maj. William BAILEY; John GWINN Esq. c/o Mr. HARRIS, merchant, York-Town; Henry HOOBER, Millstone maker; William M'AULEY, Chanceford Twp.; Robert M'CATHLAND c/o John GREER; James M'ILHENEY, Tanner, Mountjoy Twp.; Barnabas M'KEYS; Thomas M'NAUGHT c/o John GREER; John MURPHEY, Chanceford Twp.; Capt. Malcas MURRAY, Little York; Thomas MURRAY near York Town; Henry O'NEILL c/o James MARSHALL; Hugh PATTERSON, Chanceford Twp., Alexander RAMSEY; Gawin SCOTT, Chanceford Twp.; Jacob SITES, Little York; Abraham SMYTH c/o David HOSACK.

List of Letters remaining in the Post Office at York Town, 4 July 1792: James ANDERSON, cooper, Fawn Twp.; Mrs. Eleanor BEATY c/o Andrew FINLEY; Henry BLACK c/o the Rev. Mr. DOBBIN; Thomas BLACK, Monaghan Twp.; John BYERS, near Little York; John CLARK, Fawn Twp.; Peter CLARK, Fawn Twp.; Jacob COMLY c/o Thomas THORNBURGH, Esq.; Mrs. Jane CROSS, Windsor Twp.; John CROSS, Monaghan Twp.; John DEVENEY, mason, Shrewsbury Twp.; John DONNELL c/o James KELLEY, Esq.; John DUNCAN, Chanceford Twp.; James FOLIARD, Little York; John FRANCIS, Warrington Twp., John GORDON, Hopewell Twp.; William HARE c/o Alex CARNAGHAN; Owen HAUGHY, Monaghan Twp.; Joshua HOWARD, shoemaker York-Town; James KERKER c/o Aaron FINLEY, merchant; John KITTLEWELL, Warrington Twp.; James LAIRD, Chanceford Twp., John LOCKHED, Hunter's Town; David LOGAN, shoemaker, Yorktown; William LONG c/o Andrew JOHNSTON; John LONGWORTHY, Yorktown; John M'CAY, Fawn Twp.; Henry M'CORMICK, near Peach-Bottom Ferry; John M'GRIGER, Fawn Twp.; Patrick M'HUGH c/o Thomas LILLY, Esq.; William M'KEIVEY, Hopewell Twp.; John M'LAUGHLIN, Peach-Bottom Ferry; James MARIHAL, Yorktown; James MOORE, Tyrone Twp.; Capt. Malcas MURRAY, Little York; Thomas NEWMAN, Yorktown; John NICKLE, at James M'GAFFICKS; Alexander PORTER, near Slateridge meeting-house; James RAMSEY, Chanceford Twp.; Henry REBY c/o Robert Johnston CHESTER; John SEMPLE, Esq., near Peach-Bottom Ferry; Walter SMITH, Marsh Creek settlement; William SMITH, Berwick Tw.p; James SULLIVAN at David BEATY's Esq.; Robert TOWNSLEY, Mountjoy Twp.; William TURNBULL c/o the Rev. James CLARKSON; Andrew WARWICK, Hopewell Twp.; William WEBB, to be left at Willis's Mill; Dr. John WEIRE c/o Andrew WEIRE; Thomas WILKINS c/o John M'DANIEL; John WILTON c/o Joshua RUFFELL.

APPENDIX A: LETTERS AT THE YORK POST OFFICE (Taken from the York Advertiser)

List of Letters remaining at the Post Office, York-Town, 17 October 1792: William or Alexander ALLISON, Chanceford Twp.; Agnes ANDREWS, Chanceford Twp.; John ANDREWS, Chanceford Twp.; Alexander AYERS c/o Adley MATSON; Mrs. Sally BAILEY c/o Matthew DILL Esq.; William BALINTINE c/o Mr. CULBERTSON; James BANKS, Windsor Twp.; James BLACK c/o the Rev. Alexander DOBBIN; John BONNER, York Town; Samuel BOYD c/o James GRIMES; William BRACKENRIDGE, Fawn Twp.; David BRATTON, Franklin Twp.; Neal CAMPBELL c/o Thomas NEALL; Barney CARR c/o Seth DUNCAN; James CARR, Franklin Twp.; Michael CASHEDY c/o Hugh MORRISON; Michael CASLAND c/o Hugh MORRISON; David CASLOW; Andrew COCHRAN, merchant, Chanceford Twp.; George CONN c/o George IRWIN; Robert CONN c/o Samuel EDIE Esq.; Robert COWANM c/o William DOUGLASS; Thomas CROSS, Franklin Twp.; Adam CUNNINGHAM, Chanceford Twp.; James CUNNINGHAM, Newbury Twp.; Thomas DEADY c/o William DOUGHERTY; William DEERY, tanner & currier; James DERRAUGH, Fawn Twp.; Mr. DEVERALL, Huntington Twp.; Archibald DICKEY, Gettysburgh; Hugh DIVEN, Berwick Twp.; Hugh DIVEN c/o the Rev. Joseph HENDERSON; Miss Katharine DIVER c/o Capt. M'CONAUGHY; John DONNELL c/o James KELLY Esq.; Edward DOUGHERTY, Mountpleasant Twp.; John DOUGHERTY c/o Jacob GIBSON; Michael DOUGHERTY, March Creek; Manasseh DOUGLASS, Fawn Twp.; James DUNCAN, taylor, Chanceford Twp.; Robert DUCKER, Chanceford Twp.; George DUMPHY c/o Joshua RUSSELL; Samuel DUNN, Strabane Twp.; Benjamin EAKINS c/o George MILLER, painter;Adam EBERT, York Town; Arthur ERWIN, near Harris's Ferry; Josias EWART c/o Maj. TURNER; James FELLOW, Chanceford Twp.; Richard FERGUSON, Carrol's tract; David FINLEY c/o James SHORT; Samuel FINLAY c/o John SHORT; Miss Nancy FLEMING, Berwick Twp.; John FRANCIS, Warrington Twp.; Simon GILLESPY c/o James RAMSEY; Robert GRAHAM, Menallen Twp.; Thomas GRAHAM, Chanceford Twp.; John GREENAWAY or the sons of William GREENAWAY, Hunter's Town; John HANNAH, Monahan Twp.; Thomas HAUGHTEN, Chanceford Twp.; George HINDS, Hamiltonban Twp.; Thomas HOLMES, Merchant of York Town; Nicholas HOPE in Little York; Miss Lovis ISAC, near Wright's Ferry; Hugh JOHNSTON, Fawn Twp.; William KERR, Cumberland Twp.; Col. John KING, Conawago; Mrs. Jean LAIRD, Chanceford Twp.; John LINTON, Merchant, Marsh Creek; David & Robert LOGAN, Fawn Twp.; William LONG, Pine Mill; John or Matthew LONGWELL, Strabane Twp.; John LOWEIMER c/o Seth DUNCAN; Alexander M'ACHAN, Little York; Alexander M'CARTNEY c/o Henry ROWAN; Alexander M'CAUSLAND, Berwick Twp.; Samuel M'CULLOUGH, Marsh Creek; Daniel M'ELROY c/o Thomas NEILL, Merchant; Taurrnce M'FADIN in Little York; Barnabas M'GEE, Strabane Twp.; Alexander M'IVER c/o Hugh MORRISON; Charles M'KEAN, Chanceford Twp.; John M'LAUGHLIN c/o William ROSS Esq.; Thomas M'NAUGHT, Warrington Twp.; John M'NUTT c/o David M'CONAUGHY, Esq.; John M'PEAK, Marsh Creek; Bernard M'SHERRY c/o Robert JONES; Thomas MACKEY, Chanceford Twp.; John MAFFET, Marsh Creek; William MARSHALL c/o Samuel MARSHALL, Marsh Creek; John MATCHET, Chanceford Twp.; John MATHERS, Strabane Twp.; Robert MILLER, Fawn Twp.; John MITCHEL, tanner, Chanceford Twp.; George MONTGOMERY, Strabane Twp.; William MONTGOMERY c/o Col. John LAIRD; Daniel MOONY c/o John GREER; Edward MOORE, Fawn Twp.; Ingram MORRIS c/o Christian VAT, sadler; Adam MORRISON, Strabane Twp.; James MORTEN, taylor, Marsh Creek; John MUN, Fawn Twp.; John MURPHY, Chanceford Twp.; William MURROW, Hamiltonbann Twp.; John NICKLE, Chanceford Twp.; William ORR c/o Adam HENDRICKS; George OSBURN c/o William COCHRAN, Esq.; John PARKE c/o John WILSON, merchant; Mrs. Ann PARKS c/o Col. John LAIRD; Matthew PATTERSON, Fawn Twp.; Andrew & John PATTON, wheel-rights, Chanceford Twp.; John PATTY, Chanceford Twp.; James PORTER, Chanceford Twp.; James RANSON c/o Gawin SCOTT; William ROBINSON, Strabane Twp.;

Henry ROWAN, Marsh Creek; William SCOTT c/o John JONES, merchant; William SKEAKLEY; Killian SMALL, York-Town; Alexander SMART, Marsh Creek; Mr. SMITH, father of the late Capt. SMITH of York Co. levies; JAMES SMITH, Chanceford Twp.; William SMITH, Junr., Berwick Twp.; William & James STERLING, Hunter's town; Rowland STEWART, Chanceford Twp.; John THOMPSON, Fawn Twp.; Joseph THOMPSON c/o Patrick M'SHERRY; James TORBET, Fawn Twp.; William VANCE, near Gettysburg; Thomas WALKER, Strabane Twp.; Frederick WARREN; Joseph WESTON, Codorus Twp.; John WHITE c/o John GREER, merchant; Thomas WILKINS c/o John M/DANIEL; John WILSON c/o Joshua RUSSELL; John WILSON c/o Alexander TURNER.

Letters remaining at the Post Office at York Town, 13 February 1793: William ALLISON c/o James LAIRD; James ARMSTRONG, Professor in the Academy, York Town; James BRICE, Marsh Creek; Anthony BRIGS c/o Mr. IRVING, Getty's Town; Adam CARSON c/o Philip MYER; Oliver CLARK; Arthur CLOHESY, York Co.; John COMMON, near Peach Bottom Ferry; George CONN c/o George IRWIN, Little York; Thomas COOPER, near Peach Bottom Ferry; William COOPER c/o James DILL; Thomas CROSS Junr., Franklin Twp.; James DARAUGH, Fawn Twp.; William DERRY c/o James OLIVER; Thomas DILL, Monaghan Twp.; Thomas DINSMORE; Joseph DODDS, Sen., York Co.; Hugh DONAGHAY, Fawn Twp.; Seth DUNCAN, Abbot's Town; Thomas DUNN c/o the Rev. George BRINKERHOOFF; David DUNWOODY Junr., Cumberland Twp.; Thomas EWING, Franklin Twp.; Samuel, John & David FINLEY c/o James SHORT; Robert FOSTER, Manallen Twp.; John GALLAGHER c/o Hugh GALLAGHER; Charles GOLDEN, Cumberland Twp.; Robert GRAHAM, Manallen Twp.; William GRIER c/o Seth DUNCAN; Dr. Corbin GRIFFIN, York Town; Patrick HEAGERTY c/o Sandress (?) ERWIN; John HENDERSON c/o David AGNEW; George KILLINGER, near Kimmils Town; Hugh LAIRD, Chanceford Twp.; Thomas LOW, Merchant, Gettysburgh; James M'ALLISTER, Hopewell Twp.; William M'ARTHUR c/o Col. Moses M'CLEAN; Robert M'CAUSLAND, Fawn Twp.; Alexander M'CLOSKEY, Chanceford Twp.; Patrick M'CORLEY, Fawn Twp.; Ephraim M'COURTNEY, Fawn Twp.; Thomas M'CREARY & William NELSON, Chanceford Twp.; George M'DEVTT, Chanceford Twp.; Tarance M'FADIN c/o James MURRAY; James M'KEALESS, Fawn Twp.; Robert M'MULLAN, Warrington Twp.; John M'NUTT c/o David M'CONAUGHY, Esq.; William M'NUTT c/o Francis M'NUTT; Thomas MACKEY, Chanceford Twp.; Thomas MULLEDY c/o William COCHRAN, Esq.; John MURPHY, Chanceford Twp.; Kennedy MURRAY, Fawn Twp.; Capt. Malcas MURRAY, Little York; Robert ORR c/o William M'CALEY; Samuel PATTERSON c/o William NELSON, Merchant; Archibald PURDY, Muddy Creek; William PURDY c/o Joseph REED Esq.; Godfrey ROUIG, 3 miles from York; Mrs. RUMMELLS, York Town; James SMITH, Chanceford Twp.; Patrick STEWART, Hopewell Twp.; Robert STEWART, Chanceford Twp.; William TWINAM, Hamiltonban Twp. to the care of Ambrose UPDEGRAFF, Little York; William WALKER c/o James LAIRD; Patrick WALLAS c/o Joshua RUSSELL; David WILEY, Hopewell Twp.; Ezekiel WILEY, York Co. James EDIE, P. M.

Letters remaining in the Post Office, York-Town, 8 May 1793: Thomas ADAMS, York Town; William AGNEW, Mountjoy Twp.; Andrew BOYD, Marsh Creek; Thomas BRADY, Opossom Creek; Jacob BUSHOAG, (?) Bellows Maker, York Town; Thomas CANTWELL c/o Alexander IRVINE, Merchant; Widow CARSON, near Opossom CREEK; Matthew CLELLAND c/o Andrew THOMPSIN Esq.; William DAY, York Town; Jacob FAHS, York Town; John FORSITT (alias) FONITT, York Town; Mr. GANDER in Little York; John GRATT, Merchant, Hanover Town; James KELLY Esq., York Town; John KELLY, Chanceford Twp.; Dr. George KUIPLER, Chemist, York Town; Miss Kitty LEAMON, Bermudian Creek; James

LOTHER c/o Gwain SCOTT; Charles M'ALLISTER, Carrols Tract; Samuel M'CURTY, Butt's Town; James M'GAVOCK, Windsor Twp.; John M'GIMSEY (?) Student in Divinity; James M'MENNEMY c/o Hans MORRISON; George M'MULLEN, Fawn Twp.; George M'NAUGHT c/o Thomas M'NAUGHT; Thomas MACKEY, Chanceford Twp.; William MARSHALL, York Town; Paul METZGAR, Merchant, Hanover Town; John MILLER, Dover Town; Reynolds RAMSEY, York Co.; Mary Magdalen RUHLER, York Town; George SMITH, Merchant, Hanover Town; James SPEAR, near M'CALL's Ferry; Dorothy STEHR, York Town; James STEWART c/o Robert JOANSES; Peter TINKLE, York Town; Ulshu(?) UNDERWOOD, Esq., Monahan Twp.

Letters remaining at the Post Office, York-Town, 17 July 1793: William ALLISON c/o Suaw DEADE-- (?), Chanceford Twp.; Francis ARCHER c/o Rev. Mr. DOBBIN, James ARMSTRONG c/o George SHOLER, Tavernkeeper; James ARMSTRONG, Mathematician c/o Andrew JOHNSTON; George ASPER, Reading Twp.; John BARCLAY c/o Robert BLAIN; Nicholas BARNHART, York Town; Robert BARNHILL c/o Thomas NIEIF, Little York; Elijah P. BARROWS, Millers Town; Alexander BLACK c/o James BLACK; William BLAIN, Chanceford Twp.; Edmond BOYD c/o William BAILEY, Esq.; James BOWOM (?), Hanover; John BOYD c/o Joseph REED, Chanceford Twp.; William BRENHAND, Carroll's Tract; Anthony BRIGGS c/o Mr. IRWIN, Gettysburg; William BRODLEY, M'Allister's Town for William WRIGHT; John BUCHANAN c/o the Rev. Mr. DOBBIN; Robert CARSON c/o William SMITH Esq.; James CAVEREY c/o Thomas NEILL; John CHAMBERS c/o Thomas LILLY; Adam CLARK, Wilises Creek; Miss Easter CLARK c/o George KERR, Gettysburg; John CONNEL c/o Moses M'CLEAN, Esq.; Oliver CLERK c/o Mr. KERR, Gettysbug; George CONN c/o George IRWIN; Samuel CORNHILL c/o ---- REED, Esq.; Philip COROAN c/o Col. John LAIRD; William COROREN c/o Benjamin PEDAN Esq.; James CRAWFORD c/o Malcom BOGIE; Miss Katherine CULHOUN, Marsh Creek; Alexander CUNNINGHAM c/o George IRWIN; William DEAREY (DERREY?), Schoolmaster c/o Andrew DUNSMORE; Dr. David DEMSTER, Gettysburg; Dennis DEVENNY, Shrewsbury Twp.; John DEVENNY, Shrewsbury Twp.; James DICKEY, Gettysburg; Matthew DILL, Monaghan Twp.; Alexander DOWNING c/o James KELLY, Esq.; James FINLEY c/o Robert WILSON, Tavernkeeper; James FLANAGAN, Chanceford Twp.; Thomas GILMORE, Hamilton Twp.; Hugh GRAHAM c/o Robert BLAIN; Robert GRAHAM, Fawn Twp.; James GRIMES c/o Joseph REED; Samuel HAYES, Chanceford Twp.; Miss Jean HILAND c/o Robert WILSON; George HUGHES c/o William BOWNER; Samuel JAROISON(?) c/o Michael KINKAID, Marsh Creek; Samuel JOHNSTON, Blacksmith c/o William BAILEY, Esq.; Jacob KEISER c/o John ERENSTEN, Hatter; James KELLY c/o Robert WILSON; James KIRKER c/o John LARID Brogue Tavern; Col. John & James LAIRD, Chanceford Twp.; William LARIMERE, upper end of York Co.; William LONG, Taylor, York Town; Patrick M'CANON c/o Harmap UPDEGRAFF; David M'CLEARY, York Co., Waggoner; William M'CLELAN c/o Robert GRIER; John, Samuel & James M'CULOUGH c/o Joseph DICKSON; George M'CONNEL, Hamiltonban Twp.; George M'DEVID, Mountpleasant Twp.; Robert M'GINEEY, Marsh Creek; Katharine M'GLAUGHLIN c/o John FORSYTH; Archibald M'GREW, between York Town & Carlisle; William M'KESSON, York Co.; Thomas M'NANGET, Warrington Twp.; Charles M'NULTY, Mountjoy Twp.; Brian M'SHERRY c/o Robert JONES; Kearey MAGANRAN, stone layer c/o Thomas NIELL; Philip MECKLING c/o Jacob UPP; Peter MILLER, Tavernkeeper, York Town; Alexander MOORE c/o George KERR, Gettysburg; Samuel MOORE, Gettysburg; Ingraham MORRIS, M'Allister's Town; James MORTON, taylor, Marsh Creek; John MORTON, Manallen Twp.; Charles MURRAY, Fawn Twp.; Mrs. Christina MYER, Hellain Twp.; Robert NILSON c/o Samuel NILSON; Edward O'HAIL, Monaghan Twp.; Samuel OSBURN,

Schoolmaster, Strabane Twp.; John PLATT c/o George KERR, Gettysburg; Andrew PATTON, Wheelright, near M'Call's FERRY; Matthew PATTON at Wright's Ferry; David POTTER, York Co.; John POTTS c/o John LARID; Joseph REED Esq., Chanceford Twp.; Godfrey REIM, Tinman & Potter, York Town; John ROBERTSON, Berwick Twp.; Joshua RUSSELL, Marsh Creek; William SPRINCKEL c/o Daniel SPRINCKEL; James STOCKDALE, Marsh Creek; John STUART c/o the Rev. Mr. DOBBIN; Adam TERROWN, Anderson's Ferry; Paul THOMPSON c/o Robert WILSON; Robert THOMPSON c/o Robert WILSON; James TURNER c/o William EDIE; Dr. Roger WALES, Gettysburg; Henry WILLCOCKS, Printer, M'Allister's Town; Higb WILLIAMSON, Tyrone Twp.; Andrew WILSON c/o Robert GRIER; John WILSON c/o Mr. KERR, Gettysburg; Samuel WILSON c/o Joshua RUSSELL.

List of Letters in the Post Office at York Town, 1 July 1795: William ALKINS, Chanceford Twp.; Robert ANDREW, Chancedord Twp; Henry APPLEY, Tobacconist York Town; Messrs. Henry & James ARMSTRONG c/o George SHALLER; Elijah P. BARROWS, Millers Town, York Co.; John BEARY, Monaghan Twp.; John BROWN, York Town; John BUCHANAN, Chanceford Twp; John BURLEIGH c/o Thomas GURLEY, Marsh Creek; Hugh CAMPBELL, Strabane Twp. c/o Capt. JOUNISON(?); John CAMPBELL, York Town; Rev. James CLARKSON, York Co.; Alexander COBEAN, York Co.; William COLLINS c/o Rev. James CLARKSON, York Co.; Moses DAVIS, Dover twp., near Conowago; Nathaniel DEVERELL, shoemaker, near Bermudian Creek; John DONNELL, Fawn Twp.; John DOUGLAS, Chanceford Twp. c/o Rev. James CLARKSON; James DUNCAN, York; William FRANCIS near Gettys Town; William GALLAGHER, Schoolmaster c/o John GREER, York Town; James GARDNER, Huntington Twp.; Robert GEMBLE in the Barrons of York; Lawrence GIBBONS, York Town; Jacob GIBSON, York Co.; Thomas GORDON, Taylor c/o James GORDON, Peach Bottom Ferry; William HARE c/o John M'GEAN, Esq., Marsh Creek; John HENDERSON, Abbetts Town; John HERRON, Hopewell Twp.; Timothy HICKEY, near Peach Bottom Ferry; Patrick HILLON, Little York; John INNES c/o James SHORT, merchant, York Town; Richard JAMESON, Fawn Twp.; Samuel JOHNSTON, York; Rev. Daniel JONES, Monaghan Twp. c/o Mr. SHORT; Alexander KERNAGHAN c/o John M'CLEAN, Esq., Marsh Creek; Col. John LAIRD, Broueg(?) Tavern, York Co.; George LASHELLS, Strabane Twp; Jacob LISCHEY, York Co.; James LONG, Chanceford Twp.; John M'CAY, Fawn Twp.; Joseph M'GUINN, Marsh Creek or Abbots Town; William M'KASSON (M'KAFFON?), near Fair Field Town, York Co.; William M'KELWIE, Hopewell Twp.; Jacob MANLEY, Menallan Twp.; Samuel MITCHELL c/o William MITCHELL, Esq. Monaghan Twp.; Adam MORRISON, Strabane Twp.; Michael MORRISON, Hopewell Twp. c/o James SHORT, York Town; Kenedy MORROW or James MOORRW(?) c/o Jacob GIBSON, York Co.; William MURRAY, Hopewell Twp. c/o James SHORT, York; James ORBISON, Esq., York Town; Samuel OSBOURN, Strabane Twp., York Co.; Margaret RAINEY c/o the Rev. Alexander DOBBINS, Gettysburgh; John RINGLAND, Junr. c/o John FISHER, York Town; John ROBERTSON, Berwick Twp.; Patt RUSSELL c/o James ROBB, York Town; John Chr. SEIZ, York Town; Edward SHEA, Monaghan Twp.; John SMITH, Little York; John STERLING c/o William THOMPSON, Strabane Twp.; Matt(?) STEWART, Hopewell Twp.; Frederick STUMP, living 4 miles from the River Susquehannah, York Co.; Alexlander TURNER, Esq. c/o John GREER, merchant, York Town; Mrs. Jean TURNER, c/o Rev. Alexander DOBBINS, Gettysburgh, Marsh Creek; Joseph WALKER, Marsh Creek; James WILSON, Franklin Co. c/o William WAUGH in Carrols Tract, York Co.; Charles YOUNG, merchant, York Town; John YOUNG, carpenter, M'Alister's Town, York Co. Jacob SPANGLER, P. M.

APPENDIX B: LETTERS AT THE CARLISLE POST OFFICE (From the Carlisle Gazette)

List of Letters at the Post Office in Carlisle, 5 August 1791: James ADAIR, Alexander AIKEN, Joseph ALLEN, William ATCHISON, Thomas BAIRD, William BARBER, William BANE, William BARBER, William BARNHILL, John BARNS, Alexander BEATTY, Elizabeth BINGHAM, James BOGGS, William BRICE, William BROWN, Alexander BROWN, Henry BRYNAN, Anthony BURNS, James BUTLER, Sarah BUTLER, John CALDWELL, Rev. Joseph CALDWELL, George CAMPBELL, Robert CAMPBELL, Andrew CARLILE, John CARLISLE, Thomas CARSCADAN (?), James CARSON, William CARUSCHAN, John CHATHAM, Thomas CHISOLM, Adam CLELAND, William H. COAN, Jane COCHRAN, Richard COCHRAN, John COOPER, Edward COULTER, Francis COULTER, James or Patrick COULTER, James COWAN, Church COX Esq., Capt. William COX, Samuel COZBY, James CRAWFORD, John CRISTY, Thomas CROCKETT, John CROTHERS, William CROW, John CUNNINGHAM, William DASERMOND, Samuel R. DAVIS, Thomas DEEMOND, William DEETY, Robert DICK, James DICKEY, Robert DUNBAR, James ELDER, James FAIR, Thomas FLEEMAN, Nathan FOOTHORN, James GARDNER, James GARRETT, John GERTARD, John GIBSON, David GILLELAND, James GILLELAND, Brice GILMOR, James GLAIGO, William GLOVER, David GRAFTON, John GRAY, Capt. Henry GREER, John HAGAN, Hugh HANNAH, William HANNAH, John HALFPENNY, James HAMILTON, Thomas HAMILTON, Thomas HARDY c/o John HUNTER, David HARPER, John HARPER, John HAYS, Letitia HEGG, Henry HERBY, Philip HOLLAMAN, Jonathan HOOD, James HUES, Dr. Samuel HUEY, James HUMPHRIES, Robert HUNTER, William INGRAM, Ishbald IRWIN, Thomas IRWIN, Elizabeth JOHNSTON, Andrew KELLEY, James KENNEDY, John KERR, William KERRICK, Thomas KILTEY, John KINSAY, Thomas LATHERDEAL, Robert LEYBURN, William LEYBURN, William LONG, John LOUGHREY, Maac LOVERTY, Robert LUSK, John LYON, Robert LYON, George M'CANDISH, Robert M'CANU, John M. M'CASKEY, Daniel M'CAULEY, Robert M'CLELLAN, John M'CLURE, Mathew M'CLURE, William M'CLURE, James M'CORD, Archd. M'COY, Alexander M'CRACKEN, Joseph M'DONALD, John M'GRATH, Thomas M'GUIRE, Gabriel M'KINMAN, Andrew M'LAUGHLEN, Andrew M'LAUGHLIN, James M'NEELY, Hugh M'NELLY, Edward M'PIKE, John M'WILLIAMS, Robert MAFFET, William MAFFET, John MAGEE, Rev. Hugh MAGILL, Hugh MARTIN, James MARTIN, Jane MARTIN, Audly MATTSON, Henry MERCER, Robert MILHEE, James MILLAR, James MINNIS, George MITCHELL, James MITCHELL, James MOORE, John MOORE, William MOORE, Thomas MORRISON, John MORROW, William MORROW, William MURPHEY, Edward O'DONNELL, William PATTON, Thomas G. POLLARD, John POTTER, John POTTS, Patrick QUEEN, Jeremiah REED, George REID, James REID, James RIGGS, Elizabeth ROBINSON, Alexander RUTTER, Rebecca SAINTCLAIR, William SCOTT, James SEMPLE, John SHARP, Joseph SMITH, John SPEER, Archibald STEWART, Richard SWAN, Moses TEAS, Elizabeth THOMPSON, James THOMPSON, John TODD, Daniel TOLSON, John TOMB, William VANCOMPT, John WALKFIELD, Ellias WALLEN, John WHIGIM, David WHITE, William WILLIAMS, William WILLIS, Alexander WILCOX, Adam WILSON, John WILSON, William WILSON, James WOODS, John WOTK, Samuel WUINGS.

List of Letters Remaining at the Post Office at Carlisle as of 28 December 1791: Francis ALEXANDER, Joseph ALLEN, William ANDERSON, Andrew ASKEW, William ATCHISON, William BARBER, John BARNES, Robert BARNES, William BATTER(?), Alexander BEATTY, Joseph BEATTY, Thomas BELL, Thomas BELT, Samuel BENNET, John BLACK, Charles BOVARD, Daniel BOYD, Col. William BRATEN, James BRIGLAND, Henry BROAN, Daniel BROWN, George BROWN, Thomas BROWN, Robert BURNS, Nicholas BLAKE, Henry BRYNAN, Anthony BURNES, Thomas BURNS, Thomas BURRICE, James CAMBLIN, Dennis CAMPBELL, James CAMPBELL, William CAMPBELL, Alex. CAR, John CAROTHERS, Ja. CARSKADDEN, James CARTAN, John CHATAM, Henry COAN, David COFFAT, Hugh COOK, James COWAN, Robert CRAGE, Robert CREE, William CROFFAN, Esther CRORL, Thomas

CUMMINGS, John CUSACK, Jeremiah DALY, Alexander DAVIDSON, William DAVIDSON, William DEERY, William DICKSON, William DILL, Joseph DONAGHY, Edward DOUGHERTY, Hugh DRUGON, John DUNLAP, Rev. James DUNN, Robert EAKIN, Robert EATON, John EMMICK, Andrew ERWIN, Mathew & James FINDLEY, Nathaniel FISH or SITH, John FISHER, James FLEMMING, Charles FORDE, James GARDNER, Capt. GAWDY, William GEALY, John GIVEN Esq., Owen GORILNAY, James GRAHAM, Robert GRAHAM, William GRAHAM, John or William GRATTAN, John GREENWOOD, Alex. GRENTREL, John GTIER, Andrew GWYN, John HAMILTON, William HAMMOND, James HARPER, John HARPER, Jacob HARWICK, John HARWICK, John HEMPHILL, William HENERSON, Andrew HENDERSON, Mrs. HENON, John HENRY, Henry HERVEY, John HINDMAN, James HOES/HUES(?), James HOOD, Col. Daniel HUGHES, James HUMPHRIES, James HUNTER, Joseph HUNTER, Robert HUNTER, Samuel HUNTER, Robert HUTCHINSON, James KEE, Hguh KELLY, John KERR, Dennis KILLIN, William KILLGOAR, Thomas KILTY, John KINSEY, James KIRKPATRICK, Robert KNOX, L. Isaac LAVERTY, Andrew LEMY or LOWRY, Andrew LINDSAY, George LONG, William LONG, Major James LOWRY, Major Robert LOWRY, Widow LOWRY, Robert LYON, John M'ADAM, Benjamin M'AREAVEY, Hugh M'CALERY, Peter M'CARNEY, William M'CAUSLAND, Robert M'CLELLAN, John M'CLURE, Samuel M'CLURE, James M'COMB, Thomas M'CORMICK, James M'CUNE Esq., Joseph M'DONALD, James M'ENTIRE, John M'INTAIR, Bryan M'KEENE, Alexander M'KENDRY, Patrick M'KENNA, Bernard M'KEON, William M'KNIGHT, Samuel M'KOWN, Robert M'MANES, Archibald M'MILLIAN, Michael M'MULLAN, Frederick M'NAMEE, John M'NAUGHTON, James M'NEALY, Malcum M'PHERSON, Andrew M'WAINE, John M'WILLIAMS, James MACKELROY, Prussia MACLEAN, James MACLEND, Samuel MAGREGER, James MARCHBANK, Jenny MARTIN, Samuel MATHERS, James MATTHEWS, Samuel MATTHEWS, Audly MATTSON, Robert MILBY, William MILLAN, John MITCHAL, James MITCHEL, James MITCHELL, James MOORE, William MOORE, Daniel MOOREHEAD, William MOORHEAD, Robert MORDAUGH, William MORRAW, John MORROW, William MORROW, Edward MORTON, James MULLAN, Agness MURDOCK, Andrew MOZZOW, Matthew NEILLY, Charles NEWTON, Alexander NOBLE, Jane NOBLE or WOODS, Samuel PAXTON, Mr. PEARCE, Stacy POTTS, Charles PROVINCE, David QUIN, Alexander RAMSAYA, Jeremiah REED, Andrew REID, James REID, Lewis ROBERTSON, Andrew ROBINSON, Thomas ROGERS, Simon ROSS, James RUGGS, Thomas SAMSON, Matthias SAYLOR, Joseph SCOTT, William SCOTT, Francis SEMPLE, John SEMPLE, John SHERARD, John SHIELDS, James SIMMS, Alexander SKADDEN, Archibald SLOSS, Archibald SMITH, James SMITH, Alexander SPEER, William or Mathew SPEER, Rev. Mathew STEPHEN, Archibald STEWARD, Charles STEWARD, Hugh STEWARD, Thomas STEWARD, William STUART, Benjamin TAYLOR, Samuel TAYLOR, John THEKER, Mrs. General THOMPSON, Hugh THOMPSON, Robert THOMPSON, William, James and Alexander THOMPSON, William THOMPSON or Andrew M'EBWAIN, Naomi TODD, Samuel TOM, John TOMB, James TOMLINSON, Benjamin VAN SKOY, David WALKER, John WALKER, Elizabeth WALSH, Grace WARD, James WATSON, Thomas & John WILSON, Samuel WILLIAMSON, Peter WILLY, John WILTON, James YOUNG, William YOUNG.

List of Letters Remaining at the Post Office in Carlisle as of July 1st, 1792: Ignatious ADAMS, Alexander ANDERSON, John ANDERSON, John BARBER, Robert BARNES, William BEATTIE, Samuel BENNET, William BLACK, James & Thomas BOAL, Francis BOHNER (BONNER?), Adam BRANDT, Matthew BROWN, William BRYSON, Anthony BURNIES, Alexander BURNSIDE, Joseph CAMBLE, John CAROTHERS, Samuel CARR, Joseph CASTLES, Robert CLARKE, Adam CLELAND, James CLELAND, Hugh COOK, William COOK, John COOPER, James COWAN, John COWAN, Alexander CRAWFORD, Robert CRISWELL, Samuel CROSSAN(?), William CROSSAN(?), Thomas CROTHERS, Capt. E. DENNEY, Robert DICK, James DICKEY,

Michael DOYLE, Robert DUNBAR, Rev. Mr. DUBENDORFF, John DUNLAP, Robert ELLIOTT, John FALUNE, George FISHER, James FOREMAN, Thomas FORREST, George FRY, Daniel GASTON, Daniel GRAFTON, Samuel GRAY, Adam GROVER, James HAMILTON, Robert HAPHET or HACKET, Thomas HARDCASTLE, Robert HARRISON, Robert HARVEY, J. HARWICK, Joseph HENDERSON, John HENNING, William HENRY, Robert HOGG, Dr. Samuel HUEY, David HUMPHRY, Job HUNTER, Thomas HUNTER, Alexander IRWIN, Thomas IRWIN, James IRWINE, Mathew JOHNSTON, Samuel JONES Esq., Alexander KERR, David KING, Peter KURTZ, William LONG, Isaac LOVERTY, William LYON, Mathew M'BRIDE, Charles M'CAY, Sarah M'CHOWN, John M'CLEAN, Charles M'CLURE, James M'CLURE, John M'COLLUGH, James M'COMB, John M'CONIGLE, Archibald M'COOK, Arthur M'CRERY, Hugh M'CULLOUGH, John M'DANNAL, Samuel M'DOWELL, James M'ENTIRE, Charles M'GRATH, Adam M'KEE, Hugh M'KEE, Patrick M'KENNEY, Robert M'KIBBON, Gilbert M'KIMEN, Cornelius M'MAHAN, William M'MAHON, Daniel M'MULION, George M'MULLON, Alexander M'NAUGHTON, John M'NAUGHTON, John M'NEILY, James MARTIN, William MARTIN, William MASSET(?), James MATEER, James MATTHEWS, William MEEK, Dr. Adam Henry MEJER, James MILLER, Philip MILLER, John MILTNER, George MINICK, Ross MITCHELL, Jean MORROW, John MORROW, John MURRAY, Lawrence NECHILS, William NEILANCE, THomas ORR, John PIPER, Robert PORTER, Charles PROVINCE, Matthew RABB, James RAMSEY, Alex. REA, And. REED, Solomon REID, George RIDDLES, James RITHDGE(?), Lewis ROBINSON, Thomas ROGERS, John ROSS, James SIMPSON, Michael SLAVIN, Ezekiel SMITH, James SMITH, James SPEER, Charles STEWARD, Thomas STEWARD, Benjamin TAYLOR, James THOMPSON, John THOMPSON, Mathew VANLEAR, John WALKER, Benj. WALLACE, George WALLACE, Patr. WALLACE, William WALLACE, John WARDEN, Edward WARNOCK, Hugh WATSON, Part. WILLIAMS, Thomas WOODS, Wm. WOODS.

Letters remaining at the Post Office, Carlisle, PA October, 1792: John ALEXANDER; George ALLAN; Nathaniel ALLEN; Robert ALLEN; Abraham ANDERSON: Alex. ANDERSON; John ANDERSON; James ANDERSON; Archibald ARMSTRONG; Daniel BLACKHOUSE; William DEERY; George DENEERY; James DILLAP; William DINNING; Dennis DOHERTY; Samuel DOUGHERTY; Andrew DODDS; William DOWNING; James DRUMMOND; James DUNLAP; Robert DUNN; John DUNNING; James ELLAT; Robert ELWOOD; James FAIR; John FALUNE; Nathaniel FISH; William FULTAN; John FULTON; Robert GAMMET; William GEDDES; Brabazon GIBBONS; John GIBSON; Joseph GIBSON; Robert GIBSON; David GIEB(?); Nicholas GILLISPIE; John GILMORE; Robert GILNEM; William GLENN; Charles GOLDEN; Daniel GRAFTON; David GRAHAM; Hugh GRAHAM; Robert GRAHAM; John & Catharine GRAY; Robert GRAY; Alexander GREDDIN; William GRIER; James GUY; Andrew GWINN; William HAGARTY; Benjamin HALL; Hugh HALL; Isabella HALL; Jacob HALLER; Mr. HAMILTON & S. GRAHAM; Robert HAMMAND; William HANNAH; John HARPER; William HART; James HAYS; Hugh HEART; John HEART; John HENRY; Elizabeth HILTON; Andrew HINDMAN; John HOLAMS; William HOLLIDAY; James HOOD; Robert HOOD; Thomas HOUSWAING: John HUEY; David HUMPHREY; Samuel or Josias HUMPHRIES; Alex. HUNTER; Jane HUNTER; Robert HUNTER; Francis JOHNSON; John JOHNSTON; Matthew JOHNSTON; Mary JOHNSTON; Stephen JOHNSTON; William JOHNSTON; James JONES; Samuel JONES, Esq; Jane IRVIN; Thomas IRWIN; Thomas KAIN; John KELLY; Thomas KENADY; John KENNEDY; Oliver KERR; Samuel KERR; David KING; William KNOX; Capt. Robert LAIK; John LAMAND; James LAMBO; Laurence LAUGHRAN; Adam LAUGHTON; Isaac LAVERTY; Thomas LEATHERDEAL; Rachel LEE; William LEYBURG; John LIGGIT; James LONG; William LONG; Hugh & John LOWERMORE; Hamilton LOWRY; John LOWRY; Robert LUSK; John LYANS; William LYON; John LYONS; William LYONS; Benjamin M'AREVEY; Nathaniel

M'BRIAR; Bryan M'CAFFERTY; Robert M'CAIN; Sarah M'CHOWN; Joseph M'CLEAN; James M'CLENACHAN; Thomas M'CLUNE; James M'COLLAM; James M'COMB; John M'CONOGHY; James M'CORMICK; Arch. M'COWAN; James M'CRAY; John M'CULLOUGH; Hugh M'CURCHIN; Samuel M'CUTCHIN; John M'DONALD; Joseph M'ELHINEY; James M'ENTIRE; James M'FARLAND; Alexander M'GEE; William M'GINEGS; Samuel M'GOWN; John M'GRATH; William M'GUIRE; Mr. M'GUIRE (Shoemaker); James M'GURGILL; Dr. M'INTIRE; George K'KEE; William M'KEE: Edward M'KEFFERTY; Philip M'KENA; Alexander M'KENDRY; Patrick M'KENNEY; Joseph M'KIM; William M'KINNEY; James M'LAUGHLIN; William M'MAHON; William M'MICHAEL; Daniel M'MULLAN; James M'MULLAN or Malcom M'MILL; John M'NAUGHTON; Colin M'NUTT; John M'WILLIAMS; Alexander MACHARG; Charles MAGEE; John MAXWELL; William MAXWELL; John MAGIRE; John MAGRATAH; Benjamin MAIRS; William MAKLEN; John MALLIAN; George MARTIN; James MATEER; William MCLASTER; Grace MEALEY; Robert MEANS; Prussia MECLEAN; William MEEK; John MEKEN; Hugh MEKERY(?); Philip MELONE; Alexander MEWHOOD; William MILES; Thomas MILLAT; Alexander MILLER; John MILLER; Joseph MILLER; Matthew MILLER;Robert MISKELLY; James MITCHEL; Samuel MITCHEL; Henry MONTIESH; Alex. MOORE; Catharine MOORE otherwise PATTERSON; Joseph MOORE; Samuel MOORE; Hugh MORISON; Rev. Hugh MORRISON; Robert MORRISON; John MORROW; James & Robert MURDOGH; Isatolus MURPHY; Ephraim MURRAY; Francis MURRAY; John MURRAY; Samuel MURRAY; --- MURRAY, Esq.; Joseph NEEL; George NESBITT; Lawrence NICHELL; Samuel NOBLE; John O'CONN; Thomas O'CONNOR; Thomas O'MULLAN; John OLIVER; Andrew ORR; Thomas PALLEY; John PATTAN; Matthew PATTERSON; James PATTON; Mr. PEARCE; John PEDAN; Thomas POLLOCKS; Elizabeth POTTS; William PORTER; Mary POWER; Charles PROVINCE; Robert PULLUCK(?); Frederick QUIGLY; Patrick RABB; James RAINEY; David RALSTON; James RAMSAY; William RANKIN; Colling READ; John REED; John or William REED; Widow REED; John REGAN; George RIDDLE, Robert RIGHT; Anthony ROBINSON; Lewis ROBISON; Thomas ROGERS; Serg. John ROSS; George SCHNEIDER; Thomas or Betty SHEARMAN; William SHAW; John SHIELDS; Thomas SHIRLEY; Jacob SILFUS; John SIMPSON; Nathaniel SIMPSON; William SIMPSON; Michael SLAVIN; James SMITH; William SMITH, Esq.; Rev. Wm. SPEER; John STEPHENSON; James SMYTH; Hugh STEWART; James STEWART; Moses STEWART & Carry; Thomas STEWART; James THOMPSON; Serj. John THOMPSON; John THOMPSON; William THOMPSON; Naomi TODD; John TOM; Martha TURNER; William TURNER; Matthew VAN LEAR; Alexander VAUGHAN; William WADDELL; Thompson WAEHUP; Robert WALKER; George WALLACE; Patrick WALLACE; Robert WALSOP (WALLOP?) Andrew WATTS; Robert WIER; John WILEY; Archibald WILKINSON; James WILLIAMSON; John WILLIAMSON; Samuel WILLS; Thomas WILSON; William WILSON; Alexander WOOD; Thomas WOOD; Alexander or Thomas WOODBURN; William WOODS; William WRAY; James WRIGHT; Patrick WRIGHT.

Letters remaining at the Post Office, Carlisle, PA January 1793: John ANDERSON, head of the Narrows; William ANDERSON, Shearman's Valley; Sarah ARMSTRONG, Yellow Breeches; John ATWELL, Spring Well; Robert AULD; John BARCKLEY, Juniata; James BARRON c/o John STEWART;John BEATY, Wayne twp; William BELL c/o Mr. REA; David BOUES, Juniata; Samuel BOYD c/o BELL & GIVEN; Sarah BOYD c/o Mr. DUNCAN; Thomas BREADY, Pine Grove; William BROOK, Yellow Breeches; John BROWN, Yellow Breeches; Robert BUCHANAN, carpenter; Darcas BUCHANON, E. Pennsbro'; Robert BURNS c/o Adam JOHNSTON; Thomas BURRIS, Newton twp; John CALDWELL, near Carlisle; John CLARK, Yellow Breeches; Ben. CAR c/o Robert SMITH; Thomas CARRICK, Kishacoquillis; James or Pat. COULTER, Tuskarora; James COWEN, Kishacoquillis; Michael CRESASS, Carlisle; Andrew CROCKET, Yellow

Breeches; John CULBERTSON, Wayne twp; Thomas CUMMINGS c/o J. ADAIR; Jeremiah DALY, Lewistown; William DINNINGS, E. Pennsbro'; Dinnis DOUGHERTY c/o James ALEXANDER, Lewistown; Patrick DOUGHERTY c/o James LAMBERTON; Alexander DOW, Carlisle; William DRINNAN; John DUNLASS, Juniata; Dr. Adam FRANK, Carlisle; Margaret FRAZER; James FERGUSON, Milford twp; Jonathan FORSTER, Carlisle; John FULTON c/o Mr. JAMESON; Felix GILBERT, Carlisle; David GILESPY c/o William M'CRACKEN; John GILMOR, Shearman's Valley; John GLASGOW c/o William BROWN, Esq.; William GRAHAM c/o John HUNTER; William GREER c/o Hugh WILSON; Joseph HAGERTY c/o John KYLE; James HARPER, W. Pennsbro'; Thomas HEASTY(?) c/o John WRAY; Joseph HENDERSON, near Carlisle; William HENRY c/o Robert MILLER, Esq.; Robert HERVEY c/o Samuel M'COMMON; Arthur HOGAN, Bigspring; William HOLMES c/o John STEWART, Esq.; James HOOD c/o John HUNTER; Alexander HUNTER, Newton twp; Thomas HUNTER c/o Sarah M'DONALD; Robert KERR, Path Valley; John KINKEAD c/o Dr. NESBIR (?): George KLEIN, near Carlisle; Mrs. KUREYS; John LAFERTY, near Carlisle; James LAMONS, Big Spring; James LAUGHRY c/o James LAMBERTON; Henry LECKEY, near Carlisle; George LESLIE c/o John M'COY; Samuel LOGAN, Wayne twp.; James LONG c/o Mr. HUNTER; John LOUGHRY c/o John REA; Samuel LOVE c/o John HUNTER; Robert LUSK c/o John HUNTER; William LYONS, Kishacoquillia; John M'CASKEY, Big Spring; John M'CLURE c/o Samuel GREY; Rebecca M'CLURE, Strasburgh; Archibald M'COWAN c/o John HUNTER; Hugh M'COY; Thomas M'CUNE, Middle Spring; Thomas M'FETTEN c/o John HUNTER; James M'GEE; Rev. Hugh M'GILL; Thomas M'KEE, Tuskarora; William M'KEE c/o Charles M'CLURE; Charles M'KEOWN c/o John BROWN, Esq.; Margaret M'KINLEY; William M'KINNEY, Huntingdon Co; Arthur M'MACKEN, Big Spring; Collin M'NUTT, Tuskarora; Gudey M'WILLIAMS; John M'WILLIAMS, Hopewell Twp; John MILLER, near Carlisle; Rachel MILLER; Mr. MILLER, Carlisle; James MILTON, Shearman's Valley; Lydia MINSHALL, Shearman's Valley; Alexander MOORE c/o Samuel STUART; Hugh MOORE c/o John WRAY; Nancy MOOREHEAD c/o John HUNTER; Alexander MURTLAND, Wayne twp; Charles NEWTON c/o Squire QUIGLEY; Edward NIXON c/o James BROWNLEE; Thomas NORTON, Walnut Bottom; John PATTON, Tuskarora; William PETER; Isaac PLUNKET; Thomas QUIGLEY, near Harrisburgh; James RAINEY c/o Geo. LOGUE, Esq.; Samuel RAMSEY, Carlisle; William RAMSAY c/o Wm. MOORE; Joseph RAY c/o John RAY; James REILY c/o John WALKER; Col. RODGERS, ferry-house, Susquehannah; Thomas ROPER, Carlisle; Robert SCOTT, Shearman's Valley; William SCOTTARD, Long hollow; James SCOTY, Carlisle; Richard SHELDON, Valley Forge; James SIMS c/o John HUNTER; Argus SINCLAIR, Huntingdon Co, Michael SKELLY, Standing stone; Hugh SMITH c/o John UNDERWOOD; James SMITH c/o John UNDERWOOD; William SPEER c/o Dr. NISBIT; William STEEL, Huntingdon town; Samuel STIRLING, near Carlisle; Daniel SWINEY, near CARLISLE; Benjamin TAYLOR c/o John WRAY; Samuel THOMSON, Shearman's Valley; William TURBETT, Tuskarora; Jacob WAGGONER, near Carlisle; James WALKER; John WALKER; James WILLIAMS, Kishacoquillis; John WILLIAMS, ditto; John WILLIAMS, Yellow Breeches; Henry WILSON; Anthony WITHERALL, Paxton; Thomas WOOD c/o Robert SMITH; William WOODS, near Carlisle.

Letters remaining at the Post Office, Shippensburgh, Pa, Jan 1793: James ADAMS & James M'CLENSHAP(?); John BORLAND; John HERREN; William JOHN; Robert MILLER; John RIPPEY; John SKINNER. Samuel QUIGLEY, Post Master.

APPENDIX B: LETTERS AT THE CARLISLE POST OFFICE (From the Carlisle Gazette)

Letters remaining at the Post Office, Carlisle, PA June, 1793: Thomas ALCHLEY, Mrs. AULD, James ANDERSON, John ANDERSON, Sarah ARMSTRONG, Wm. ATHENHURST, John ATWALL, Robert AULD, David BANES; Wm. BARBER; John BARCLAY; James BARRON; John BEATTY; David BELL; James BLACK; Thomas BLAYER, Sarah BODY; John BONNER; David BOWER; Samuel BOYD, William BOYD; Thomas BRADY; John BREDEN, William BROOK; James BROWN; John BROWN; Henry BURCHSTEAD; Thomas BURRIS; John CALHOON; John CAMPBELL; Benjamin CAR; John CAROTHERS; Thomas CAROTHERS; Samuel CHESTNUT; John CHRISTY; Robert CHRISTY; George CLARK; Robert COCKRAN; Patrick COLLINS; William COON; John CONNELLY; Samuel COXBEY; James COWEN; Samuel COYLEY; Thomas CRAWFORD; John CREERY; Mrs. Jenny CREIGHEAD; Robert CRISTWELL; Thomas CROCKET; Edmond CROSSEN; John CULBERTSON, Esq.; John CULBERTSON, Senr.; Thomas CUMMINGS; Hugh CUNNINGHAM; William CUNNINGHAM; William DAVIDSON; Michael DEECHAN; Widow DENNY; Archibald DICKEY; James DILLAN; Dr. Ezra DOTY; Dennis DOUGHERTY; John DOUGLASS; William DOWLING: William DRENNAN; Daniel DUNLAP; Edward DUNN; James ELDER; Christy ERWIN; James FERGUSON; Thomas FLOVEN; John FORSYTH; Robert FORSYTH; John FRENCH; James GARDENER; John GIBSON; William GILEY; Samuel GILMORE; John GIVEN; William GREER; Major James GRIEAR [sic]; Robert GUINEY; Andrew GWYNN; George HAMILTON; Robert HAMILTON; Joseph HEAGERTHY; Thomas HEASLEY; Thomas HEASTINGS; Robert HINDMAN; James HOLMES; Mary HOLMES; William HOLMES; James HOOD; Robert HUEY; Robert HUGBEY; Josiah HUMPHRYES; Alexander HUNTER; John HUNTER; Thomas HUNTER; James HUSTON; Robert HUSTON; Samuel HUSTON; Arthur JOHNSTON; John JOHNSTON; Stephen JOHNSTON; THomas JOHNSTON; Percival KEAN; William KERR; John KINCAID; Thomas KING; Michael KLITCH; Mrs. KURYS; John KYLE; Thomas LAUGHLIN; James LEAVY; Henry LECKEY; James LEMON; William LINCH; John LISERTY (LIFERTY?); James LLOYD; Samuel LOGAN; James LONG; James LOVE; Samuel LOVE; William M'ATEE; Margaret M'AVOY; James M'BEE; William M'CHERRY; Robert M'CLELLAND; John M'CLURE: Thomas M'CLURE; Robert M'COLLOK; John M'CONAUGHEY; Mary M'CORMICK; Archibald M'COWAN; John & George M'DOYLE; Ester M'ELDOWNY; Robert M'FETTERS; Charles M'GAGLTAGEN; George M'KEE; William M'KEE; James M'KELISPI(?); John M'KIN; William M'KINNEY; John M'KOAN; Charles M'KOWN; John M'LAUGHLIN; Arthur M'MACKIN; Charles M'MANUS; James M'NAB; Robert M'NAUGHT; William M'NEELANDS; John M'NEIL; Patrick M'NICKLE; Patrick M'NULTY; Collin M'NUTT; John M'NUT; Gudy(?) M'WILLIAMS; John M'WILLIAMS; William MAIN; Robert MARTIN; John MELLON; Naomi MILLER; Rachel MILLER; Samuel MILLER; James MITCHELL; Thomas MITCHELTREE; James MITTEN; James MOAK; Henry MOON; Alexander MOORE; Hugh MOORE; Robert MOORE; Nancy MOOREHEAD; John MORROW; Roger MULHOLLAND; Robert MURDOCH; Alexander MURTLAND; Thomas NEIL; James NICHOLSON; James NICKLE; William NOLAND; John NORRIS; Thomas OLIVER; James PATTON; James PAULEY; Edard PRITCHARD; Charles PROVINCE; Thomas QUIGLEY; Robert RALSTON; Samuel RAMSAY; William RAMSAY; Joseph RAY; Alexander REA; James REILY; John & Peter REN?; Colonel RODGERS; Thomas ROPER; Robert SCOUT; John SCOTT; Michael SHELLY; James SIMPSON; Angus SINCLAIR; George SMITH; Hugh SMITH; James SMITH; George STEEL; Robert STEEL; John STONER; William STUART; Benjamin TAYLOR; Robert THOMPSON; Thomas TOMPSON; Edward TILGHMAN; James TURNER; Patrick WALLACE; George WEIR; Jacob WELSH; Robert WHITEHILL; James WILEY; Adam WILSON; John WILSON; William WILSON; Anthony WOOD; Alexander & Thomas WOODBURN.

APPENDIX B: LETTERS AT THE CARLISLE POST OFFICE (From the Carlisle Gazette)

Letters remaining at the Post Office, Carlisle, Pa., August 1793: John ALEXANDER d/o John MONTGOMERY, Esq.; John ALLEN, Derry twp; Joseph ALLEN, Allen twp; Sarah ARMSTRONG, Yellow Breeches; Mrs. AULD c/o William HUNTER; Samuel BARBER, West-Pennsborough; James BARRON c/o John STEWART; John BEARD c/o John WEBBER; William BEGLEY, Big Aughwick; James BLACK, Lewisville; Sarah BLACK c/o John CREIGH; William BLACK c/o Samuel GRAY; Thomas BLAYER c/o James GIVEN; William BOYD, Shearman's Valley; Mathew BRADY; Eleanor BROWN c/o Rev. D. DAVIDSON; Hugh BROWN c/o John CREIGH; Thomas BROWN c/o Mr. ALEXANDER; Doteat(?) BUCHANAN c/o James POLLOCK; John CAIN; Jean CAMPBELL, Big Spring; Laughlin CAMPBELL; Capt. Thomas CAMPBELL, Monaghan twp; William CAMPBELL, Shearman's Valley; Alexander CARNACHAN c/o John CREIGH; John CAROTHERS, Middleton Twp.; Thomas CAROTHERS c/o Maj. FINLEY; Henry CARTON c/o Ephraim STEEL; James CATHCART; Luke CRAWFORD c/o John WRAY; Robert CRAWFORD; George CLARK near Carlisle; John CLARK, near Carlisle; John COLHOON, Carlisle; Sussauna CONOLEY, Carlisle; George CONYNGHAM, Toboyne twp.; Jean COOPER c/o Samuel TATE; Samuel COTTON c/o John WALKER; Henry CRAIG; Jenny CREIGHEAD; Michael CRESAP, student; John CULBERTSON; William DENNING c/o Edward MORTON; Archibald DICKEY, Gettystown; James DICKEY, Juniata; John DICKEY; Richard DIMSEY c/ol John CREIGH; Hugh DOUGHTERY, West Pennsborough; Edward DOUGHERTY c/o John CALDWELL; James DOUGHERTY c/o John WEBBER; Robenny DUNLAP c/o James BELL; Thomas ELLIOT, Shearman's Valley; Adam ERWIN; Andrew FERGUSON c/o John WRAY; William FERRIS c/o William ANDERSON; Mathew & James FINLEY c/o Ephraim STEEL; John FLEMING c/o John ANDERSON; Samuel F--NTON, Big Spring; Adam GAMBLE c/o John CREIGH; Henry GERVAN c/o Ephraim STEEL; Joseph GHORMLEY c/o John CREIGH; William GILEY s/o James GIVEN; Philip GILLAND; John GILMOR c/o Robert GRAYSON; Alexander GIVENS c/o William RAMSEY; Patrick GLACKEN c/o Thomas HUNTER; John GREGG c/o John M'COY; John GREER; Samuel GREGG c/o William HUNTER; Andrew GWINN c/o John WEBBER; John HAHN, Carlisle; Daniel HAMILL, cooper; Archibald HAMILTON c/o Samuel TATE; Hance HARPER or HARBER c/o J. HUNTER; Mathew HARPER c/o J. HUNTER; John HASLET; Mary HASLER; Thomas HASTINGS c/o J. REA; James HENDERSON c/o William BART; John HEYANDR; James HOLMES c/o J. OLIVER; Mary HOLMES, Carlisle; William HOLMES c/o J. STUART; James HOOD c/o J. HUNTER; Francis HUGHES c/o J. CAROTHERS; Thomas HUGHES c/o J. HUGHES; John HUNTER c/o R. HUSTON; Alexander HUNTER; Thomas HUNTER c/o Sarah M'CONNELL; James HUSTON c/o J. CREIGH; Joseph Turner JAMES; Thomas JOHNSTON c/o John HUNTER; Thomas JORDAN; Ralph KELLY c/o J. WEBSTER; Samuel KERR; Michael KILCH(?) c/o R. WHITEHILL; Mrs. KILGRITH (?) c/o E. MOFFOT. Robert KILGORE; Robert KNOX c/o William HUNTER; ---- KROUTZ, Carlisle; Andrew KURN. Remainder in our next. [No further remainder appeared in next or subsequent issues.]

Letters remaining at the Post Office, Carlisle, Pa., October 1793: John ALLEN; James ANDERSON; Joshua ANDERSON; William ANDERSON; Archibald ARMSTRONG; Christopher ARMSTRONG; Sarah ARMSTRONG; William ARMSTRONG; Robert BARID; Samuel BARNHILL; Robert BARR; Samuel BARR; William BARR; Albert BARRETT; James BARRON; John BATLAND; Patrick BENNETT; Hugh BILLEY; James BLACK; Sarah BLACK; William BLACK; William BLAIR; Thomas BLAYER; Charles BRADLEY; Mathew BRADLEY; Michael BRADLEY; James BREADY; Robert BREDEN; William BROWN; John BRUSTER; John CAIN; Robert CALLENDER; Samuel CAMMEL; Laughlin CAMPBELL; Capt. Thomas CAMPBELL; William CAMPBELL; Alexander CARNSHAN; John CAROTHERS; Benjamin CARR; Biddy CARR; James CARSAN; James CATHCART; Joseph CHIDERS; Thomas CHISOLM; John CLARK; Jane CLEMENTS; John COGAN; Margaret COMMINGS; John CONNER;

Sussanna CONOLLY; Thomas COOPER; Samuel COTTON; John COWAN; Henry CRAIG; David CRAWFORD; James CRAWFORD; Robert CRAWFORD; William CRAWFORD; Jenny CREIGHEAD; Michael CRESAP; Robert CRISTWELL; Samuel CULBERTSTON; Charles CUMMING; Robert DALLRUMSEL; David DERRICKSON; Archibald DICKEY; John DICKEY; Richard DIMSEY; Henry DIXON; William DOAK; Dennis DOUGHERTY; Edward DOUGHERTY; James DOUGHERTY; William DOUGHLASS; John DUNLAP; Robenny DUNLAP; Isaac DURBORRAWS; Joseph EATON; Alexander EMMIT; Adam ERWIN; William ERWIN; William FEATON; Hance FERGUSON; James FERGUSON; Roger FINLEY; Thomas FIARMAN; Bernard FISHEG; Ben. FISHER; John FLEMING; Thomas FULTON; William FULTON; William GALBREATH; James GILEY; William GILEY; Philip GILLAND; David GILLESPIE; Henry GIVAN; Alexander GIVEAR?; William GLENN; Edward GOUDEY; Alexander GRAHAM; Patrick GRAHAM; John GREER; Samuel GREGG; Robert HASLET; Andrew GWINN; Hugh HAYES; Thomas HEASSINGS; Edward HELSERTY; James HEMPHILL; Thomas HENDERSON; John HESLERT; James HILL; John HOGERTY; George HOLMES; James HOLMES; Mary HOLMES; William HOLMES; James HOOD; Robert HOOD; John HOPKINS; John HOSECK; James HOSTON; Thomas HOY; William HUGHES; John HENRY; John HUMES; Jean HUNTER; Joseph HUNTER; Thomas HUNTER; William HUNTER; John HYLANDS; William IDARE?; James IRWIN; John JAMESON; Joseph JOHNSON; James JOHNSTON; Mary JOHNSTON; [some names obliterated by spot on paper] --- JORDAN; James KEAEOY; Ann KENEDY; Thomas KENNEDY; Robert KILGORE; Mary KILLGRISS?; John KING; Michael KITCH; Johanna ? KNOCK; John LAMBERTON; Abraham LATIMORE; Thomas LAUGHLIN; James LAUGHREY; John LAUGHREY; George LAWSON; Alexander LECKEY; John LEE; Archibald LEECK; John LEEPER; David T. LEWIS; William LIGGITT; David LINCH; Luke LINSAY; James LOVE; James LUKE; William M'ATEER; John M'BRIDE; Mary M'CARTY; Elizabeth M'CLEERY; Robert M'CLELAND; James M'CLUER; David M'CLURE, Esq.; William M'COLLOUGH; John M'CONAUGHEY; Samuel M'DONALD; Robert M'DOWELL; Robert M'FARE; Jane M'FETRAGE; Robert M'FEWLIS; Anthony M'GAHN; Robert M'GINNESS; John M'GULGGAN; John M'HOSEY; Bernard M'KEAS; John M'KEAS; Thomas M'KEE; John M'KIM; David M'KINLEY; William M'KNIGHT; Cornelius M'MAHON; Thomas M'MURRAY; Malcom M'NEAL; Alexander M'NICKLE; Collie M'NUTT; John M'PHEETERS; John M'QUE; Heenry M'WILLIAMS; Stephen MAGURK; Robert MARSHALL; James MARTIN; Samuel MATHEWS; William MATHEWS; Adley MATSON; William MAXWELL; Joseph MEANS; John MEEK; William MELON; James METEIR; Joseph MILLAN; Naomi MILLER; Robert MILLER; Robert MITCHELL; Thomas MITCHELL; Andrew MORROW; William MONTGOMERY; David or Agness MOODY; Alexander MOORE; John MOORE; Joseph MOORE; William MOORE; Rev. Hugh MORRISON; Hugh MULHOLIAN; Alexander NAUGHTON; Joseph NEAL; Daniel NEIFF; James NELSON; Thomas NICKLE; John O'HARA; Mary OFFICER; William OLIVER; John ORR; John PARKER; John PARKHILL; James PATTON; John PAXTON; Samuel PAXTON; Moses PORTER; Pricilla PRESTICE; James QUIGLEY; John QUIGLEY; James RAINEY; William REED; George REID; William RENESON; Henry RICHARD; William RIDDLE; Anthony ROBINSON; Jane ROGERS; John ROGERS; Thomas ROPER; John SHARP; William SHERRARD; Joseph SIMPSON; William SIMPSON; George SMITH; John SMITH; William SMITH; Richard SPARKS; Alexander SPEERS; James STAFORD; Mathew STEPHEN; George STEVENSON; Samuel STIRLING; Robert STORY; Henry STUART; Robert STUART; Neal SWEENY; Charles TALLFORD; Albert TAYLOR; Benjamin TAYLOR; William TEMPLE; Hugh THOMPSON; David TOMB; John TOMB; Nathaniel TORBET; John TRUSDEL; James WALKER; James WALLACE; Nathaniel WALLIS; Hugh WATSON; Joseph WATSON; Daniel WELSH; James WHITE; John WHITE; Stephen WHITE; Ephraim WILLIAMS; Henry WILSON; James WILSON; Joseph WILSON; Thomas WILSON; William WILSON; Rev. Mr. WILSON; John WOOD; Thomas WOOD;

Alexander of Thomas WOODBURN; James WOODBURN; Joseph WOOK; David WORK; James WRAY; Robert WRAY; William WRAY; James YOUNG; William YOUNG.

Letters remaining at the Post Office, Carlisle, Pa., January 1794: Thomas ADAMS; James ANDERSON; Robert ANDERSON, West Pennsbro'; Robert ARMSTRONG; Sarah ARMSTRONG, Yellow Breeches; William ATHINGHURST; Robert BAIRD, Shearman's Valley; William BARNHILL, James BARRAON, Shearman's Valley; William BEARS; William BEATTY, Schoolmaster; William BILTLAND(?), Juniata; Joseph BLAIN, Shearman's Valley; Thomas BOALS(?), John BORLAND, James BREADY, carpenter; William BROOKS, Yellow Breeches; John BROWN, William BRYSON, Newton twp.; William BUCHANAN, carpenter; Adam BUCHANAN, Huntingdon; Robert BURN; William CALDWELL, Mathew CAMPBELL, Juniata; Christopher CAROTHERS . John CAROTHERFS, Middleton; Oliver CARR, James CARSKADEN, Shearman's Valley; Joseph CASTLES, Mifflin; Joseph CHILDERS, Shearman's Valley; Arthur CLARK; Alexander CLINTON; Henry CONNELLY, Big Spring; William COOK, Greenwood Twp.; Joseph CORBETT, Wayne; Samuel COTTON (?); John COULTER, Mifflin Co.; John COWAN; Rev. John CRAIGE, Big Spring; Alexander CRAWFORD; James CRAWFORD, Carlisle; James CRAWFORD, Hopewell; Luke CRAWFORD; William CRAWFORD; Patrick CREIGHTON, Andrew CROUSE; Samuel CULBERT; Charles CUNNING; Henry CUNNINGHAM; Hugh CUNNINGHAM; Robert DALRUMPLE, Richard DIMSY; James DONNELLY; James or Patrick DONNELLY; James DOUGHERTY; John DUNBARR; Thomas FAIRMAN; Hance FERGUSON, Sheraman's Valley; --- FINLEY c/o Robert BROWN; Benjamin FISHER; Bernard FISHER; Hugh FLETCHER; William & George FOSTER, Shearman's Valley; James FOSTER, Walnut Bottom; James FOWLER; Andrew FREELAND; Henry FULTON; Thomas FULTON; Duncan GALBREATH; John GALBREATH; William GALBREATH, West-Pennsbro'; Hugh GHORMLEY, Shearman's Valley; William GILCHRIST; William GILEY; Brice GILMORE; James GLENN, West-Pennsbro'; Edward GOUDY; Alexander GRAHAM; James GRAHAM; John GRAY; John GREER; Samuel GREGG; Robert GRIMES; Patrick GUINAS; Andrew GWINN; Arthur HAGGAN or HIGGINS, West-Pennsbro'; William HALL; Robert HASLET; Enoch HASTINGS & John WILSON, Mifflin; James HOLMES; Jesse HUNT; John HUNTER, Yellow-Breeches; Samuel HUNTER; William IDARE, Shearman's Valley; David IRWIN; Rev. John JAMESON; Andrew JOHNSTON; Arthur JOHNSTON, Yellow Breeches; Francis JOHNSTON; James JOHNSTON, Big Spring; John JOHNSTON; Robert JOHNSTON; Thomas JOHNSTON, Shearman's Valley; Hance KENNEDY; Alexander KERR, Tuskarora; Mrs. KILLGRIST, East-Pennsbro'; John KYLE; Johannetta KNOCK, East-Pennsbro'; Mathew LARID, Conodoquinet; David LAUGHLIN, Hopewell; Joseph LAUGHLIN; Thomas LAUGHLIN; Archibald LEECH; David Thomson LEWIS; James LOGAN, Shearman's Valley; John M'CALLEY; Peter M'CARNY, in Juniata, 224 miles northwards of Philadelphia; John M'COLLOUGH, near Big Spring; William M'CONNEL, Standing stone; John M'COY; John M'FADDEN; William M'FALL; Robert M'FELIN; Mrs. M'KEE, Shearman's Valley; Thomas M'KEE, Shearman's Valley; William M'NEELENCE; Alexander M'NICKLE; Adley MATSON; William MAXWELL, Hopewell; George MILLER; Thomas MITCHEL; Hugh MONTGOMERY; James MOORE; Ruth MOORE (See Nathaniel TORBETT); John MORROW, Newton; Martin MOTZER, Shearman's Valley; Samuel MURDAGH, Wayne; John MURRAY; Alexander NAUGHTON; Joseph NEEL, Mifflin Co.; John NELSON; James NIBLOCK; John NICKLE; Thomas NICOL; James O'NEAL; John ORR; William ORR; Sammuel or James PATTERSON, Juniatta; John PATTON, Big Spring; Phillip PENDERGRASS, hatter; James PORTER; John or Wm. PORTER, Monaghan; James QUIGLEY, Hopewell; Patrick QUINN, West-Pennsbro'; Matthew RABB, West-Pennsbro'; James RANEY; John REED, Newton; George REED; William REED; Peter RODGERS; Thomas ROPER; David ROULSTON; John

SCHOULLAR; William SCOTT, Sinking-spring; Neal SHACKEY; George SMITH; John SMITH, Newton; William SMITH; Matthew STEEL; John STEPHEN, Wayne; Rev. Matthew STEPHENS, Mifflin; William STEVENSON; Robert STEWART; Robert STEWART, Shearman's Valley; Thomas H. STEWART, Juniata; Robert STORY; James TAYLOR Esq., Juniata; John or Robert TAYLOR; William TELFAIR; William TEMPLE; John THOMPSON, shoemaker; William THOMPSON, Mifflin; David TOMB; John TOMB; Nathaniel TORBETT, husband to Ruth MOORE; John WALKER; Col. WALKER & William BROWN, Mifflin; Patrick WALLACE; Samuel WALLACE, Allen twp.; Thomas WARWICK, Mifflin; Joseph WATSON; Samuel WEAKLEY, Walnut Bottom; David WHITE, Middle-spring; James WHITE; Stephen WHITE, Lewistown; James WIDNEY, Path Valley; Andrew WILSON, near STRASBURGH; Edward WILSON; Henry WILSON; James WILSON, Huntingdon; John WILSON & Enoch HASTINGS, Mifflin; Joseph WILSON; William WILSON, Yellow Breeches; James WOOD; Thomas WOOD; James YOUNG.

Letters Remaining at the Post Office, Carlisle, Pa., May 1794: James ADAMS c/o Ephraim STEEL; James ALEXANDER c/o Ephraim STEEL; Robert ANDERSON c/o Thomas FOSTER; Robert ARMSTRONG c/o Jas. CRAWFORD, currier, Carlisle; William BARNHILL c/o Jas. LAMBERTON; James BARRON, c/o Jas. STEWART, hatter; William BEATTY, Newville; BELL & GIVEN, merchant, Carlisle; WIlliam BILSLANE c/o John M'CULLOCH; David BOWER c/o William PETRIKIN; William BRATTON, Carlisle; William BROOKS c/o Thomas FOSTER; Adam BUCHANAN c/o Matthew SIMPSON, Huntington; Robert BURN c/o Adam JOHNSTON, Carlisle; William CALDWELL c/o John HAY; John CAMPBEL c/o James LAMBERTON; Robert CAMPBEL c/o John HUNTER, Carlisle; John CAMPBELL c/o John UNDERWOOD; Oliver CAR c/o Mr. HUNTER; Col. John CAROTHERS, near Carlisle; Joseph CASTLES c/o Robert DICK; Samuel CATTON c/o John WALKER; Joseph CHILDERS, Shearman's Valley; Arthur CLARK, Bridgetown, Cumberland Co.; John CLARK c/o Persey KEAN; Alexander CLINTON c/o Edwd. MAGUARAN, merchant, Carlisle; John COLBRIT c/o John IRVIN; John CONLEY c/o John HUNTER; John CONNOR c/o James LAMBERTON; Thomas COOPER c/o John RODGERS; Samuel COSBY, near Mount Rock; James or Patt COULTER, Tuscarora; John COULTER, Spring Creek furnace, Mifflin Co.; John COWDON c/o Andrew KENNEDY; John CRAWFORD c/o Robert CLARK; John CREARY c/o John HAY; Patrick CREIGHTON, near Carlisle; James CUBBER c/o John HUNTER; Hugh CUNNINGHAM c/o John WALKER; Jeremiah DALY, Lewistown; Michael DELANY, Shearman's Valley; Samuel DENMAN c/o Robert HUSTON, Carlisle; James DILLAP c/o General WATTS; Richard DIMSEY c/o John CREIGH, Carlisle; Robert DONAVAN, Franklin Co.; James DONNELLY c/o Thomas HUNTER, store keeper Carlisle; Joseph DUNCAN, merchant, Shippensburgh; Revd. Samuel DUPENDORFF, Carlisle; William FAIRMAN c/o John WRAY, Carlisle; William FINTON c/o John HUNTER; Benjamin FISHER c/o H. WILSON, merchant, Carlisle; Andrew FREELAND, Carlisle; William FULTON, Big-spring c/o John HUNTER; John GALBRAITH c/o John HUNTER; Messrs. GARDNER & MARS c/o Jacob RHOM; James GLEN c/o John ALEXANDER; James GRAHAM c/o Joseph REED; Alexander GRAHAM c/o William M'CRACKEN; Samuel GREGG c/o William HUNTER; Edward GUOY c/o John BARBER; Andrew GWIN c/o John WEBBER; William HALL c/o Mr. M'CRACKEN; John HARPER, near Carlisle; Bartholomew HEITLE c/o Jacob WAGGONER; Robert HENDERSON c/o Thomas FOSTER; William HENDERSON Esq.; William HENEY c/o Robert MILLER; Arthur HIGGENS c/o Thomas KENNEDY; Robert or James HOLMES c/o John HUNTER; James HOLMES c/o John OLIVER; George HOLMES c/o Thomas NICHOL; Mary HOLMES, Carlisle; Ditrich HSHLER, house carpenter, Carlisle; Major John HULING, near Carlisle; John HUNTER c/o Robert HUSTON; Thomas HUNTER, Carlisle; William HUNTER, blue dyer, Carlisle; Joseph Turner JAMES, Carlisle; Leonard KELLER,

Carlisle; Thomas KERR, Huntington; John KING c/o Samuel FINDLEY; Robvert— KNOX, student, Carlisle; John KYLE c/o John HUNTER; Hugh LAIRD, Cumberland Co.; Austine LEAKE, Carlisle; Archibald LEECH c/o John WEBBER; William LINCH, near Carlisle; James LUNGAN, Shearmans Valley; James M'CALLEY c/o James LAMBERTON; Joseph M'CLINTOCK, Shearmans Valley; Daniel M'CONNEL c/o John HUNTER; John M'CONNEL c/o John BULBERSON; Robert M'CRACKEN c/o John HUNTER; John M'CREARY c/o John WRAY; Dr. M'CULLOCH, Big-spring; Nicholas M'CURTY, Bucks Co.; James M'DEVITT; John M'DONNELL c/o Ephraim STEEL; John M'FADDEN c/o Thomas BUCHANAN; Jane M'FARTRIDGE c/o Mr. HUNTER; Robert M'FEELERS (?), Path Valley; Robert M'GINNIS c/o James LAMBERTON; James M'KEOWN c/o John HUNTER; William M'KNOT, Path Valley; Collin M'KNUT c/o Mr. MILLER; Alexander M'NAUGHTON c/o William HUNTER; Patrick MACANULTY c/o Gabriel GLEN; Rosanna MAGAW c/o Major BUTLER; Charles MAGEE c/o James LAMBERTON; John MAGUIGGAN c/o Brice GILMOUR; James MATTHEWS c/o George KLINE, Printers; Samuel MATTHEWS c/o Esq. FINDLY; James MAZE c/o John GANNON; John MEIN c/o Robert LEYBURN; John MILLER c/o John UNDERWOOD; James MITCHEL c/o John HOLMES; Thomas or Josias MITCHEL c/o James M'CORD; Thomas MITCHEL c/o William M'CRACKEN; John MOOR, Bedford Co.; Robert MORRISON, student, Carlisle; Alexander MORROW Esq. c/o Samuel MILLS; Thomas MORROW c/o Hugh SWENY; William MORROW c/o Samuel WILSON; Esther or Ann MULE, Downey, Carlisle; James MULLEN c/o John HUNTER; Joseph MULLEN, Juniata; Samuel MURDAGH c/o Robert GIBSON; Jonathan MURPHY, Fort Cumberland; Philip MURPHY c/o John MILLER; John MURRAY c/o Joseph ANDERSON; James NIBLOCK c/o George REED; Henry O'NEAL c/o John HUNTER; David OFFICER c/o John OFFICER; William ORR c/o John HUNTER; Samuel or James PATTERSON c/o Dr. STEVENSON, Carlisle; James PAXTON c/o Ephraim STEEL, Carlisle; John PEEBLES, Big-spring, cabinet maker; William PETRIIN, Carlisle; John or WIlliam PORTER c/o Ephraim STEEL, Carlisle; John POTTER c/o John M. CXESNEY, Harrigburgh; James QUIGLEY, Hopewell twp.; James RAIMEY c/o George LOGUE Esq.; James RIDDLE, Newcastle, merchant; Peter RODGERS c/o John M'KEE, Cumberland Co.; John RODGERS, merchant, Brownsville; James RUTLIDGE c/o James CRAWFORD, Carlisle; William SCOTT c/o John WEBBER; John SCOULLER, near Big-Spring; James SEMPLE c/o James STERRET; Neal SHACKEY c/o William BLAIR; Joseph SHANNON c/o Mr. WEISER; William SHERRARD c/o Robert MORRISON near Carlisle; Margaret SIMRALL, Hopewell Twp.; James SMILY c/o James ANDERSON; Mary SMITH, near Trents Gap; Nathaniel SMITH c/o John SMITH; William & Samuel STEEL, Huntingdon; John STEPHEN c/o Rev. Matthew STEPHEN; Archibald STEWART c/o Samuel STEWART; James STEWART c/o William EAKEN; Robert STEWART c/o Mr. SEMPLE; William STRITCH, Mifflin Co.; David TOMB c/o John CREIGH; John TOMB c/o John CREIGH; George WAKE, Captain Sparks' company; John WALKER, Carlisle; Samuel WALLACE c/o Thomas FOSTER; Edmond WARD, near Harrisburgh; Austin & Jesse WHARTON, students; David WHITE c/o Thomas FOSTER; James WHITE, Cumberland Co.; John WHITE, near Carlisle; James WILKIN c/o John CULBERSON; Joseph WILKIN, Pine Creek Twp.; James WILKINS c/o James SMILEY; Edward WILLSON c/o Robert GRAYSON; Henry WILSON c/o John MAGUARAN; Hugh WILSON c/o Mr. THOMPSON; Daniel WONDERLEY, near Carlisle; Thomas WOOD c/o Robert SMITH; James WOODBURN c/o Alexander LACKEY; James YOUNG from Ireland.

Letters Remaining in the Post Office, Carlisle, Pa., July 1794: John ---; Abraham ADAMS c/o Charles HUSTON; Thomas ALEXANDER, P.M.; Robert or Joseph ALLEN, Allan twp.; Joseph ANDERSON c/o Jno. MORROW; Edward BAILEY, Carlisle; William BEAN c/o Alexander M'BRIDE; William BEATTY c/o

APPENDIX B: LETTERS AT THE CARLISLE POST OFFICE (From the Carlisle Gazette)

John HUNTER; William BEATY c/o Robert SMITH, Carlisle; Nathaniel BECK c/o David M'CLURE Esq.; Thomas BELL c/o John WRAY; William BLACK c/o Samuel GRAY, weaver; Runnel BLAIR, near Mount Rock; Michael BRADLEY, York or Carlisle; Robert REDEN c/o Col.. CANNON; Hugh BROWN c/o John CREIGH; Joseph BROWN c/o Patrick M'SHERRY; Alexander BUCHANAN, Big-Spring; Robert BURROS c/o John DUNBAR; Jenny CAMPBELL c/o Rev. WILSON; John CAMPBELL, Carlisle; John CAMPBELL, Monahan twp.; John CAROTHERS, near Carlisle; Thomas & Margaret CARRICK c/o William SMITH Esq.; James CASTELS c/o Robert DICK; John CLARK, Allen Twp.; George CLARKE, near Carlisle; John CLARKE c/o Percy CAIN; William Henry COAN c/o Robert MILLER Esq.; Patrick COLLINS c/o Robert HUSTON; David CRAWFORD c/o Samuel FINLEY; Robert DICK, Greenwood Twp.; Edward DOUGHERTY c/o Robert GRAYSON; William DOUGLASS c/o David M'CLURE; John DUNBAR c/o John HUNTER; Robert DUNCAN, Big Spring; James or Thomas FAIRMAN c/o John WRAY; David FORQUER, Carlisle; James FOWLY c/o Thomas DUNCAN Esq.; John GIBSON c/o Mr. GORDAN Esq.; John GILMORE c/o Robert GRAYSON; William GLENDENNING c/o Dr. M'CULLOUGH; Alexander GLENN, Walnut Bottom; David GOLLAWAY c/o John HUNTER; John GRAY c/o James LAMBERTON; William GREACEN c/o William WAKLEY; Alexander GREDEN c/o George BURLEY, Carlisle; John GREER c/o John BROWN; Ann GREGORY c/o Jacob CRAVER; Frederick HARDER, Greenwood; Hugh HART c/o Rev. Hugh M'GILL; Thomas HASTINGS c/o John WRAY; James HIGGENS c/o John STEEL Esq., Carlisle; James HITE, Mifflin Co.; Betsy HOCH c/o George WORMLEY; Robert HOGGE c/o Ephraim STEEL; Robert HOLLIDAY, Carlisle; Thomas HOY c/o Robert GRAYSON; John HUCY c/o James GALBREATH; James HUDDLESTON c/o Ephraim STEEL; John HUDDLESTON c/o Ephraim STEEL; John HUMES, Middleton; John HUNTER c/o Robert HUSTON; Nathaniel HUNTER c/o John HUNTER; Thomas HUNTER c/o Thomas BUCHANAN Esq.; Nullet JACKSON c/o Mr. POLLOCK; Archibald JAMISON, Big-Spring; John JAMISON c/o Henry QUIGLY Esq.; Daniel JOHNSTON c/o Abraham LOCHRIDGE; Thomas JOHNSTON c/o John HUNTER; John JOHNSTONE c/o James LAMBERTON; Agness JORDAN, Carlisle; Alexander KARR, Lack twp.; Samuel KEATON c/o John WALKER, I.K.; James KENNEDY c/o Samuel LAIRD Esq.; Robert KENNEDY, near Carlisle; Thomas KENNEDY c/o Alexander M'KEEHAN; Thomas KENNEDY c/o William FINLEY (free); John KING c/o Samuel FINLEY Esq.; James KIRKPATRICK, Big-Spring; John LAMB c/o James LAMBERTON; David LINDSEY, Carlisle; George LONG c/o Robert HAZLET; John LONG c/o Robert HAZLET; Sarah LONG, Shearmans Valley; John M'BRIDE, Rye twp.; Hugh M'CAY c/o Andrew HOLMES; Patrick M'CENNEY, Carlisle; Samuel M'CHINNEY c/o Jerry M'KIBBEN; Thomas M'CLEARY c/o Abraham LOUGHRIDGE; Robert M'CLELLAND c/o John CANNON Esq.; James M'CLUCKY, Huntingdon Co.; Archibald M'CLURE c/o Henry BIRCHSTEAD; Francis M'COLLAM c/o James GIVEN; Patrick M'CONMY c/o John WRAY; Alexander M'CONNEL, Huntington; James M'CONNEL, Mifflin Co.; Neal M'COY c/o Ephraim STEEL; James M'DEWIT, Carlisle; John M'DONALD, Walnut Bottom; Samuel M'DOWEL c/o Jeremiah M'KIBBEN; Elizabeth M'FARLAND c/o John HUMER; Polly M'GAFFEY c/o Samuel M'GAFFEY; Anthony M'GAHAN c/o John WALKER; Samuel M'GAHEY c/o Robert HUSTON; Widow M'GARRACH c/o Col. James POTTER; John M'GLAUGHLIN c/o James LAMBERTON; Alexander M'ILROY c/o John HUNTER; Robert M'KIBBEN c/o Jeremiah M'KIBBEN; Hugh M'MULLIN c/o George WEIRS; Henry M'NULLY c/o William M'CRACKEN; Arthur M'SORLY c/o John HUNTER; William MARTIN c/o George M'MULLIN; George MATTHEWS, Carlisle; Thomas MILIKIN c/o William BROWN Esq.; Thomas MITCHEL c/o James LEEPER, John MONTGOMERY c/o Adam JOHNSTONE, John MOORE, Path Valley; Thomas MOORE c/o Esq. M'CLURE; William MORROW c/o David BLANE; Alexander MURSLAND(?) c/o Ephraim STEEL; Daniel NEIL; John NELSON c/o John HUNTER; Lewis OBRIAN, Carlisle;

John ORR, Carlisle; George OTENBERGER, Carlisle; William PARK c/o Esq. BROWN; Isabella PHILIPS, Carlisle; William PLAT c/o James LAMERTON, John & James QUINN c/o John HUNTER; Matthew RABB c/o Robert HUSTON; Thomas RAMSEY c/o William DAVIDSON; John REED c/o John HUNTER; John REED, N. Twp.; William REED c/o John HUNTER; John RIDDLE, Mifflin Co.; William RIDDLE c/o James SEABURN; Stephen ROPER c/o John SMITH; Thomas ROPER c/o John SMITH; Robert SAMPLE Esq., near Carlisle; John SCCULAR, N. twp.; Thomas SCOTT c/o Robert GRAYSON; Alexander SHAW c/o James LAMBERTON; James SHAW c/o Alexander SHARP; John & William SHERIFF, near Carlisle; Samuel SIMISON, Carlisle; Elizabeth SINGER, Carlisle; James SMILEY c/o Robert LAYBURN; Col. Abraham SMITH, Huntingdon Co.; Archibald SMITH c/o James LAMBERTON; Alexander STAFFORD, Cumberland Co.; Samuel STEVENSON c/o James LAMBERTON; Archibald STUART c/o Samuel STUART; John STUART, Mifflin Co.; William THOMPSON c/o General WATT; John UNDERWOOD, Carlisle; John VANCE c/o Ephriam STEEL; James WALKER c/o Samuel FINLAY; James WALLACE, High Sheriff; Joseph WARDON c/o John CRIEGH; Samuel WEAKLEY c/o William LYONS; David WHITE c/o Miss PETRIKIN; John WHITING, near Carlisle; Edward WIGGENS c/o Robert GRAYSON; Ephraim & Catharine WILLIAMS c/o David MITCHEL; David WILSON c/o Wm. BROWN; Edward WILSON c/o Robert GRAYSON; John WILSON c/o John HUNTER; James YOUNG c/o Mr. GREENFIELD; William YOUNG, Mifflin Co.

Letters Remaining at the Post Office, Carlisle, Pa., January 1795: James ADAMS c/o John WEBBER; William ADAMS c/o John CREIGH; James ALLEN c/o Mr. JAMESON, Path Valley; John ANDERSON, store keeper, Carlisle; Andrew ARMSTRONG c/o John HUNTER; John BARR c/o John HUNTER; William BEATTY c/o William BUCHANAN; William & James BEER c/o Robert HUSTON; Thomas BELL c/o Col. James FOTTER; William BELL c/o William WILLIAMS; Jacob BOWMAN c/o David LINDSAY; Daniel BOYLE c/o John HUNTER; Barney BRADLEY c/o William CREERY; Peter BRICKER, Allan Twp.; Robert BROWN c/o John UNDERWOOD; John BUTLAR c/o Joseph BUTLAR; Richard CAIRNS c/o John WALKER; James CALHOON, inn keeper; Arthur CHAMBERS, near Harrisburgh; John COHANN c/o Joseph POSTLETHWAIT; John COMBE, Buffaloe Valley; John CONNELLY c/o John HUNTER; Alexander CRAWFORD, Shearmans Valley; James CRAWFORD, Shermans Valley; John CRAWFORD, Shermans Valley; John CRAWFORD c/o Robert BROWN; Thomas CRAWFORD, Shermans Valley; Andrew CUNNINGHAM c/o Gen. WATTS; George CUNNINGHAM c/o Thomas CURFCADON; George CUNNINGHAM c/o John MORROW; James CUNNINGHAM c/o James MITCHEL; Col. John DAVIDSON c/o George DAVIDSON; John DAVIDSON, Mountrock; Patrick DOAKE c/o Hugh WILSON; Phoeby DOUDS c/o Ensign MARTIN; George DOUGHERTY c/o John CAREY; John DOUGHERTY, Soap Boiler, Carlisle; James DUNBAR c/o John UNDERWOOD; Joseph EATON c/o Adam JOHNSTON; James ELDER c/o John ANDERSON; Samuel FINLEY, Newville; William FINTON c/o John HUNTER; John GAW c/o Robert LEYBURN; James GELEY c/o John HUNTER; James GLENDENING c/o John HUNTER; William GODFREY c/o John HOLMES; Thomas GORDON c/o Daniel MONTGOMERY; Edward GORRELL c/o James BROWN; Samuel HAWTHORN c/o James LAMBERTON; Joseph HENDERSON c/o Samuel ALEXANDER; David HOGG, near Carlisle; William HOOD c/o John HUGHES; William HORTON, Carlisle; Major HULLING, collector of excise; Thomas HUNTER c/o John HUNTER; William HUNTER, Shermans valley; James IRVINE c/o John WALKER; William JAMESON c/o Francis SILVERS; John KEAN, Surveyor; Phillip KELLY c/o James STRAWBRIDGE; Mr. LE CLEREY c/o Jacob WISER; Mr. A. LEXAMBOREE, Huntingdon; James LUNGAN, Shermans Valley; Mathew M'CLURE c/o John WRAY; Henry M'CULLY c/o Thomas M'CULLEY; Dennis M'CURDY; John M'DANIEL c/o David WATTS Esq.; John M'ELREE c/o John HUNTER; Robert M'FATE c/o Thomas

HUNTER; Joseph M'FERRAN c/o Rev. LINN; John M'GETTIGAN, Carlisle; Daniel M'GUIRE, Newville; Hugh M'JULLIN c/o George WIRES; John M'KEE c/o Mr. MAGAWRIN; William M'MURRAY, Carlisle; Dr. M'NAUGHTON; John M'NAUGHTON, Shermans Valley; William M'NELLANS c/o John WEBER; Archibald M'SOARDS c/o Thomas HAMILTON; Charles MAGEE c/o George STEVENSON; Samuel MARSHALL, Huntingdon; William MARTIN c/o James RAMSEY; Adley MATSON c/o Ephraim STEEL; Mary MICHAEL, Penn twp.; Thomas MILLER c/o Frederick WATTS; Jane MOORE c/o Robert GRAYSON; Richard MORROW, Carlisle; Edward MORTON c/o John HOLMES; Edward NIXON c/o Adam JOHNSTONE; David PARKS c/o Robert HUNTER; William PEART, Carlisle; Samuel POWER, Shermans Valley; Samuel RAMSAY, near Carlisle; John REED c/o John HUNTER; Mathew ROBERTSON, Carlisle; Robert RUSSEL c/o Robert GRAYSON; John SCOTT c/o James CRAWFORD; Joseph SEMPLE, Middleton twp.; Widow SHADE, Carlisle; Archibald SMITH c/o James LAMBERTON; William SPRIGGS, Dickinson College; Rev. Mathew STEPHENS, Juniata; George STEVENSON c/o Ephraim STEEL; Hugh STEWART c/o William HUNTER; Hugh SWENY c/o Robert BLAINE; John THOMPSON c/o David M'CLURE; William WADDLE c/o Mr. BEEN; Robert WALKER c/o Mathew SIMPSON; Patrick WALLACE c/o Hugh WILSON; John WATTS c/o Frederick WATTS; Moses WELSH c/o John UNDERWOOD.

Letters Remaining at the Post Office, Carlisle, Pa. "since December 1794." Matthew ADAMS c/o Rev. Hugh MAGILL; Joseph ALLEN c/o Thomas FOSTER; Jain ANDERSON c/o John UNDERWOOD; John ANDERSON c/o John UNDERWOOD; Thomas ANDERSON Esq., Mifflin Co.; David AYRES, near Lisburn; John BAIRD c/o William BROWN Esq.; Robert BARR c/o John HUNTER; Monsieur BAUDRY, Carlisle; Thomas BEALE Esq., Mifflin Co.; Alexander BEATTY c/o John HUNTER; Alexander BEER c/o Major James LAMBERTON; William BLACK, Patterson's, 14 miles from Carlisle; Mathew BORLAND c/o Col. Samuel LYON; John BOTTON(?), Newville; Adam BOUTNET c/o Roboert SMITH; James BOYD c/o Thomas FOSTER, inn keeper; John BRECKER c/o Jacob WISER; John BREDEN c/o John CANNON; James BREWER c/o Gen. WATTS; John BRISBANE c/o Joseph SIBNEY; Robert BROWN c/o Robert HUSTON, merchant; William BROWN c/o David WALKER, Esq.; John BUCHANAN, Lewistown; William CAMELIN, near Carlisle; Peter CARHART, near Carlisle; Alexander CARNAHAN, Marsh Creek; John CARRICK c/o William BROWN; Margaret or Robert CARRICK c/o William BROWN Esq.; Robert CARRICK c/o William BROWN Esq.; John CLARK c/o Persy KAIN; Rev. CLARSON c/o James YOUNG, carpenter; David COCHRAN c/o Ephraim STEEL; Patrick COLLINS, merchant, Newville; Samuel Judson COOLEDGE Esq., Carlisle; William COWAN c/o Robert MILLER Esq.; James CRAWFORD, Huntingdon; Robert CREE, Junior, Sherman Valley; Elizabeth CROCKETT c/o Robert SMITH; John CULBERTSON Esq., Mifflin Co.; James CUMMINS, Carlisle; Dr. John CUTHBERSON, Carlisle; Robert DAVIDSON c/o Joseph ALLEN; Samuel DAVIDSON c/o Mr. MAGAURAN; William DAVIDSON c/o John HUNTER; Henry L. DAVIS, Carlisle; John DAVIS, Mifflin; James DERMOT, Huntingdon; John DIXON, Carlisle; Patrick DOAK c/o Captain HOLMES; John DONALDSON c/o John DOUGLASS; Charles DONOLSON c/o Robert SMITH; Dr. Ezra DOTY, Mifflin; John DOUGLAS c/o David M'CLURE Esq.; John ERVIN, Carlisle; William FERGUSON c/o John MILLER, inn keeper; Stephen FOULK, T. Gap; Sarah FOWLER c/o Thomas PATTON; William FRENCH, near Carlisle; James GALEY, Hopewell twp.; Dr. John GIBBINS, Carlisle; Widow GIBSON c/o Gilbert SEAWRIGHT; Felix GILBERT, Carlisle College; David GILLESPIE c/o William M'CRACKEN; John GILMORE c/o Robert GRAYSON; James GILSON, near Carlisle; Andrew GIVIN c/o John WEBBER; James GLASGOW, Marsh Creek; George GODFREY, Carlisle Barracks; Hamilton GRAHAM c/o Mr. GRAY; Robert GRAHAM c/o Ephraim STEEL; William GRAHAM c/o John HUNTER; James GRAY c/o

Samuel GRAY; John GRIER c/o John BREW; William HANNAH, Biggspring; John HANNAL, Tuscarora; Ebenezer HARBERT, Jumpers mill; John HARPER c/o William ELLIOTT; Sarah HARRISON, Shearmans Valley; Hugh HART c/o Rev. Hugh MAGILL; John HENEREY, Carlisle; John HENRY c/o Robert HAZLET, merchant; Patrick HERVEY c/o John HUNTER; Arthur HIGGINS, Biggspring; Samuel HOG c/o John HOLMES; John HOGG c/o Ephraim STEEL; Robert HOLLIDAY c/o John IRVINE R.M.; James HOOD c/o John HUNTER; William HUDLESON c/o Samuel GOURSEY; John Montgomery HUDLESTON c/o Ephraim STEEL; John HUGHES c/o Dr. JOHNSTON; Thomas HULIN Esq., Juniata; James HUNTER c/o John HUNTER; William HUNTER c/o John FOORD; William HUNTER Sen., Biggspring; Robert HUSTON; Gerrard IRVINE, Lisburn; John IRVINE c/o Robert HOLLIDAY; Alexander JACKSON; Andrew JOHNSTON c/o John MOORE Y.B.; Francis JOHNSTON c/o Joseph ANDERSON; James JOHNSTON, Biggspring; Capt. John JOHNSTON c/o Col. STEEVENSON; Robert JOHNSTON, Carlisle; Thomas JOHNSTON, Tuscaroroa; Joshua JONES, Carlisle; James KEE c/o John WRAY; James KELLEY c/o Daniel DUNLAP; Joseph KELLY c/o Daniel DUNLAP; Sampson KELLY c/o Daniel DUNLAP; Joseph KELSO, student Carlisle; Robert KENNEDY, Middleton Twp.; William KENNEDY c/o LYONS Esq.; Samuel KNOX, Carrols Tract; Edward LACKEY, Coppersmith; Gibbard LEHMAN, Carlisle; Thomas LOGHEAD c/o Andrew PARKER; John LOGUE c/o James HAY, merchant; Robert LOOHLIN(?) c/o Andrew GREGG; Thomas LYONS c/o Charles COPER; Hugh M'CALLEY c/o Robert BROWN; William M'CANDLESS c/o William M'CRACKEN; John Bawn M'CAUGHEN, Carlisle; Francis M'CAY c/o John M'CAY; Hugh M'CORMICK, Carlisle; Neil M'COY c/o Ephraim STEEL; William M'CRACKEN, Inn keeper; Samuel M'DOWEL c/o Jeremiah M'KIBBEN; Francis M'ELDUFF c/o John MOORE; John M'FADDEN c/o Daniel DUNLAP; Major William M'FARLAND, Yellow Breeches; Col. William M'FARLANE, Biggspring; Robert M'FATE, Carlisle; Rober M'FEELY c/o John HUNTER; William M'GAHAN c/o Maj. WALKER; Alexander G'GAHEY c/o William BROWN, Esq.; James M'GAUGHEY, Marsh Creek; Mathew M'GOLRICK c/o Alexander M'BRIDE; John M'KEE c/o Thomas GRAY; Daniel M'KINLEY, Carlisle; Margaret M'KINLEY, Carlisle; Charles M'MANNEE(?) c/o Adam JOHNSTON; Hugh M'ULLEN c/o James LAMBERTON; James or Hugh M'MUSSEN(?), Burn Cabbins; John M'VOY c/o James LAMBERTON; John MAGILL c/o William THOMPSON; David MAKEE, Carlisle; David MARTIN c/o William BROWN Esq.; George MARTIN, Clarksgap; Josiah MARTIN c/o John MILLER, T.K.; William MARTIN, Linen weaver; Jean MATHEWS c/o Rev. William LOGAN; William MATTHEWS, Carlisle; Grace MEALEY c/o Robert HAZLET; John MEBBAN c/o John POLLOCK; James MILDS, Carlisle; Joseph MILLER c/o Col. William M'DONALD; Martha MILLER c/o Robert SMITH; Matthew MILLER, Tuscarora Valley; Robert MILLER c/o Simon ROSS; Mick MONAGAN c/o David or Francis IRVIN; James MONTGOMERY, Cohonon(?); John MONTGOMERY, painter, Carlisle; James MOORE c/o John HUNTER; James MOORE c/o Robert SMITH; James MOORE, Carlisle; William MOORE, Carlisle; John MORRA c/o William WALLACE; William MORRISON, Carlisle; Agnes MURDOCK c/o Dr. NESBIT; Daniel NEILL, Cumberland Co.; Joseph NIELL c/o William BROWN; William NOBLE c/o William HUNTER; Thomas NORTON c/o James POLLOCK Esq.; Henry O'NEILL c/o John HUNTER; Thomas OLIVER c/o John WRAY; Robert PATTERSON, Kishacoquillis Valley; Thomas PATTERSON; Nathan PATTON c/o John HUNTER; Capt. John PEEBLES, Big Spring; William PORTER c/o John WRAY; James POTTER Esq., Penns Valley; Hugh RACHFORD, Westpennsborough; William REA c/o David WALKER, Esq.; John REED c/o John HUNTER; John REED c/o William HANNA; William REID c/o Samuel WEAKLY; Peter REILLY, Huntington; William RENNISON c/o Robert MILLER Esq.; William RIDDLE c/o George KLINE; Samuel ROBINSON c/o William HUNTER; Elisabeth ROBINSON, Carlisle; Agness SEXTON c/o William AKINS; Robert SHANNON c/o John HUNTER; John SHARP, near

Carlisle; John SHIELDS c/o James ALCORN; Frederick SHUPP, near Harris Ferry; Archibald SMITH c/o James LAMBERTON; John SMITH c/o John HUNTER; Joseph SMITH, Racoon Valley; David SNIDER, miller near Carlisle; George Snider, near Carlisle; John SPEAR c/o John BARBER; John SPRATT, Shemans Valley; William SPRIGG or William HARPER; William C. (G?) SPRIGG, Carlisle; George STESEL c/o John CREIGH; John STEEL c/o Thomas FOSTER; John STEPHENS, Mifflin; Joseph STEPHENS, Mifflin; Rev. Matthew STEPHENS, Mifflin; David STEWART Esq., Huntingdon; Philip STRIKER, near Carlisle; Elizabeth STUART, near Carlisle; Mary STUART c/o Major James LAMBERTON; John STUART c/o William BROWN, Esq.; Robert STUART, Blaines Mill; Robert STUART, York Co.; Alexander (THOMPSON?) c/o Ephraim STEEL, Thomas HUNTER, merchant, Carlisle; Alexander THOMPSON, Carlisle; James THOMPSON, York Co.; Thomas THORP c/o Mrs. Tweedle GROFFER; John TRIMBLE c/o Richard BOVARD, merchant; Samuel TURBETT, merchant, Tuscarora; Alexander WALKER, Tuscarora; David WALKER, Esq. c/o William BROWN, Esq.; David WALKER Esq., Carlisle Barracks; Miss Mary WALLACE, Carlisle; Patrick WALLACE c/o Hugh WILSON; Ludwick WALTMAN; Joseph WARDEN c/o John CREIGH, S.K.; John WARK; John WATSON, Mifflin; William WATSON, Lewistown; Andrew WATT c/o James YOUNG; John WATT; John WHELAN, Mifflin Co.; James WILKIN; John WILKIN c/o John ANDERSON, merchant; James WILLSON c/o Alexander M'CONNEL, Esq.; John WILSON c/o John HUNTER; Nathaniel WILSON c/o John WEBBER; Lt. George WOODS, Carlisle Barracks; James YOUNG c/o John HUNTER; James YOUNG c/o William YOUNG.

Letters Remaining at the Post Office, Carlisle, Pa., August 1795: Robert ALCORN c/o Capt. BLAIR; James ALEXANDER c/o Ephraim STEEL; T. ALEXANDER, P.M.; Mary ALLEN c/o Ephraim STEEL; John ANDERSON, Yellow Breeches; William ANDERSON, Shearmans Valley; Joseph ARCHER; John ARNEL c/o William BROWN; Joseph BAIRD c/o Ephraim STEEL; John BARBER, Carlisle; Robert BARCLAY c/o John PENTER; James & Robert BARR c/o William BROWN; William BARR c/o James GIVEN; Mr. CAUDRY, Champagnfields; Thomas BEALE, Mifflin Co.; Alexander BEATTY c/o John HULER; John BLACK c/o Robert FORSYTH; William BLACK c/o Squire BROWN; William BLACK c/o Widow PATTERSON; John BLACKWOOD c/o John HUNTER; William BLACKWOOD c/o John HUNTER; Rannel BLAIR c/o Margaret MURPHEY; Rev. James BLYTH, Carlisle; William BOIL c/o Samuel BOYD; James BRADLEY c/o Squire M'CLELLAN; William BRADLEY, Wheelright; George BROWN; John BROWN c/o Alexander M'CONNEL; Robert BROWN c/o Robert HUSTON; James BROWNLEE, Carlisle; James BUTLER c/o Mr. MILLER; James BYERS, Cumberland Co.; Pat CAIN c/o John HUNTER; Widow CALDWEL c/o Ephraim STEEL; Mary CAMPBEL c/o Robert HUTCHISON; Jane CAMPBLE c/o John HUNTER; Daniel CLARK c/o Gilbert M'ROWAN; Ninan COCHRAN, Fort Cumberland; Mary CONNEL c/o John HUGHES; James CRAWFORD c/o Major William M'FARLAND; Robert CRISWELL c/o Ephraim STEEL; Roboert CROKES c/o John GLEN; Samuel CROSBY c/o Daniel DUNLAP; William CROSSEN, Lewistown; William CROW c/o John CREIGH; George CUNNINGHAM c/o Thomas CARFEADON; James CUNNINGHAM c/o Ralph STERRET; Robert DALRYMPLE c/o James LAMBERTON; John DARRAGH; John DAVIS c/o Thomas MURPHEY; William DINNING c/o Edward MORTON; James DODDS c/o John HUNTER; John EDWARDS c/o Col. John CONNER; Thomas ELLIOT c/o Stephen DUNCAN; James ERRAND c/o Robert LYBURN; James ERWIN c/o Robert LYBURN; John EWING c/o David M'MOUTRE; William FAIRMAN c/o John WRAY; James FENTON c/o Gen. WATTS; James & Matthew FINLEY c/o Ephraim STEEL; Robert FORGY c/o John CULBERTSON; Thomas FOSTER, near Mount Rock; William FULTON c/o Samuel M'CULLOUGH; James GARRET; Henry GASS, near Carlisle; James GATLEY, Hopewell Twp.; James GEDDES; William GILBY c/o James

GIVEN; Robert GILSILLEN c/o James LAMBERTON; John GRAHAM c/o William BROWN; William GRAHAM; Thomas GRAY, Monoghan; Robert GRAYSON, Carlisle; Richard GREENFIELD, nailor, Carlisle; William GREER c/o John HUNTER; Patrick GUIN; Edward GUY c/o John BARBER; Jenny Betty HAMIL, Carlisle; Archibald HAMILTON c/o Joseph JENKINS; Widow HARPER c/o James MURPHEY; Thomas HASTINGS c/o John WRAY; James HAZLET c/o Moses WILLIAMSON; Bernard HEGANS c/o David WALKER; James HEMPHILL c/o John PATTON; Joseph HENDERSON c/o Samuel ALEXANDER; John HENERY c/o James M'FARLAND; John or William HEYLAND c/o Rev. H. MORRISON; Thomas HILLHOUSE c/o Robert HUSTON; Bryan HOGAN c/o David WALKER; Andrew HOLMES, near Carlisle; George HOLMES c/o John HUNTER; John HUMES c/o Robert HUSTON; Jane HUNTER, Carlisle; John HUNTER c/o James LAMBERTON; Margaret HUNTER c/o John CARSON; Nathaniel HUNTER; Nathaniel & Thomas HUNTER c/o John HUNTER; Robert HUSTON c/o James WOODBURN; William HUSTON c/o Ephraim STEEL; John IRVINE, Lewistown; John JAFFRES c/o Mr. LINN; Thomas JOHNSON c/o John HUNTER; Thomas JOHNSON c/o Ephraim STEEL; Thomas JONES, Carlisle; Samuel JORDAN c/o Daniel DUNLAP; Andrew KERR, Frankstown; John KERR c/o Stephen DUNCAN; James KIRKPATRICK c/o John HUNTER; Mary KIRTY c/o Rev. WILLSON; Samuel KNOX c/o Mr. COOPER; Robert KYLE c/o Robert MACKEY; Sarah LABBEC c/o Mr. SLOUGH; John LAMBERTON c/o James LAMBERTON; John LAUGHLIN c/o John WILLS; Thomas LEMERY, Esq.; James LIKEEN c/o Adam NEAL; Anthony LIPSETT c/o John BARTON; John LISLE c/o Richard GREENFIELD; Andrew LONG c/o Matthew STEPHEN; Mathew LOUDON c/o Archibald LOUDON; Mary LOUGHBRIDGE c/o John WATSON; Robert LUSK c/o John HUNTER; William LYONS c/o Squire BROWN; John M'ADAM; John M'AND c/o Ephraim STEEL; Patrick M'ANULTY, Bigspring; Elizabeth M'CABE c/o Robert GRAYSON; James M'CANN c/o Robert LYBURN; Alexander M'CLEERY c/o Rev. LONG; Thomas M'CLEERY c/o Abraham LOCHRIDGE; Thomas M'CLEERY c/o John MORRISON; John M'CLOSKY c/o James GIVEN; John M'CLURE c/o John KINCADE; Sarah M'CLUSKY c/o Rev. COOPER; John M'CULLOGH c/o John HUNTER; Hugh M'CULLOUGH c/o James LAMBERTON; Thomas & John M'CULLY c/o William WORK; James M'DONAL c/o Samuel GRAY; Joseph M'DONALD c/o Samuel GRAY; John or George M'DOWEL c/o Ephraim STEEL; Samuel M'DOWEL c/o John PIPER; Samuel M'EENY c/o James M'KIBBEN; Johney M'FADDEN, near Carlisle; Roger M'FEELY c/o John HUNTER; Joseph M'FERSON c/o Robert COOPER; Daniel M'GAUGHEY c/o James LAMBERTON; Rolance(?) M'GONAGLE c/o George LOGUE; Joseph or Margaret M'ILHENY c/o H. M'CUMMIN; Alexander M'ILROY; John M'ILROY; John M'KEE, Carlisle; John M'KENNEN c/o Robert LYBURN; William M'KLEISTER c/o Robert SMITH; Peter M'LAUGHLIN c/o Dr. NESBIT; James M'MATH c/o John HUNTER; Eneas M'MULLEN c/o James JAMESON; Hugh M'MULLEN c/o Geroge WEIRS; Michael M'MULLEN c/o William PURDY; Hugh M'MULLIN c/o Mr. WILSON; William M'NEILANCE c/o John WEBBER; Henry M'NULLEY c/o Robert PATTERSON; John M'NUTT, Huntingdon Co.; John M'WILLIAMS c/o Robert HUSTON; Patrick MAGARY c/o John LAWSHE; John MAGAW c/o Richard GIBSON; Benjamin MAIRES c/o Thomas BLAIR; Agness MANSON c/o Thomas M'FERRANT; Mathew MATHERS c/o John HUNTER; William & Samuel MATHEWS c/o Esquire FINLAY; William MAXWELL; Robert MEANS c/o Ephraim STEEL; Robert MEGAGHEY c/o John BELL; James MELLON c/o John M'DONNAL; James MILDS, Carlisle; Thomas MILIKEN c/o James PATTON; Robert MILLER c/o Simon ROSS; John MONTGOMERY c/o Col. PATTON; Margaret MONTGOMERY c/o Hugh M'CUMMIN; James MOORE c/o Robert SMITH; James MOORE; John MOORE c/o Thomas SCOTT; John MOORE, Carpenter; John MOORE c/o James ANDERSON; Samuel MOORE, Path Valley; William MOORE, Blacksmith; William MOORE c/o Robert GRAYSON; Thomas MORELAND c/o THomas MURPHEY; Hugh MORRISON, merchant, Stonetown; John MORROW c/o William WALLACE; John MORTON, at Forgy Clarks; Willilam MORTON c/o David SCOBEY;

William MORTON c/o Edward MORTON; William NEILSON, Shearmans Valley; John O'CONON c/o James LAMBERTON; Hugh O'NEIL c/o John HUNTER; James ODAIR c/o Stephen DUNCAN; John ORR c/o James PHILIPS; Lettice ORR c/o Samuel M'CULLOUGH; Christian & John PALSLEY, near Carlisle; William PARK c/o Mr. KENNEY; John PATTEN c/o John HUNTER; Mary PATTERSON c/o Col. PATTEN; James PETTIGREW c/o Archibald LOUDON; Isabel PHILIPS, Carlisle; David POAK c/o James LAMBERTON; Patrick PORTER c/o John NORRIS; Patrick QUIN c/o Daniel M'GAHEY; John REED c/o William HANNAH; Joseph RINKEN c/o Mathew STEPHEN; Adam RITCHEY c/o Mr. MEBLAHAN; Elizabeth ROBINSON c/o Edward MORTON; Arthur ROBINSON c/o John WATSON; John ROBINSON c/o John WATSON; John ROBINSON c/o Gen. WATTS; Alexander ROGERS c/o George KLINE; David ROSS c/o John HUNTER; Stewart ROWAN c/o John CREIGH; William SANDS c/o John SANDS; Edward SCANLON c/o Col. CANON; Joseph SCOTT c/o Robert HUSTON; William SCOTT; William SCOTT c/o Esquire CAROTHERS; David SEMPLE c/o Thomas M'CLELAND; James SHAW c/o Alexander SHARP; James SHERIDAN, Cumberland Co.; Alexander SHERLOCK, Tuscarora; Elizabeth SKINNER c/o John CALDWELL; David SMITH c/o Stephen DUNCAN; John SMITH c/o John HARPER; William SMITH c/o Daniel DUNLAP; James SPEER c/o John CREIGH; John SPROTT c/o John HUNTER; John SPROTT, Shearmans Valley; John STEEL c/o Capt. Thomas BLAIR; Rev. Mathew STEPHENS, Juniata; Hugh STEWART c/o James GIVIN; James STEWART c/o Robert FORSYTH; Robert STEWART c/o Samuel EDDY; Samuel STEWART, Carlisle; Charles SWENEY c/o Abraham LOUGHBRIDGE; Robert TAYLOR c/o John WRAY; George & James THOMPSON c/o Major BROWN; John TOMB; William TRINDLE c/o John CREIGH; John TRUSDALE c/o Stephen DUNCAN; William TURNER c/o Daniel DUNLAP; William WALKER c/o David WALKER; Benjamin WALLACE c/o Ephraim STEEL; Patrick WALLACE c/o William WALLACE; Jacob WALTERS c/o George KLINE; Thomas WARRICK c/o John WATSON; John WATSON c/o Daniel WEAKLEY; William WILLS c/o William BROWN; John YOUNG c/o Isaac HORNER.

Letters Remaining at the Post Office, Carlisle, Pa., December 1795: James ADAMS c/o Allan CUNNINGHAM; Mathew ADAMS c/o Hugh HART; John ALEXANDER c/o Robert PATTERSON; Thomas ALEXANDER, P.M.; Joseph ALLAN c/o Andrew GREGG; Andrew ARMSTRONG c/o William ARMSTRONG; Mathew ANDERSON, Big-spring; Jane BARID c/o Mrs. HOLMES; John BARR c/o James LAMBERTON; Thomas BASKIN c/o Gen. WATT; Mr. BAUDRY, Carlisle; Thomas BEALE, Esq., Tuscarora; John BEATTY c/o William BUCHANAN; William BEATY, Mount Rock; Thomas BELL c/o Col. POTTER; John BELL c/o David STEWART, Esq.; John BIERBOW, Juniata; William BLACK c/o Robert PATTERSON; James BLAINE c/o Thomas BLAINE; Adam BRATTON, near Carlisle; Joseph or Walter BREDEN, Carlisle; Hugh BREKEN, Mifflin; Daniel BROLLEY c/o Esq. QUIGLEY; James BROWN, tanner, Carlisle; John BROWN c/o Alexander M'CONNEL, Esq.; John CADWALLADER Esq., Carlisle; Samuel CALDWELL, Carlisle; William CAMBELL c/o Robert SMITH; Robert CAMPBELL c/o John HUNTER; Willian CANDLISH c/o William M'CRACKEN; John CANNON Esq., Huntingdon; John CAROTHERS Esq., near Carlisle; Margaret CAROTHERS, Carlisle; Samuel CATON c/o John WALKER; Walter CHARTRES(?) c/o John NOBLE; Patrick CHESNUT c/o James ADAMES; John CHRISTY c/o Joseph M'CLELLAN; James CLARK c/o William SMITH, York Co.; John CLARK c/o Percival KEAN; John CONNELY; Capt. William COX, Greenwood; James CRAMPSEY c/o Robert HUSTON; Robert CRISWELL c/o John WRAY; Edward CROFFIN; Robert CROSS, Tuscarora; William CUMMIN c/o William BROWN Esq.; William DAVIDSON & Thomas RAMSEY c/o James LAMBERTON; Samuel DAVIS, merchant Thompson's town; James DENNY c/o George LOGUE Esq.; Alexander DONALDSON c/o David M'MONTRIE; Sarah DONNAL c/o Gen. WATT; Dr. Ezra DOTY, Mifflin; James DOUGHERTY, near Carlisle;

APPENDIX B: LETTERS AT THE CARLISLE POST OFFICE (From the Carlisle Gazette)

John DUFF c/o Samuel WILLSON; George DUFFELD, Lewistown; James DUNBAR c/o John UNDERWOOD; Robert DUNBAR c/o John BELL; William & James DUNCAN c/o John HUNTER; John DUNLAP, near Lisburn; Edward DUNN c/o Col. ELLIOT; Michael EGOLIFF, Baker, Carlisle; Robert ELKIN c/o John UNDERWOOD; Messrs. ELLIOT & STEELE, Lewistown; Patrick ELLIOT c/o Robert PATTERSON; William ELLIOT, Lewistown; Alexander EMMIT c/o William BROWN, Esq.; Thomas EWART c/o Adam JOHNSTON; Thomas FAIRMAN c/o John WRAY; William FENTON c/o John HUNTER; Thomas FERGESON c/o Samuel FINLEY, Esq.; RICHARD FINLEY c/o John LAMBERTON; James FLEMING c/o William BROWN, Esq.; Robert FORGEY c/o John CULBERTSON; Paul FRASER, Shermans-valley; John FRENCH c/o Mr. WOODBARN; James GARLAN, Carlisle; James GAW, in Carlisle; JOhn GIBSON, son to Robert GIBSON, decd.; Alon GILKISON or James GEALY; Richard GILSON, near Carlisle; James GLEN c/o James DUNLAP; Neal GRAHAM c/o Isaac THOMAS; Barney GRAHAM c/o Samuel DAVIS; John GREER c/o John BROWN; Frederick HARPER, Esq., Greenwood; Thomas HARRIS c/o John WATSON; Hugh HART c/o Revd. Hugh M'GILL; Mary HAZITT, Carlisle; Widow HEMPHILL c/o John BARBER; James HENDERSON c/o James CRAWFORD, currier; James HENDERSON c/o Samuel EDMISTON, Esq.; Samuel HENDERSON c/o John GLEN; Dermond HOGANS c/o David WATSON; Ann HOLMES c/o Gen. WATT; James HUDDLESTON, Tuscarora; Jonathan HUDSON, Carlisle; Robert HUNTER c/o William BROWN, Esq.; James IRVINE c/o George FREY; James IRVINE c/o Robert LOVE; Jared IRWIN, Lisburn; John JEMISON c/o Esq. QUIGLEY; Frances JOHNSTON c/o William AKENS; Stephen JOHNSTON c/o John CREIGH; Dominick KEAN; Joseph KENNEDY, near Carlisle; Alexander KERR, Tuscarora; Samuel KERR, Huntingdon; Robert KILERIST, Shermans-valley; Henry LECKY, Shermans-valley; John LEE; Thomas LEE c/o John HUNTER; JOhn LEWIS c/o Mr. HESLEY; Henry LICKLY c/o Ephraim STEEL; Edward LITTLE, Carlisle; James LOVE c/o John HAYS; Thomas LYONS c/o Charles COOPER; Mathew M'CABE c/o Mr. STEEL, printer; John M'CAUGHAN c/o Hugh WILSON; James M'CLINTONCK c/o Robert WHITEHILL; John M'CORMICK, East Pennsborough; Francis M'COY c/o John M'COY; George M'CULLAUGH c/o Adam M'KEE; Robert M'CUTCHEN; John M'CUTCHIN c/o William HARPER; John M'DOWELL; Joseph M'ELHINEY c/o Hugh M'COMMONS; James M'ELROUGH c/o James GIVEN; Alexander M'ELROY; Neal M'ELWAIN, Pennsborough twp.; Jean M'ELWEE c/o Gen. WATT; Hugh M'FADIN c/o Robert CHAMBERS; Jean M'FARLAND c/o Revd. Mathew STEPHENS; Thomas M'FARLANE; Jean M'FETRICH c/o John HUNTER; John M'GARVEY c/o Col. ELLIOT; John M'GAW c/o Mr. GILSON; Manases M'GLAUGHLIN c/o William BROWN Esq.; James M'GUINLEY; Daniel M'GUIRE, Newville; Adam M'KEE c/o James REED; George M'KEE c/o James MILLER; Michael M'KEEHAN c/o James BLACK; John M'KENNAN c/o Robert LEYBURN; Robert M'KIBBIN c/o Jeremiah M'KIBBIN; John M'LANDBURGH c/o William M'CRACKEN; Henry M'LAUGHLIN c/o George FREY; Peter M'LAUGHLIN, Huntingdon; David M'MURTRIE Esq., Huntingdon; Henry M'WILLIAMS; Wililam MAFFET c/o JOhn CANNON Esq.; William MAHON; James MAIZE; Agness MANSON c/o Revd. Thomas M'FERRIN; George MARTIN; Michael MARTIN; Robert MARTIN; DJames MATTEER c/o John GREGG; James MATTER c/o John CREIGH; John Craig MILLER; Messrs. MILLIKEN & MENVILL, North Yarmouth; William MONTGOMERY c/o Thomas FOSTER; Andrew MOORE, Dickinson College; James MOORE c/o Esq. FINLEY; Thomas MOORLAND c/o Thomas MURPHEY; Dennis MORRISON; John MURPHEY c/o James LAMBERTON; William MURRAY c/o Revd. Mr. WILSON; Joseph NEEL c/o William BROWN, Esq.; John NORRIS, Lewistown; Thomas NORTON, Carlisle; Patrick NUGENT, Juniata; Esther O'BRINES c/o John CREIGH; Elizabeth ORR c/o John POTTS, Path Valley; William PARK c/o Mathew KENNEDY; James PARR c/o Robert GRAYSON; John PORTER, C. County; Moses PORTER c/o Gen. WATT; Patrick PORTER; Col. James POTTER, Mifflin; Thomas PROVINCE; John PURDY;

Patrick QUEN c/o James LAMBERTON; Thomas RAMSAY & William DAVIDSON c/o James LAMBERTON; James REDMAN, Tuscarora; William REED c/o Ephraim STEEL; Alexander REID c/o Esq. FINDLEY; George REID c/o Robert NILSON; James RES c/o Esq. BELL; William RIDDLE c/o George KLINE; Elizabeth ROBINSON; George ROBINSON Esq., Shermans Valley; Henry ROBINSON, James ROBINSON, merchant, Carlisle; Jeremiah ROBINSON c/o James JAMESON; Alexander ROGERS; George E. ROSS, attorney at law; James RYND c/o James LAMBERTON; SAMBOURNE c/o Col. PATTON, Mifflin; Mary SANDERSON, near Carlisle; Charles SEMPLE; David SEMPLE; Francis SEMPLE; James SEMPLE c/o William BROWN, Esq; John SEMPLE; Samuel SEMPLE; Captain SERVICE, Huntingdon; John SHIELDS c/o Revd. Robert DAVIDSON; John SKINNER c/o George SKINNER; David SMITH, Carlisle; John SMITH, Carlisle; John SMITH, Carpenter; John SMITH, shoemaker, Carlisle; Nathan SMYTH c/o William BARR; William SMYTH, York Co.; David SNIDER, Miller; Archibald SPEER c/o John BARBER; David STAIRS c/o Francis ELLIS; William STEEL, merchant; John STEPHEN; Joseph STEPHEN c/o Revd. Mathew STEPEHN; Rev. Mathew STEVEN, Juniata; George STEVENSON c/o William THOMSON; Hugh STUART c/o James GIVEN; Isabella STUART, Shermans-valley; Moses STUART c/o John HUNTER; William STUART c/o William LYONS, Esq.; William SWARBRIG, Carlisle; Richard THOMAS c/o John ARTHUR; Archibald THOMPSON, Huntingdon; James THOMSON c/o David MILLER; Robert TOMSON c/o Joseph ANDERSON; William THOMSON, Newton twp.; Rebecca TREGO, Mount Rock; John VANCE c/o Ephraim STEEL; Banjamin WALLACE s/o Ephraim STEEL; Francis WARD; Frances WATKINS, Huntingdon; Samuel WATT c/o Joseph STEEL; Samuel WATT c/o Thomas JONES; Lewis WHITE; James WHITE c/o John M'CONNELL, Esq.; Edward WIGGINS c/o James HENDERSON; Rev. David WILEY, Mifflin; John WILKINS c/o John ANDERSON; James WITHROW c/o Robert FORSYTH; David WORK c/o George RIDDLE.

INDEX (to the paragraph number)

INDEX (to the paragraph number)

INDEX (to the paragraph number)

INDEX (to the paragraph number)

INDEX (to the paragraph number)

INDEX (to the paragraph number)

INDEX (to the paragraph number)

INDEX (to the paragraph number)

INDEX (to the paragraph number)

INDEX (to the paragraph number)

INDEX (to the paragraph number)

INDEX (to the paragraph number)

INDEX (to the paragraph number)

INDEX (to the paragraph number)

INDEX (to the paragraph number)

INDEX (to the paragraph number)

INDEX (to the paragraph number)

INDEX (to the paragraph number)

INDEX (to the paragraph number)

INDEX (to the paragraph number)

INDEX (to the paragraph number)